STANDARD
STRUCTURAL
DETAILS ——

FOR

BUILDING

CONSTRUCTION

STANDARD STRUCTURAL DETAILS

FOR

BUILDING

CONSTRUCTION

MORTON NEWMAN
Civil Engineer

McGRAW-HILL BOOK COMPANY

New York   St. Louis   San Francisco   Düsseldorf   Johannesburg
Kuala Lumpur   London   Mexico   Montreal   New Delhi
Panama   Rio de Janeiro   Singapore   Sydney   Toronto

TO MY MOTHER

PREFACE

The purpose of this book is to provide a graphic means of communication between architects, engineers, contractors, and students who are engaged in the design and construction of buildings. The four basic structural materials that are employed in building construction are wood, concrete, masonry, and steel. In the application of these materials many standard details and methods of construction have been developed. For several years the author found it quite useful to collect and index standard structural details for the preparation of structural drawings of buildings. The use of structural graphic standards reduced the cost of production of structural drawings and also helped to facilitate the communication of information between all of the personnel who were involved in the design and construction of a building. No claim is made for the originality of the details in this book, as they are standard methods of construction and they are extensively used throughout the construction industry.

This book consists of a series of drawings of standard structural details that are most frequently employed in building construction. The details are presented individually and in their most basic and general form. A brief description is given for each detail pertaining to the material used, the type of condition shown, and its method of construction. In no instance should this book be considered or used as a substitute for the engineer or as a shortcut method of engineering. It is the function of the engineer to verify the use of any detail and to determine the sizes, dimensions, and all other pertinent information that will be essential to its use in a particular building design. The details are separated and arranged into four chapters with respect to the type of construction materials used. The titles of the chapters are Wood, Concrete, Masonry, and Steel. In some instances two types of construction materials are used in the same detail. The author endeavored to place each detail in the related chapter and in the sequence of its use in building construction so that it could be readily located. Also, the index for this book has been set up so that any particular detail that may be sought can be easily located.

The engineering information presented in this book is in accordance with the basic requirements of The American Institute of Steel Construction, The American Concrete Institute, The International Conference of Building Officials Uniform Building Code, "The West Coast Lumbermen's Douglas Fir Use Book," and The Concrete Masonry Association of California. Standard details and construction methods evolve from the structural design requirements. Many excellent books on structural design and analysis are available to the practicing engineer and student; there is also a great need for applied practical information related to structural drafting and the use of construction materials. Expanding technology in the fields of building engineering and construction has created a situation which demands that the structural drawings be more complete and therefore more complex. The purpose of structural drawings is to communicate the engineer's design requirements to the various contractors and material fabricators.

To achieve total communication, the structural drawings should be clear and complete, the general presentation of information should be in a logical sequence, all sections and details should be shown and clearly referenced, and any field conditions should be considered on the drawings. A good set of structural drawings will ensure that the building is constructed in accordance with the engineering design requirements and that construction delays and unnecessary additional costs are avoided.

The engineer's work is the prime factor in the successful design and construction of a building; however, in the final event, his work is directly dependent upon the intelligence and integrity of the men on the construction job, particularly at the supervisory level. Poor fieldwork in terms of accuracy and material quality control will negate a great deal of engineering effort. Building construction requires a high degree of teamwork between the engineers and the contractors. Each party should have a working knowledge of the other's functions and responsibilities. The author hopes that this book will serve as a communication tool that will improve the quality of engineering and construction. Also, engineering and architectural students can use this book as a source of information to familiarize themselves with the methods and materials of construction. As the student uses the information presented in this book, he will increase his ability to translate structural engineering calculations into practical applications.

I would like to acknowledge the very able assistance of Bruce L. Ward who drew the details shown on the following pages and assisted in assembling the information into a book form. Also, I would like to thank Jack Clark for his advice and encouragement, and acknowledge the assistance of Bogdan Todorovic in the early stages of this book.

Morton Newman
Civil Engineer

CONTENTS

LIST OF TABLES

ABBREVIATIONS

Adjustable	Adjust.	Double	Dbl.
Alternate	Alt.	Drawing	Drwg.
American Concrete Institute	A.C.I.		
American Institute of	A.I.S.C.	Each	Ea.
Steel Construction		Elevation	El. or Elev.
American Society of	A.S.T.M.	Engineer	Engr.
Testing and Materials		Equal	Eq.
Architect	Arch.	Equipment	Equip.
Area	A.	Existing	Exist.
		Expand	Exp.
Beam	Bm.	Expose	Expo.
Block	Blk.	Exterior	Ext.
Blocking	Blkg.		
Bottom	Bott.	Fillet	Fill.
Building	Bldg.	Finish	Fin.
		Floor	Flr.
Calculations	Calcs.	Foot	Ft.
Ceiling	Ceil.	Footing	Ftg.
Cement	Cem.	Foundation	Fdn.
Center Line	C.L.	Framing	Frmg.
Channel Stud	C.S.		
Civil Engineer	C.E.	Gauge	Ga.
Clear	Clr.	Glued Laminated	Gl. Lam.
Column	Col.	Grade	Gr.
Concrete	Conc.	Grout	Grt.
Connection	Conn.	Gypsum	Gyp.
Construction	Constr.		
Continuous	Cont.	Hanger	Hngr.
Cubic	Cu.	Height	Ht.
		Hook	Hk.
Deflection	Defl.	Horizontal	Horiz.
Depression	Depr.		
Detail	Det.		
Diagonal	Diag.	Inch	In.
Diameter	Dia.	Inclusive	Incl.
Dimension	Dim.	Inside Diameter	I.D.
Discontinuous	Disc.	Interior	Int.

Joint	Jnt.	Roof	Rf.
Joist	Jst.	Room	Rm.
		Round	ϕ
Lag Screw	L.S.		
Laminated	Lam.	Schedule	Sched.
Lateral	Lat.	Section	Sect.
Light Weight	Lt. Wt.	Section Modulus	S.
		Seismic	Seis.
Machine	Mach.	Sheathing	Shtg.
Masonry	Mas.	Sheet	Sht.
Maximum	Max.	Spacing	Spcg.
Membrane	Memb.	Specification	Spec.
Metal	Met. or Mtl.	Spiral	Sp.
Minimum	Min.	Stagger	Stgr.
Moment of Inertia	I	Standard	Std.
		Steel	Stl.
Nails	d (penny)	Steel Joist	S.J.
Natural	Nat.	Stiffener	Stiff.
Number	No. or #	Stirrup	Stirr.
		Structural	Struct.
On Center	O.C.	Structural Steel Tube	S.S.T.
Opening	Opng.	Square	Sq.
Opposite	Opp.	Symmetrical	Sym.
Outside Diameter	O.D.		
		Thick	Thk.
Panels	Pnls.	Through	Thru.
Partition	Part.	Tread	Tr.
Penetration	Pen.		
Plaster	Plas.	Ultimate	Ult.
Plate	Pl.	Ultimate Stress Design	U.S.D.
Plywood	Plywd.	Uniform Building Code	U.B.C.
Pounds per Cubic Foot	P.C.F.	Utility	Util.
Pounds per Square Foot	P.S.F.		
Pounds per Square Inch	P.S.I.	Vertical	Vert.
Pressure	Press.	Volume	Vol.
Radius	R.	Waterproof	W.P.
Rafter	Rftr.	Weight	Wt.
Rectangular	Rect.	Welded Wire Fabric	W.W.F.
Reinforcing	Reinf.	Wide Flange	W.F.
Required	Reqd.	With	W/
Riser	R.	Working Stress Design	W.S.D.

STANDARD
STRUCTURAL
DETAILS ——————
    FOR

    BUILDING

    CONSTRUCTION

1

WOOD

The details presented in this chapter pertain generally to buildings of wood frame construction. The drawings are arranged in the sequence of their use in the construction of a building. The general categories of the details are post and footing connections, floor and roof structural diaphragms, stair sections and details, wood stud wall sections and connections, roof framing sections, beam and floor connections and sections, post and beam connections, lateral force connections of beams to wood stud walls, wood framing and steel beam connections, and glued laminated wood or heavy timber details.

The species of wood used in the drawings is not designated, since the availability of the different species of wood used in construction varies for each particular geographic region. Local building codes or the applicable construction design criteria specify the allowable working stress values for each species of wood used. Building codes also regulate the control of structural lumber by requiring stress grade marks from a responsible agency on each member and on plywood panels. The allowable stress requirement of wood members is only one of the factors that is involved in the use of wood as a structural material. Protection against moisture and

decay may be necessary, depending on the climate conditions in which the wood is used. Wood will not be subject to decay when the moisture content is less than 20%; however, decay caused by excessive moisture will definitely occur when the moisture content is greater than 25%. The following structural details of foundations are drawn to eliminate the possibility of excessive moisture in the floor joists. Wood mudsills or ledgers that are in contact with concrete or masonry should be pressure treated or constructed of a species of naturally durable lumber. Also, interior floors, ceilings, and attic spaces should be ventilated to eliminate moisture condensation. Another source of damage to wood structures is the presence of termites. The termite is an insect similar to the ant, that can destroy wood by devouring the cellulose material. Attacks by large numbers of termites can be prevented by creating a barrier between the ground moisture and the wood members. Termite barriers are made of 26-gauge galvanized sheet metal and are installed to protect the top of the foundation from the ground surface. There are also many commercial chemical solutions that can be added to the adjacent ground to prevent termite intrusion. Since lumber is susceptible to decay from moisture and termites, it must also be protected while it is stored on the job site prior to its use in the construction. This can be accomplished by maintaining the lumber at least 6″ above the ground surface and keeping it covered with a waterproof material.

Wood structural framing requires that the members be accurately cut to size and fit together with even bearing surfaces. Special care should be taken in the design and the construction to allow for wood shrinkage and the deflections of the members. The wood members used in the details in this chapter are mill-cut to standard sizes; however, they are designated by their nominal, or rough, size. Table 1–1 gives the nominal dimension and the net dimension of wood members with four sides surfaced.

Table 1–1. American Standard Lumber Dimensions S4S

Nominal, or rough, dimension, in.	Standard surfaced four sides, or actual net dimension, in.
1	¾
2	1⅝
3	2⅝
4	3⅝
6	5½
8	7½
10	9½
12	11½
14	13½
16	15½
18	17½

The details in this chapter are used for commercial and residential wood framed structures. The roof and the floors are framed with rafters or joists, which are usually spaced 12″, 16″, or 24″ apart, depending on their span, the unit load on the member, and the allowable working stress of the wood. When the rafters or joists are used to support plaster ceilings, the deflection of the members should be limited to prevent surface cracks. The floor and roof framing members should have an end bearing length of 1½″ on wood or metal and 3″ on concrete or masonry, except as shown in Detail 1–14. The floor joists should be laterally braced by blocking or cross bridging as shown in Detail 1–8. The distance between rows of bridging should not exceed 8′0″. The end blocking or rim joists, as shown in Details 1–15, 1–16, and 1–21 through 1–24, may be used to brace the floor joists laterally at the walls. Floor joists may be notched for piping, provided the notch does not exceed ⅙ of the depth of the joist and is not located within the middle ⅓ of the span. Holes may be bored in floor joists for piping or electrical cable, provided the hole is not closer than 2″ from the top or the bottom of the joist. When floor joists are notched at the ends, the notch should not exceed ¼ of the joist depth. Wood subfloors are nailed to the top of the floor joists as shown in Details 1–7 and 1–10. Detail 1–9(a) shows a special type of roof sheathing for prefabricated panelized roof construction.

Interior and exterior walls of wood buildings are constructed with vertical studs. The size and spacing of the studs (bearing or non-bearing wall) depend on the load to be supported by the wall, the height of the wall, and the lateral forces normal to the surface of the wall. Interior partitions or non-bearing walls may be constructed with 2″ × 4″ studs spaced at 24″ o.c.; however, studs are usually spaced at 16″ o.c. to accommodate the wall-covering materials. Non-bearing partitions are supported by double floor joists as shown in Detail 1–10 and are connected at the top to the floor joists or rafters as shown in Detail 1–19(a) and (b). Exterior walls and bearing walls are framed with 2″ × 4″ studs at 24″ o.c. for one-story buildings, 2″ × 4″ studs at 16″ o.c. for two-story buildings. When the stud height is greater than 6′0″ and it is supporting loads from two stories above, the studs should be 2″ × 6″ or 3″ × 4″ at 16″ o.c. The studs in exterior walls and bearing walls should be placed with the larger dimension perpendicular to the wall. The bottom of the studs are nailed to a sole plate 2″ thick and equal to the depth of the studs; the top of the studs are connected to a double 2″ plate as shown in Detail 1–26. Stud walls should be continuously blocked at midheight as a fire stop. Details 2–1 through 2–13 show the various concrete foundation conditions for wood stud walls. Stud wall corners and intersections should be framed with at least three studs nailed together to make a solid member. The walls are laterally braced by 1″ × 4″ let-in braces spaced not more than 25′0″ o.c. and set at each corner and intersection of the walls.

Details 1–7 and 1–9(a) and (b) are specifically concerned with plywood as a roof or floor sheathing material. Douglas fir plywood panels are manufactured by laminating and gluing together an odd number of layers of Douglas fir veneer sheets. The veneer sheets are usually ⅛″ thick and are laminated so that the surface grain of the adjacent layers are perpendicular to each other. Standard plywood panels are 48″ × 96″ with the exposed surface grain on each side running in the direction of the length of the panel. The strength of the wood running in the direction of the surface grain of the panel is much greater than the strength of the cross-grain plies, which only serve as a filler material between the laminations; therefore, plywood should be placed so that the surface grain is perpendicular to the framing members. Two types of Douglas fir plywood are manufactured, interior-type and exterior-type plywood, their classification depending on the glue used in their fabrication. The exterior-type plywood uses a waterproof adhesive. Structural plywood is designated as Exterior Type "Commercial Standard CS 45" of the United States Department of Commerce or Commercial Standard CS 122 for Western Softwood Plywood. Vertical and horizontal structural diaphragms are constructed by nailing the plywood panels to the framing members. The capacity of the diaphragm to resist lateral force depends on the thickness of the plywood, the size and spacing of the nails to the panel edges and the diaphragm edges, and the panel-edge blocking.

Details 1–86(a) to 1–95 are drawings of glued laminated wood or heavy timber construction. Building codes specify heavy timber as structural wood members of sufficient width and depth to qualify as slow-burning construction. The fire rating for heavy timber varies in different building codes; however, the National Board of Fire Underwriters recommends the following nominal dimensions for heavy-timber construction: columns shall not be less than 8″ in any dimension; beams and girders shall not be less than 6″ in width or 10″ in depth; floors shall be constructed of tongue and grooved planks not less than 3″ thick and covered with 1″ thick flooring laid perpendicular or diagonal to the subfloor planks; roof sheathing shall be not less than 3″ thick tongue and grooved planks.

Glued laminated wood members are often used for heavy timber construction since their nominal dimensions can readily conform to building-code requirements. These members are factory fabricated and consist of vertically laminated, nominal 2″ thick boards of various combinations of structural lumber, each board being glued to the adjacent board. Two types of adhesives are used in the manufacture of glued laminated structural members. When the moisture content of the member exceeds 15% or when it is exposed to the weather, the boards are laminated with an exterior-type phenol resorcinol glue. A fortified casein glue is used to fabricate members that are used in the interior of a building or that are not exposed to excessive moisture. The allowable working stresses of glued laminated structural members depend on the number of laminations and the structural grade of the laminated boards. Since these members are manufactured to meet the engineer's design requirements, it is recommended that they be shop-drawn and detailed before they are fabricated.

Quite often glued laminated wood members are left exposed to attain an architectural affect. In such instances the finished appearance of the wood is important and should be specified as either architectural or premium-finished. Also, the member should be delivered to the job site in a protective wrapping which should not be removed until after the member is in place. Glued laminated members that are not used in an exposed situation may have an industrial-finished appearance and need only a protective wrapping against excessive moisture.

Wood framing members and floor sheathing that are nominally 1″ and 2″ in width are connected by wire nails. Common wire nails are most often used in framed construction, although other types of nails are available where stronger withdrawal-type connections may be required. Nails are generally employed to react principally in shear caused by lateral loading of the connection. The lateral resistance value of a nail depends on the nail diameter and the depth of penetration into the member to be joined. When a force is applied parallel to the nail, a withdrawal resistance will occur which is much less than the lateral resistance; therefore, this type of connection should be avoided. Nails that are driven into a member at an angle of approximately 30° to the surface grain are called toenails and will have ⅔ of the normal lateral-resistance value. Nails should penetrate the connected member at least ½ the length of the nail, all connections should have at least two nails, and nails should be at least ½ the nail length apart and be not less than ¼ of the nail length from the edge of the member. Many of the drawings in this chapter call for metal clips. These clips are a commercially standard piece of hardware and are commonly used to join wood members when a high connection resistance is required. The clips are made of 18-gauge sheet metal in various left- and right-hand configurations and are basically used for light wood framed connections. Table 1–2 shows the various common wire nail sizes and lengths. Table 1–3 gives the recommended light framed nailing schedule for the different types of connections. Plywood roof and floor sheathing nails are not specified in this table since they are determined by the shear to be resisted by the diaphragm.

The use of metal bolts to connect wood members to each other and to other structural materials such as concrete, masonry, and steel is a common and economical method of construction. Bolts connecting wood members are capable of resisting forces applied both parallel and lateral to the shank of the bolt by bearing and shear. In the following drawings in this chapter

Table 1–2. Common Wire-nail Sizes

Size of nail, d	Standard length, in.	Wire gauge
6	2	11½
8	2½	10¼
10	3	9
12	3¼	9
16	3½	8
20	4	6
30	4½	5
40	5	4
50	5½	3
60	6	2

the bolts are used to connect metal plates to wood posts and beams, to connect wood members to each other, and to connect wood framing to steel beams. Flat washers should be used in bolted wood connections when metal side plates are not specifically designated.

The washers are either round or square and are made of malleable iron. The size and the thickness of a washer are determined by calculation and depend on the bolt tension when the bolt is tightened or loaded and on the bearing stress normal to the wood surface. Heavy timber construction often requires that the washers be made of cast iron; however, the washers are not

Table 1–3. Recommended Nailing Schedule

Connection	Nailing	Nail size, d
Joist to sill or girder	Toenail	2–16
Bridging to joist	Toenail	2–8
1 × 6 subfloor to joist	Face nail	2–8
2 subfloor to joist or girder	—	2–16
Plate to joist or blocking	—	16 at 16″ O.C.
Stud to plate	End nail	2–16
Stud to plate	Toenail	3–16 or 4–8
Top plates spike together:		
Laps and intersections	—	16 at 24″ O.C.
Ceiling joists:		
To plate	Toenail	2–16
Laps over partitions	Toenail	3–16
To parallel alternate rafters	Toenail	3–16
Rafter to plate	—	3–16
Continuous 1″ brace to stud	—	2–8
2″ cut in bracing to stud	—	2–16
1″ sheathing to bearing	—	2–8
Corner studs and angles	—	16 at 30″ O.C.

designated in the following wood details. The strength of a bolted wood connection depends on the thickness of the members, the number and the size of the bolts, the species of the wood, the angle of the resisted force to the grain of the members, the use of metal side plates or other standard hardware connectors, and the arrangement of the bolt spacing in the connection. It is important that the bolt spacing and the edge distance be sufficient to ensure that the wood will not split and to allow enough bearing area. Each bolt should be installed through a predrilled hole 1/16″ larger than the bolt shank diameter.

Lag screws are often used in lieu of bolts when it is not possible or convenient to obtain full penetration by a bolt through a wood member. The capacity of lag screws to resist lateral forces and withdrawal depends on the same factors as do bolts in wood members; however, lag screws will not resist as much force as an equal size bolt. A lag screw should be installed in a predrilled hole approximately 70% of the shank diameter of the screw, and it should penetrate the member to be joined at least ½ of the screw length or eight shank diameters.

In general, wood is a highly versatile and inexpensive construction material. Except for glued laminated members, wood can be fabricated and assembled on the job site. The contractor must have clear and complete structural drawings of the framing and connections to avoid the inefficient use of labor and materials.

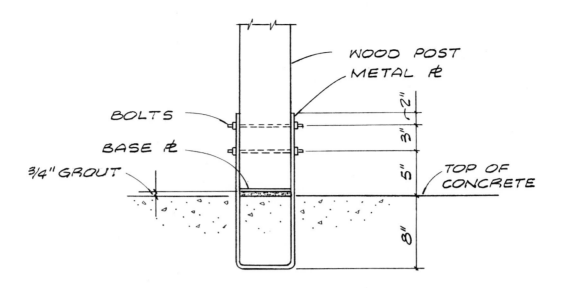

Detail 1-1(a). A wood post connected to a concrete foundation using a U-shaped metal plate bolted to the post and embedded in the concrete. The base plate should be the same size as the post.

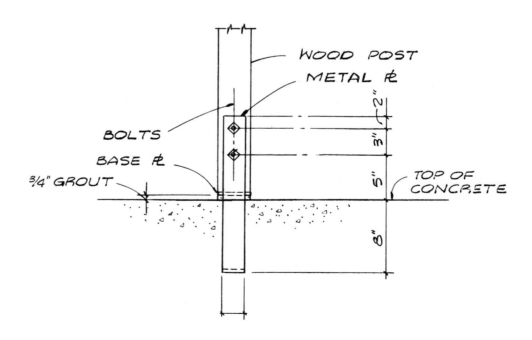

Detail 1-1(b). A side view of Detail 1-1(a). The length of the metal plate and the thickness of the bolts are determined by calculation.

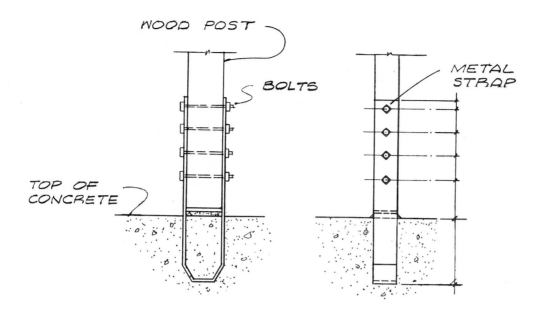

Detail 1-2. A wood-post connection to a concrete foundation using a U-shaped metal plate and bolts. The number of bolts and the size of the plate permit the post to resist tension or compression.

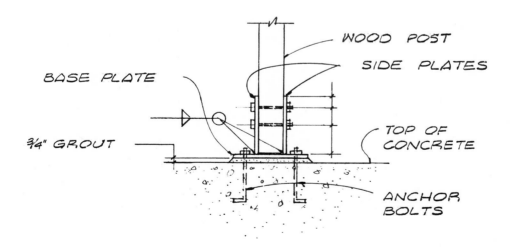

Detail 1-3. A wood-post connection to a concrete foundation. The metal side plates are bolted through the post and welded to the base plate.

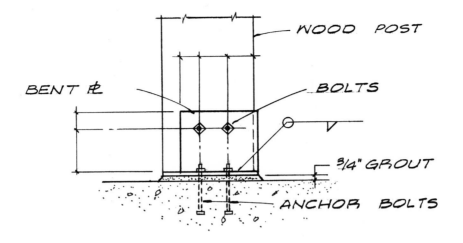

Detail 1-4(a). A wood-post connection to a concrete foundation. The metal shoe plate connection can resist lateral loads at the base of the post.

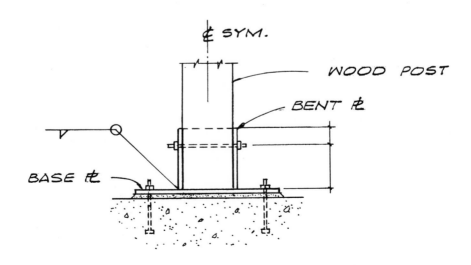

Detail 1-4(b). A front view of Detail 1-4(a).

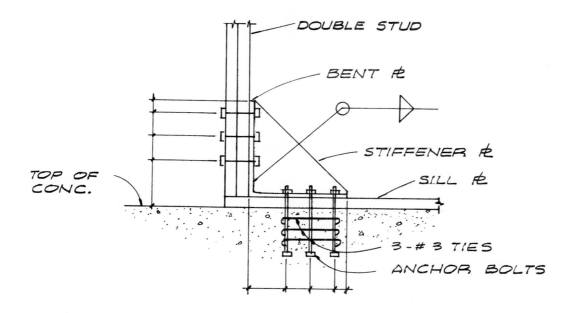

Detail 1-5. A structural tie-down connection for ends or corners of wood stud walls that are used to resist lateral forces. The bolts through the double studs and into the concrete permit the wall to resist uplift forces caused by lateral loads applied parallel to the wall. The number of bolts and the size of metal plates are determined by calculation.

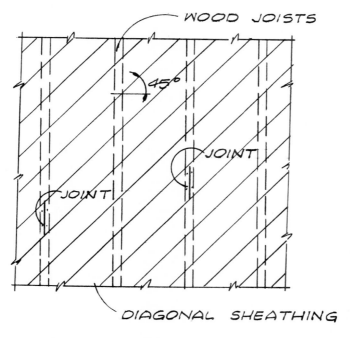

Detail 1-6. A plan of diagonal sheathing boards nailed to wood rafters or floor joists. The sheathing can act as a diaphragm to resist lateral force when it is nailed to the rafters or joists. The sheathing board should be 1″ × 6″ or 1″ × 8″ members, and the joints of adjacent boards should be separated by two rafters or joists. Each board should be nailed to a rafter or joist with a minimum of two 8d nails.

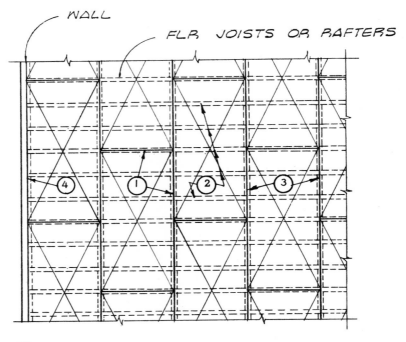

WALL

FLR. JOISTS OR RAFTERS

① EDGE NAILING

② FIELD NAILING

③ PANEL EDGE TO BLOCKING

④ BOUNDARY NAILING

Detail 1-7. A plan of floor or roof sheathing using 4′0″ × 8′0″ plywood panels. The ability of the sheathing to act as a diaphragm to resist lateral force depends on the thickness of the plywood and the size and spacing of the nails. The numbers circled on the plan permit the nailing to be scheduled. The plywood is laid with the surface grain perpendicular to the framing members.

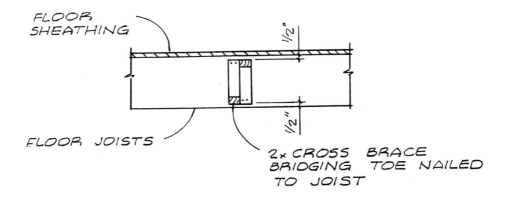

FLOOR SHEATHING

½″

FLOOR JOISTS

½″

2x CROSS BRACE BRIDGING TOE NAILED TO JOIST

Detail 1-8. A section of cross bracing acting as bridging between floor joists or roof rafters. The spacing of the rows of bridging is specified by the local building code.

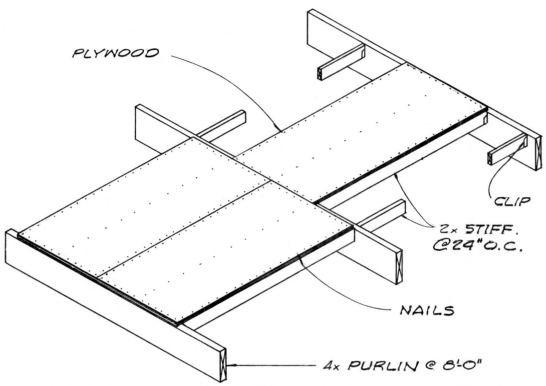

PLYWOOD

CLIP

2x STIFF. @24" O.C.

NAILS

4x PURLIN @ 8'-0"

Detail 1-9(a). An isometric view of a plywood panelized roof system. 4'0" × 8'0" plywood panels are delivered to the job site with prenailed 2" × 4" wood stiffeners nailed to the edge and to the middle of the panel. The panels are installed and nailed in place to the 4" wide wood purlins which are spaced at 8'0" o.c. The size and spacing of the nails to the purlin members depends on the required lateral resistance of the plywood sheathing acting as a diaphragm.

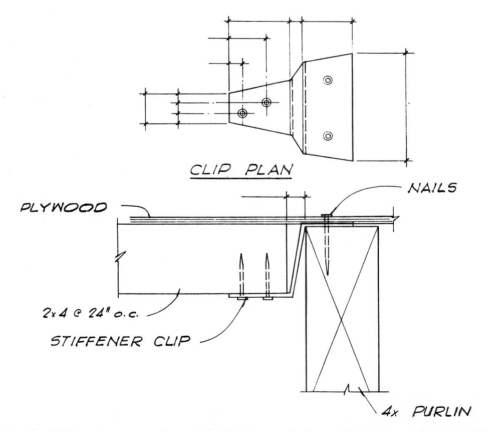

CLIP PLAN

NAILS

PLYWOOD

2x4 @ 24" o.c.

STIFFENER CLIP

4x PURLIN

Detail 1-9(b). Two views of a standard sheet metal clip used to connect the 2" × 4" stiffeners to the purlins shown in Detail 1-9(a). The size of the clip depends on the load to be supported on the roof.

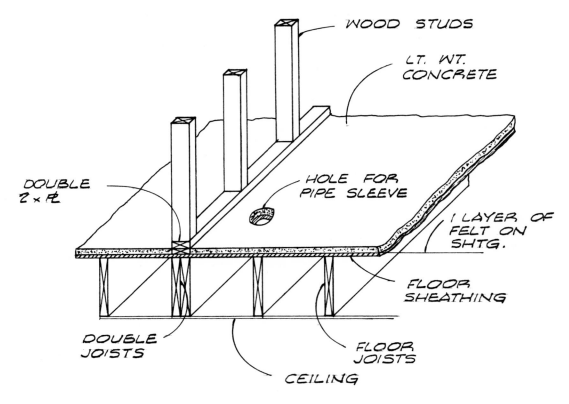

Detail 1-10. An isometric view of a wood floor with 1⅝″ thick concrete cover. Double joists are placed under the wood stud wall. The double plate at the base of the wood stud wall is optional; a single plate may be used. The plate at the base of the wood stud wall is used as a concrete screed. The concrete is poured over one layer of 15 lb. building felt.

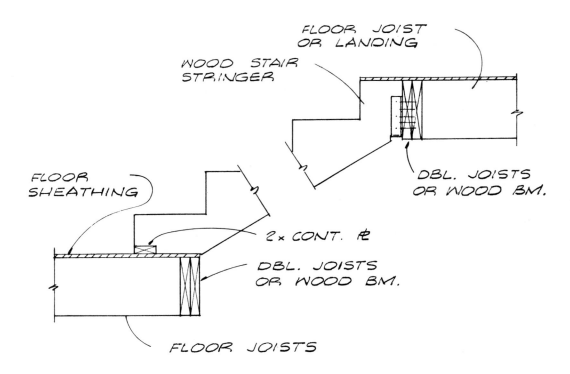

Detail 1-11. A section of a wood floor and stair stringer. The size and spacing of the wood stringers are determined by the load and span of the stairs. The base of the stringer is connected to the floor by toenailing the floor joist through the floor sheathing. The top of the stringer is connected to the double joist with a standard joist hanger.

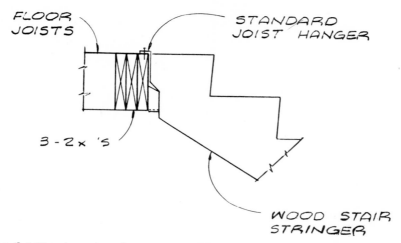

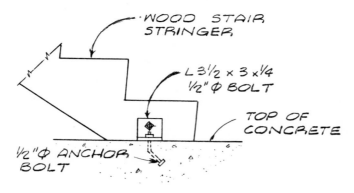

Detail 1-12. A section of a connection of a wood stringer to a triple-joist floor beam. The stringer is connected to the beam with a standard joist hanger.

Detail 1-13. A connection of the base of a wood stringer to a concrete floor slab. Each stringer is connected to the concrete slab by a clip angle with one bolt through each leg of the angle.

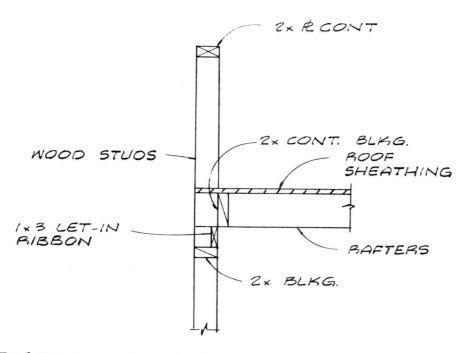

Detail 1-14. A section of a wood stud parapet wall and roof. The parapet is constructed by extending the wood studs above the top of the roof sheathing. The rafters and studs are blocked as shown to transfer the roof diaphragm stress into the wall. The rafters bear on the 1″ × 3″ let-in ribbon.

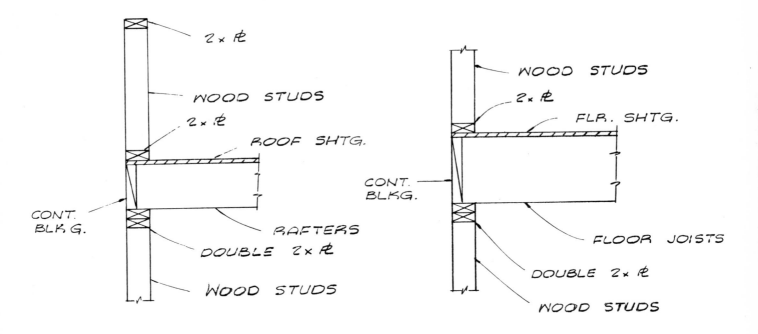

Detail 1-15. A section of a wood stud parapet wall and roof. The rafters bear on the wall double plates and are laterally braced by the continuous blocking.

Detail 1-16(a). A section of an exterior wood stud wall and floor joists. The joists bear on the wall double plates and are continuously blocked to complete the connection between the floor and the wall.

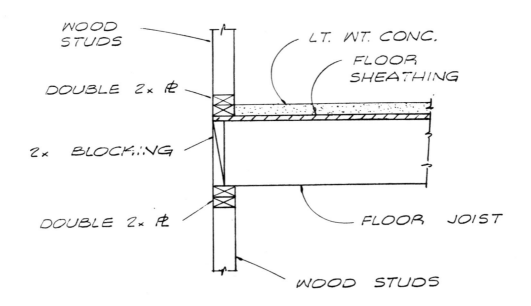

Detail 1-16(b). A section of an exterior wood stud wall and floor joists as shown in Detail 1-16(a). The floor sheathing is covered with light-weight concrete. The double plate of the stud wall on the floor is optional; a single plate may be used.

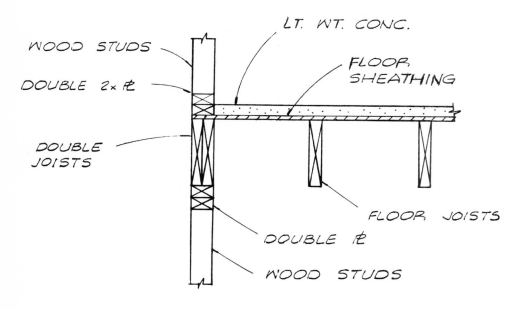

WOOD STUDS

DOUBLE 2 × ℔

DOUBLE JOISTS

LT. WT. CONC.

FLOOR SHEATHING

FLOOR JOISTS

DOUBLE ℔

WOOD STUDS

Detail 1-17. A section of an exterior wood stud wall, floor joists, and light-weight concrete over the floor sheathing. The joists span parallel to the wall. The double plate of the stud wall on the floor is optional; a single plate may be used.

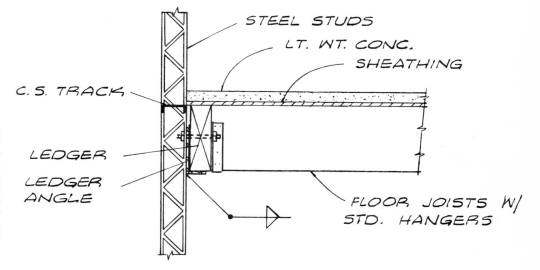

STEEL STUDS

LT. WT. CONC.

SHEATHING

C. S. TRACK

LEDGER

LEDGER ANGLE

FLOOR JOISTS W/ STD. HANGERS

Detail 1-18(a). A section of an exterior steel stud wall, wood floor joists, and light-weight concrete over wood floor sheathing. A 4″ wide wood ledger is bolted to a continuous bent metal plate or ledger angle. The angle is welded to each stud to permit the transfer of lateral force from the floor diaphragm to the wall. The channel stud track between the studs acts as a strut in the wall.

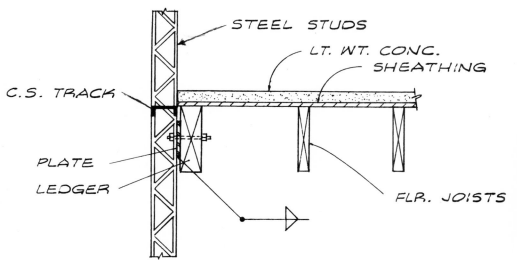

STEEL STUDS

LT. WT. CONC.

SHEATHING

C. S. TRACK

PLATE

LEDGER

FLR. JOISTS

Detail 1-18(b). A section of an exterior steel stud wall, wood floor joists, and light-weight concrete over wood floor sheathing. The floor joists span parallel to the wall. A 4″ wide wood ledger is bolted to a continuous plate. The plate is welded to each stud to permit the transfer of lateral force from the floor diaphragm to the wall. The channel stud track between the studs acts as a strut in the wall.

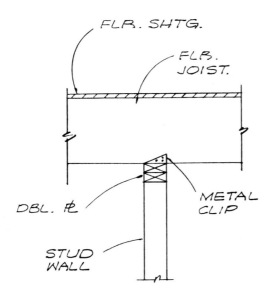

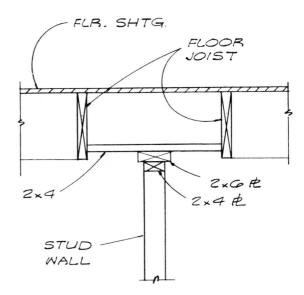

Detail 1-19(a). A section of a wood floor and floor joists which span parallel to a nonbearing wood stud partition wall. The top of the studs of the partition are connected to the floor joists as shown. The 2″ × 6″ continuous plate is nailed to the 2″ × 4″ members between the floor joists.

Detail 1-19(b). A section of a wood floor and floor joists that span perpendicular to a nonbearing wood stud partition wall. The double plate at the top of the studs is connected to the floor joists by toenails or with a sheet metal clip as shown.

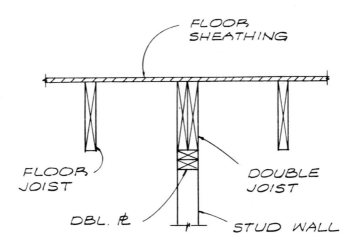

Detail 1-20. A section of a wood stud wall, floor sheathing, and floor joists. The double plate at the top of the wall is toenailed to the double floor joists.

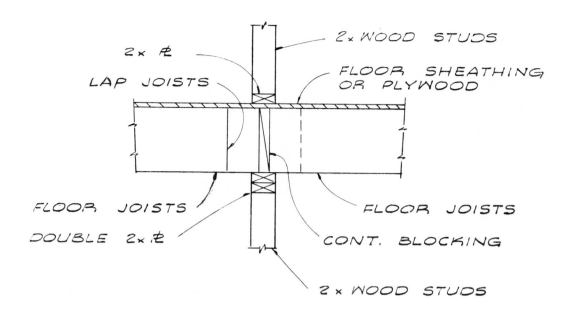

Detail 1-21. A section of an interior wood stud wall, floor sheathing and floor joists. The floor joists are lapped and nailed together and bear on the double plate at the top of the wall. The continuous blocking of the floor joists supports the wood stud wall and provides a means of transferring diaphragm loads from the floor to the walls.

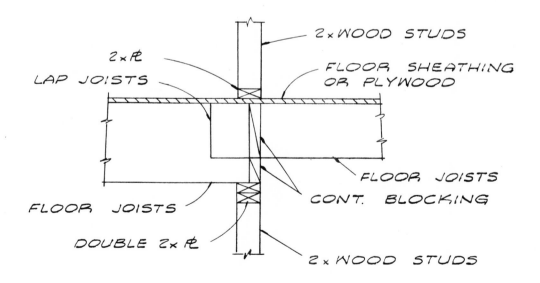

Detail 1-22. A section of an interior wood stud wall, floor sheathing, and floor joists. The wood floor joists on each side of the stud wall are unequal in depth. An extra continuous block is provided to support the smaller joist. The continuous blocking of the floor joists provides a means of transfer of the diaphragm load from the floor to the wall.

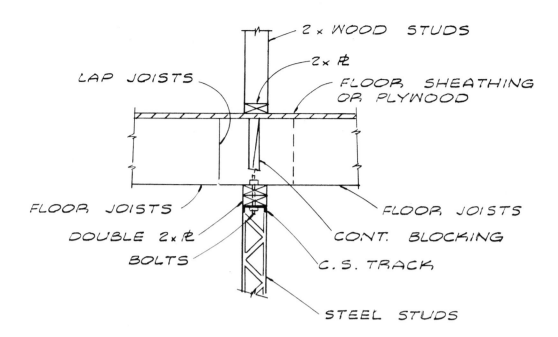

Detail 1-23(a). A section of an interior steel stud bearing wall, supporting wood floor joists and a wood stud wall. The floor joists are lapped and nailed together and bear on the double plate of the steel stud wall. The double 2″ × 4″ plate is bolted to the channel track at the top of the steel stud wall as shown. The continuous blocking provides a means of transfer of the diaphragm load to the steel stud wall.

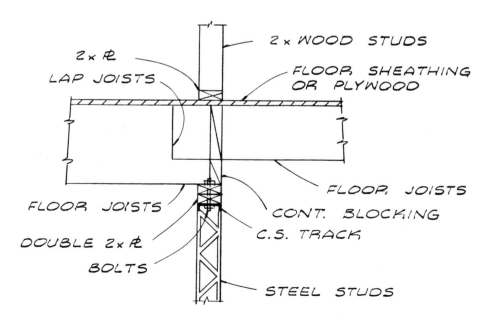

Detail 1-23(b). A section of an interior steel stud bearing wall supporting wood floor joists and a wood stud wall. The floor joists are lapped and nailed together and bear on the double plate of the steel stud wall. The wood floor joists on each side of the steel stud wall are unequal in depth. An extra continuous block is provided to support the smaller joists. The double 2″ × 4″ plate is bolted to the channel track at the top of the steel stud wall as shown. The continuous blocking provides a means of transfer of the floor diaphragm load to the steel stud wall.

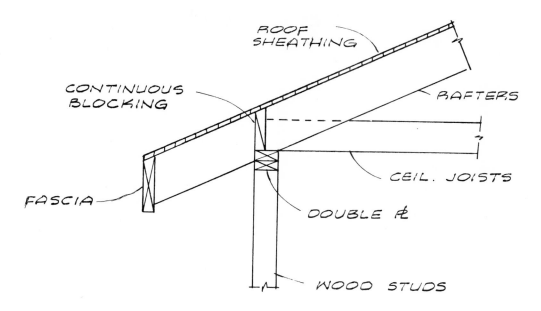

Detail 1-24. A section of an exterior wood stud wall and a wood roof eave. The roof rafters and the ceiling joists are nailed to the double plate at the top of the wall. Continuous blocking is provided to transfer the roof diaphragm load to the wall.

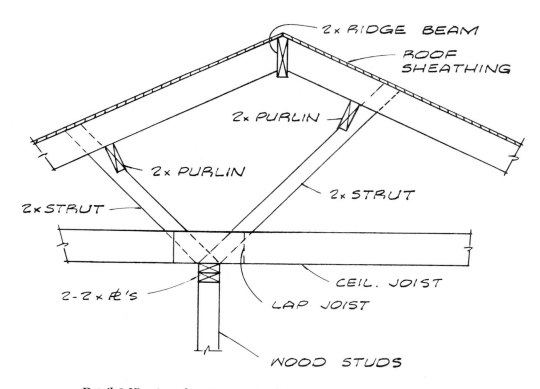

Detail 1-25. A roof section supported by an interior wood stud wall. The 2″ wide struts supporting the roof to the wall should not slope more than 45° from the vertical. The wood struts are spaced at 4′0″ o.c. and the intermediate rafters are supported by the 2″ wide continuous purlins.

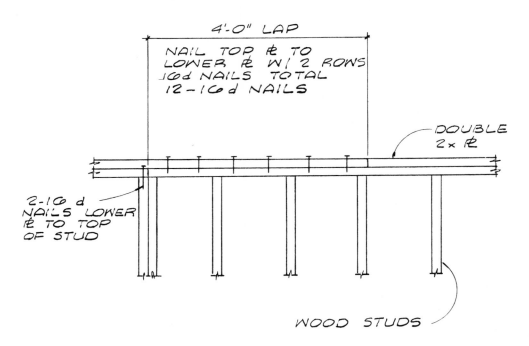

Detail 1-26. A lap splice of the top double plates of a wood stud wall. The width of the plates are equal to the width of the studs. The studs of the wall are tied together at the top with a double plate to transfer lateral force from a floor or roof diaphragm to the wall. The double plates must be properly lapped and nailed to make the total element effective in the transfer of lateral force.

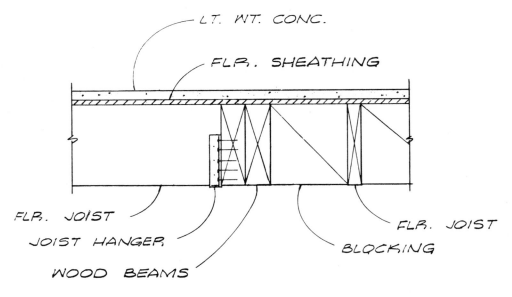

Detail 1-27. A section of a laterally laminated wood beam, wood floor joists, and light-weight concrete on a wood floor. The joists are supported by the beam on the left side and span parallel to the beam on the right side. The beam is laterally laminated as shown in Detail 1-35(a).

Detail 1-28. A section of a wood beam, an exterior wood stud wall and light weight concrete on a wood floor. The joists span parallel to the beam. The double plate of the stud wall on the floor is optional; a single plate may be used.

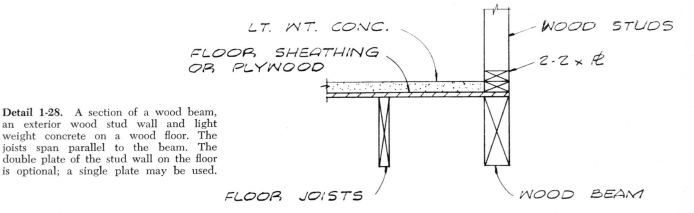

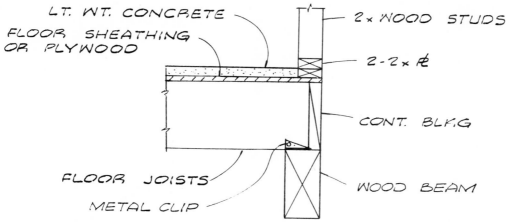

LT. WT. CONCRETE

FLOOR SHEATHING
OR PLYWOOD

2 x WOOD STUDS

2-2 x ℞

CONT. BLK.G

FLOOR JOISTS

METAL CLIP

WOOD BEAM

Detail 1-29(a). A section of a wood beam, an exterior wood stud wall, floor joists, and light-weight concrete on a wood floor. The floor joists are connected to the wood beam by toenailing or by a sheet metal clip as shown. The continuous blocking may be substituted with a continuous rim member provided that the floor joists have sufficient bearing area on the wood beam.

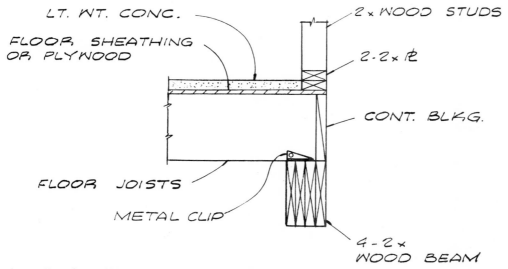

LT. WT. CONC.

FLOOR SHEATHING
OR PLYWOOD

2 x WOOD STUDS

2-2 x ℞

CONT. BLK.G.

FLOOR JOISTS

METAL CLIP

4 - 2 x
WOOD BEAM

Detail 1-29(b). A section of a laterally laminated wood beam supporting an exterior wood stud wall, floor joists, and light-weight concrete on a wood floor. The floor joists are connected to the wood beam by toenails or by a sheet metal clip as shown. The continuous blocking may be substituted with a continuous rim member provided that the floor joists have sufficient bearing area on the wood beam. The wood beam is laminated as shown in Detail 1-35(a).

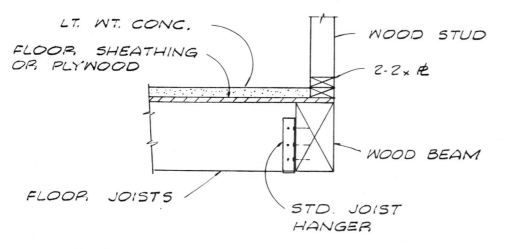

LT. WT. CONC.

FLOOR SHEATHING
OR PLYWOOD

WOOD STUD

2-2 x ℞

WOOD BEAM

FLOOR JOISTS

STD. JOIST
HANGER

Detail 1-30. A section of a wood beam supporting an exterior wood stud wall, floor joists, and light-weight concrete on a wood floor. The floor joists are connected to the beam with standard joist hangers. The double plate of the stud wall on the floor is optional; a single plate may be used.

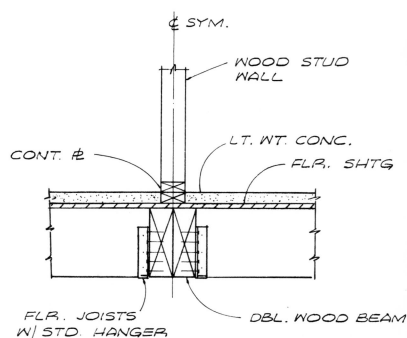

¢ SYM.

FLR. SHTG.

LT. WT. CONC.

DOUBLE WOOD BEAM

FLR. JOIST W/ STD. HANGER

Detail 1-31. A section of a laterally laminated wood beam supporting floor joists and light-weight concrete on a wood floor. The wood beam is laminated as shown in Detail 1-35(a).

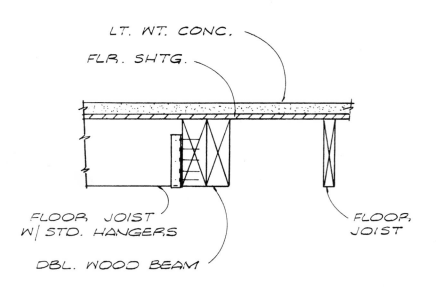

LT. WT. CONC.

FLR. SHTG.

FLOOR JOIST W/ STD. HANGERS

DBL. WOOD BEAM

FLOOR JOIST

Detail 1-32. A section of a laterally laminated wood beam supporting floor joists on the left side and light-weight concrete on a wood floor. The floor joists on the right side span parallel to the laminated beam. The beam is laminated as shown in Detail 1-35(a).

¢ SYM.

WOOD STUD WALL

LT. WT. CONC.

FLR. SHTG

CONT. ℞

FLR. JOISTS W/ STD. HANGER

DBL. WOOD BEAM

Detail 1-33. A section of a laterally laminated wood beam supporting floor joists, a wood stud wall, and light-weight concrete on a wood floor. The beam is laminated as shown in Detail 1-35(a). The double plate of the stud wall on the floor is optional; a single plate may be used.

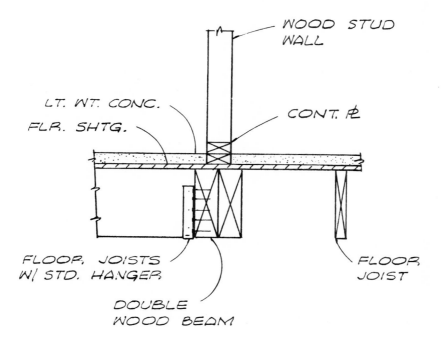

WOOD STUD WALL

LT. WT. CONC.

FLR. SHTG.

CONT. ℞

FLOOR JOISTS W/ STD. HANGER

FLOOR JOIST

DOUBLE WOOD BEAM

Detail 1-34. A section of a laterally laminated wood beam supporting floor joists, a wood stud wall, and light-weight concrete on a wood floor. The floor joists on the right side span parallel to the laminated beam. The beam is laminated as shown in Detail 1-35(a). The double plate of the stud wall on the floor is optional; a single plate may be used.

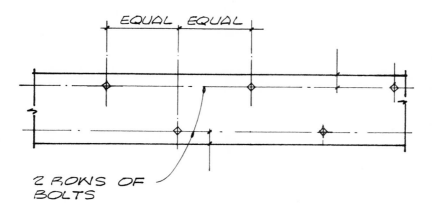

EQUAL   EQUAL

2 ROWS OF BOLTS

Detail 1-35(a). An elevation of a laterally laminated wood beam showing the bolts and spacing required. See Detail 1-35(b).

3 OR MORE 2× OR 2 - 4× WOOD MEMBERS

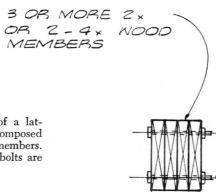

Detail 1-35(b). A section of a laterally laminated wood beam composed of a 2″ wide or 4″ wide members. The size and spacing of the bolts are determined by calculation.

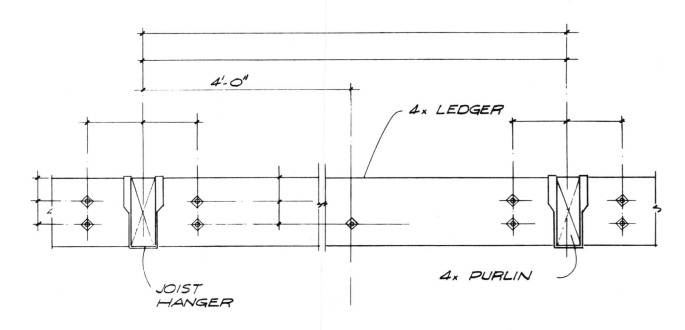

4'-0"

4x LEDGER

JOIST
HANGER

4x PURLIN

Detail 1-36. An elevation of a 4″ wide wood ledger and bolts. The ledger may be bolted to a masonry or concrete wall. The size and spacing of the bolts are determined by calculation. The purlins are also shown in Detail 1-9(a). Detail 2-70 shows a section of the ledger.

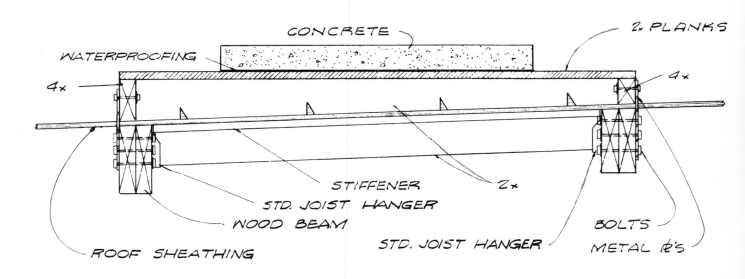

CONCRETE

2x PLANKS

WATERPROOFING

4x

4x

STIFFENER

2x

STD. JOIST HANGER

WOOD BEAM

STD. JOIST HANGER

BOLTS

METAL Ŕ'S

ROOF SHEATHING

Detail 1-37. A section of a wood platform used to support mechanical equipment on a plywood panelized roof. See Detail 1-9(a). The platform is supported by and connected to the roof beams with metal straps bolted as shown. The connections should be capable of resisting lateral loads caused by wind or seismic forces. The concrete slab on the platform serves to dampen vibrational forces caused by the operation of mechanical equipment.

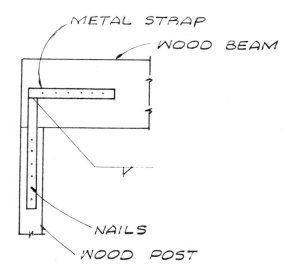

Detail 1-38(a). An end connection of a wood beam to a wood post. The connection is made with metal side plates and nails on each side of the post and beam.

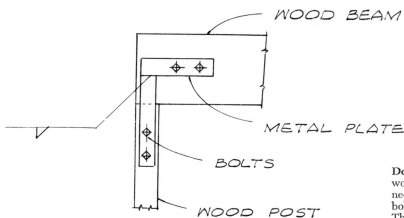

Detail 1-38(b). An end connection of a wood beam to a wood post. The connection is made with metal side plates and bolts on each side of the post and beam. The size and spacing of the bolts are determined by calculation.

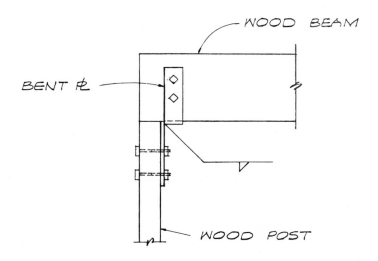

Detail 1-39. An end connection of a wood beam to a wood post. The method of the connection allows the beam and the post to be of different widths.

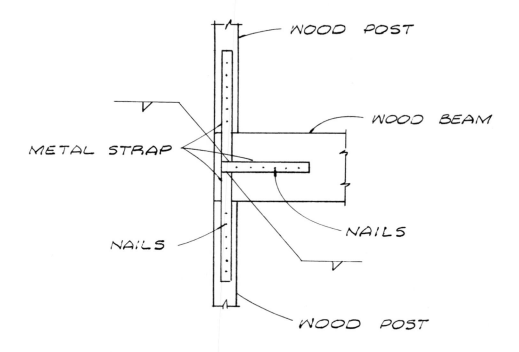

Detail 1-40(a). An end connection of a wood beam to wood posts. The connection is made with metal side plates and nails to each side of the beam and the posts.

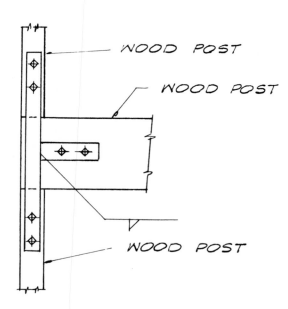

Detail 1-40(b). An end connection of a wood beam to wood posts. The connection is made with metal side plates and bolts through each side of the beam and posts.

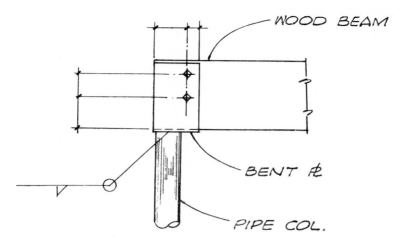

Detail 1-41(a). An end connection of a wood beam to a steel pipe column. The U-shaped metal plate is bolted through the wood beam and welded to the top of the pipe column.

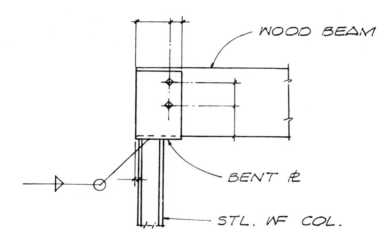

Detail 1-41(b). An end connection of a wood beam to a wide flange steel column. The U-shaped metal plate is bolted through the wood beam and welded to the top of the wide flange column.

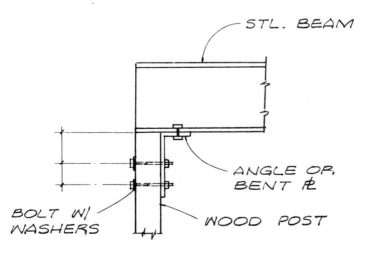

Detail 1-42. An end connection of a steel beam to a wood post. The vertical leg of the connection angle is bolted to the post with two bolts as shown. The horizontal leg of the connection angle is bolted to the bottom flange of the steel beam with two bolts, one bolt on each side of the beam web.

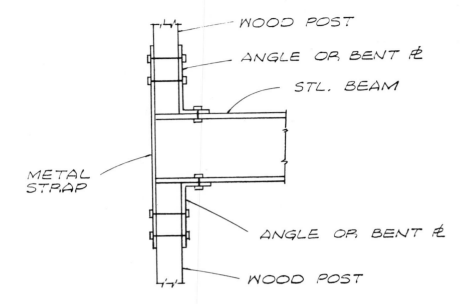

Detail 1-43. An end connection of a steel beam to wood posts. The vertical legs of the connection angles at the top and bottom of the steel beam are bolted to the posts with two bolts as shown. The horizontal legs of the connection angles are bolted to the top and bottom flanges of the steel beam with two bolts, one bolt on each side of the beam web. The metal strap on the face of the posts connects the top post to the bottom post.

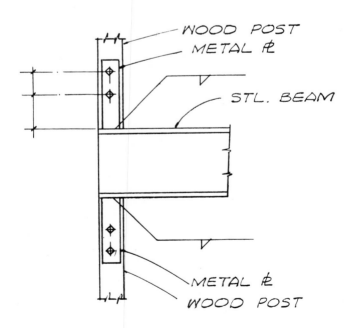

Detail 1-44. An end connection of a steel beam to wood posts. The plates on each side of the posts are welded to the top and bottom flanges of the beam.

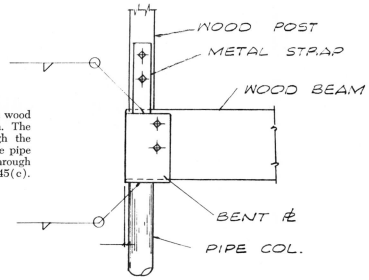

Detail 1-45(a). An end connection of a wood beam and post to a steel pipe column. The U-shaped metal plate is bolted through the wood beam and welded to the top of the pipe column. The metal plates are bolted through each side of the wood post. See Detail 1-45(c).

WOOD POST

METAL STRAP

WOOD BEAM

BENT ℞

PIPE COL.

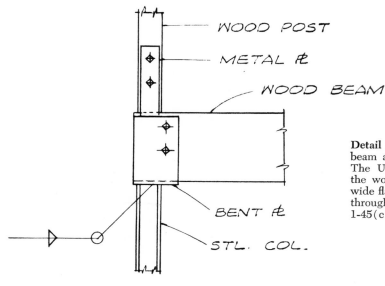

WOOD POST

METAL ℞

WOOD BEAM

BENT ℞

STL. COL.

Detail 1-45(b). An end connection of a wood beam and post to a wide flange steel column. The U-shaped metal plate is bolted through the wood beam and welded to the top of the wide flange column. The metal plates are bolted through each side of the wood post. See Detail 1-45(c).

WOOD POST

SHIM AS REQD

Detail 1-45(c). A section of Details 1-45(a) and 1-55. Wood shim plates are added between the metal side plates and the post.

PIPE COL. OR STL. WF COL.

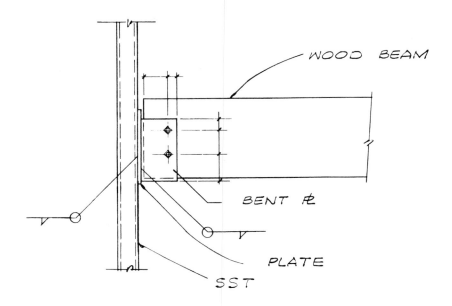

Detail 1-46. An end connection of a wood beam to a continuous structural steel tube column. The plate at the face of the column serves to adapt the width of the beam to the width of the column. The U-shaped metal plate is bolted through the beam and welded to the plate on the face of the column.

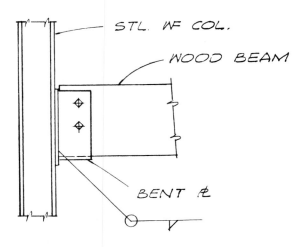

Detail 1-47. An end connection of a wood beam to a continuous wide-flange steel column. The metal plate at the face of the column serves to adapt the width of the beam to the width of the column. The U-shaped metal plate is bolted through the beam and welded to the plate on the face of the column.

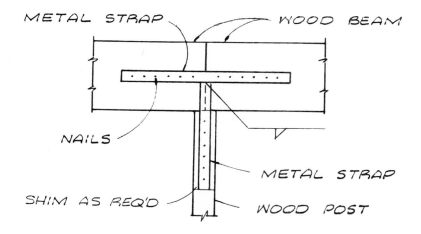

Detail 1-48(a). A wood beam and post connection. The metal straps are nailed to each side of the beam and post. The beams should set on the post to allow sufficient bearing area between the post and the beam. Wood shim plates are added to the sides of the post when the width of the beam is greater than the width of the post.

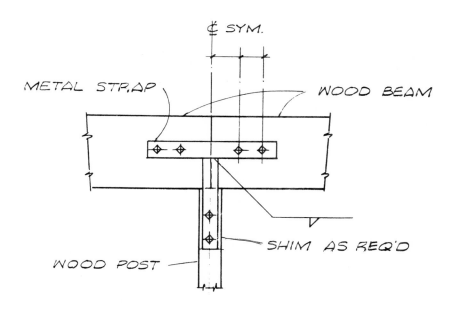

Detail 1-48(b). A wood beam and post connection. The metal straps are bolted through each side of the beams and post. The beams should set on the post to allow sufficient bearing area between the post and the beam. Wood shim plates are added to the sides of the post when the width of the beam is greater than the width of the post.

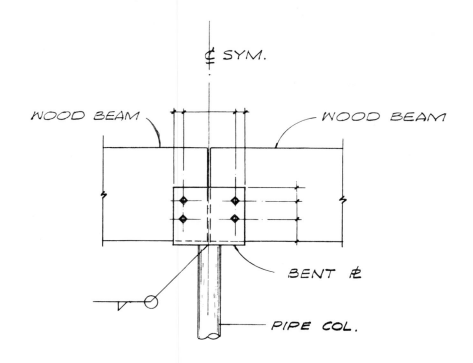

WOOD BEAM

WOOD BEAM

BENT ℞

PIPE COL.

¢ SYM.

Detail 1-49(a). A connection of wood beams to a steel pipe column. The U-shaped metal plate is bolted through the beams and welded to the top of the pipe column.

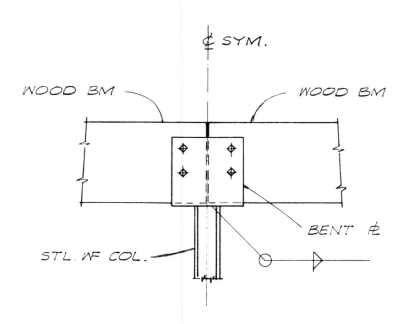

WOOD BM

WOOD BM

BENT ℞

STL. WF COL.

¢ SYM.

Detail 1-49(b). A connection of wood beams to a wide flange steel column. The U-shaped metal plate is bolted through the beams and welded to the top of the wide flange column.

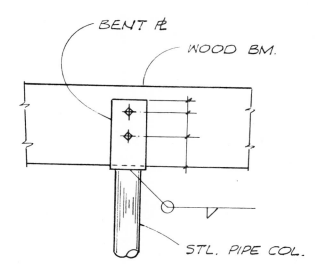

Detail 1-50(a). A connection of a cantilevered or continuous wood beam to a steel pipe column. The U-shaped metal plate is bolted through the beam and welded to the top of the pipe column.

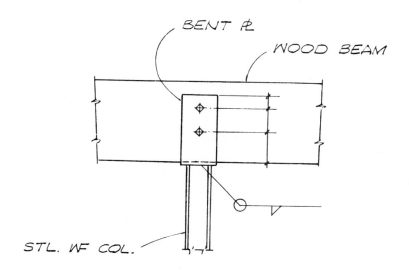

Detail 1-50(b). A connection of a cantilevered or continuous wood beam to a wide flange steel column. The U-shaped metal plate is bolted through the beam and welded to the top of the wide flange column.

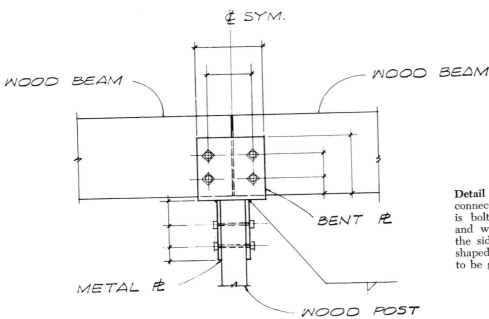

WOOD BEAM

WOOD BEAM

¢ SYM.

BENT ℔

METAL ℔

WOOD POST

Detail 1-51. A wood beam and post connection. The U-shaped metal plate is bolted through the wood beams and welded to the metal plates on the sides of the wood post. The U-shaped plate allows the beam width to be greater than the post width.

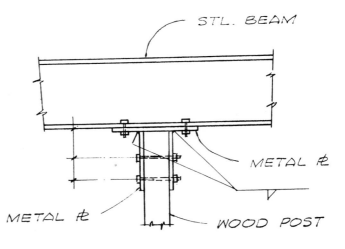

STL. BEAM

METAL ℔

METAL ℔

WOOD POST

Detail 1-52. A connection of a wood post supporting a cantilevered or continuous steel beam. The horizontal plate at the top of the post is bolted to the bottom flange of the steel beam with two bolts on each side of the beam web. The metal plates bolted through each side of the post are welded to the horizontal plate as shown.

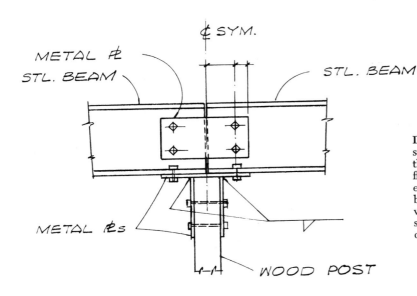

¢ SYM.

METAL ℔
STL. BEAM

STL. BEAM

METAL ℔s

WOOD POST

Detail 1-53. A connection of a wood post supporting steel beams. The horizontal plate at the top of the post is bolted to the bottom flange of the steel beams with two bolts on each side of the beam web. The metal plates bolted through each side of the post are welded to the horizontal plate as shown. The steel beams are connected by plates bolted on each side of the beam web.

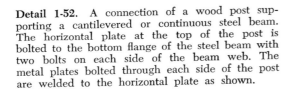

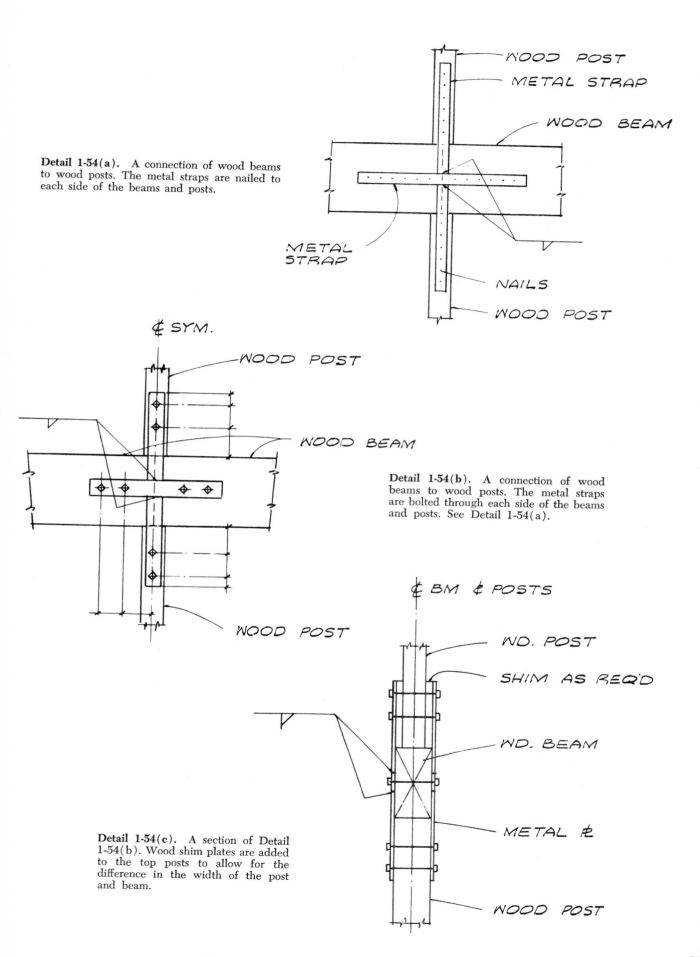

Detail 1-54(a). A connection of wood beams to wood posts. The metal straps are nailed to each side of the beams and posts.

WOOD POST
METAL STRAP
WOOD BEAM
METAL STRAP
NAILS
WOOD POST

℄ SYM.
WOOD POST
WOOD BEAM
WOOD POST

Detail 1-54(b). A connection of wood beams to wood posts. The metal straps are bolted through each side of the beams and posts. See Detail 1-54(a).

℄ BM ℄ POSTS
WD. POST
SHIM AS REQ'D
WD. BEAM
METAL ℄
WOOD POST

Detail 1-54(c). A section of Detail 1-54(b). Wood shim plates are added to the top posts to allow for the difference in the width of the post and beam.

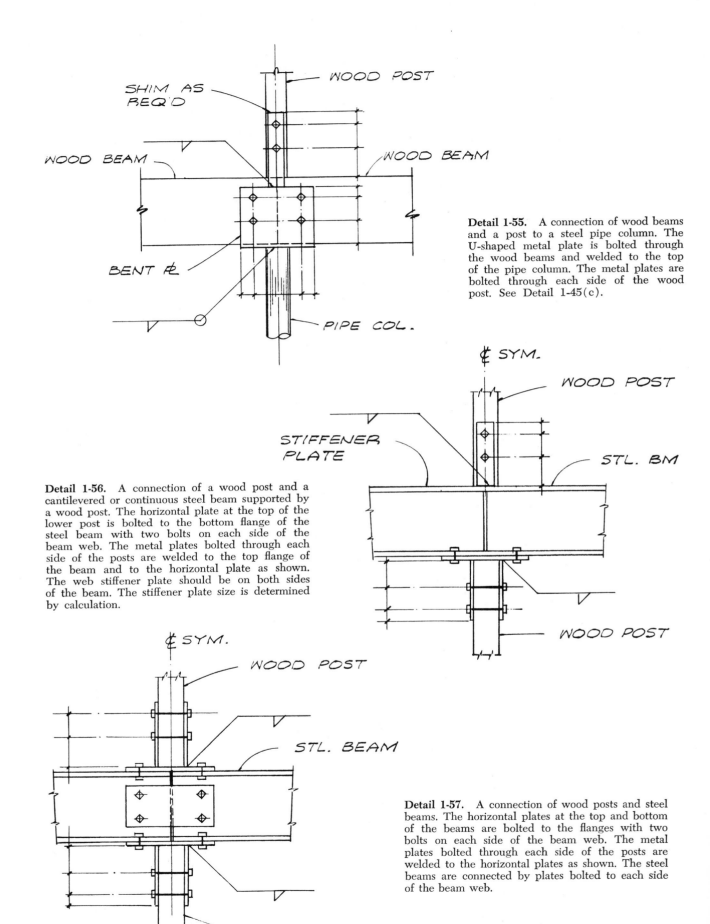

SHIM AS REQ'D

WOOD POST

WOOD BEAM

WOOD BEAM

BENT ℄

PIPE COL.

Detail 1-55. A connection of wood beams and a post to a steel pipe column. The U-shaped metal plate is bolted through the wood beams and welded to the top of the pipe column. The metal plates are bolted through each side of the wood post. See Detail 1-45(c).

℄ SYM.

WOOD POST

STIFFENER PLATE

STL. BM

Detail 1-56. A connection of a wood post and a cantilevered or continuous steel beam supported by a wood post. The horizontal plate at the top of the lower post is bolted to the bottom flange of the steel beam with two bolts on each side of the beam web. The metal plates bolted through each side of the posts are welded to the top flange of the beam and to the horizontal plate as shown. The web stiffener plate should be on both sides of the beam. The stiffener plate size is determined by calculation.

WOOD POST

℄ SYM.

WOOD POST

STL. BEAM

Detail 1-57. A connection of wood posts and steel beams. The horizontal plates at the top and bottom of the beams are bolted to the flanges with two bolts on each side of the beam web. The metal plates bolted through each side of the posts are welded to the horizontal plates as shown. The steel beams are connected by plates bolted to each side of the beam web.

WOOD POST

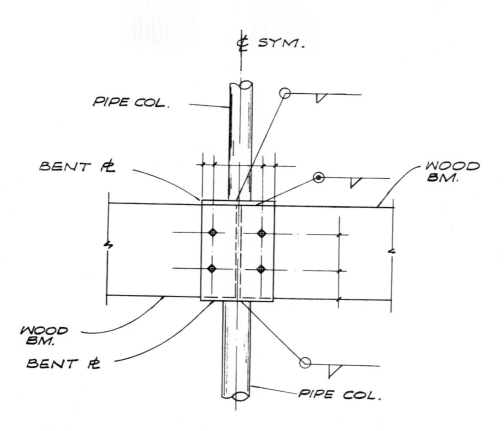

Detail 1-58(a). A connection of wood beams and steel pipe columns. The L-shaped metal plates are bolted through the beams and welded to the top and bottom of the pipe columns as shown. See Detail 1-58(b).

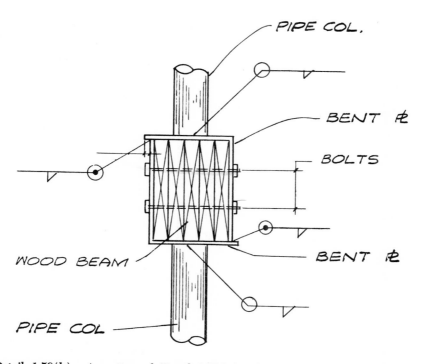

Detail 1-58(b). A section of Detail 1-58(a). The wood beam that is shown is composed of laterally laminated 2″ wide members. See Detail 1-35(b). The L-shaped side plates bear on each other to transfer the vertical column load if the wood beams compress or shrink away from the metal plates.

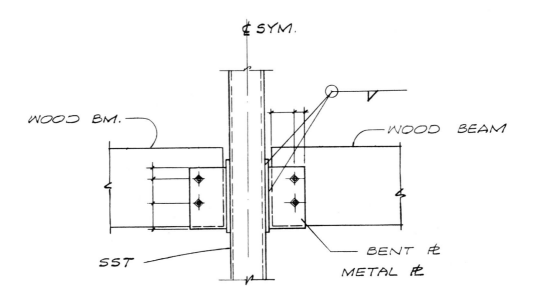

Detail 1-59. Connection of wood beams to a continuous structural steel tube column. The metal plates at each face of the column serve to adapt the width of the beams to the width of the column. The U-shaped metal plates are bolted through the beams and welded to the face of the column plates.

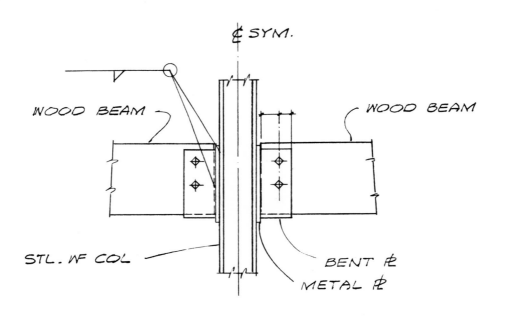

Detail 1-60. A connection of wood beams to a continuous wide flange steel column. The metal plates at each face of the column serve to adapt the width of the beams to the width of the column. The U-shaped metal plates are bolted through the beams and welded to the face of the column plates.

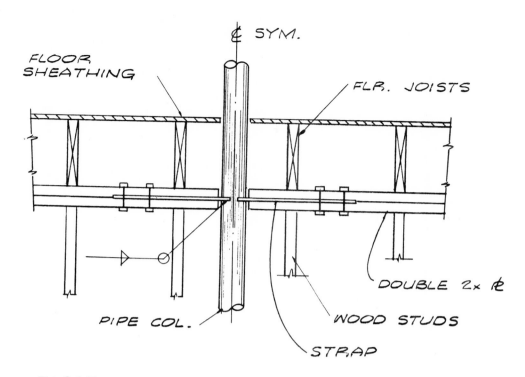

FLOOR SHEATHING

FLR. JOISTS

₵ SYM.

DOUBLE 2x ℓ

PIPE COL.

WOOD STUDS

STRAP

Detail 1-61. A steel pipe column connected to a wood stud wall. The connection is made to the double plates at the top of the wall to reduce the slenderness ratio of the pipe column. The connection is effective only in the direction parallel to the wall.

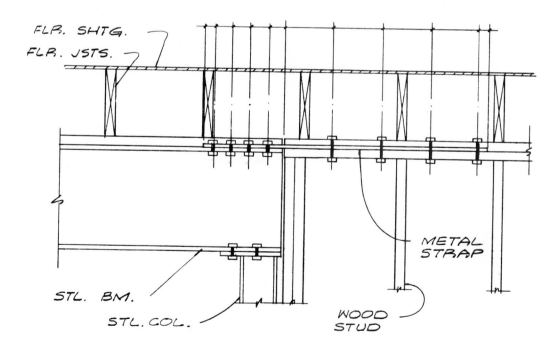

FLR. SHTG.

FLR. JSTS.

METAL STRAP

STL. BM.

STL. COL.

WOOD STUD

Detail 1-62. An end connection of a steel beam to a wood stud wall. The wood stud wall resists lateral forces that are transferred from the floor diaphragm to the steel beam. The lateral force is transferred to the wall through the metal strap that is bolted to the top flange of the beam and the double plates at the top of the wall. The strap may be welded to the beam in lieu of the bolts as shown.

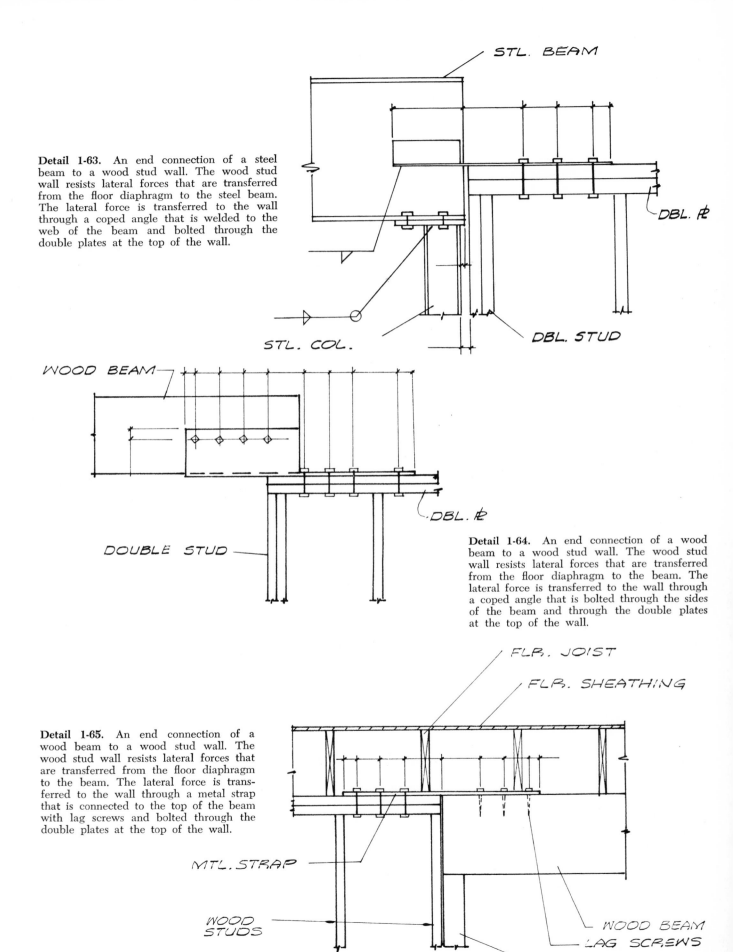

STL. BEAM

Detail 1-63. An end connection of a steel beam to a wood stud wall. The wood stud wall resists lateral forces that are transferred from the floor diaphragm to the steel beam. The lateral force is transferred to the wall through a coped angle that is welded to the web of the beam and bolted through the double plates at the top of the wall.

DBL. ℞

STL. COL.

DBL. STUD

WOOD BEAM

DBL. ℞

DOUBLE STUD

Detail 1-64. An end connection of a wood beam to a wood stud wall. The wood stud wall resists lateral forces that are transferred from the floor diaphragm to the beam. The lateral force is transferred to the wall through a coped angle that is bolted through the sides of the beam and through the double plates at the top of the wall.

FLR. JOIST

FLR. SHEATHING

Detail 1-65. An end connection of a wood beam to a wood stud wall. The wood stud wall resists lateral forces that are transferred from the floor diaphragm to the beam. The lateral force is transferred to the wall through a metal strap that is connected to the top of the beam with lag screws and bolted through the double plates at the top of the wall.

MTL. STRAP

WOOD STUDS

WOOD BEAM

LAG SCREWS

WOOD POST

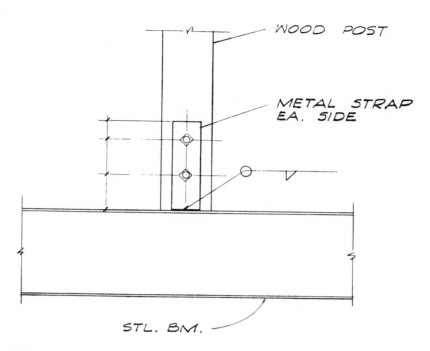

Detail 1-66(a). A wood post supported by a steel beam. The metal plates bolted through each side of the post are welded to the top flange of the beam.

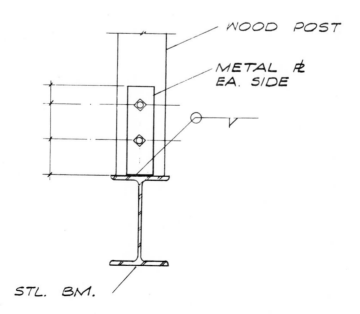

Detail 1-66(b). A wood post supported by a steel beam. The metal plates bolted through each side of the post are welded to the top flange of the beam.

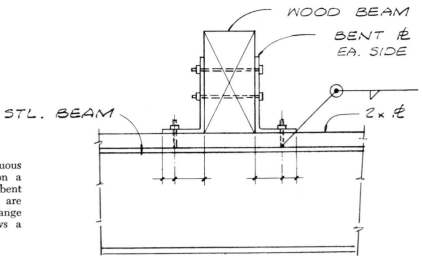

Detail 1-67(a). A connection of a continuous or cantilevered wood beam supported on a steel beam. The horizontal legs of the bent plates on each side of the wood beam are connected with bolts welded to the top flange of the steel beam. Detail 1-67(b) shows a section of this connection.

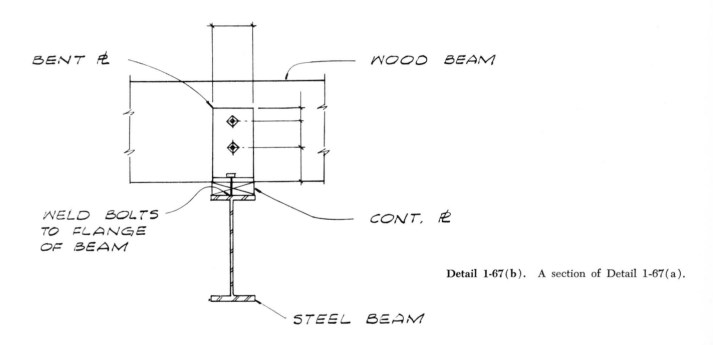

Detail 1-67(b). A section of Detail 1-67(a).

Detail 1-68. An intersection connection of a wood beam to a steel beam. A metal plate is welded to the edges of the steel beam flanges as shown. A U-shaped metal plate is welded to the flat plate and bolted through the wood beam. The steel beam may require web stiffener plates depending on the wood beam reaction.

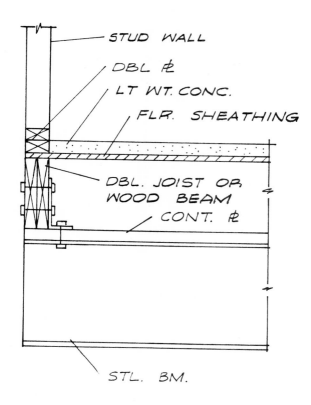

STUD WALL

DBL. ℀

LT WT. CONC.

FLR. SHEATHING

DBL. JOIST OR
WOOD BEAM

CONT. ℀

STL. BM.

Detail 1-69. A section of double wood floor joists supporting a wood stud wall on a steel beam. The double joist is connected to the steel beam by a clip angle that is bolted to the top flange of the beam with one bolt on each side of the beam web.

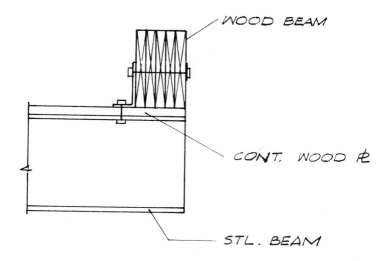

WOOD BEAM

CONT. WOOD ℀

STL. BEAM

Detail 1-70. A connection of a wood beam to the top of a steel beam. The laterally laminated wood beam is composed of 2″ wide members. See Detail 1-35(b). The wood beam is connected to the steel beam by a clip angle that is bolted to the top flange of the steel beam with one bolt on each side of the beam web.

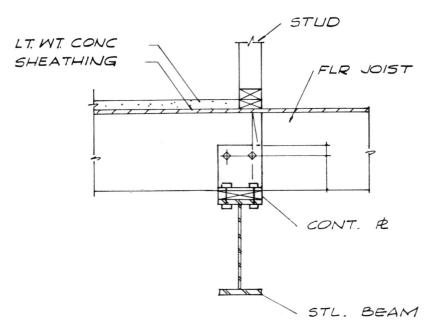

LT. WT. CONC
SHEATHING

STUD

FLR JOIST

CONT. ℞

STL. BEAM

Detail 1-71. A section of a steel beam supporting cantilevered wood floor joists. The clip angles are spaced at 4′0″ o.c. and connect the floor joists to the top of the steel beam. The clip angles have two bolts through each leg.

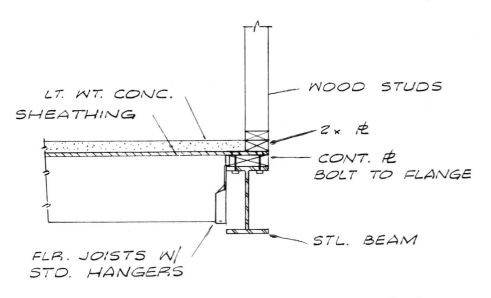

LT. WT. CONC.
SHEATHING

WOOD STUDS

2 × ℞

CONT. ℞
BOLT TO FLANGE

STL. BEAM

FLR. JOISTS W/
STD. HANGERS

Detail 1-72. A section of a steel beam supporting an exterior wood stud wall, floor joists, and light-weight concrete on a wood floor. The floor joists are supported by the beam with standard joist hangers welded to the top flange. The wood nailer plate is bolted to the top flange of the beam with ⅝″ dia. bolts spaced at 4′0″ o.c., staggered on each side of the beam web. The double plate of the stud wall on the floor is optional; a single plate may be used.

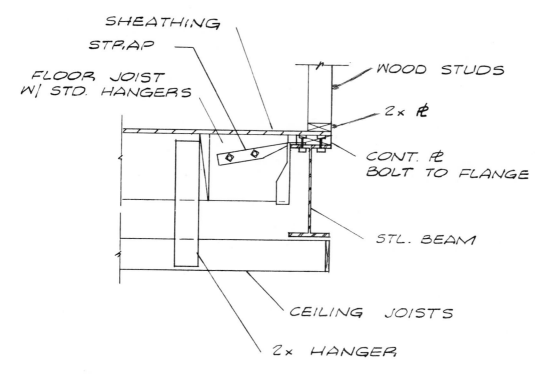

SHEATHING

STRAP

FLOOR JOIST
W/ STD. HANGERS

WOOD STUDS

2x ℔

CONT. ℔
BOLT TO FLANGE

STL. BEAM

CEILING JOISTS

2x HANGER

Detail 1-73. A section of a steel beam supporting an exterior wood stud wall, floor joists, and a suspended ceiling. The detail is similar to Detail 1-72. The ceiling joists are suspended from the floor joists by a wood hanger. The hanger spacing determines the span of the ceiling joists.

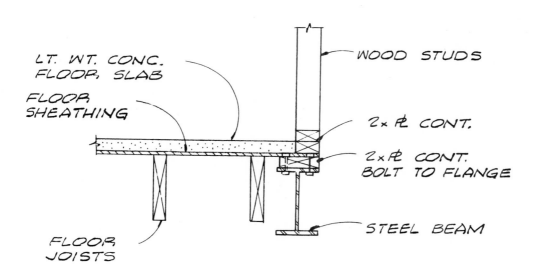

LT. WT. CONC.
FLOOR SLAB

FLOOR
SHEATHING

WOOD STUDS

2x ℔ CONT.

2x ℔ CONT.
BOLT TO FLANGE

STEEL BEAM

FLOOR
JOISTS

Detail 1-74. A section of a steel beam supporting an exterior wood stud wall, floor joists, and light-weight concrete on a wood floor. The floor joists span parallel to the steel beam. The wood nailer plate is bolted to the top flange of the beam with ⅝" dia. bolts spaced at 4'0" o.c., staggered on each side of the beam web. The double plate of the stud wall on the floor is optional; a single plate may be used.

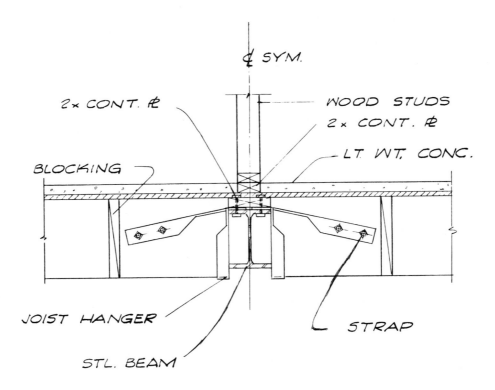

Detail 1-75. A section of a steel beam supporting an interior wood stud wall, floor joists, and light-weight concrete on a wood floor. The joists are supported by the beam with standard joist hangers welded to the top flange. The wood nailer plate is bolted to the top flange of the beam with ⅝″ dia. bolts spaced at 4′0″ o.c., staggered on each side of the beam web. A twisted metal strap or coped angle spaced at 4′0″ o.c. is welded to each side of the beam and bolted to a joist to transfer the floor diaphragm stress to the steel beam.

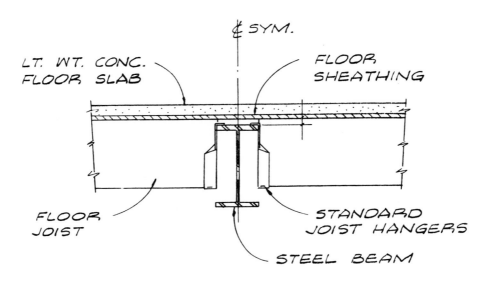

Detail 1-76. A section of a steel beam supporting wood floor joists and light-weight concrete on the wood floor. The floor joists are supported by the beam with standard joist hangers welded to the top flange. A space is provided between the top flange of the steel beam and the bottom side of the floor sheathing to allow for the wood shrinkage.

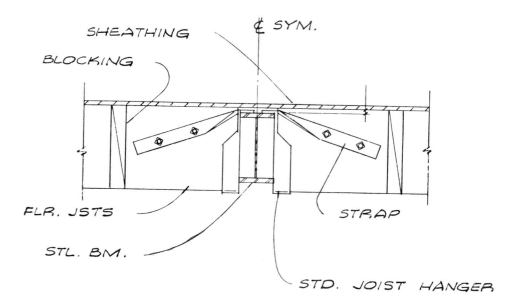

SHEATHING

BLOCKING

℄ SYM.

FLR. JSTS

STL. BM.

STRAP

STD. JOIST HANGER

Detail 1-77. A section of a steel beam supporting wood floor joists and a wood floor. The floor joists are supported by the beam with standard joist hangers welded to the top flange. A twisted metal strap spaced at 4'0" o.c. is welded to each side of the beam and bolted to a joist to transfer the floor diaphragm stress to the beam. A space is provided between the top flange of the steel beam and the bottom side of the floor sheathing to allow for the wood shrinkage.

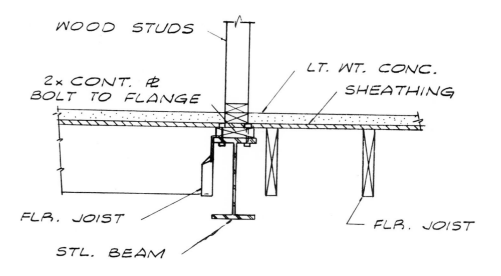

WOOD STUDS

2× CONT. ℔ BOLT TO FLANGE

LT. WT. CONC.

SHEATHING

FLR. JOIST

STL. BEAM

FLR. JOIST

Detail 1-78. A section of a steel beam supporting an interior wood stud wall, floor joists, and light-weight concrete on a wood floor. The floor joists on the left side of the beam are supported by the beam with standard joist hangers welded to the top flange. The floor joists on the right side of the beam span parallel to the beam. The wood nailer plate is bolted to the top flange of the beam with ⅝" dia. bolts spaced at 4'0" o.c., staggered on each side of the beam web. The double wood plate of the stud wall on the floor is optional; a single plate may be used.

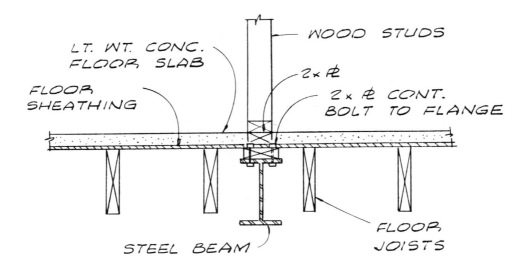

LT. WT. CONC. FLOOR SLAB

FLOOR SHEATHING

WOOD STUDS

2 x ℔

2 x ℔ CONT. BOLT TO FLANGE

STEEL BEAM

FLOOR JOISTS

Detail 1-79. A section of a steel beam supporting an interior wood stud wall and light-weight concrete on a wood floor. The floor joists span parallel to the beam. The wood nailer plate is bolted to the top flange of the beam with ⅝" dia. bolts spaced at 4'0" o.c., staggered on each side of the beam web. The double plate of the stud wall on the floor is optional; a single plate may be used.

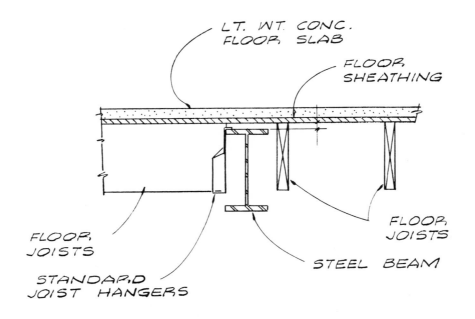

LT. WT. CONC. FLOOR SLAB

FLOOR SHEATHING

FLOOR JOISTS

STANDARD JOIST HANGERS

FLOOR JOISTS

STEEL BEAM

Detail 1-80. A section of a steel beam supporting floor joists and light-weight concrete on a wood floor. The floor joists on the left side are supported by the beam with standard joist hangers welded to the top flange. The floor joists on the right side span parallel to the beam. A space is provided between the top flange of the steel beam and the bottom side of the floor sheathing to allow for the wood shrinkage.

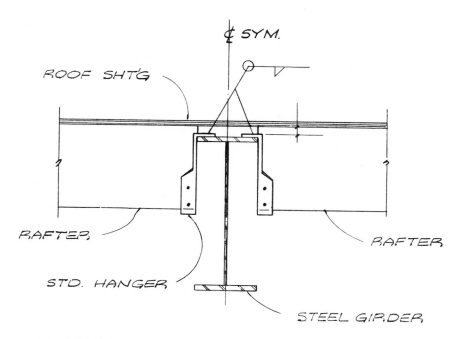

Detail 1-81(a). A section of a roof girder supporting wood rafters and roof sheathing. The rafters are supported by the girder with standard joist hangers welded to the top flange. A space is provided between the top flange of the steel girder and the bottom side of the sheathing to allow for the wood shrinkage.

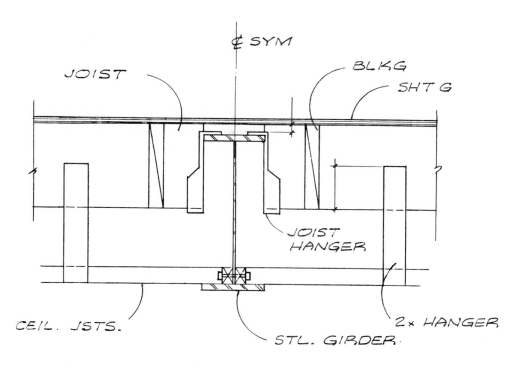

Detail 1-81(b). A section of a roof girder as shown in Detail 1-81(a) and a suspended ceiling. The ceiling joists are suspended from the rafters by wood hangers. The hanger spacing determines the span of the ceiling joists.

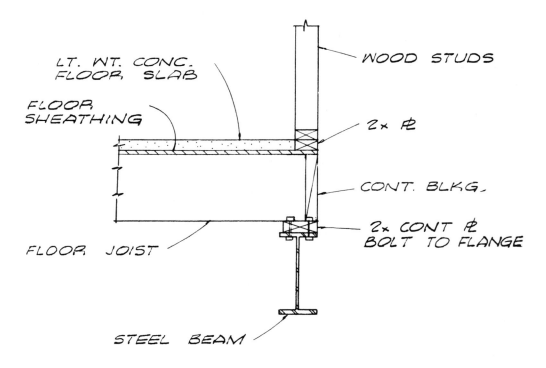

Detail 1-82(a). A section of a steel beam supporting an exterior wood stud wall, wood floor joists, and light-weight concrete on a wood floor. The joists are continuously blocked and bear on the nailer plate. The wood nailer plate is bolted to the top flange of the beam with ⅝″ dia. bolts spaced at 4′0″ o.c., staggered on each side of the beam web. The double plate of the stud wall on the floor is optional; a single plate may be used.

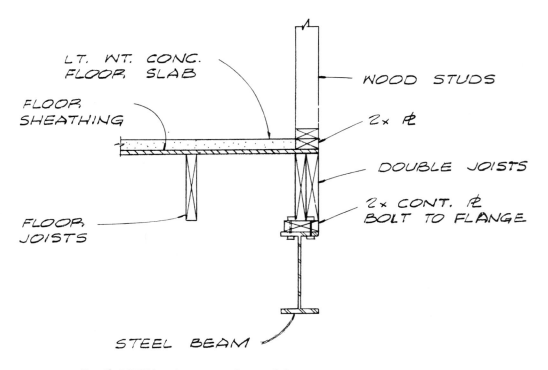

Detail 1-82(b). A section of a steel beam supporting an exterior wood stud wall and light-weight concrete on a wood floor. The joists span parallel to the beam. The double joists support the wood stud wall on the beam. The wood nailer plate is bolted to the top flange of the beam with ⅝″ dia. bolts spaced at 4′0″ o.c., staggered on each side of the beam web. The double plate of the stud wall on the floor is optional; a single plate may be used.

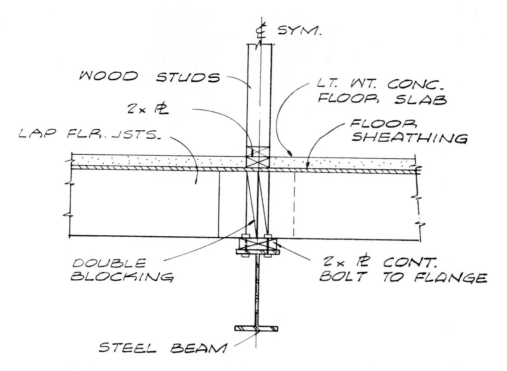

WOOD STUDS

LT. WT. CONC. FLOOR SLAB

2 × $\mathcal{L}$

LAP FLR. JSTS.

FLOOR SHEATHING

DOUBLE BLOCKING

2 × $\mathcal{L}$ CONT. BOLT TO FLANGE

STEEL BEAM

$\mathcal{C}$ SYM.

Detail 1-83. A section of a steel beam supporting an interior wood stud wall, floor joists, and light-weight concrete on a wood floor. The floor joists are lapped and bear on the top flange wood nailer. The continuous double blocking transfers the floor diaphragm stress to the beam. The wood nailer plate is bolted to the top flange of the beam with ⅝″ dia. bolts spaced at 4′0″ o.c., staggered on each side of the beam web. The double plate of the stud wall on the floor is optional; a single plate may be used.

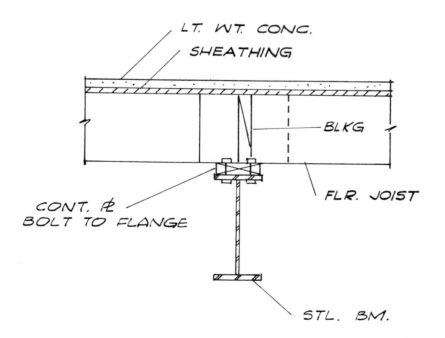

LT. WT. CONC.

SHEATHING

BLKG

CONT. $\mathcal{L}$ BOLT TO FLANGE

FLR. JOIST

STL. BM.

Detail 1-84. A section of a steel beam supporting wood floor joists and light-weight concrete on a wood floor. The joists are lapped and blocked and bear on the wood nailer at the top flange of the beam. The wood nailer plate is bolted to the top flange of the beam with ⅝″ dia. bolts spaced at 4′0″ o.c., staggered on each side of the beam web.

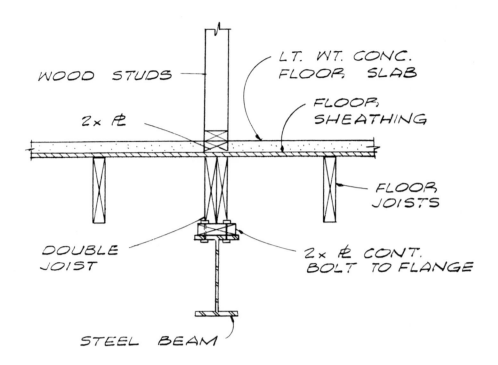

WOOD STUDS

2× Pℓ

LT. WT. CONC.
FLOOR SLAB

FLOOR,
SHEATHING

FLOOR,
JOISTS

DOUBLE
JOIST

2× Pℓ CONT.
BOLT TO FLANGE

STEEL BEAM

Detail 1-85(a). A section of a steel beam supporting an interior wood stud wall, wood floor joists, and light-weight concrete on a wood floor. The floor joists on the right side span parallel to the beam. The double continuous blocking transfers the floor diaphragm stress to the steel beam. The wood nailer plate is bolted to the top flange of the beam with ⅝" dia. bolts spaced at 4'0" o.c., staggered on each side of the beam web. The double plate of the stud wall on the floor is optional; a single plate may be used.

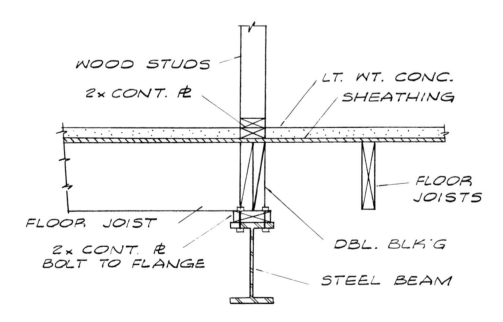

WOOD STUDS

2× CONT. Pℓ

LT. WT. CONC.
SHEATHING

FLOOR
JOISTS

FLOOR JOIST

2× CONT. Pℓ
BOLT TO FLANGE

DBL. BLK'G

STEEL BEAM

Detail 1-85(b) A section of a steel beam supporting an interior wood stud wall and light-weight concrete on a wood floor. The floor joists span parallel to the beam. The double joists transfer the weight of the wood stud wall to the beam. The wood nailer plate is bolted to the top flange of the beam with ⅝" dia. bolts spaced at 4'0" o.c., staggered on each side of the beam web. The double plate of the stud wall on the floor is optional; a single plate may be used.

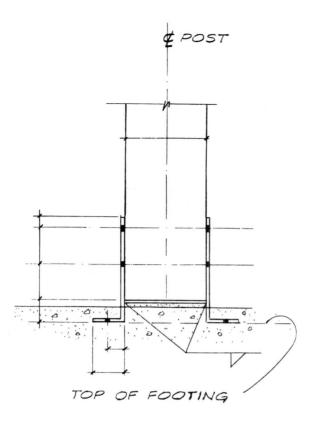

Detail 1-86(a). A connection of a glued laminated wood post to a concrete foundation. See Detail 1-86(b).

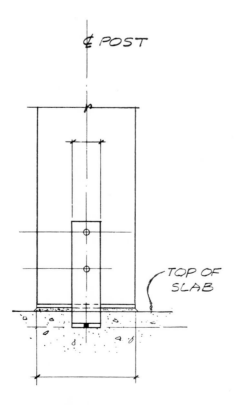

Detail 1-86(b). A side view of the metal connection plates shown in Detail 1-86(a).

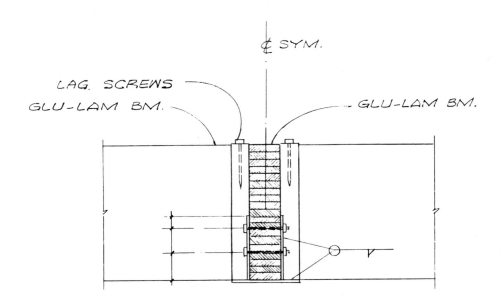

Detail 1-87(a). An intersection of two glued laminated wood beams. The beam shown in section is supported by the beam shown in elevation. A metal strap hanger is connected to the top of the supporting beam with lag screws and bolted through the sides of the beam shown in section. See Detail 1-87(b).

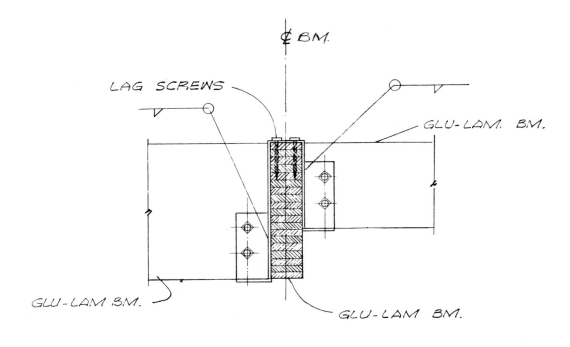

Detail 1-87(b). A section of Detail 1-87(a). The beams on each side of the supporting beam are shown in elevation. The metal strap hanger plates are designed to act in tension.

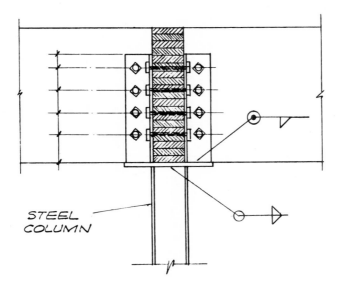

Detail 1-88(a). A wide flange steel column supporting the intersection of four glued laminated wood beams. See Detail 1-88(b).

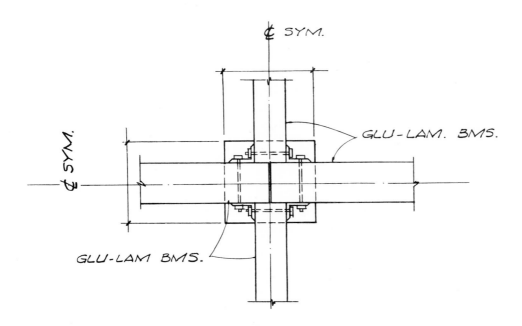

Detail 1-88(b). A plan of Detail 1-88(a) showing the intersection of four glued laminated wood beams on a wide flange steel column. The beams are connected with clip angles and bolts. The angles are welded to the cap plate at the top of the column.

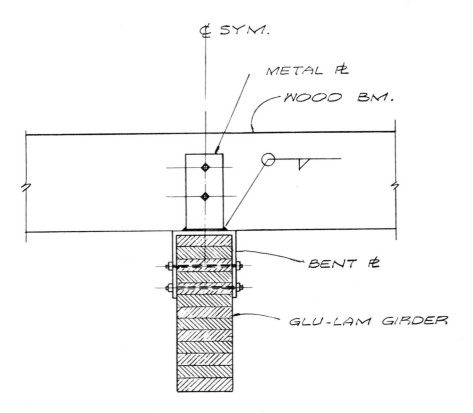

Detail 1-89(a). A section of a glued laminated wood girder supporting a glued laminated wood beam. The beam is connected to the top of the girder by metal side plates bolted through the girder and through the beam. See Detail 1-89(b).

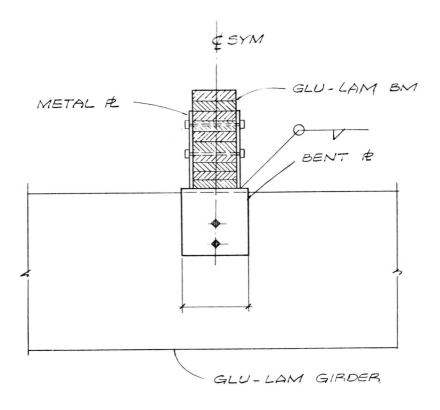

Detail 1-89(b). A section of Detail 1-89(a) showing the glued laminated wood beam in section.

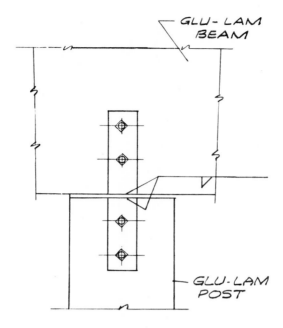

Detail 1-90(a). A connection of a continuous glued laminated wood beam and a wood post. The metal side plates are bolted through the beam and through the post. The side plates are welded to the horizontal plate at the top of the post. See Detail 1-90(b).

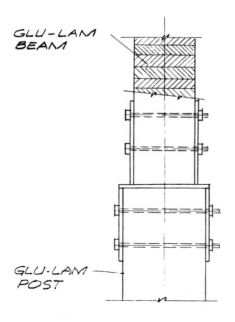

Detail 1-90(b). A section of Detail 1-90(a).

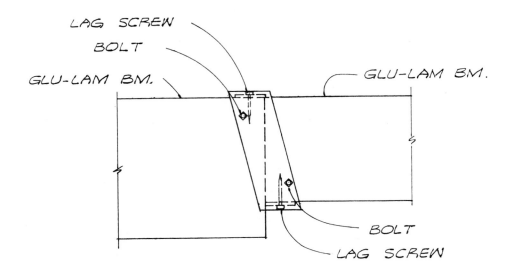

LAG SCREW

BOLT

GLU-LAM BM.

GLU-LAM BM.

BOLT

LAG SCREW

Detail 1-91(a). A connection of two glued laminated wood beams. The metal strap hanger is connected to the top of the left beam and suspends the end of the right beam. The beams are equal in width. See Detail 1-91(b).

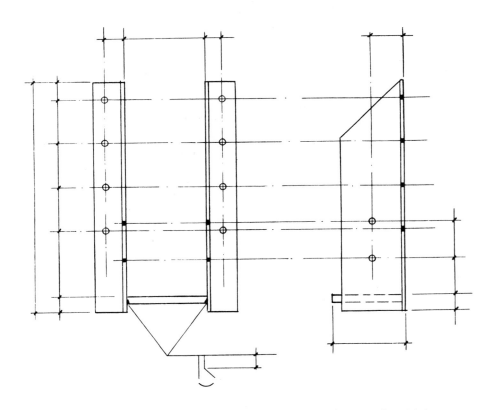

Detail 1-91(b). Two views of a metal strap hanger used in Detail 1-91(a). The hanger is bolted through the sides of the beams and lag screwed at top and bottom of the beams.

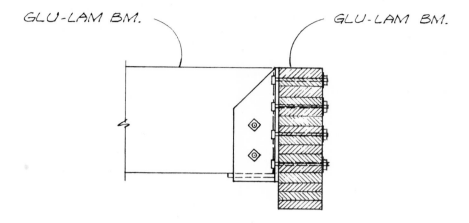

GLU-LAM BM.   GLU-LAM BM.

Detail 1-92(a). A connection of a glued laminated wood beam supported by a glued laminated wood girder. The beam is connected to the girder with metal angle plates and a shelf plate. See Detail 1-92(b).

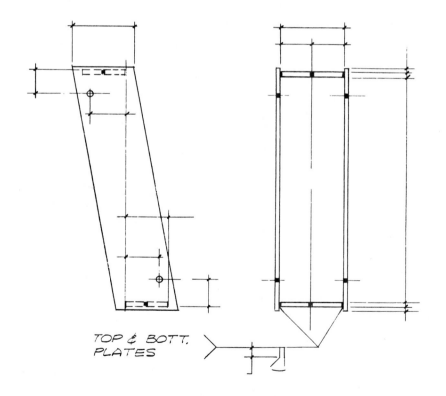

TOP & BOTT.
PLATES

Detail 1-92(b). Two views of the connecting angles and shelf plate used in Detail 1-92(a). The size of the plates and bolts used to connect the beam to the girder is determined by calculation.

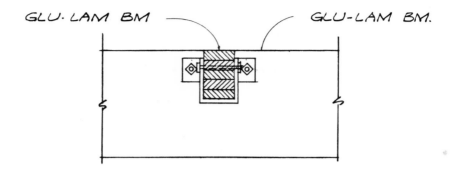

Detail 1-93(a). A connection of a wood purlin to a glued laminated wood beam. See Detail 1-93(b).

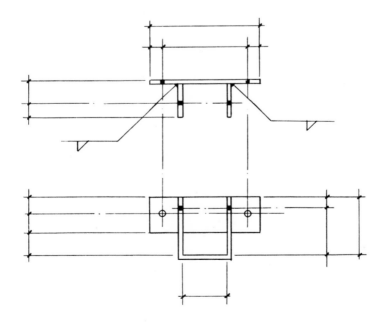

Detail 1-93(b). Two views of the connecting plates shown in Detail 1-93(a). The size of the plates and bolts used to connect the purlin to the beam are determined by calculation.

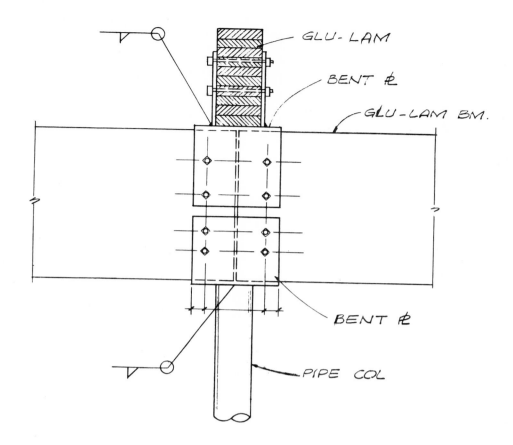

GLU-LAM

BENT ℄

GLU-LAM BM.

BENT ℄

PIPE COL

Detail 1-94. A connection of a glued laminated wood beam and girder supported by a steel pipe column. The beams are connected to the girder similar to Detail 1-89(a). The pipe column is connected to the wood girder similar to Detail 1-49(a).

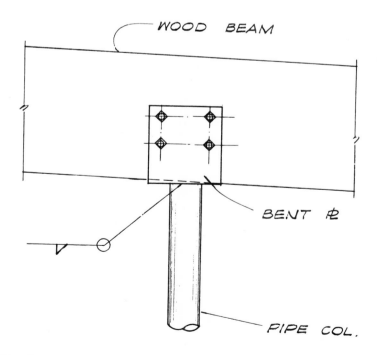

WOOD BEAM

BENT ℄

PIPE COL.

Detail 1-95. A steel pipe column supporting a cantilevered glued laminated wood beam. The beam is connected to the pipe column similar to Detail 1-49(a).

2

CONCRETE

The details shown in this chapter pertain to reinforced concrete construction. Since each of the following drawings is presented in its most general form, many of the dimensions and structural sizes are omitted. It is required that these dimensions and sizes be determined by engineering design calculation for each specific condition of use of the detail.

The details are arranged in the following general categories: continuous footings for walls, grade beams, pit walls, basement walls, wall openings, retaining walls, beam sections, poured-in-place belled caissons, spread footings, pile caps, column sections, slab sections, wall pilasters, and precast wall sections. Several of the details presented in this chapter are composed of concrete and other construction materials such as wood, masonry, and steel. These details are included in this particular chapter because their basic application in building relates to reinforced concrete construction.

The type and the strength of the concrete required for the construction of the details in this chapter are not specified. The requirements for structural concrete of a building depends upon the concrete durability, watertightness, and resistance to deterioration; the economics of the construction; and the strength of the concrete that will be needed to resist the dead and live loads. Structural concrete strength is determined

by its capacity to resist compression and is expressed as a unit compressive stress in terms of pounds per square inch. The unit compressive stress that is used to specify the strength of a concrete mixture 28 days after it is placed or molded for test samples is denoted as f'_c. The values of f'_c for the various water and cement mixtures of concrete are verified by testing the compression resistance of a certain number of standard size specimen samples. The American Society of Testing Materials specifies definite and rigid requirements for the testing procedures of concrete specimen. The specimen samples are taken from fresh concrete batches and molded into cylinders 6″ in diameter and 12″ high or are taken from cores of existing concrete. These test cylinders are subjected to loads to determine their ultimate compressive strength at 7 days and at 28 days after the sample is molded and cured. The results of the tests of a number of specimen of a particular concrete mixture can give a comparatively wide range of values for the compressive strength. In order to obtain a valid value of the f'_c, it is necessary to test several specimen samples of a mixture and correlate the results mathematically. The statistical standard deviation and the coefficient of variation are used to indicate the degree of quality control of the concrete mixture. The standard deviation is obtained by subtracting the square root of the average of the squares of all the test result values from the common average value. The coefficient of variation is a percentage determined by dividing the standard deviation by the mean value of the test results. Proper quality control of concrete mixtures should produce concrete with an average compressive strength of 15% greater than the f'_c for working stress designs and 25% greater for ultimate stress designs. The design, testing, sampling, and evaluating of concrete mixtures is performed by a responsible laboratory using definite standards of procedure.

Structural concrete is generally specified by the water-cement ratio of the mixture, the value of f'_c, and the weight or the volume proportions of the mixture. Concrete is composed of a mixture of cement, water, coarse aggregate, fine aggregate, and, in certain cases, chemical admixtures. The type and quality of cement used in commercial structural concrete is Type I portland cement, which is produced in accordance with rigid A.S.T.M. standards. Other types of commercial cements are available; however, Type I cement is most commonly used in building construction. Fine aggregate and coarse aggregate are two different materials in the concrete mixture; however, both are used as chemically inert fillers to increase the volume of the mixture. Coarse aggregates consist of particles of crushed rock greater than ¼″ but usually not larger than 1½″. Fine aggregates consist of graded natural sand and particles of crushed rock less than ¼″. Various types of aggregate can be employed in concrete to achieve a specific quality that may be required as a condition of the use of the concrete; for example, concrete used for fireproofing or thermal insulation requires a light-weight mixture. Many commercial chemical admixtures are also available for use in structural concrete. These admixtures are used to produce a specific quality in the finished concrete such as water-tightness, hard exterior surfaces, color, and high early strength immediately after the concrete is placed.

The water-cement ratio of a concrete mixture is the primary factor in determining the compressive strength of the hardened concrete. The water and cement combine chemically to create a physical paste which adheres to and binds the aggregates. The result of this chemical and physical phenomenon is a concrete mixture that will act as a monolithic material after it hardens. The water-cement ratio is usually specified as the number of gallons of water per sack of cement. This ratio can also be expressed in terms of weight or in the number of cubic feet of water and the number of cubic feet of cement. One cubic foot of water equals 7.48 gal.; one standard sack of cement equals 1 cu ft. These values are given to demonstrate arithmetically that a water-cement ratio of 7.5 gal. of water per sack of cement will contain approximately 1 cu. ft. of water per cubic foot of cement. The compressive strength of concrete is inversely proportional to the water-cement ratio; that is, as the water-cement ratio increases, the f'_c value decreases. The f'_c values of structural concrete range between 2000 and 5000 psi and are usually designated in 500 psi increments, except for $f'_c = 3750$ psi.

Efficient methods for the proper placing of concrete depend upon the plasticity or workability of the wet mixture. The degree of plasticity of wet concrete is determined by a slump test. This test is performed by measuring the subsidence or vertical displacement of a sample of the wet concrete mixture. The sample is formed in a metal truncated cone 12″ high with top and bottom diameters equal to 4″ and 8″, respectively. The results of the test are given as the number of inches of vertical displacement that is measured immediately after the cone form is removed. The amount of slump should vary between 2″ and 6″. The required degree of plasticity depends on the clearance between reinforcing bars, the size of the coarse aggregate, the method of delivering the concrete to the forms, and the intricacy of the formwork. The A.C.I. Building Code recommends a maximum slump of 4″ and a minimum slump of 1″ with respect to the various structural elements of the building.

The minimum slump value should be maintained for construction of concrete ramps, sloping walls, and slabs. When the slump is high, the wet concrete mixture will be loose and thus permit the coarse aggregates to separate from the cement paste; when the slump is low, the wet concrete mixture may be stiff and will create internal void spaces in the hardened concrete. Very often the wet concrete must be mechanically vibrated or rodded as it is placed to prevent the formation of internal voids and to ensure that the reinforcing bars are completely surrounded by concrete. Mechanical vibrating should be performed with care so that the designed positions of the reinforcing bars will not be altered. The design of reinforced concrete is based on the condition that the concrete material is homogeneous and well consolidated when it is placed; if this condition is met, the concrete will react as a monolithic material when it hardens. A positive physical bond must exist between the reinforcement and the concrete. Internal voids that are caused by poor consolidation will seriously reduce the structural bonding of the two different materials. Also, reinforcement surfaces should be free of excessive rust and mill scale, paint, soil, or other substances that will reduce the bond capacity. To ensure good consolidation, concrete should be placed in continuous layers of uniform depth; it should not be dropped into place from a height greater than 5.0' and it should not be chuted into place at a steep angle for long distances. Concrete mixes that are composed of small size aggregates are often used when the clearance dimensions between the reinforcing bars and between the forms are small. As the concrete is being placed, it should be continuously moved away from the sides of the forms to allow the smaller size aggregates to settle near the exposed surfaces and thus give the structure a smooth finish and eliminate surface voids.

After concrete is placed, it must be cured to obtain a uniform hardness. The curing process consists of creating an external and internal condition of temperature and moisture that will be favorable to the uniform hardening of the concrete. The time rate of hardening is not constant; it proceeds quite rapidly immediately after the concrete is placed, and it will attain approximately 70% of its f'_c value within the first seven days. The concrete will continue to harden at a progressively slower rate for a long period of time; however, it should attain at least the f'_c value within 28 days after it is in place. Cold weather, that is, temperatures less than 40°F, will retard the water and cement chemical reaction required to produce the cement paste in the mixture. Hot weather, that is, temperatures greater than 90°F, will cause the exposed surface moisture to evaporate, which will result in uneven hardening and surface cracks. The

method and length of time required to cure a particular concrete construction should be determined with regard to the temperature and moisture conditions at the job site at the time the concrete is placed. The concrete should be kept moist for at least one day immediately after it is placed, and it should be prevented from rapid drying for seven days. High-early-strength concrete mixtures require only a three day curing period.

The form work for a concrete structure is constructed to reflect the architectural- and engineering-designed configuration. Although concrete forms are generally designed and constructed by the contractor, the resident engineer or building inspector should verify that the forms satisfy two main conditions: (1) that the form structure is safe and (2) that the forms meet the architectural and engineering design requirements as they are shown on the working drawings. Since the formwork is often used as a working deck during construction, it should be designed and constructed to resist vertical and lateral forces. Many form failures are the result of improper or insufficient lateral bracing that was required to plumb the structure and to resist the lateral forces caused during construction. The contractor must provide sufficient vertical support shores of the form structure to prevent excessive deflections or the overstressing of any form members. The sides of beams, columns, and walls should be braced against the hydrostatic pressure exerted by the wet concrete mixture. These side forms may be removed as soon as the concrete attains its initial hardness; however, the vertical supporting members should not be removed until the concrete attains a strength capable of supporting the dead load of the structure and any construction live loads that may occur. The contact surfaces of the forms are coated with a heavy oil to prevent the concrete from adhering to the forms and to permit the forms to be removed without damaging the exposed concrete surfaces. Also, the sharp corners of rectangular columns, walls, and beams are formed with a 45° chamfer strip to eliminate the possibility of spalling the concrete when the forms are removed. Damaged concrete surfaces, surface voids, and form tie holes are patched with a patching mortar that is composed of the same proportions of sand and cement as the poured concrete. The surface finish of poured concrete depends on the degree of exposure of the members and the architectural quality of the building. The A.C.I. Standard 301–66 defines the various methods and criteria for concrete surface finishes.

Structural reinforced concrete members are used to resist external loads by reacting by bending, by compression, or by a combination of both bending and compression. The ability of plain concrete to resist tensile stress is quite low and undependable. In the analysis and design of reinforced concrete it is assumed that the concrete material offers no resistance to tensile stress and that the tension is resisted only by the reinforcing steel. Reinforcing steel is also used to resist compression in a member acting in flexure or compression when the unit compression exceeds the permissible compressive stress of the concrete.

The structural analysis is mathematically performed by the "transformed section method." This method is based on the assumptions that (1) the concrete resists compression, (2) the reinforcing steel resists tension and compression, (3) the concrete cannot resist tension, (4) the reinforcing steel and the concrete are bonded together and therefore react together, (5) the reinforcing steel and the concrete are individually elastic. When a reinforced concrete member deflects or deforms from an externally applied load, the unit stress in the reinforcing steel is directly proportional to the unit stress in the concrete. The proportional relationship between the two materials is denoted as n. The value n of a concrete mixture is defined as the ratio of the modulus of elasticity of the reinforcing steel E_s and the modulus of elasticity of the concrete E_c, or $n = 30{,}000/f'_c$. It can be seen in the last equation that n is inversely proportional to the value of f'_c. The values of n vary from 15.0 for $f'_c = 2000$ psi for $n = 6.0$ for $f'_c = 5000$ psi. The reinforcing steel area of a concrete beam or column can be converted or transformed into an equivalent cross section of concrete by multiplying the cross-sectional area of the reinforcement, A_s by the value of n. After the reinforced concrete is transformed into an analogous homogeneous concrete member, it can be structurally analyzed by the use of the basic rules of mechanics and equilibrium.

The working stress design (W.S.D.) method, as applied to reinforced concrete members, is performed by using maximum allowable working stresses of the materials, the actual dead load, and a specified live load. The various building codes and design criteria specify the maximum allowable design stress for concrete and reinforcing steel. These stresses are determined by dividing the yield point stress of the material by a factor of safety. Reinforced concrete structures designed by the working stress design method do not utilize the full stress capacity of the materials because the factor of safety is applied generally both to the working stresses of each material and to the loads.

Another method of reinforced concrete structural design is called the ultimate strength design (U.S.D.) method. This method is based upon designing the members to the yield point stress of the materials and by individually increasing the dead load and the live load by a particular load factor instead of by a single general safety factor. The ultimate strength design method is currently being adopted by many building codes and design criteria since it can effect a significant economy in the use of concrete and reinforcing steel and also create a structure that will more realistically react to the design loading.

Table 2–1 shows the various reinforcing steel strength values and their respective A.S.T.M. specification titles and numbers.

Reinforcing steel bars are manufactured in standard sizes which are designated by a number. Each designation number represents the number of eighths of an inch of the nominal diameter of a deformed reinforcing bar, for example, #5 or #6. Plain reinforcing bars, that is, bars that are not deformed, are designated as the diameter in inches, for example, ½″ or ⅝″. Reinforcing bars that are ¼″ in diameter are never deformed and are always designated as #2 bars. Reinforcing bars that are manufactured with a raised surface pattern are referred to as deformed bars. These surface projections serve to increase the contact area between the concrete and the reinforcing steel, and they also provide a mechanical device to increase the bar bond capacity. Welded wire fabric consists of cold-drawn wire arranged in a rectangular pattern and welded at the points of intersection. The size and the spacing of the wire can be varied in either direction. The welded wire fabric shown on the following drawings is $6 \times 6 - 10/10$; the 6×6 indicates that the wires are 6″ o.c. in each direction, and the 10/10 indicates that the wires are 10 gauge in each direc-

Table 2-1. Concrete Reinforcing Steel for A.S.T.M. Specifications

Minimum yield-point strength, psi	Grade of steel	A.S.T.M. specification title	A.S.T.M. Spec. No.
40,000	Intermediate	Specifications for Billet-steel Bars for Concrete Reinforcement	A 15
	Intermediate	Specifications for Axle-steel Bars for Concrete Reinforcement	A 160
	Intermediate	Specifications for Special Large Size Deformed Billet-steel Bars for Concrete Reinforcement	A 408
50,000	Hard	Specifications for Billet-steel Bars for Concrete Reinforcement	A 15
	Regular	Specifications for Rail-steel Bars for Concrete Reinforcement	A 16
	Hard	Specifications for Axle-steel Bars for Concrete Reinforcement	A 160
	Hard	Specifications for Special Large Size Deformed Billet-steel Bars for Concrete Reinforcement	A 408
60,000		Specifications for Deformed Billet-steel Bars for Concrete Reinforcement with 60,000 psi Minimum Yield Strength	A 432
		Specifications for Deformed Rail Steel Bars for Concrete Reinforcement with 60,000 psi Minimum Yield Strength	A 61
70,000		Specifications for Cold-drawn Steel Wire for Concrete Reinforcement	A 82
75,000		Specifications for High-strength Deformed Billet Steel Bars for Concrete Reinforcement with 75,000 psi Minimum Yield Strength	A 431
Bars and rod mats		Specifications for Fabricated Steel Bar or Rod Mats for Concrete Reinforcement	A 184
Welded wire fabric		Specifications for Welded Steel Wire Fabric for Concrete Reinforcement	A 185

tion. Cold-drawn wire or plain reinforcing rod that is used for round column spiral reinforcement is designated as the rod diameter in inches. Table 2-2 shows the reinforcing bar designation numbers and their dimensions. Bar sizes #3 to #11, inclusive, are manufactured in accordance with A.S.T.M. Spec. No. A 305; bars #14S and #18S are special size large bars and are manufactured in accordance with A.S.T.M. Spec. No. A 408.

Table 2-2. Concrete Reinforcing Steel Bar Sizes and Dimensions

Deformed-bar designation	Weight, lb. per ft.	Diameter, in.	Cross-section area, sq. in.	Perimeter, in.	Max. outside dia., in.
#2	0.167	0.250	0.05	0.786	
#3	0.376	0.375	0.11	1.178	7/16
#4	0.668	0.500	0.20	1.571	9/16
#5	1.043	0.625	0.31	1.963	11/16
#6	1.502	0.750	0.44	2.356	7/8
#7	2.044	0.875	0.60	2.749	1
#8	2.670	1.000	0.79	3.142	1 1/8
#9	3.400	1.128	1.00	3.544	1 1/4
#10	4.303	1.270	1.27	3.990	1 7/16
#11	5.313	1.410	1.56	4.430	1 5/8
#14S	7.65	1.693	2.25	5.32	1 15/16
#18S	13.60	2.257	4.00	7.09	2 1/2

Reinforcing bars should be accurately placed to ensure that the completed construction will reflect the enginer's design. Small inaccuracies may appreciably increase the stress in a member and thus cause serious surface cracks; therefore the engineer must rely a great deal on the intelligence and the integrity of the men who are constructing his designs. Shop drawings prepared from the information given on the engineer's working drawings will help to coordinate the fieldwork with the structural design. The engineer responsible for the structural design should check the shop drawings for dimensions, reinforcing bar sizes, and the details for placing the reinforcing bars. It is also a good practice for the engineer to visit the job site during the construction to inspect the accuracy of the placing of the reinforcing steel. The A.C.I. Specification for Structural Concrete for Buildings No. 301–66 Section 504 recommends allowable fabrication and placing tolerances for reinforcement. The bars should be wired together and secured in place to prevent any movement that may be caused by placing the concrete. Galvanized metal or concrete block bar chairs are used to support the reinforcement in the forms to obtain the required concrete cover. In no instance should these chairs be used to support form boards or construction loads other than the weight of the reinforcing bars. Table 2–3 gives the recommended concrete cover for reinforcing bars in the

Table 2–3. Minimum Clear Cover of Concrete for Reinforcing Steel

Location of reinforcement in concrete	Clear distance
Reinforcement in footings and other structural members in which the concrete is poured directly against the ground	3"
Formed concrete surfaces to be exposed to weather or in contact with the ground for bar sizes greater than #5	2"
Formed concrete surfaces to be exposed to weather or in contact with the ground for bar sizes #5 or less	1½"
Slabs and walls not exposed to weather or in contact with the ground	¾"
Beams and girders not exposed to weather or in contact with the ground	1½"
Floor joists with a maximum clear spacing of 30"	¾"
Column spirals or ties (not less than 1½ times the maximum size of the coarse aggregate or . . .)	1½"

Note: Except for concrete slabs or joists, the concrete cover protection shall not be less than the nominal diameter of the reinforcing bar.

Table 2–4. Minimum Clear Spacing Distance between Reinforcing Bars

Space between bars	Clear distance
Clear distance between parallel bars except in columns and layers of bars in beams and girders	Not less than the nominal diameter of the bars, or 1⅓ times the size of the coarse aggregate, or not less than 1"
Clear distance between layers of reinforcement in beams or girders; the bars in each layer shall be directly above and below the bars in the adjacent layer	Not less than 1"
Clear distance between bars in walls and slabs	Not more than three times the wall or slab thickness or more than 18"
Clear distance between bars in spirally reinforced and tied columns	1½ times the nominal bar diameter, 1½ times the maximum size of the coarse aggregate, or not less than 1½"

Note: The clear distances above also apply for the clear distances between contact splices and adjacent splices of reinforcing bars.

various structural members. Table 2–4 gives the recommended clear distances between reinforcing bars.

Reinforcing bars can be connected either by a lapped splice or by a butt welded connection. Splices should not be made at points of critical stress in the member, or at points which are not specified on the working drawings, without the authorization of the design engineer. Lapped splices acting in tension or compression should not be made with reinforcing bars larger in size than #11. If deformed reinforcing bars are used and $f'_c = 3000$ psi, the recommended length of lap in a splice is as follows: tension splices, not less than 24, 30, and 36 bar diameters for specified yield strengths of 40,000, 50,000, and 60,000 psi, respectively; compression splices, not less than 24, 30, and 36 bar diameters for specified yield strengths of 40,000, 50,000, and 60,000 psi, respectively. These bar diameter lengths should be doubled for plain reinforcing bars and increased by ⅓ for f'_c less than 3000 psi. The minimum length of lap should not be less than 1'0". Welded splices are usually made for large size reinforcing bars. This is done by butt welding the square cut ends together so that the connection is capable of resisting 125% of the specified yield strength of the bar in tension. Various mechanical bar connectors are available; however, their use would depend upon the approval of the engineer and their acceptability by the design criteria.

The preceding information is only a brief description of some of the aspects of reinforced concrete when it is used as a construction material. The design, construction, and quality control of reinforced concrete is a very complex field. This material is presented as a guide for the use of the structural details in this chapter. The American Concrete Institute and the Portland Cement Association have compiled a large amount of information on many subjects that are concerned with reinforced concrete construction. Material from Building Code for Reinforced Concrete (A.C.I. 318–63) has been included by permission of the American Concrete Institute. These standards are subject to revision whenever the studies of the committees responsible indicate that developments in concrete design and construction warrant any change. Working drawings are made to communicate the design requirements and configurations to the contractor. These drawings should be supplemented by shop drawings of the individual reinforcing bars and their method of placement. The accuracy of design, the quality of workmanship, and the quality control of the construction materials are important factors in reinforced concrete design and construction. Once the reinforcing steel and the concrete are finally placed, a total commitment is made by the engineer, the job-site inspector, the laboratory testing the materials, and the contractor. The owner of the building must be able to rely on the responsibility of this commitment. Responsibility of construction must follow progressively and in sequence from the design engineer to the contractor.

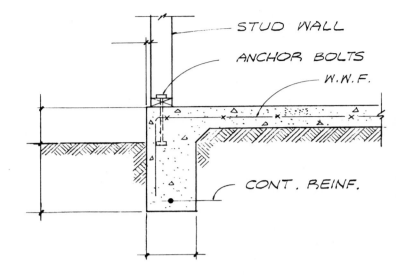

STUD WALL

ANCHOR BOLTS

W.W.F.

CONT. REINF.

Detail 2-1(a). A section of a continuous concrete footing for an exterior wood stud wall. The stud wall is set back to allow the exterior wall covering to meet the face of the concrete. The depth and width of the footing depend on the soil conditions.

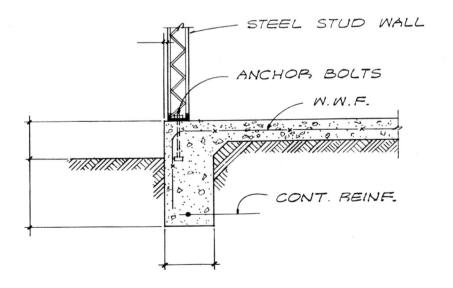

STEEL STUD WALL

ANCHOR BOLTS

W.W.F.

CONT. REINF.

Detail 2-1(b). A section of a continuous concrete footing for an exterior steel stud wall. The stud wall is set back to allow the exterior wall covering to meet the face of the concrete. The depth and width of the footing depend on the soil conditions.

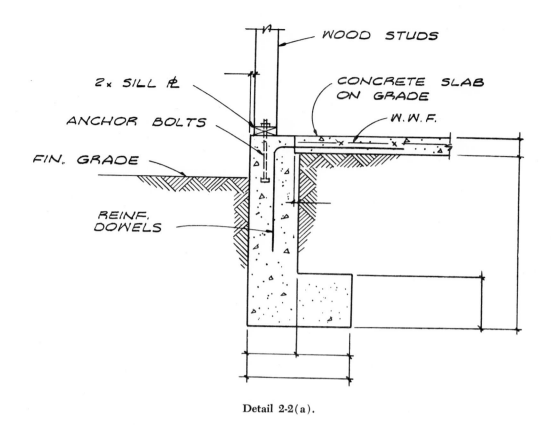

Detail 2-2(a).

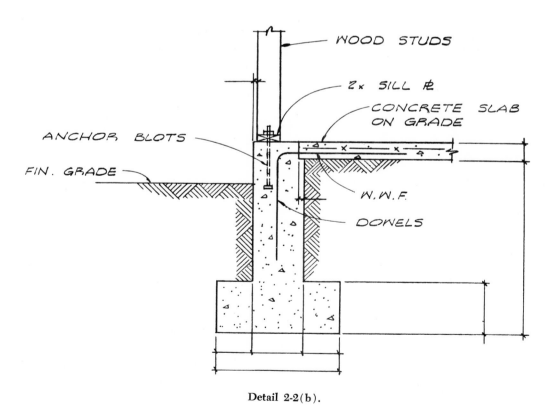

Detail 2-2(b).

Details 2-2(a) and (b). A section of a continuous concrete footing for
an exterior wood stud wall. The footing is connected to the slab on grade
by reinforcing dowels. The stud wall is set back to allow the exterior wall
covering to meet the face of the concrete. The depth and width of the
footing depend on the soil conditions.

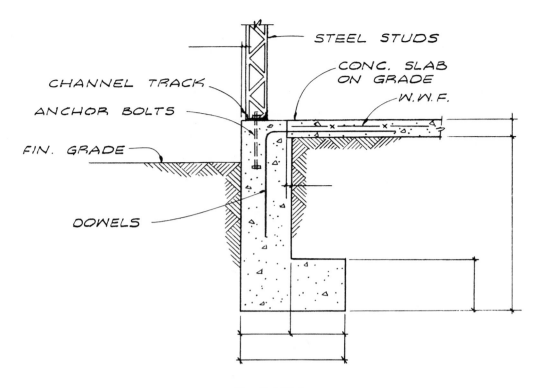

Detail 2-3(a).

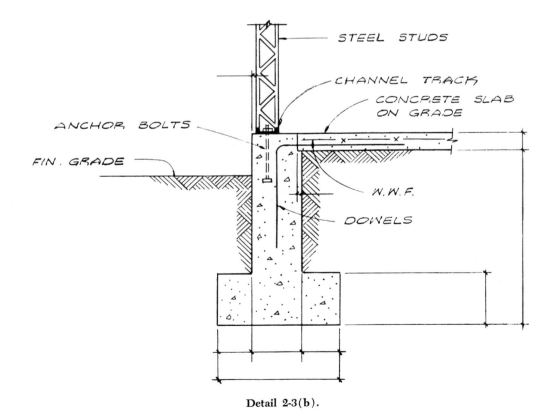

Detail 2-3(b).

Details 2-3(a) and (b). A section of a continuous concrete footing for an exterior steel stud wall. The footing is connected to the slab on grade with reinforcing dowels. The steel studs are set back to allow the exterior wall covering to meet the face of the concrete. The depth and width of the footing depend on the soil conditions.

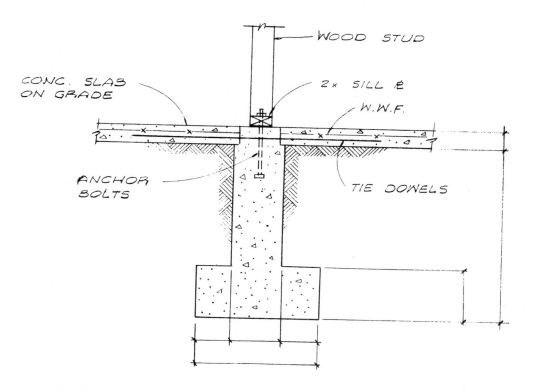

Detail 2-4. A section of a continuous concrete footing for an interior wood stud wall. The concrete slab on grade is connected across the top of the footing by reinforcing dowels. The depth and width of the footing depend on the soil conditions.

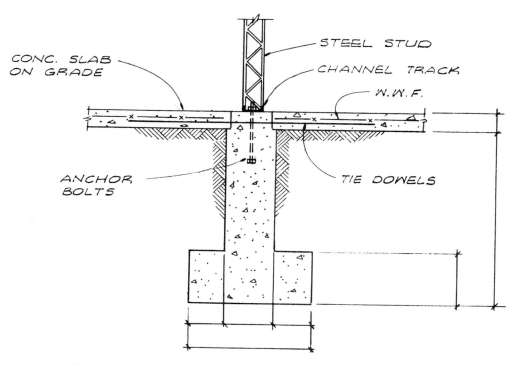

Detail 2-5. A section of a continuous concrete footing for an interior steel stud wall. The concrete slab on grade is connected across the top of the footing by reinforcing dowels. The depth and width of the footing depend on the soil conditions.

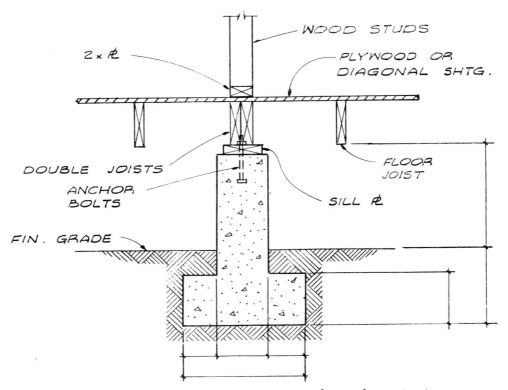

Detail 2-6. A section of a continuous concrete footing for an interior wood stud wall. The floor joists span parallel to the footing. The weight of the wall is transferred to the concrete footing by the double joists. The clear distance between the finished grade and the bottom of the floor joists is determined by the local building code. The depth and width of the footing depend on the soil conditions.

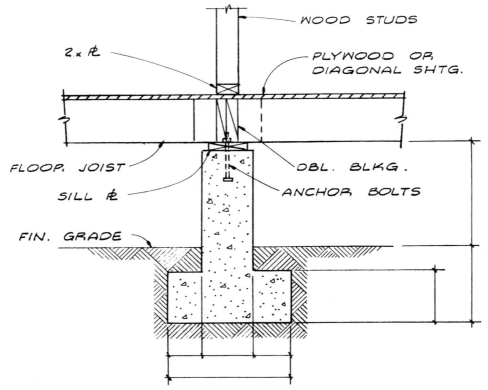

Detail 2-7. A section of a continuous concrete footing for an interior wood stud wall and floor joists. The floor joists are lapped and nailed together. The distance between the bottom of the floor joists and the finished grade is determined by the local building code. The depth and width of the footing depend on the soil conditions.

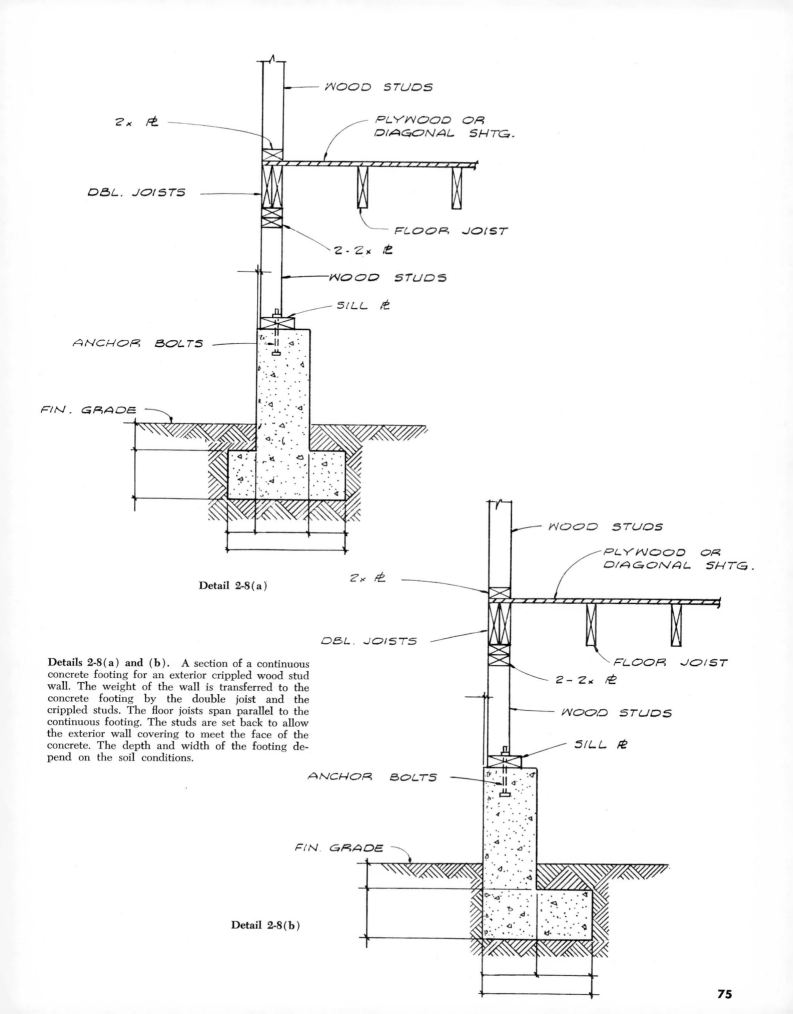

WOOD STUDS

2 × ₽

PLYWOOD OR DIAGONAL SHTG.

DBL. JOISTS

FLOOR JOIST

2 · 2 × ₽

WOOD STUDS

SILL ₽

ANCHOR BOLTS

FIN. GRADE

Detail 2-8(a)

Details 2-8(a) and (b). A section of a continuous concrete footing for an exterior crippled wood stud wall. The weight of the wall is transferred to the concrete footing by the double joist and the crippled studs. The floor joists span parallel to the continuous footing. The studs are set back to allow the exterior wall covering to meet the face of the concrete. The depth and width of the footing depend on the soil conditions.

WOOD STUDS

PLYWOOD OR DIAGONAL SHTG.

2 × ₽

DBL. JOISTS

FLOOR JOIST

2 - 2 × ₽

WOOD STUDS

SILL ₽

ANCHOR BOLTS

FIN. GRADE

Detail 2-8(b)

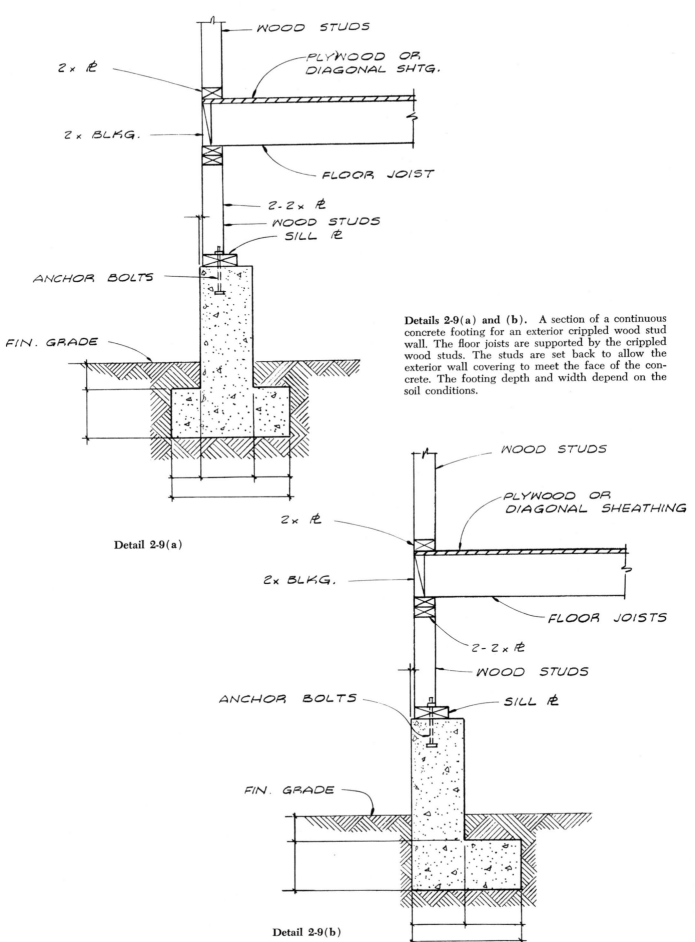

WOOD STUDS

PLYWOOD OR DIAGONAL SHTG.

2 x ℔

2 x BLKG.

FLOOR JOIST

2-2 x ℔

WOOD STUDS

SILL ℔

ANCHOR BOLTS

FIN. GRADE

Details 2-9(a) and (b). A section of a continuous concrete footing for an exterior crippled wood stud wall. The floor joists are supported by the crippled wood studs. The studs are set back to allow the exterior wall covering to meet the face of the concrete. The footing depth and width depend on the soil conditions.

Detail 2-9(a)

WOOD STUDS

PLYWOOD OR DIAGONAL SHEATHING

2 x ℔

2 x BLKG.

FLOOR JOISTS

2-2 x ℔

WOOD STUDS

ANCHOR BOLTS

SILL ℔

FIN. GRADE

Detail 2-9(b)

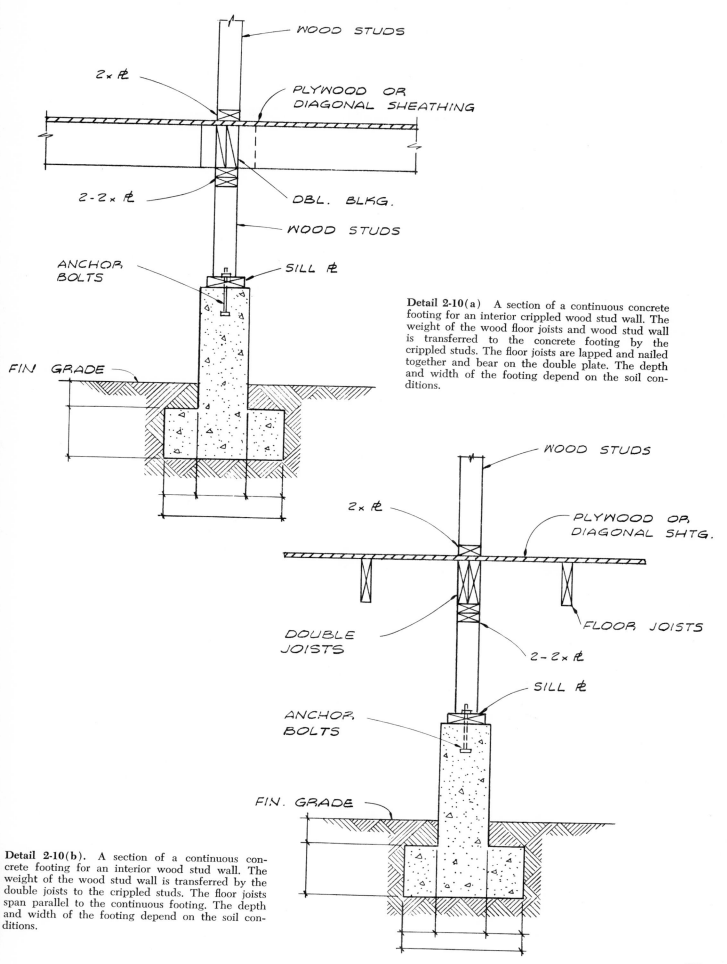

WOOD STUDS

2 x ℄

PLYWOOD OR DIAGONAL SHEATHING

2-2 x ℄

DBL. BLKG.

WOOD STUDS

ANCHOR BOLTS

SILL ℄

FIN GRADE

Detail 2-10(a) A section of a continuous concrete footing for an interior crippled wood stud wall. The weight of the wood floor joists and wood stud wall is transferred to the concrete footing by the crippled studs. The floor joists are lapped and nailed together and bear on the double plate. The depth and width of the footing depend on the soil conditions.

WOOD STUDS

2 x ℄

PLYWOOD OR DIAGONAL SHTG.

DOUBLE JOISTS

FLOOR JOISTS

2-2 x ℄

SILL ℄

ANCHOR BOLTS

FIN. GRADE

Detail 2-10(b). A section of a continuous concrete footing for an interior wood stud wall. The weight of the wood stud wall is transferred by the double joists to the crippled studs. The floor joists span parallel to the continuous footing. The depth and width of the footing depend on the soil conditions.

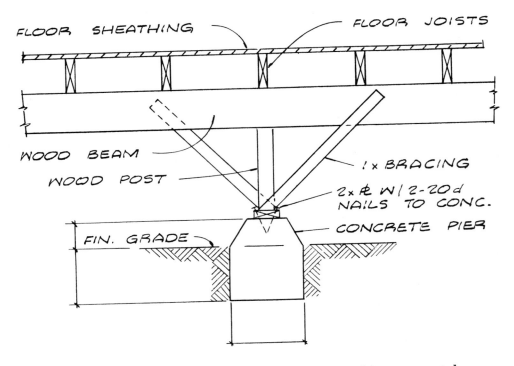

FLOOR SHEATHING — — FLOOR JOISTS

WOOD BEAM

WOOD POST

/ x BRACING

2x ℓ W/ 2-20d NAILS TO CONC.

FIN. GRADE

CONCRETE PIER

Detail 2-11(a). An elevation of wood floor joists and beams supported over the finished grade. The depth and size of the supporting concrete pier depends on the soil conditions. See Detail 2-11(b).

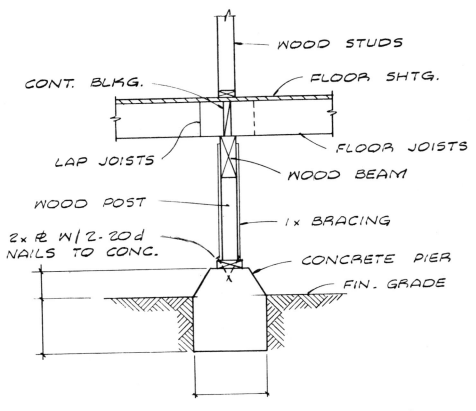

WOOD STUDS

CONT. BLKG.

FLOOR SHTG.

LAP JOISTS

FLOOR JOISTS

WOOD BEAM

WOOD POST

/ x BRACING

2x ℓ W/ 2- 20d NAILS TO CONC.

CONCRETE PIER

FIN. GRADE

Detail 2-11(b). A section of Detail 2-11(a). The floor joists lap over the wood beam and are nailed together. The 1"-wide diagonal braces on each side of the wood post restrain the floor laterally. The bracing may be omitted if the posts are short and the floor is laterally restrained by a continuous footing.

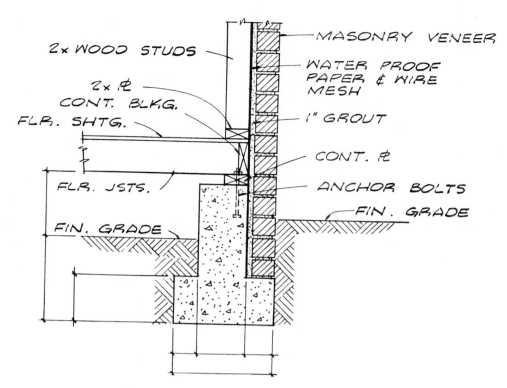

2x WOOD STUDS

2x ℄
CONT. BLKG.
FLR. SHTG.

FLR. JSTS.

FIN. GRADE

MASONRY VENEER

WATER PROOF PAPER & WIRE MESH

1" GROUT

CONT. ℄

ANCHOR BOLTS

FIN. GRADE

Detail 2-12(a). A section of a continuous concrete footing for an exterior wood stud wall with an exterior masonry veneer surface. The floor joists bear on the sill plate. The distance between the finished grade and the bottom of the floor joists is determined by the local building code. The masonry veneer is connected to the wood studs as shown. The depth and width of the footing depend on the soil conditions.

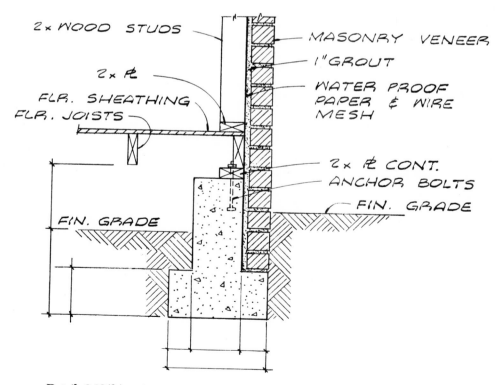

2x WOOD STUDS

2x ℄
FLR. SHEATHING
FLR. JOISTS

FIN. GRADE

MASONRY VENEER

1" GROUT

WATER PROOF PAPER & WIRE MESH

2x ℄ CONT.
ANCHOR BOLTS

FIN. GRADE

Detail 2-12(b). A section of a continuous concrete footing for an exterior wood stud wall with an exterior masonry veneer surface. The floor joists span parallel to the wall. The double joist transfers the weight of the wall to the continuous footing. The distance between the finished grade and the bottom of the floor joists is determined by the local building code. The masonry veneer is connected to the wood studs as shown. The depth and width of the footing depend on the soil conditions.

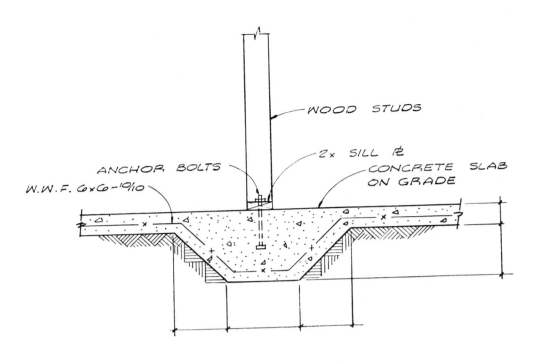

Detail 2-13(a). A section of a non-bearing wood stud wall on a concrete slab on grade. The increased width and depth of the concrete slab depend on the soil conditions.

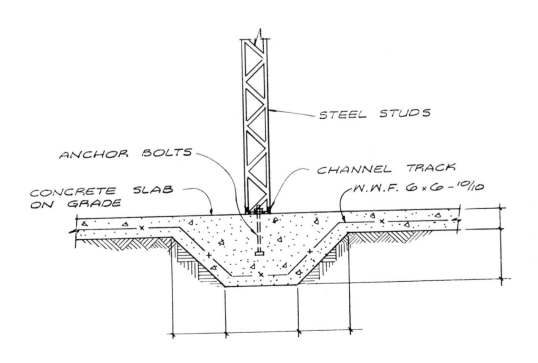

Detail 2-13(b). A section of a non-bearing steel stud wall on a concrete slab on grade. The increased width and depth of the concrete slab depend on the soil conditions.

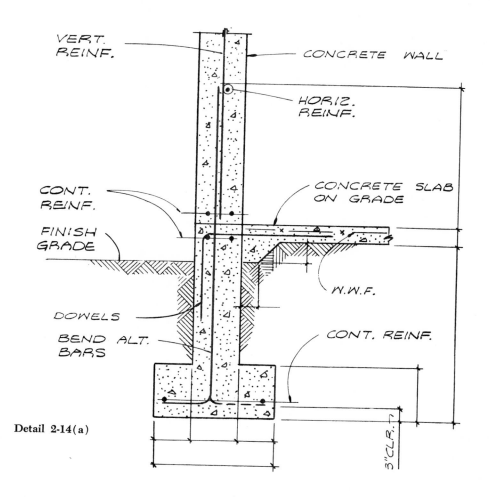

VERT. REINF.

CONCRETE WALL

HORIZ. REINF.

CONT. REINF.

CONCRETE SLAB ON GRADE

FINISH GRADE

W.W.F.

DOWELS

BEND ALT. BARS

CONT. REINF.

3" CLR.

Detail 2-14(a)

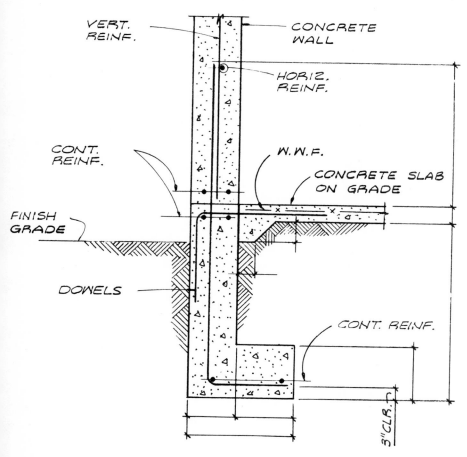

VERT. REINF.

CONCRETE WALL

HORIZ. REINF.

CONT. REINF.

W.W.F.

CONCRETE SLAB ON GRADE

FINISH GRADE

DOWELS

CONT. REINF.

3" CLR.

Detail 2-14(b)

Details 2-14(a) and (b). A section of a continuous concrete footing for an exterior concrete wall. The footing is connected to the concrete slab on grade and to the concrete wall above grade by reinforcing dowels. The reinforcing dowels lap the wall vertical reinforcement 40 bar diameters or not less than 24". The size and spacing of the reinforcing steel is determined by calculation. The depth and width of the footing depend on the soil conditions.

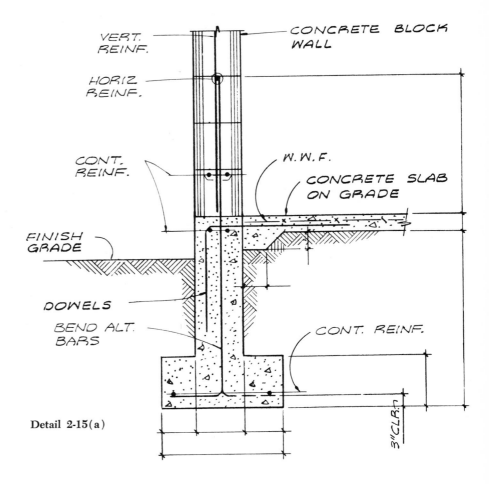

VERT. REINF.

HORIZ. REINF.

CONCRETE BLOCK WALL

CONT. REINF.

W.W.F.

CONCRETE SLAB ON GRADE

FINISH GRADE

DOWELS

BEND ALT. BARS

CONT. REINF.

3" CLR.

Detail 2-15(a)

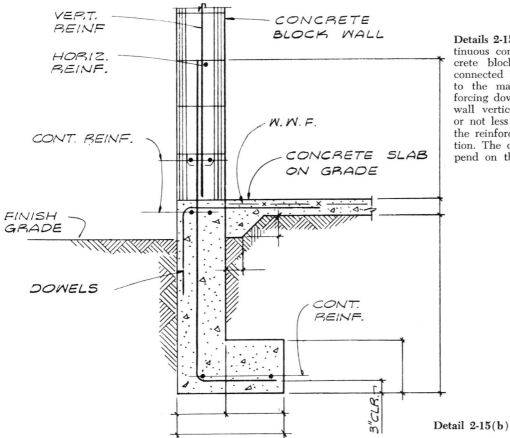

VERT. REINF

HORIZ. REINF.

CONT. REINF.

FINISH GRADE

DOWELS

CONCRETE BLOCK WALL

W.W.F.

CONCRETE SLAB ON GRADE

CONT. REINF.

3" CLR.

Detail 2-15(b)

Details 2-15(a) and (b). A section of a continuous concrete footing and an exterior concrete block masonry wall. The footing is connected to the concrete slab on grade and to the masonry wall above grade by reinforcing dowels. The reinforcing dowels lap the wall vertical reinforcement 30 bar diameters or not less than 24″. The size and spacing of the reinforcing steel is determined by calculation. The depth and width of the footing depend on the soil conditions.

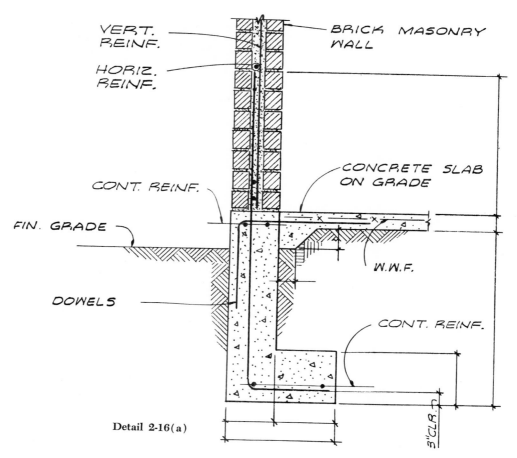

VERT. REINF.

HORIZ. REINF.

BRICK MASONRY WALL

CONT. REINF.

CONCRETE SLAB ON GRADE

FIN. GRADE

W.W.F.

DOWELS

CONT. REINF.

3" CLR.

Detail 2-16(a)

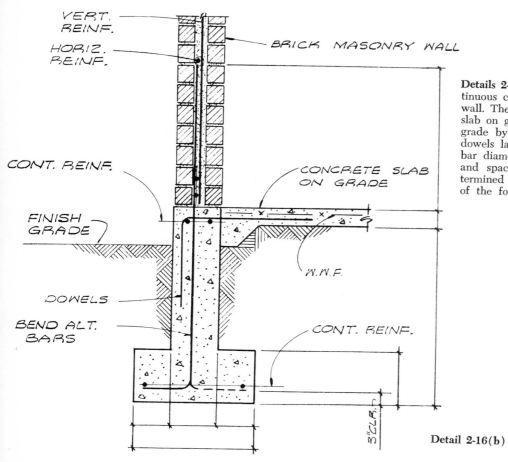

VERT. REINF.

HORIZ. REINF.

BRICK MASONRY WALL

CONT. REINF.

CONCRETE SLAB ON GRADE

FINISH GRADE

W.W.F.

DOWELS

BEND ALT. BARS

CONT. REINF.

3" CLR.

Detail 2-16(b)

Details 2-16(a) and (b). A section of a continuous concrete footing and an exterior brick wall. The footing is connected to the concrete slab on grade and to the masonry wall above grade by reinforcing dowels. The reinforcing dowels lap the wall vertical reinforcement 30 bar diameters or not less than 24". The size and spacing of the reinforcing steel is determined by calculation. The depth and width of the footing depend on the soil conditions.

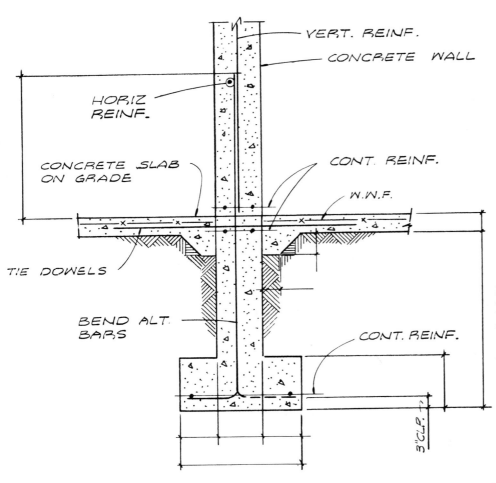

VERT. REINF.

CONCRETE WALL

HORIZ REINF.

CONCRETE SLAB ON GRADE

CONT. REINF.

W.W.F.

TIE DOWELS

BEND ALT. BARS

CONT. REINF.

3"CLR.

Detail 2-17(a). A section of a continuous concrete footing and an interior concrete wall. The concrete slab on grade is connected across the top of the footing by reinforcing dowels. The footing is connected to the concrete wall above grade with reinforcing dowels. The reinforcing dowels lap the wall vertical reinforcement 40 bar diameters or not less than 24". The size and spacing of the reinforcing steel is determined by calculation. The depth and width of the footing depend on the soil conditions.

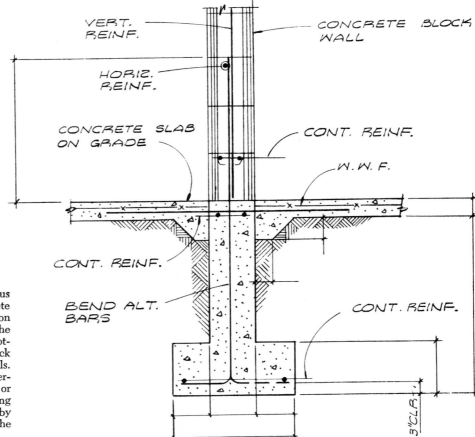

VERT. REINF.

CONCRETE BLOCK WALL

HORIZ. REINF.

CONCRETE SLAB ON GRADE

CONT. REINF.

W.W.F.

CONT. REINF.

BEND ALT. BARS

CONT. REINF.

3"CLR.

Detail 2-17(b). A section of a continuous concrete footing and an interior concrete block masonry wall. The concrete slab on grade is connected across the top of the footing with reinforcing dowels. The footing is connected to the concrete block wall above grade with reinforcing dowels. The reinforcing dowels lap the wall vertical reinforcement 30 bar diameters or not less than 24". The size and spacing of the reinforcing steel is determined by calculation. The depth and width of the footing depend on the soil conditions.

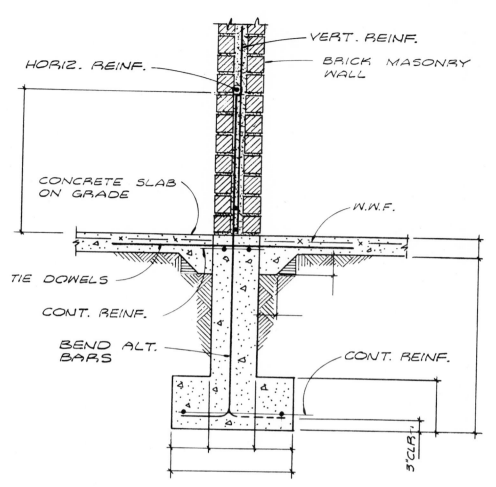

Labels on diagram:
HORIZ. REINF.
VERT. REINF.
BRICK MASONRY WALL
CONCRETE SLAB ON GRADE
W.W.F.
TIE DOWELS
CONT. REINF.
BEND ALT. BARS
CONT. REINF.
3" CLR.

Detail 2-17(c). A section of a continuous concrete footing and an interior brick wall. The concrete slab on grade is connected across the top of the footing with reinforcing dowels. The footing is connected to the brick wall above grade with reinforcing dowels. The reinforcing dowels lap the wall vertical reinforcement 30 bar diameters or not less than 24″. The size and spacing of the reinforcing steel is determined by calculation. The depth and width of the footing depend on the soil condition.

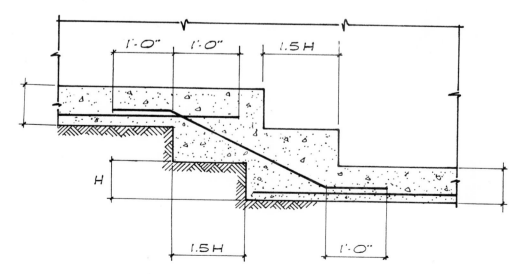

Labels on diagram:
1'-0"
1'-0"
1.5 H
H
1.5 H
1'-0"

Detail 2-18. An elevation of a stepped continuous footing. The length of the run of the step is 1½ times the height of the rise of the step. The footing reinforcing bars are lapped in accordance with the local building code.

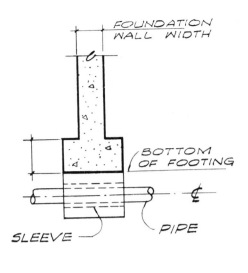

FOUNDATION
WALL WIDTH

BOTTOM
OF FOOTING

℄

SLEEVE — PIPE

SECTION

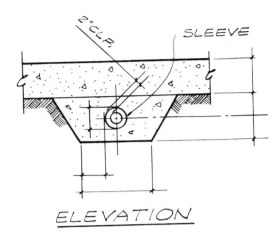

2" CLR. SLEEVE

ELEVATION

Detail 2-19(a). A section showing a steel pipe passing through and below a continuous concrete footing. The pipe is sleeved to prevent damage caused by possible footing deflection. An additional depth and width of concrete covers the pipe sleeve and allows sufficient bearing of the continuous footing. See Detail 2-19(b).

Detail 2-19(b). A section of Detail 2-19(a).

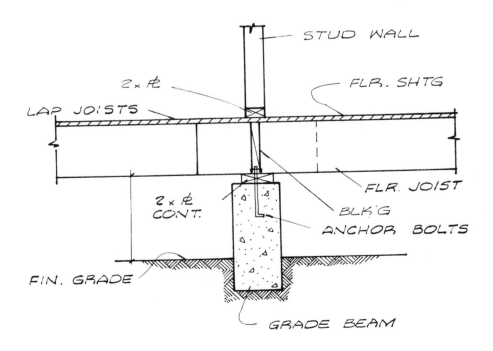

STUD WALL

2 × ℔

FLR. SHTG

LAP JOISTS

2 × ℔
CONT.

FLR. JOIST

BLK'G

ANCHOR BOLTS

FIN. GRADE

GRADE BEAM

Detail 2-20. A section of a concrete grade beam supporting an interior wood stud wall and floor joists. The floor joists are lapped and nailed together. The reinforcing steel in the grade beam is not shown. The distance between the finished grade and the bottom of the floor joists is determined by the local building code.

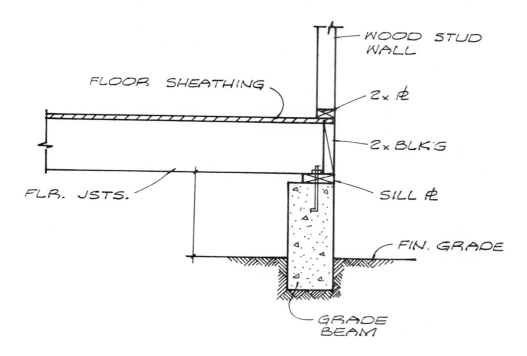

Detail 2-21(a). A section of a concrete grade beam supporting an exterior wood stud wall and floor joists. The reinforcing steel in the grade beam is not shown. The distance between finished grade and the bottom of the floor joists is determined by the local building code.

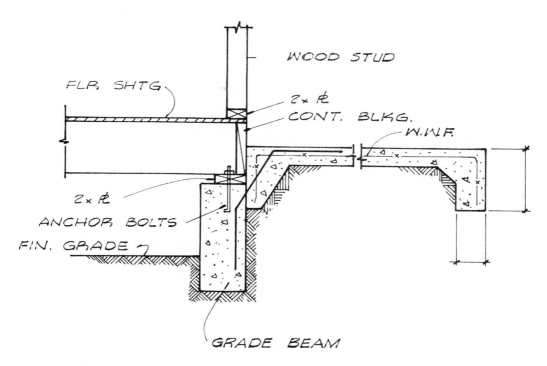

Detail 2-21(b). A section of a concrete grade beam supporting an exterior wood stud wall and floor joists. The reinforcing steel in the grade beam is not shown. The distance between finished grade and the bottom of the floor joists is determined by the local building code. The exterior concrete slab on grade is connected to the grade beam by reinforcing dowels as shown.

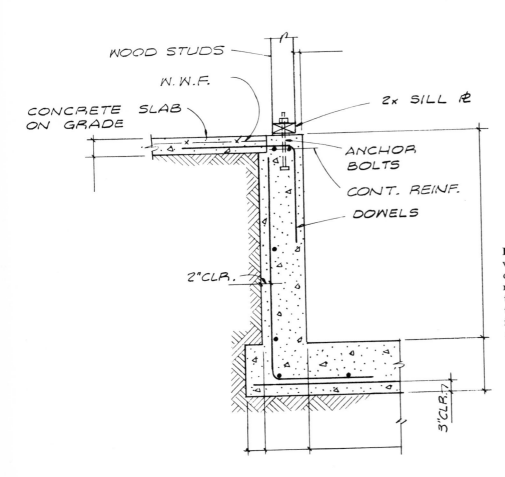

WOOD STUDS

W.W.F.

CONCRETE SLAB
ON GRADE

2x SILL ℙ

ANCHOR
BOLTS

CONT. REINF.

DOWELS

2"CLR.

3"CLR.

Detail 2-22(a). A section of a concrete pit wall and a wood stud wall. The pit wall is connected to the concrete slab on grade with reinforcing dowels. The stud wall is set back to allow the wall covering to meet the face of the concrete. The size and spacing of the reinforcing steel in the pit wall and the footing are determined by calculation.

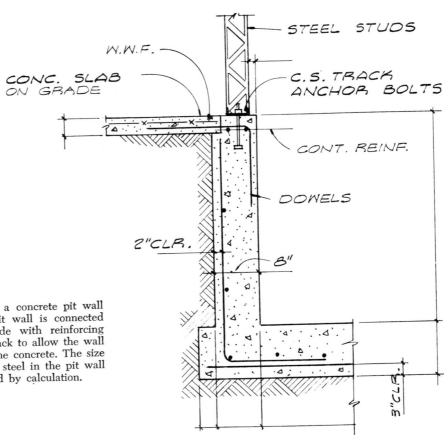

STEEL STUDS

W.W.F.

CONC. SLAB
ON GRADE

C.S. TRACK
ANCHOR BOLTS

CONT. REINF.

DOWELS

2"CLR.

8"

3"CLR.

Detail 2-22(b). A section of a concrete pit wall and a steel stud wall. The pit wall is connected to the concrete slab on grade with reinforcing dowels. The stud wall is set back to allow the wall covering to meet the face of the concrete. The size and spacing of the reinforcing steel in the pit wall and the footing are determined by calculation.

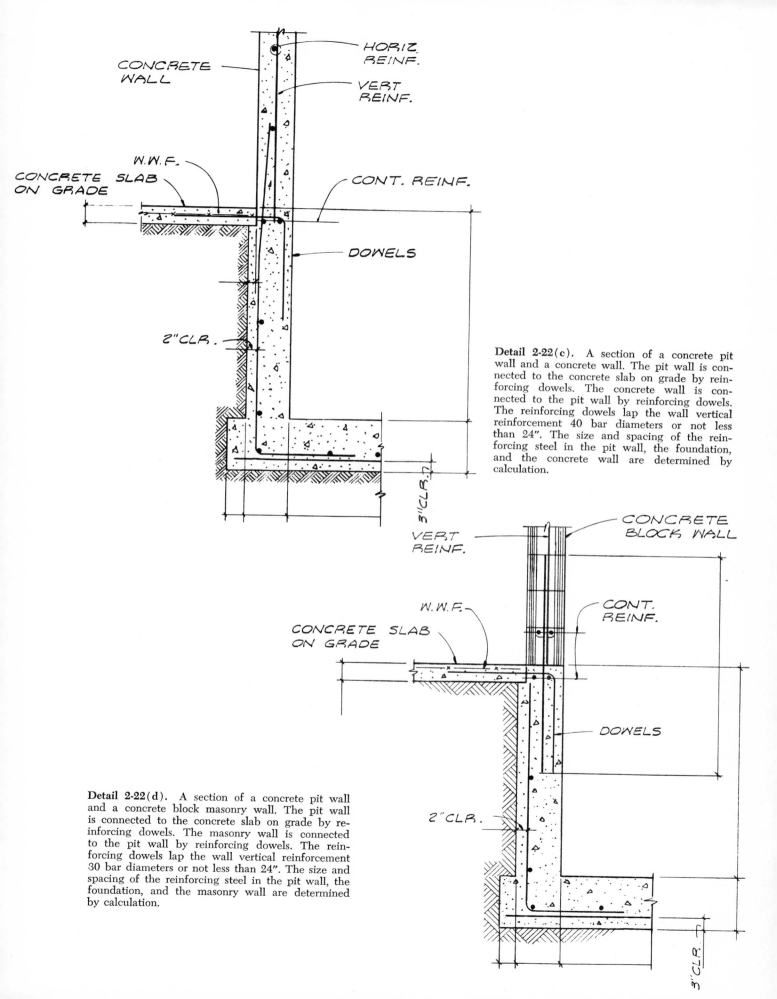

CONCRETE WALL

HORIZ. REINF.

VERT. REINF.

W.W.F.

CONCRETE SLAB ON GRADE

CONT. REINF.

DOWELS

2" CLR.

3" CLR.

Detail 2-22(c). A section of a concrete pit wall and a concrete wall. The pit wall is connected to the concrete slab on grade by reinforcing dowels. The concrete wall is connected to the pit wall by reinforcing dowels. The reinforcing dowels lap the wall vertical reinforcement 40 bar diameters or not less than 24″. The size and spacing of the reinforcing steel in the pit wall, the foundation, and the concrete wall are determined by calculation.

CONCRETE BLOCK WALL

VERT. REINF.

CONT. REINF.

W.W.F.

CONCRETE SLAB ON GRADE

DOWELS

2" CLR.

3" CLR.

Detail 2-22(d). A section of a concrete pit wall and a concrete block masonry wall. The pit wall is connected to the concrete slab on grade by reinforcing dowels. The masonry wall is connected to the pit wall by reinforcing dowels. The reinforcing dowels lap the wall vertical reinforcement 30 bar diameters or not less than 24″. The size and spacing of the reinforcing steel in the pit wall, the foundation, and the masonry wall are determined by calculation.

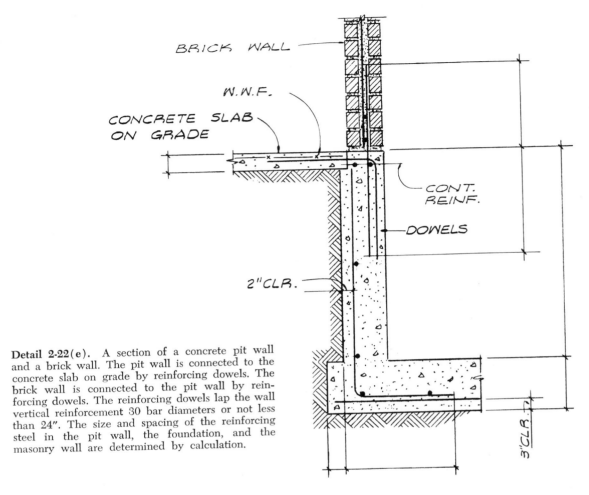

BRICK WALL

W.W.F.

CONCRETE SLAB
ON GRADE

CONT.
REINF.

DOWELS

2"CLR.

3"CLR.

Detail 2-22(e). A section of a concrete pit wall and a brick wall. The pit wall is connected to the concrete slab on grade by reinforcing dowels. The brick wall is connected to the pit wall by reinforcing dowels. The reinforcing dowels lap the wall vertical reinforcement 30 bar diameters or not less than 24". The size and spacing of the reinforcing steel in the pit wall, the foundation, and the masonry wall are determined by calculation.

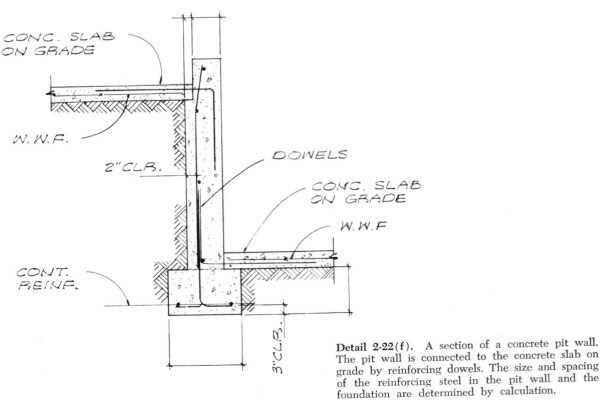

CONC. SLAB
ON GRADE

W.W.F.

2"CLR.

DOWELS

CONC. SLAB
ON GRADE

W.W.F

CONT.
REINF.

3"CLR.

Detail 2-22(f). A section of a concrete pit wall. The pit wall is connected to the concrete slab on grade by reinforcing dowels. The size and spacing of the reinforcing steel in the pit wall and the foundation are determined by calculation.

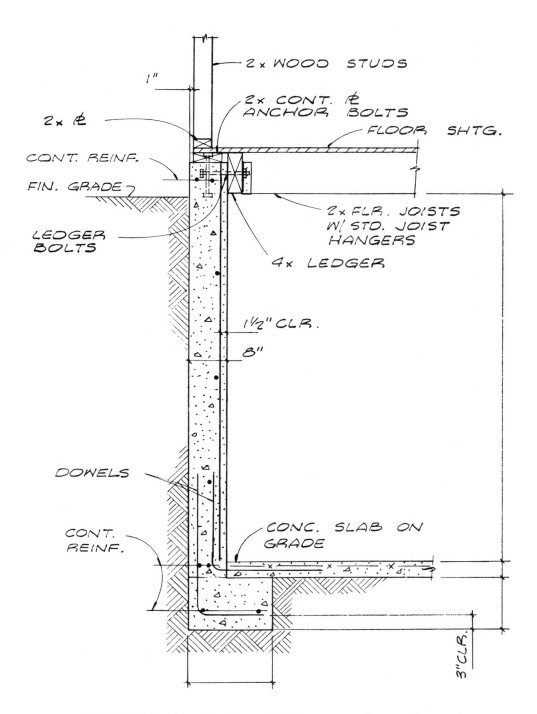

Detail 2-23(a). A section of a concrete basement wall supporting wood floor joists and an exterior wood stud wall. The stud wall is set back to allow the exterior wall covering to meet the face of the concrete. The floor joists are connected to a 4″ wide wood ledger by joist hangers. The ledger is bolted to the wall. The size and spacing of the ledger bolts are determined by calculation. The size and spacing of the reinforcing steel in the concrete wall are determined by calculation. The depth and the width of the wall footing depend on the soil conditions.

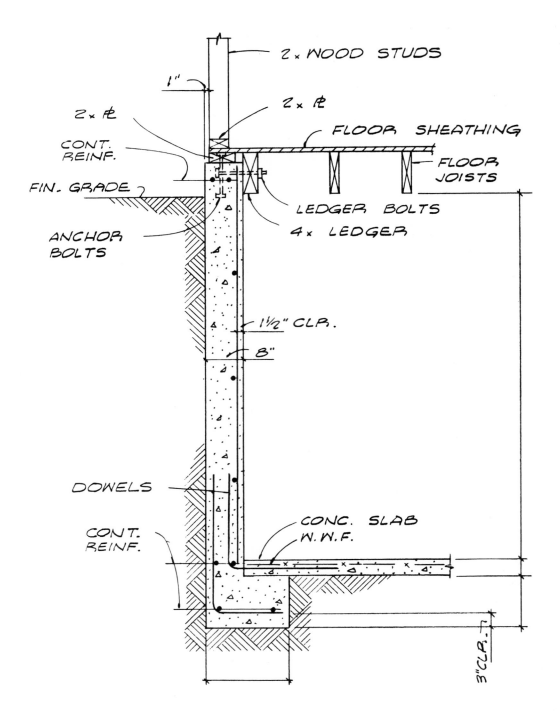

Detail 2-23(b). A section of a concrete basement wall, wood floor joists and an exterior wood stud wall. The stud wall is set back to allow the exterior wall covering to meet the face of the concrete. The floor joists span parallel to the wall. The floor sheathing is nailed to a 4″ wide wood ledger which is bolted to the concrete wall. The size and spacing of the ledger bolts and the size and spacing of the reinforcing steel in the concrete wall are determined by calculation. The depth and the width of the wall footing depend on soil conditions.

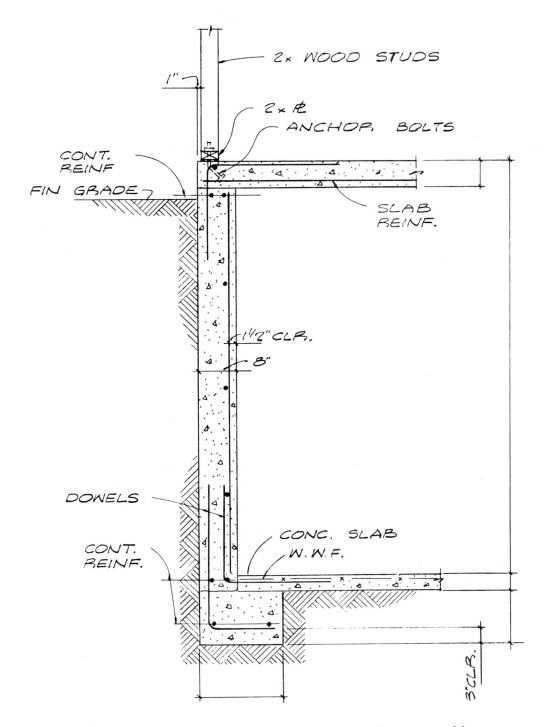

Detail 2-24(a). A section of a concrete basement wall, a concrete slab, and an exterior wood stud wall. The stud wall is set back to allow the exterior wall covering to meet the face of the concrete. The slab is connected to the wall with reinforcing dowels. The size and spacing of the reinforcing steel in the wall are determined by calculation. The depth and the width of the wall footing depend on the soil conditions.

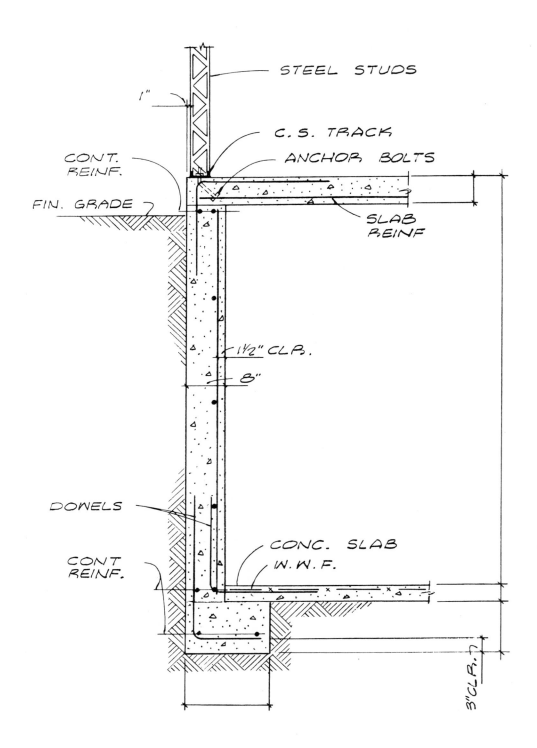

Detail 2-24(b). A section of a concrete basement wall, a concrete slab, and an exterior steel stud wall. The stud wall is set back to allow the exterior wall covering to meet the face of the concrete. The slab is connected to the wall with reinforcing dowels. The size and spacing of the reinforcing steel in the wall are determined by calculation. The depth and the width of the wall footing depend on the soil conditions.

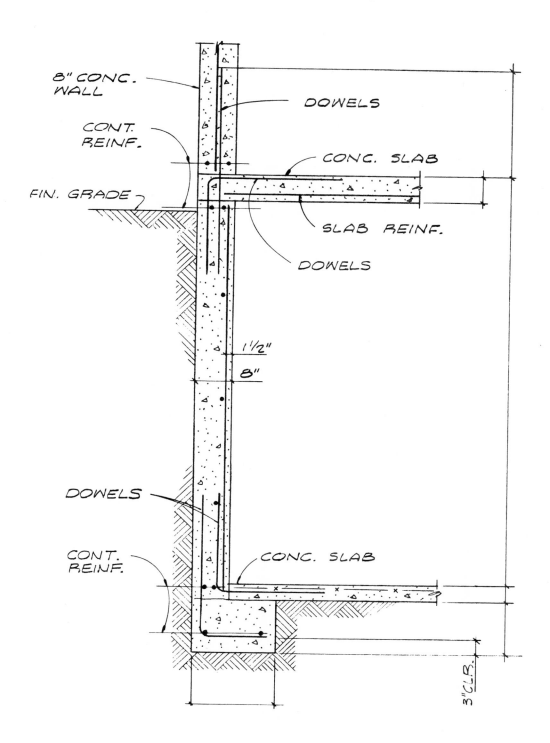

Detail 2-24(c). A section of a concrete basement wall supporting a concrete slab and a concrete wall. The slab and wall above grade are connected to the basement wall with reinforcing dowels lapped 40 bar diameters or not less than 24″. The size and spacing of the reinforcing steel in the wall are determined by calculation. The depth and the width of the wall footing depend on the soil conditions.

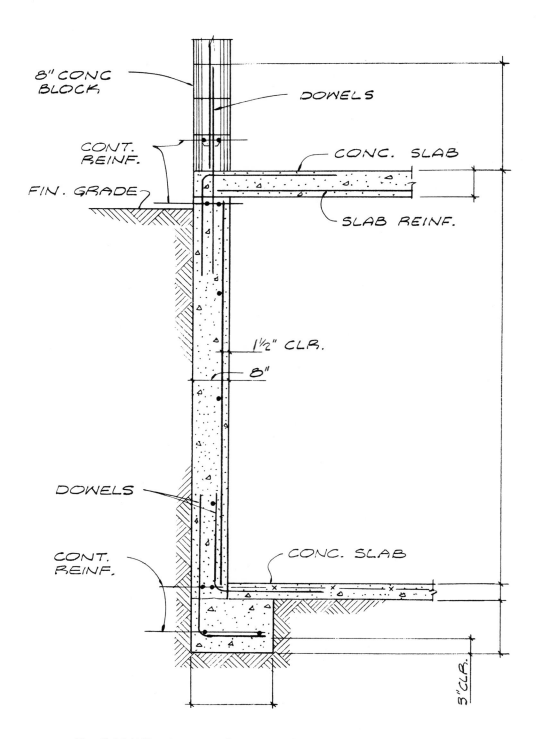

8" CONC BLOCK

DOWELS

CONT. REINF.

CONC. SLAB

FIN. GRADE

SLAB REINF.

1½" CLR.

8"

DOWELS

CONT. REINF.

CONC. SLAB

3" CLR.

Detail 2-24(d). A section of a concrete basement wall supporting a concrete slab and a concrete block masonry wall. The concrete slab and the masonry wall are connected to the basement wall with reinforcing dowels. The reinforcing dowels lap 40 bar diameters into the concrete and 30 bar diameters into the masonry or not less than 24". The size and spacing of the reinforcing steel in the wall are determined by calculation. The depth and the width of the wall footing depend on the soil conditions.

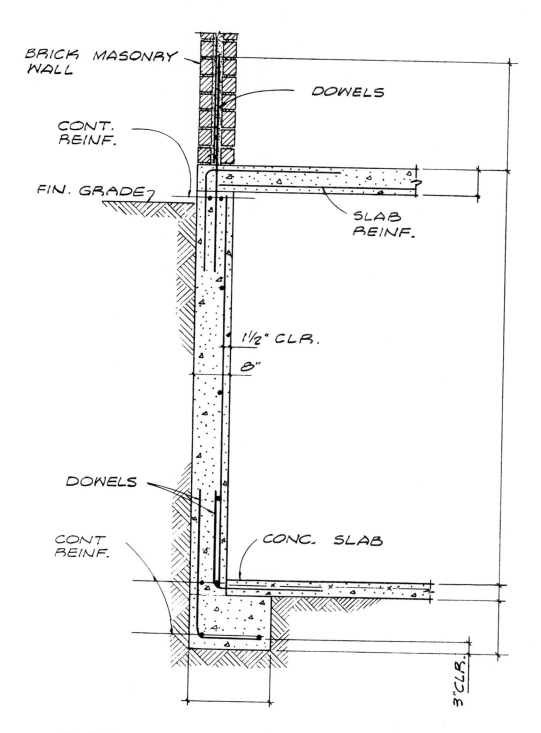

Detail 2-24(e). A section of a concrete wall supporting a concrete slab and a brick wall. The concrete slab and the brick wall are connected to the basement wall with reinforcing dowels. The reinforcing dowels lap 40 bar diameters into the concrete and 30 bar diameters into the masonry or not less than 24″. The size and spacing of the reinforcing steel in the wall are determined by calculation. The depth and the width of the wall footing depend on the soil conditions.

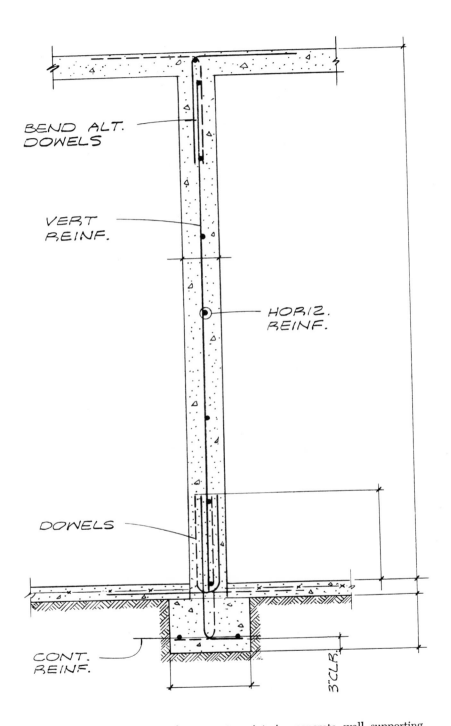

BEND ALT.
DOWELS

VERT
REINF.

HORIZ.
REINF.

DOWELS

CONT.
REINF.

3"CLR.

Detail 2-25. A section of a one story interior concrete wall supporting a concrete slab. The wall is connected to the slab at the top of the wall and to the footing at the bottom of the wall with reinforcing dowels bent in alternate directions. The size and spacing of the wall reinforcement are determined by calculation. Concrete walls greater than 8″ thick require reinforcement on each face. The depth and the width of the wall footing depend on the soil conditions.

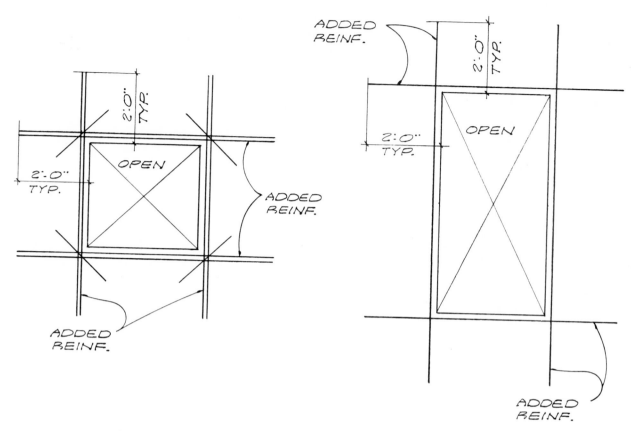

Detail 2-26(a). Elevations of openings in concrete walls. Additional reinforcing steel is placed at the edges of the wall opening. The added vertical and horizontal bars extend a minimum of 24″ past the edge of the opening. The diagonal bars at the corners are optional. See Detail 2-26(b).

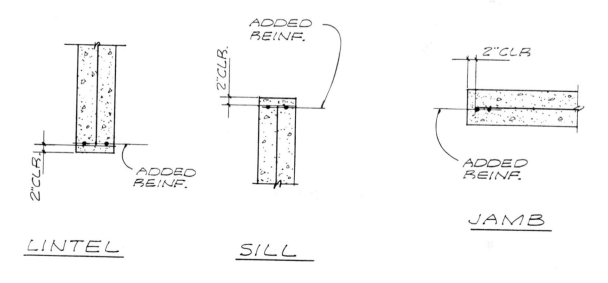

LINTEL   SILL   JAMB

Detail 2-26(b). Sections of a concrete wall opening, lintel, jamb, and sill. The sill and jamb edges are nominally reinforced with two bars. The lintel may require more than two reinforcing bars depending on the span of the opening and the load to be supported.

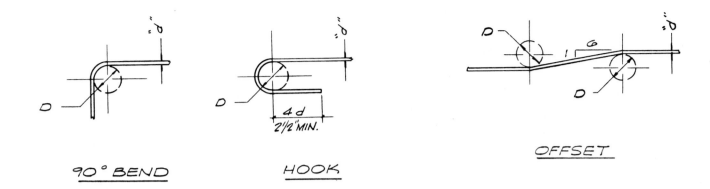

90° BEND   HOOK   OFFSET

TYPICAL REINF. BAR BENDS

D = BAR DIAM.
d = BEND DIAM.
MIN D = 6d FOR #7 BARS OR SMALLER
    D = 8d FOR #8 BARS OR LARGER
    D = 5d FOR STIRRUPS AND TIES

Detail 2-27(a). Details of reinforcing bar standard bends and hooks.

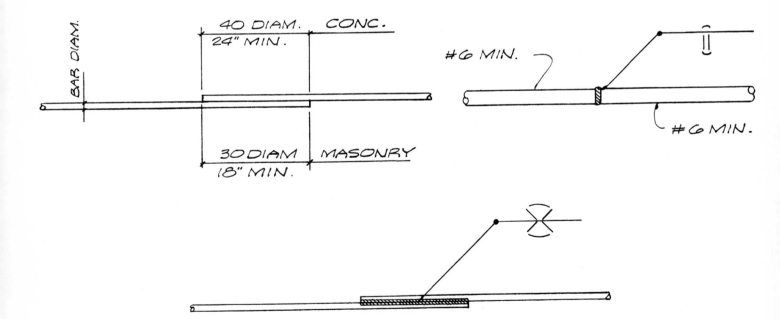

Detail 2-27(b). Details of reinforcing bar lap splices and welded splices.

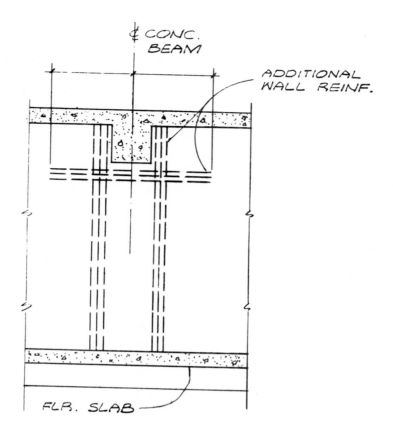

Detail 2-28. A section of a concrete beam supported by a concrete wall. The beam reaction on the wall is supported by added reinforcement in the wall as shown. The size and spacing of the added reinforcement are determined by calculation.

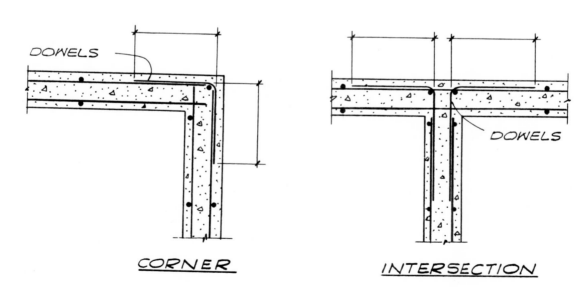

Detail 2-29(a). A plan section of the reinforcing steel intersection of concrete wall bond beams. The reinforcing bars are lapped 40 bar diameters or not less than 24″.

Detail 2-29(b). A plan section of the reinforcing steel at the corner of a concrete wall bond beam. The bond beams are connected by reinforcing dowels of the same size as the bond beam reinforcing bars. The length of the lap splice is 40 bar diameters or not less than 24″.

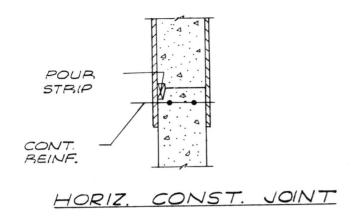

POUR STRIP

CONT. REINF.

HORIZ. CONST. JOINT

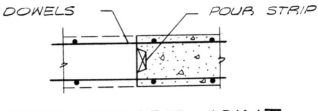

DOWELS — POUR STRIP

VERT. CONST. JOINT

Detail 2-30(a). Sections of concrete wall construction joints. The location of a concrete construction joint for thermal expansion and contraction or because of a concrete pour stop is determined by the engineer. All surface laitance must be removed from the previous pour before a new concrete pour is made. It may be necessary to waterproof a concrete wall construction joint, depending on the conditions of use of the wall. Construction joints in concrete walls should not be made at points of high bending or high shear unless it is specifically provided for in the design of the wall.

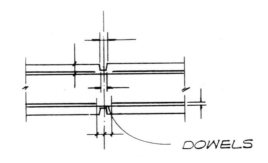

DOWELS

TYP. CONTROL JT.

Detail 2-30(b). A section of a vertical control joint in a concrete wall. The location of the wall control joint is determined by the engineer. Control joints should not be located at points of high bending or shear unless it is specifically provided for in the design of the wall.

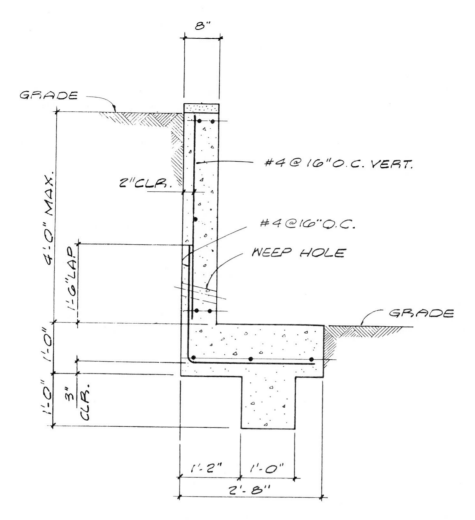

8"

GRADE

#4 @ 16" O.C. VERT.

2" CLR.

4'-0" MAX.

1'-6" LAP

#4 @ 16" O.C.

WEEP HOLE

GRADE

1'-0" 1'-0"

3" CLR.

1'-2"   1'-0"

2'-8"

Detail 2-31(a).   Stem height 4'0".

Detail 2-31. Sections of concrete retaining walls with soil at the exterior face of the stem. The wall retains a flat grade with no surcharge. The wall dimensions and reinforcing steel size and spacing are determined by calculation. Two #4 horizontal continuous reinforcing bars are placed at the top and at the bottom of the wall stem. The minimum horizontal reinforcement in the stem wall and the footing is #4 at 24" o.c. A 3" dia. galvanized iron pipe space at 8'0" o.c. is placed at the base of the stem to act as a weep hole. The cement cap at the top of the wall is optional. The walls are designed for 30 lb per cu ft equivalent fluid pressure and a maximum soil pressure of 1500 lb per sq ft. The resultant of the forces passes through the middle ⅓ of the wall footing. The walls are designed to resist sliding and overturning. The overturning safety factor is 1.5. The concrete design stress is $f'c = 2000$ psi.

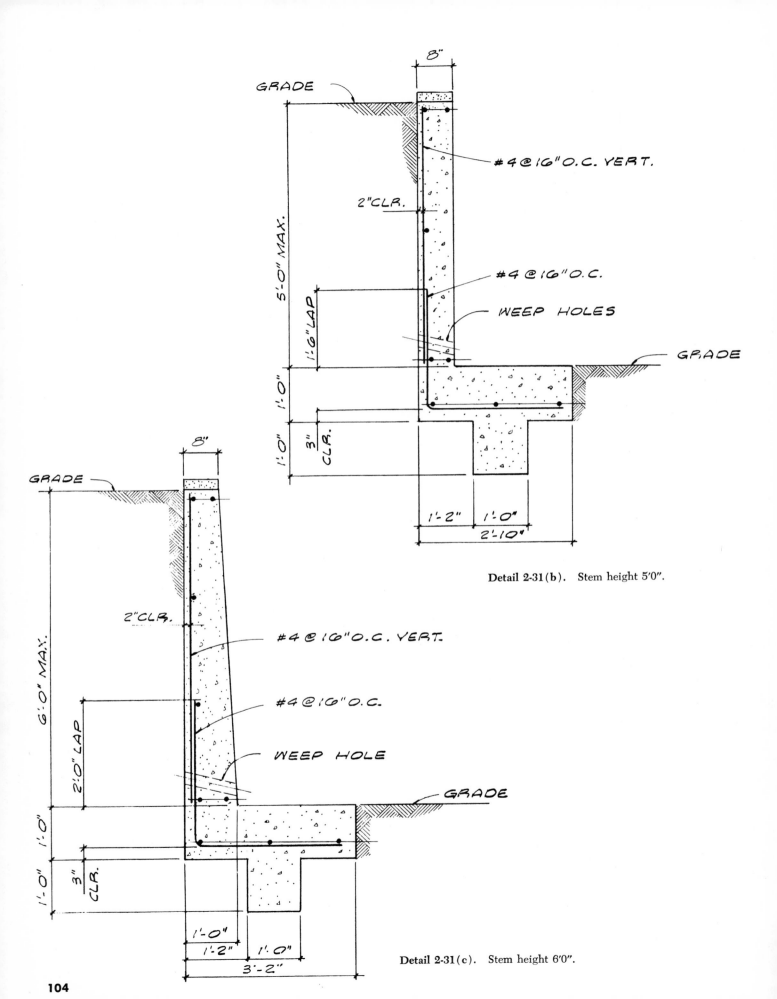

8"

GRADE

#4 @ 16" O.C. VERT.

2" CLR.

5'-0" MAX.

1'-6" LAP

#4 @ 16" O.C.

WEEP HOLES

GRADE

1'-0"

1'-0"

3" CLR.

1'-2"   1'-0"

2'-10"

Detail 2-31(b).   Stem height 5'0".

GRADE

8"

2" CLR.

#4 @ 16" O.C. VERT.

6'-0" MAX.

#4 @ 16" O.C.

2'-0" LAP

WEEP HOLE

GRADE

1'-0"

1'-0"

3" CLR.

1'-0"

1'-2"   1'-0"

3'-2"

Detail 2-31(c).   Stem height 6'0".

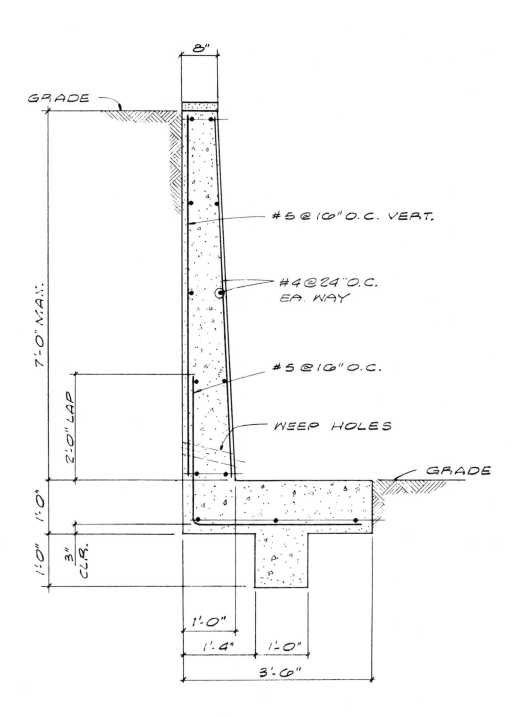

8"

GRADE

#5 @ 16" O.C. VERT.

#4 @ 24" O.C.
EA. WAY

#5 @ 16" O.C.

WEEP HOLES

GRADE

7'-0" MAX.

2'-0" LAP

1'-0"

1'-0"

3"
CLR.

1'-0"

1'-4"   1'-0"

3'-6"

Detail 2-31(d).   Stem height 7'0".

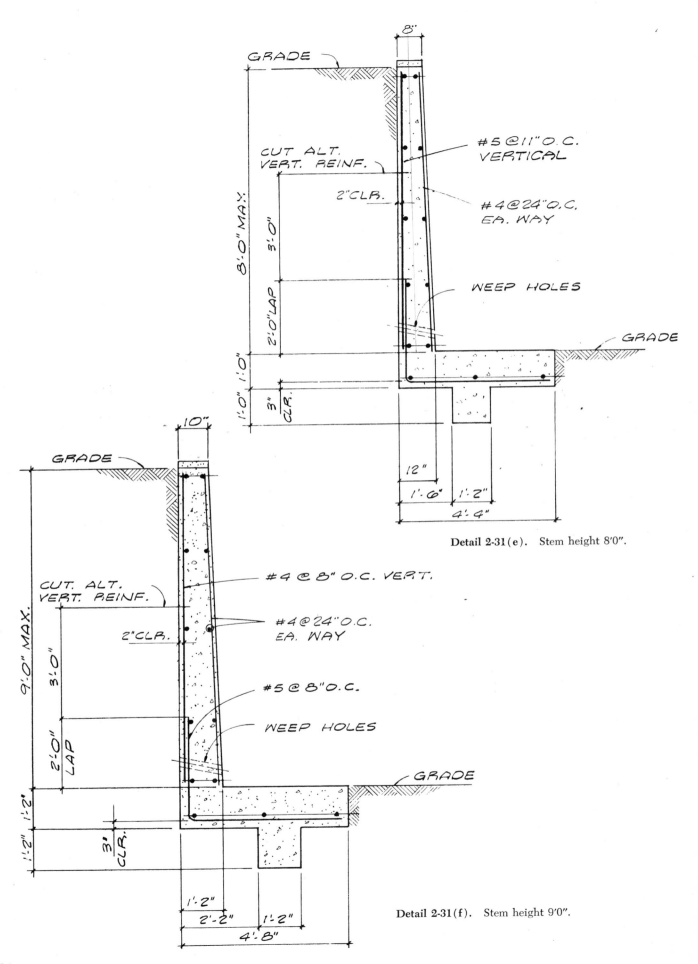

GRADE

8"

CUT ALT.
VERT. REINF.

#5 @ 11" O.C.
VERTICAL

2"CLR.

#4 @ 24" O.C.
EA. WAY

8'-0" MAX.

3'-0"

2'-0" LAP

WEEP HOLES

GRADE

1'-0" 1'-0"

3"
CLR.

12"

1'-6" 1'-2"

4'-4"

Detail 2-31(e). Stem height 8'0".

GRADE

10"

CUT ALT.
VERT. REINF.

#4 @ 8" O.C. VERT.

2"CLR.

#4 @ 24" O.C.
EA. WAY

9'-0" MAX.

3'-0"

2'-0" LAP

#5 @ 8" O.C.

WEEP HOLES

GRADE

1'-2"

1'-2"

3"
CLR.

1'-2"

2'-2" 1'-2"

4'-8"

Detail 2-31(f). Stem height 9'0".

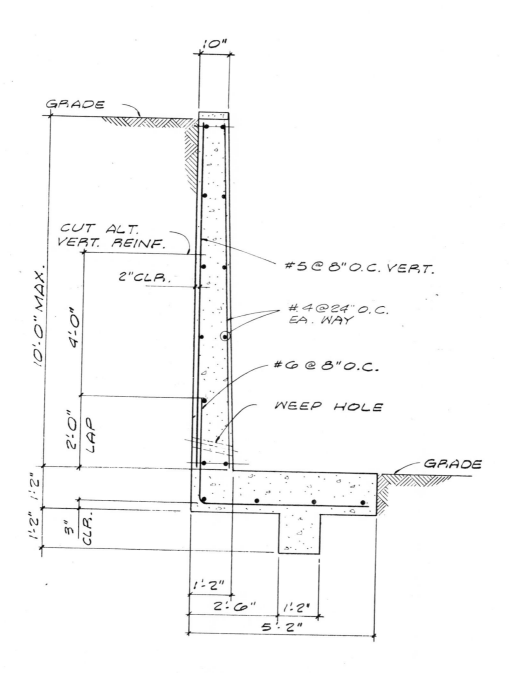

Detail 2-31(g). Stem height 10′0″.

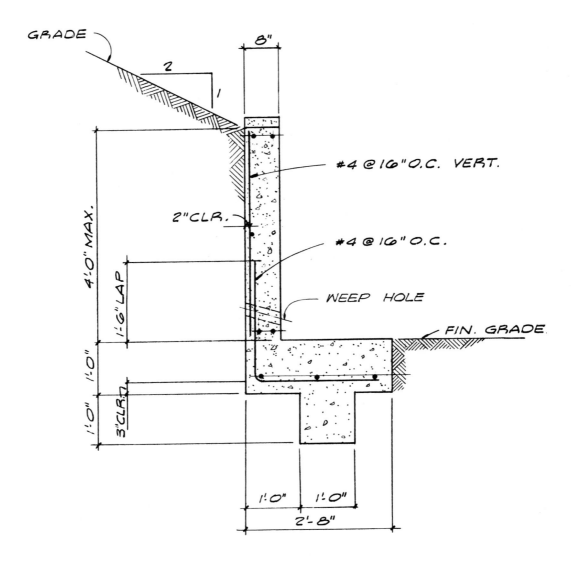

GRADE

8"

2

1

#4 @ 16" O.C. VERT.

2" CLR.

#4 @ 16" O.C.

WEEP HOLE

FIN. GRADE

4'-0" MAX.

1'-6" LAP

1'-0"

1'-0"

3" CLR.

1'-0"

1'-0"

2'-8"

Detail 2-32(a). Stem height 4'0".

Detail 2-32. Sections of concrete retaining walls with soil at the exterior face of the stem. The walls retain a grade slope of two horizontal to one vertical and no surcharge. The wall dimensions and reinforcing steel size and spacing are determined by calculation. Two #4 horizontal continuous reinforcing bars are placed at the top and the bottom of the wall stem. The minimum horizontal reinforcement in the stem wall and the footing is #4 at 24" o.c. A 3" dia. galvanized iron pipe spaced at 8'0" o.c. is placed at the base of the stem to act as a weep hole. The cement cap at the top of the wall is optional. The walls are designed for 43 lb per cu ft equivalent fluid pressure and a maximum soil pressure of 1500 lb per sq ft. The resultant of the forces passes through the middle $\frac{1}{3}$ of the wall footing. The walls are designed to resist sliding and overturning. The overturning safety factor is 1.5. The concrete design stress is $f'c = 2000$ psi.

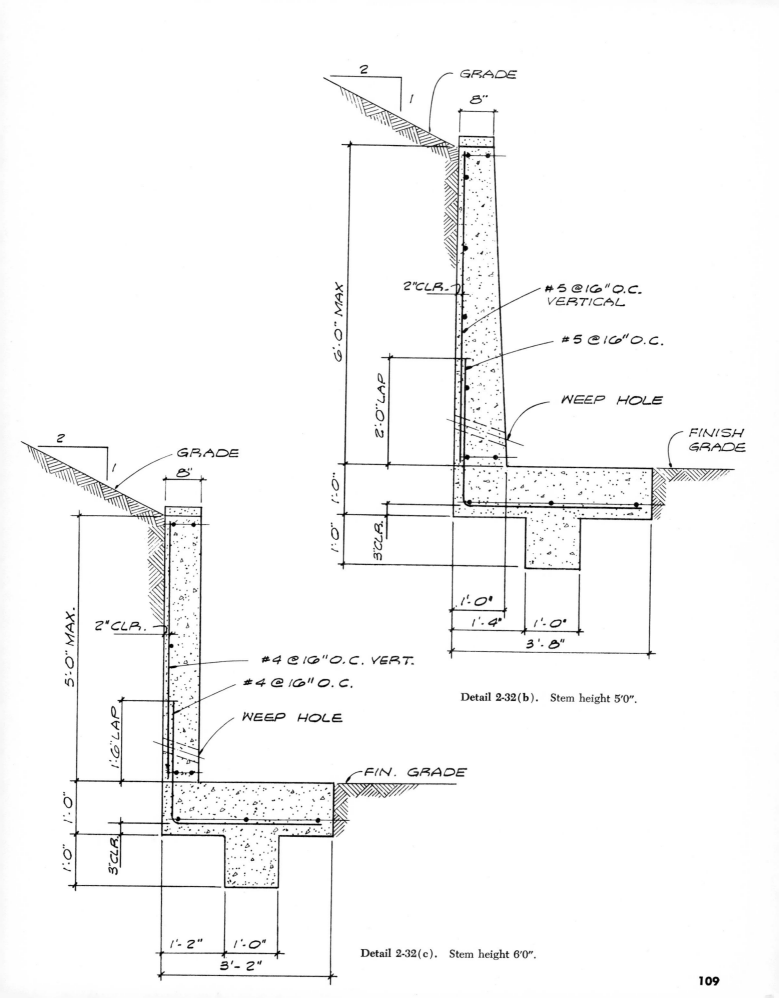

GRADE

2
1

8"

6'-0" MAX

2"CLR.

#5 @ 16" O.C.
VERTICAL

#5 @ 16" O.C.

2'-0" LAP

WEEP HOLE

FINISH
GRADE

1'-0"

1'-0"

3" CLR.

1'-0"

1'-4"   1'-0"

3'-8"

Detail 2-32(b).   Stem height 5'0".

GRADE

2
1

8"

5'-0" MAX.

2"CLR.

#4 @ 16" O.C. VERT.

#4 @ 16" O.C.

WEEP HOLE

1'-6" LAP

FIN. GRADE

1'-0"

1'-0"

3" CLR.

1'-2"   1'-0"

3'-2"

Detail 2-32(c).   Stem height 6'0".

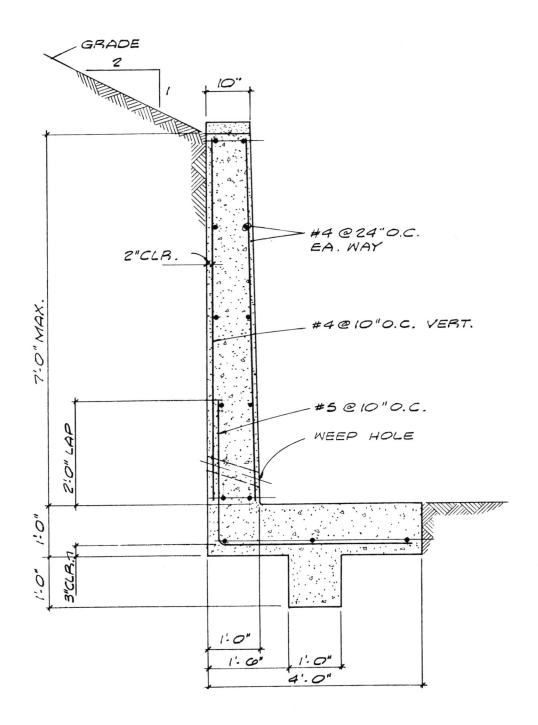

GRADE
2
1

10"

#4 @ 24" O.C.
EA. WAY

2" CLR.

#4 @ 10" O.C. VERT.

#5 @ 10" O.C.

WEEP HOLE

7'-0" MAX.

2'-0" LAP

1'-0"

1'-0"

3" CLR.

1'-0"

1'-0"

1'-0"

4'-0"

Detail 2-32(d). Stem height 7'0".

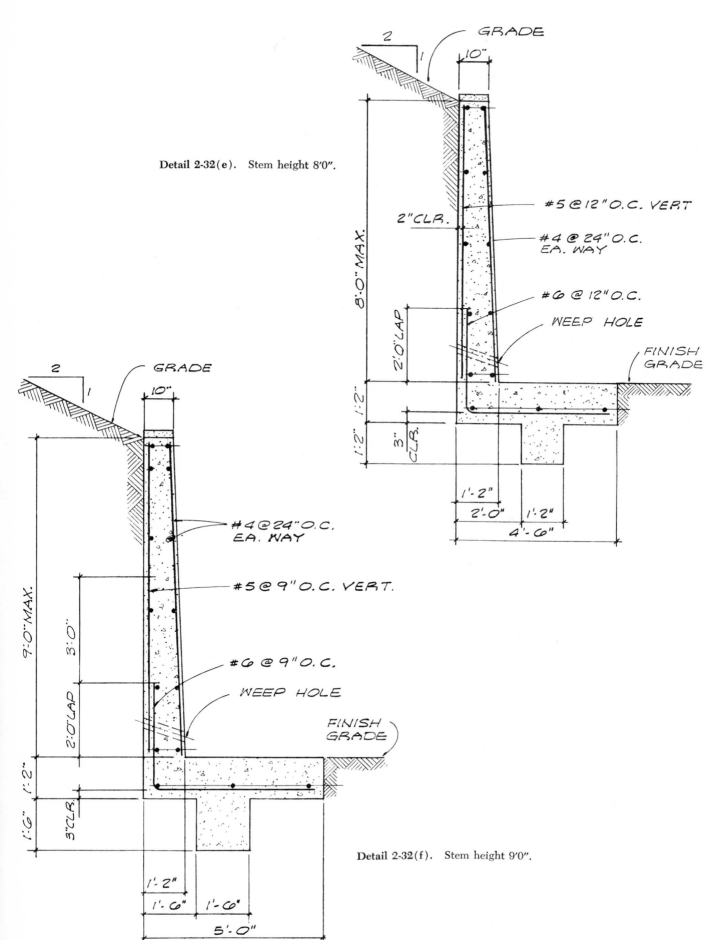

Detail 2-32(e). Stem height 8'0".

GRADE

2 / 1

10"

8'-0" MAX.

#5 @ 12" O.C. VERT

2" CLR.

#4 @ 24" O.C. EA. WAY

2'0" LAP

#6 @ 12" O.C.

WEEP HOLE

FINISH GRADE

1'-2"

1'-2"

3" CLR.

1'-2"

2'-0"

1'-2"

4'-0"

GRADE

2 / 1

10"

9'-0" MAX.

#4 @ 24" O.C. EA. WAY

3'-0"

#5 @ 9" O.C. VERT.

2'0" LAP

#6 @ 9" O.C.

WEEP HOLE

FINISH GRADE

1'-6" 1'-2"

3" CLR.

Detail 2-32(f). Stem height 9'0".

1'-2"

1'-6"

1'-6"

5'-0"

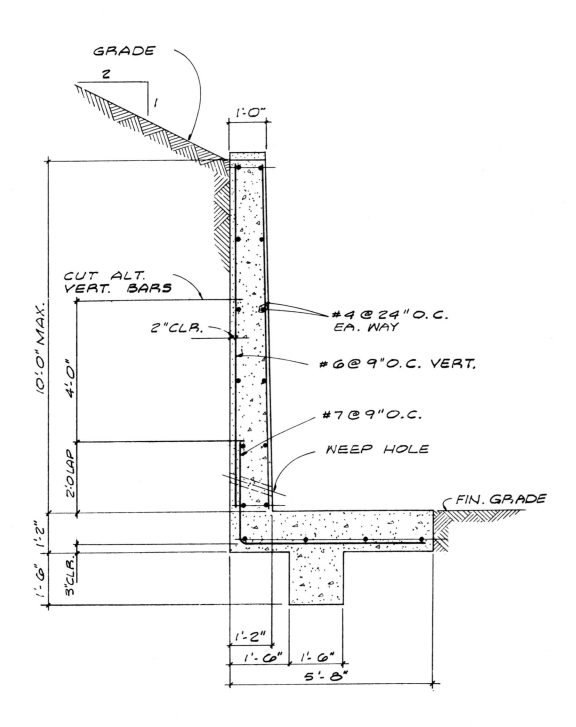

GRADE

2

1

1'-0"

10'-0" MAX.

4'-0"

2'-0" LAP

1'-2"

1'-6"

3" CLR.

CUT ALT.
VERT. BARS

2" CLR.

#4 @ 24" O.C.
EA. WAY

#6 @ 9" O.C. VERT.

#7 @ 9" O.C.

WEEP HOLE

FIN. GRADE

1'-2"

1'-6"

1'-6"

5'-8"

Detail 2-32(g).   Stem height 10'0".

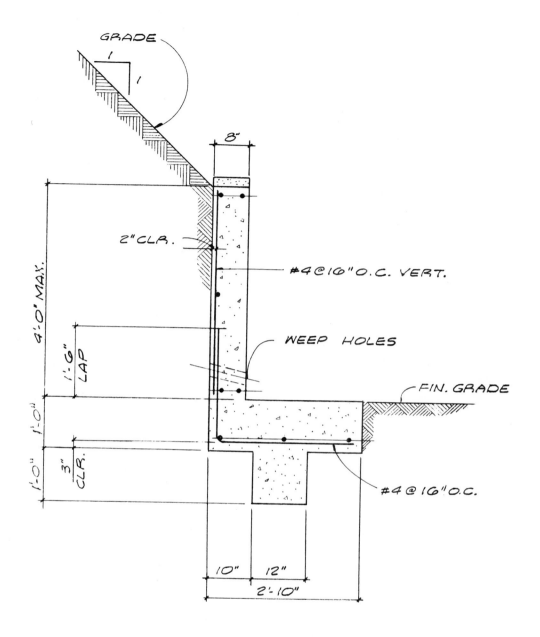

GRADE

8"

2" CLR.

#4 @ 16" O.C. VERT.

4'-0" MAX.

1'-6" LAP

WEEP HOLES

FIN. GRADE

1'-0" 1'-0"

3" CLR.

#4 @ 16" O.C.

10"   12"

2'-10"

Detail 2-33(a).   Stem height 4'0".

Detail 2-33. Sections of concrete retaining walls with soil at the exterior face of the stem. The wall retains a sloping grade with one horizontal to one vertical and no surcharge. The wall dimensions and reinforcing steel size and spacing are determined by calculation. Two #4 horizontal continuous reinforcing bars are placed at the top and the bottom of the wall stem. The minimum horizontal reinforcement in the stem wall and the footing is #4 at 24" o.c. A 3" dia. galvanized iron pipe spaced at 8'0" o.c. is placed at the base of the stem to act as a weep hole. The cement cap at the top of the wall is optional. The walls are designed for 80 lb per cu ft equivalent fluid pressure and a maximum soil pressure of 1500 lb per sq ft. The resultant of forces passes through the middle ⅓ of the wall footing. The walls are designed to resist sliding and overturning. The overturning safety factor is 1.5. The concrete design stress is $f'c = 2000$ psi.

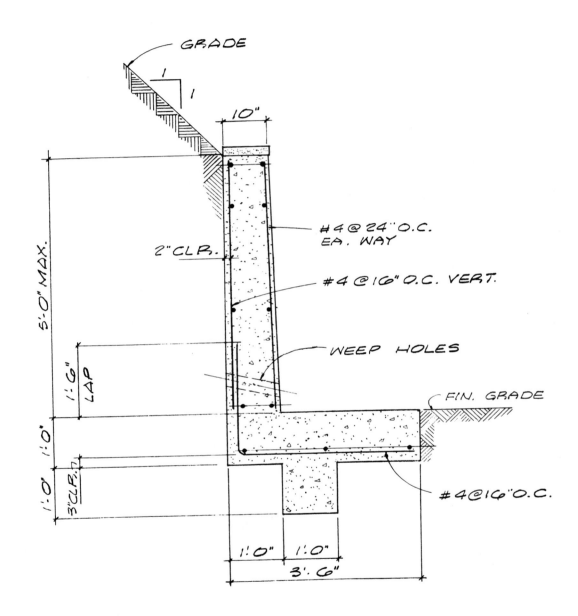

GRADE

10"

#4@24"O.C.
EA. WAY

2"CLR.

#4 @ 16" O.C. VERT.

5'-0" MAX.

1'-6" LAP

WEEP HOLES

FIN. GRADE

1'-0"

1'-0"

3"CLR.

#4@16"O.C.

1'-0"   1'-0"

3'-6"

Detail 2-33(b).   Stem height 5'0".

114

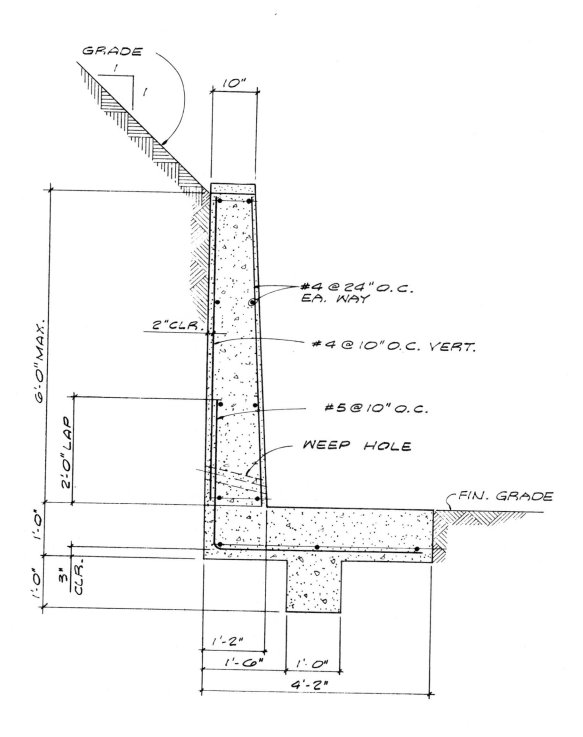

GRADE

10"

#4 @ 24" O.C. EA. WAY

2" CLR.

#4 @ 10" O.C. VERT.

#5 @ 10" O.C.

WEEP HOLE

FIN. GRADE

6'-0" MAX.

2'-0" LAP

1'-0"

1'-0"

3" CLR.

1'-2"

1'-6"

1'-0"

4'-2"

Detail 2-33(c).   Stem height 6'0".

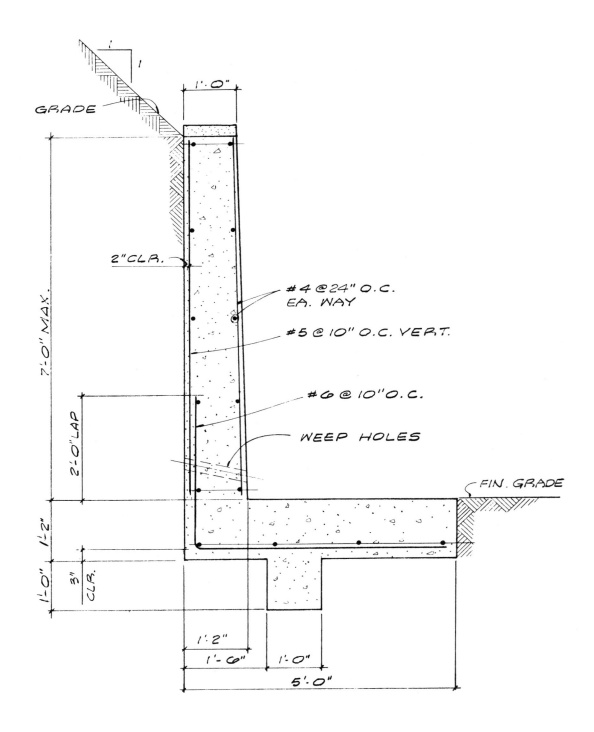

GRADE

1'-0"

2"CLR.

#4 @ 24" O.C.
EA. WAY

#5 @ 10" O.C. VERT.

7'-0" MAX.

#6 @ 10" O.C.

WEEP HOLES

2'-0" LAP

FIN. GRADE

1'-2"

1'-0"

3"
CLR.

1'-2"

1'-6"   1'-0"

5'-0"

Detail 2-33(d). Stem height 7'0".

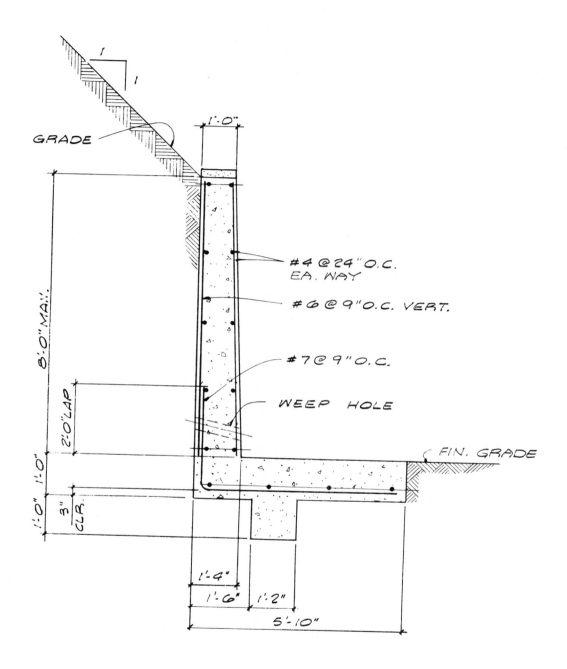

GRADE

1

1

1'-0"

#4 @ 24" O.C.
EA. WAY

#6 @ 9" O.C. VERT.

#7 @ 9" O.C.

WEEP HOLE

FIN. GRADE

8'-0" MAX.

2'-0" LAP

1'-0"

1'-0"

3" CLR.

1'-4"

1'-6"   1'-2"

5'-10"

Detail 2-33(e). Stem height 8'0".

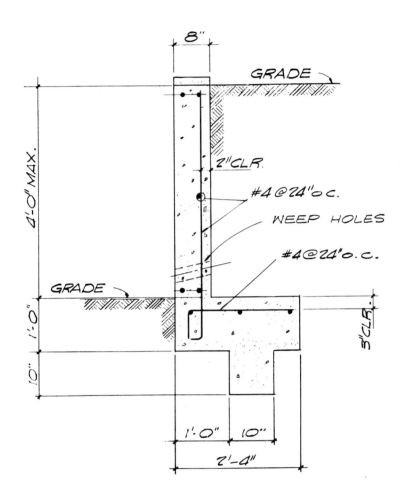

8"

GRADE

4'-0" MAX.

2"CLR.

#4@24"o.c.

WEEP HOLES

#4@24"o.c.

3"CLR.

GRADE

1'-0"

10"

1'-0" | 10"

2'-4"

Detail 2-34(a).   Stem height 4'0".

Detail 2-34. Sections of concrete retaining walls with soil at the interior face of the stem. The walls retain a flat grade with no surcharge. The wall dimensions and reinforcing steel size and spacing are determined by calculation. Two #4 horizontal continuous reinforcing bars are placed at the top and the bottom of the wall stem. The minimum horizontal reinforcement in the stem wall and the footing is #4 at 24" o.c. A 3" dia. galvanized iron pipe spaced at 8'0" o.c. is placed at the base of the stem to act as a weep hole. The cement cap at the top of the wall is optional. The walls are designed for a 30 lb per cu ft equivalent fluid pressure and a maximum soil pressure of 1500 lb per sq ft. The resultant of the forces passes through the middle $\frac{1}{3}$ of the wall footing. The walls are designed to resist sliding and overturning. The overturning safety factor is 1.5. The concrete design stress is $f'c = 2000$ psi.

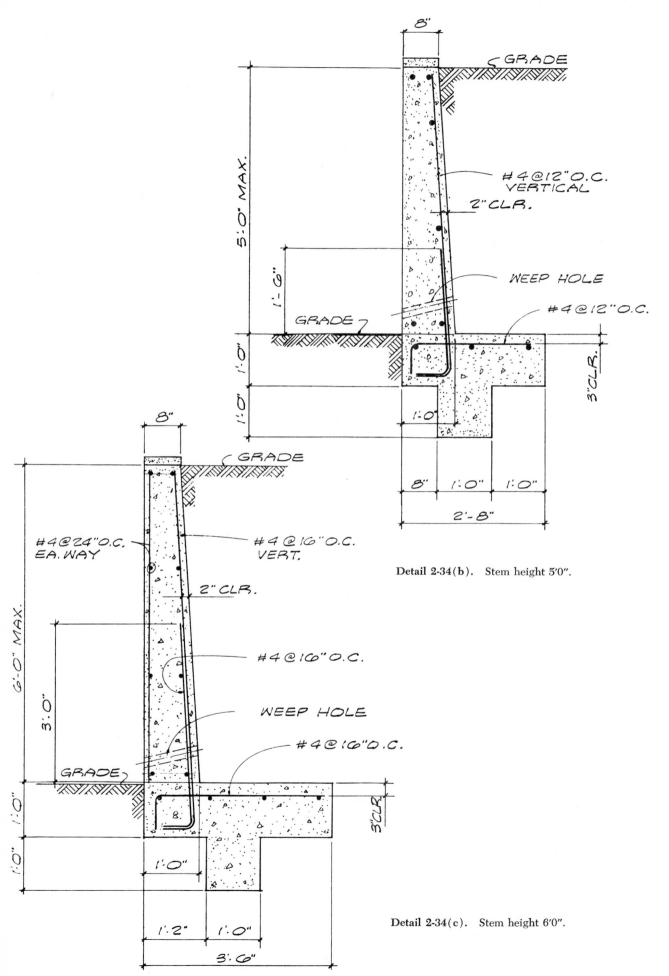

8"

GRADE

#4@12"O.C.
VERTICAL

2" CLR.

WEEP HOLE

#4@12"O.C.

5'-0" MAX.

1'-6"

GRADE

1'-0"

1'-0"

3"CLR.

1'-0"

8"   1'-0"   1'-0"

2'-8"

Detail 2-34(b).   Stem height 5'0".

8"

GRADE

#4@24"O.C.
EA. WAY

#4@16"O.C.
VERT.

2" CLR.

#4@16"O.C.

WEEP HOLE

#4@16"O.C.

6'-0" MAX.

3'-0"

GRADE

1'-0"

1'-0"

3"CLR.

1'-0"

1'-2"   1'-0"

3'-6"

Detail 2-34(c).   Stem height 6'0".

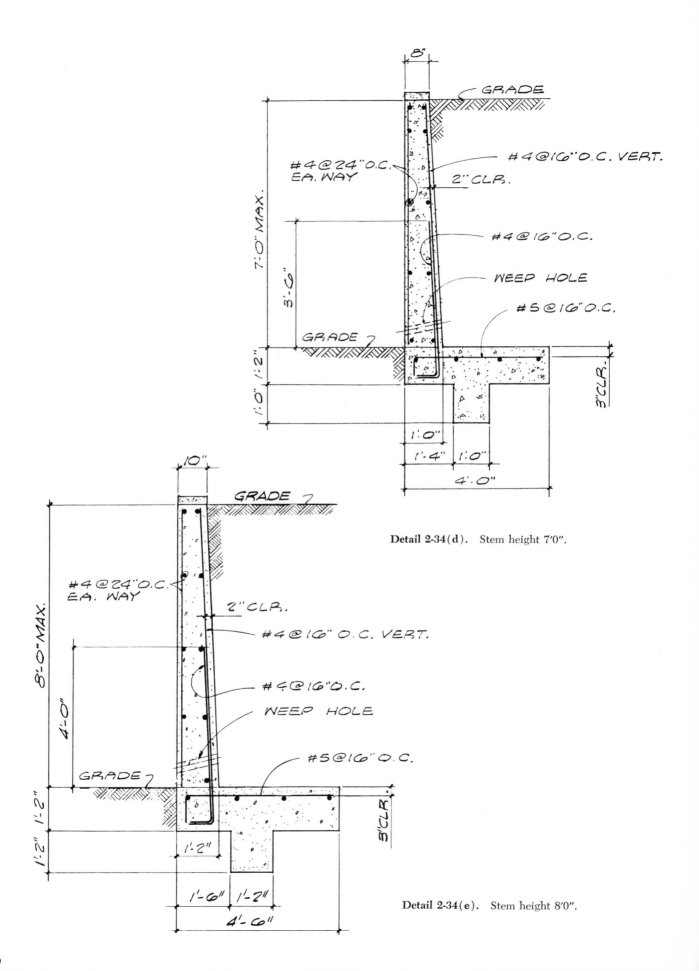

Detail 2-34(d). Stem height 7'0".

Detail 2-34(e). Stem height 8'0".

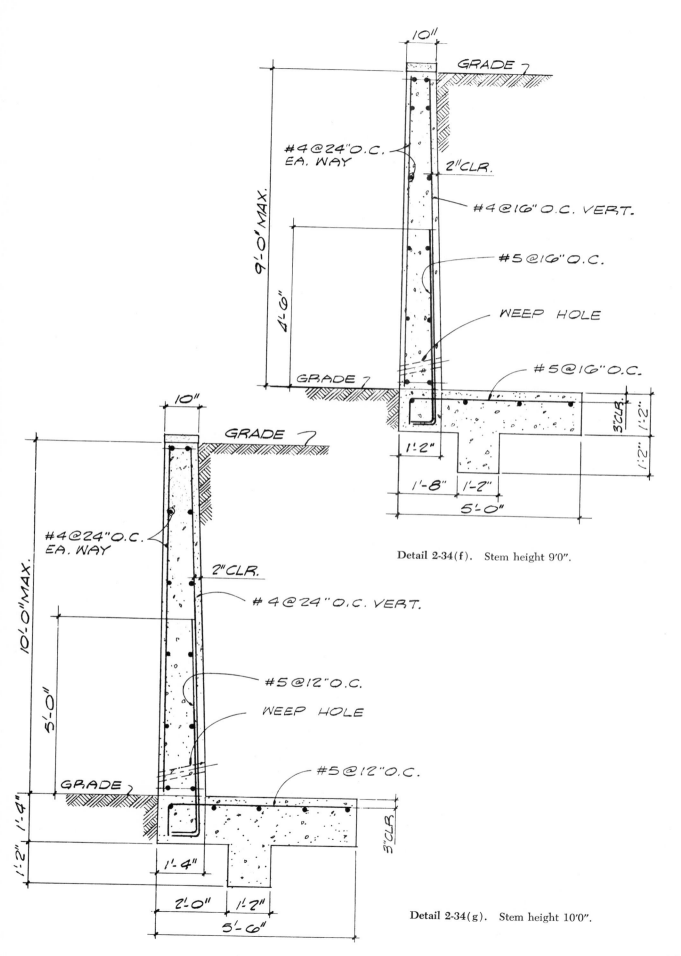

#4 @ 24" O.C. EA. WAY

2" CLR.

#4 @ 16" O.C. VERT.

#5 @ 16" O.C.

WEEP HOLE

#5 @ 16" O.C.

GRADE

GRADE

9'-0" MAX.

4'-6"

10"

10"

3" CLR.

1'-2"

1'-2"

1'-2"

1'-8"

1'-2"

5'-0"

Detail 2-34(f). Stem height 9'0".

#4 @ 24" O.C. EA. WAY

2" CLR.

#4 @ 24" O.C. VERT.

#5 @ 12" O.C.

WEEP HOLE

#5 @ 12" O.C.

GRADE

GRADE

10'-0" MAX.

5'-0"

10"

3" CLR.

1'-4"

1'-2"

1'-4"

2'-0"

1'-2"

5'-6"

Detail 2-34(g). Stem height 10'0".

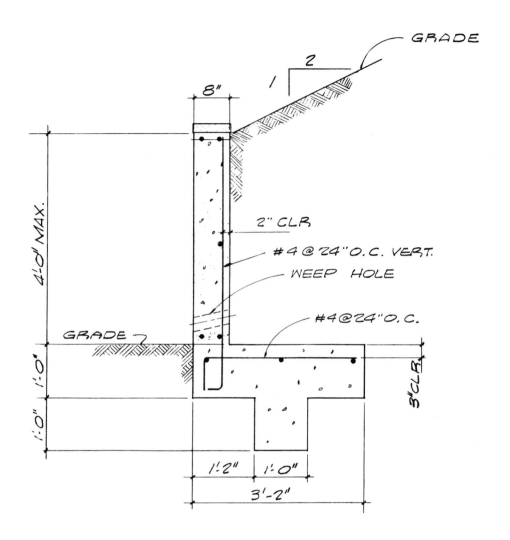

Detail 2-35(a). Stem height 4'0".

Detail 2-35. Sections of concrete retaining walls with soil at the interior face of the stem. The wall retains a sloping grade of two horizontal to one vertical and no surcharge. The wall dimensions and reinforcing steel size and spacing are determined by calculation. Two #4 horizontal continuous reinforcing bars are placed at the top and the bottom of the stem. The minimum horizontal reinforcement in the stem wall and the footing is #4 at 24" o.c. A 3" dia. galvanized iron pipe spaced at 8'0" o.c. is placed at the base of the stem to act as a weep hole. The cement cap at the top of the wall is optional. The walls are designed for 43 lb per cu ft equivalent fluid pressure and a maximum soil pressure of 1500 lb per sq ft. The resultant of the forces passes through the middle ⅓ of the wall footing. The walls are designed to resist sliding and overturning. The overturning safety factor is 1.5. The concrete design stress is $f'c = 2000$ psi.

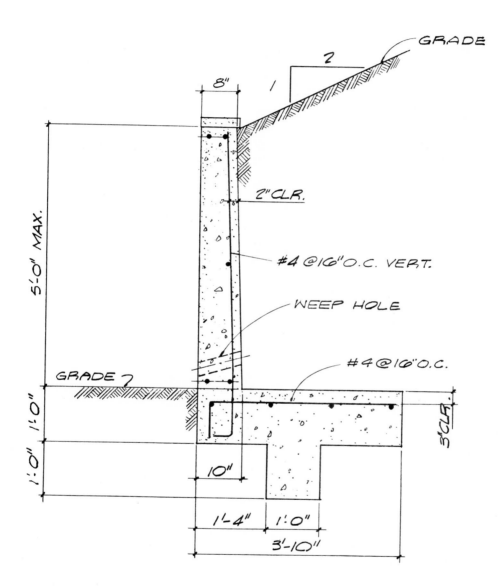

GRADE

8"

2" CLR.

#4 @ 16" O.C. VERT.

WEEP HOLE

#4 @ 16" O.C.

3" CLR.

5'-0" MAX.

GRADE

1'-0"

1'-0"

10"

1'-4"

1'-0"

3'-10"

Detail 2-35(b).   Stem height 5' 0".

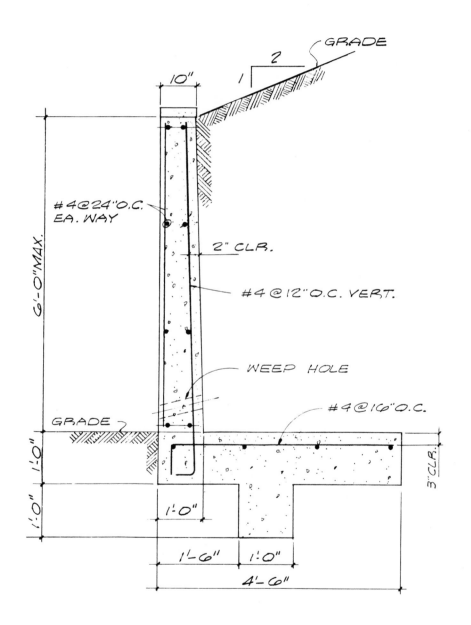

Detail 2-35(c).   Stem height 6'0".

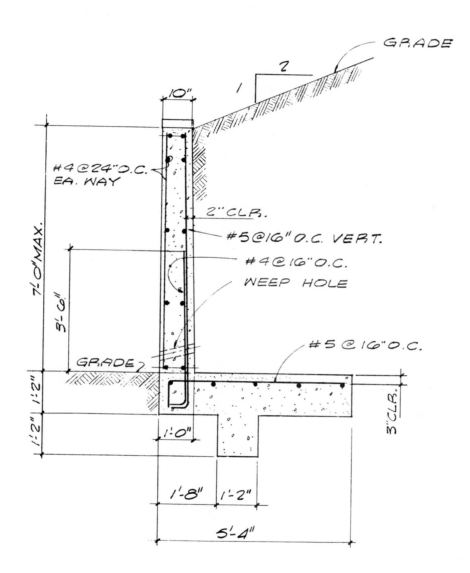

GRADE

2

1

10"

#4 @ 24" O.C.
EA. WAY

2" CLR.

#5 @ 16" O.C. VERT.

#4 @ 16" O.C.

WEEP HOLE

#5 @ 16" O.C.

7'-0" MAX.

5'-6"

GRADE

1'-2" | 1'-2"

1'-2"

3" CLR.

1'-0"

1'-8" | 1'-2"

5'-4"

Detail 2-35(d).   Stem height 7'0".

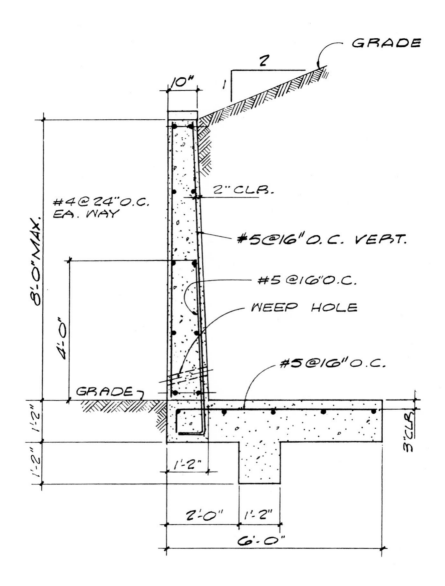

GRADE

10"

2
1

#4@24"O.C.
EA. WAY

8'-0" MAX.

4'-0"

2" CLR.

#5@16" O.C. VERT.

#5 @16"O.C.

WEEP HOLE

#5 @16" O.C.

GRADE

1'-2"

1'-2"

3"CLR.

1'-2"

2'-0"

1'-2"

6'-0"

Detail 2-35(e). Stem height 8'0".

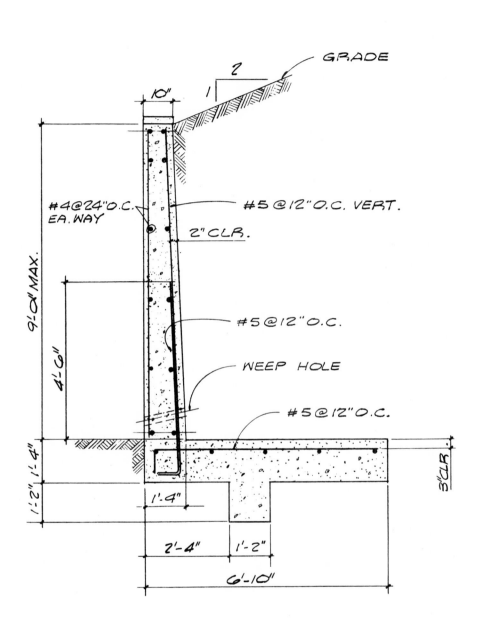

GRADE

10"

#4@24"O.C. EA.WAY

#5@12"O.C. VERT.

2"CLR.

9'-0" MAX.

4'-6"

#5@12"O.C.

WEEP HOLE

#5@12"O.C.

3"CLR.

1'-4"

1'-4"

1'-2"

2'-4"

1'-2"

2'-4"

1'-2"

6'-10"

Detail 2-35(f). Stem height 9'0".

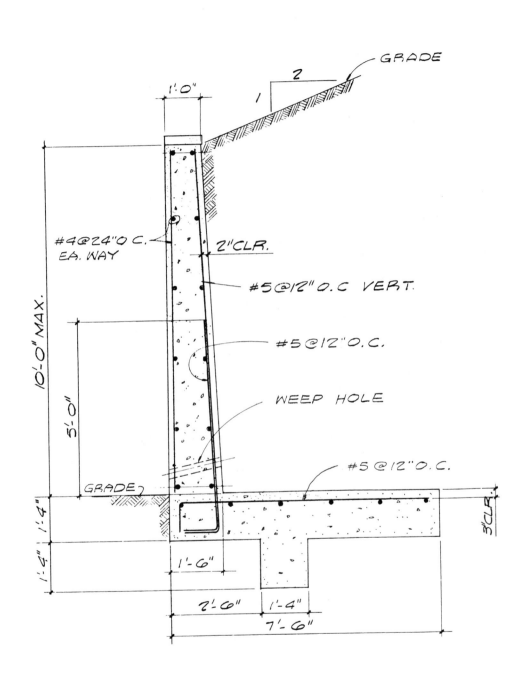

GRADE

1'-0"

2

1

#4@24"0 C.
EA. WAY

2"CLR.

#5@12"0.C VERT.

#5@12"0.C.

WEEP HOLE

#5@12"O.C.

10'-0" MAX.

5'-0"

GRADE

1'-4"

1'-4"

3"CLR.

1'-6"

2'-6"

1'-4"

7'-6"

Detail 2-35(g).   Stem height 10'0"

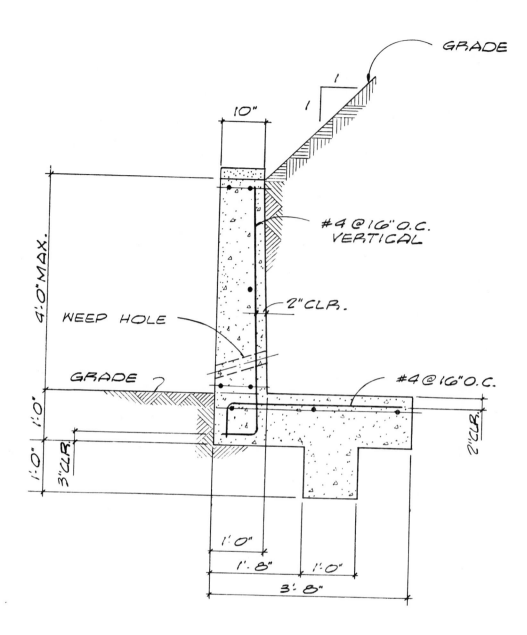

GRADE

10"

#4 @ 16" O.C.
VERTICAL

4'0" MAX.

WEEP HOLE

2" CLR.

GRADE

#4 @ 16" O.C.

2" CLR.

1'0" 1'0"

3" CLR.

1'0"

1'.8"   1'0"

3'.8"

Detail 2-36(a).   Stem height 4'0".

Detail 2-36.   Sections of concrete retaining walls with soil at the interior
face of the stem. The wall retains a sloping grade of one horizontal to one
vertical and no surcharge. The wall dimensions and reinforcing steel size
and spacing are determined by calculation. Two #4 horizontal continuous
reinforcing bars are placed at the top and the bottom of the wall stem.
The minimum horizontal reinforcement in the stem wall and footing is
#4 at 24" o.c. A 3" dia. galvanized iron pipe spaced at 8'0" o.c. is
placed at the base of the stem to act as a weep hole. The cement cap
at the top of the wall is optional. The walls are designed for 80 lb per
cu ft equivalent fluid pressure and a maximum soil pressure of 1500 lb
per sq ft. The resultant of the forces passes through the middle $\frac{1}{3}$ of the
wall footing. The walls are designed to resist sliding and overturning. The
overturning safety factor is 1.5. The concrete design stress is $f'c = 2000$ psi.

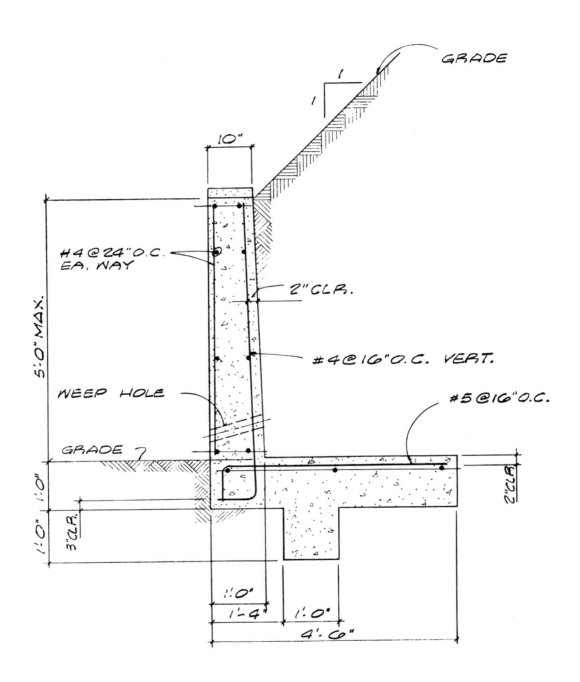

GRADE

10"

#4@24"O.C.
EA. WAY

2"CLR.

#4@16"O.C. VERT.

#5@16"O.C.

5'0" MAX.

WEEP HOLE

GRADE

1'-0"

1'-0"

3"CLR.

2"CLR.

1'-0"

1'-4"

1'-0"

4'-6"

Detail 2-36(b). Stem height 5'0".

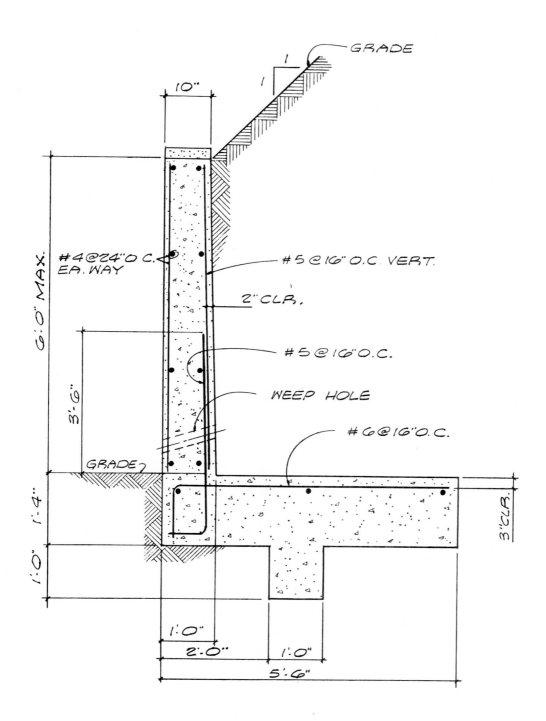

GRADE

10"

#4@24"0.C. EA. WAY

6'-0" MAX.

#5 @ 16" O.C. VERT.

2" CLR.

#5 @ 16" O.C.

3'-6"

WEEP HOLE

#6 @ 16" O.C.

GRADE

1'-4"

3" CLR.

1'-0"

1'-0"

2'-0"

1'-0"

5'-6"

Detail 2-36(c). Stem height 6'0".

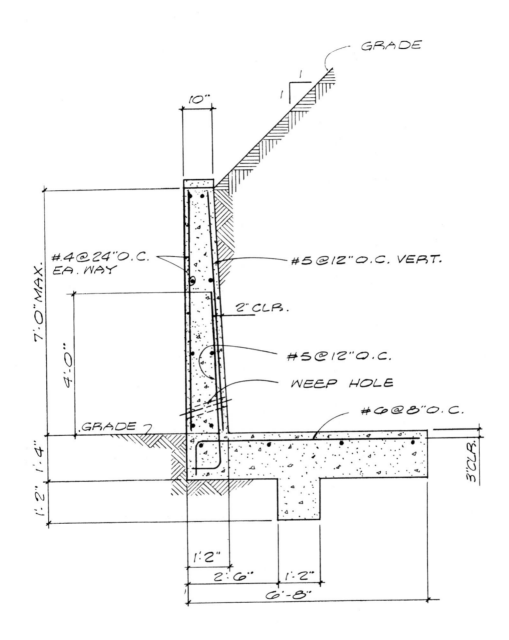

GRADE

10"

#4@24"O.C.
EA. WAY

#5@12"O.C. VERT.

2" CLR.

#5@12"O.C.

WEEP HOLE

#6@8"O.C.

7'-0"MAX.

4'-0"

GRADE

1'-2" 1'-4"

3"CLR.

1'-2"

2'-6"   1'-2"

6'-8"

Detail 2-36(d). Stem height 7'0".

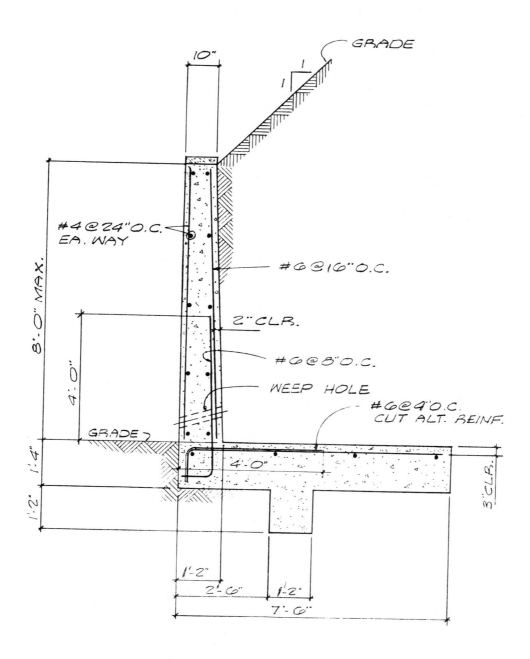

GRADE

10"

#4@24"O.C.
EA. WAY

#6@16"O.C.

2"CLR.

#6@8"O.C.

WEEP HOLE

#6@4'O.C.
CUT ALT. REINF.

8'-0" MAX.

4'-0"

GRADE

1'-4"

1'-2"

GRADE

4'-0"

3"CLR.

1'-2"

2'-6"

1'-2"

7'-6"

Detail 2-36(e).   Stem height 8'0"

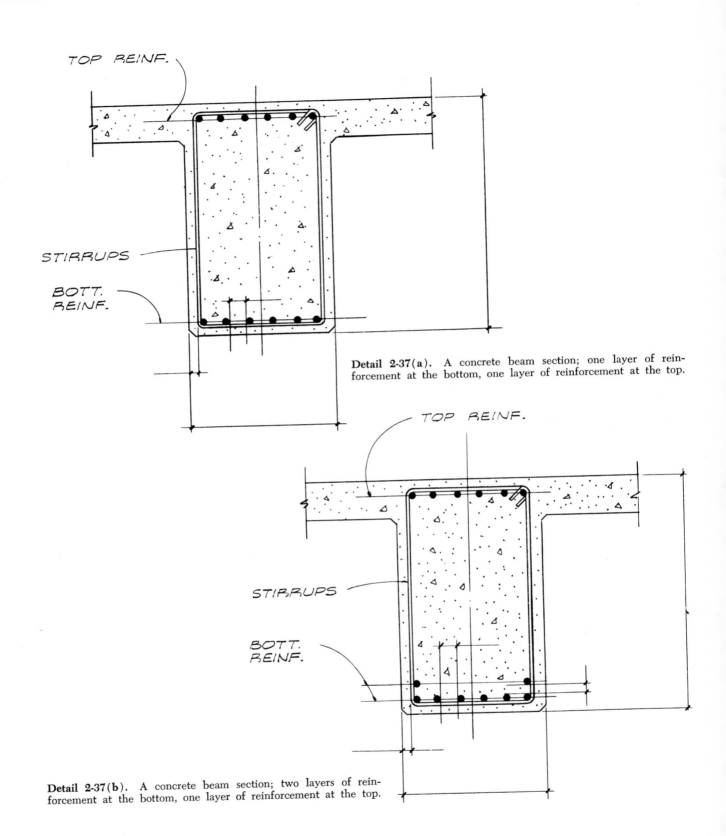

TOP REINF.

STIRRUPS

BOTT. REINF.

Detail 2-37(a). A concrete beam section; one layer of reinforcement at the bottom, one layer of reinforcement at the top.

TOP REINF.

STIRRUPS

BOTT. REINF.

Detail 2-37(b). A concrete beam section; two layers of reinforcement at the bottom, one layer of reinforcement at the top.

Detail 2-37. Sections of concrete beams with various combinations of top and bottom reinforcing steel. The minimum horizontal clear distance between reinforcing bars is the diameter of the bar, or 1⅓ times the maximum size of the coarse aggregate or not less than 1″. The minimum concrete coverage of the reinforcing steel is 1½″. The concrete cover over the reinforcing steel may be increased to obtain a higher fire rating of the beam. The clear vertical distance between layers of reinforcement is the diameter of the bar, or 1⅓ times the size of the coarse aggregate or not less than 1″. The bars of each layer should be placed directly in line with each other.

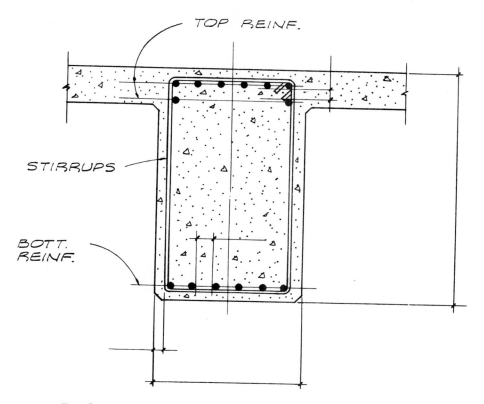

Detail 2-37(c). A concrete beam section; three layers of reinforcement at the bottom, one layer of reinforcement at the top.

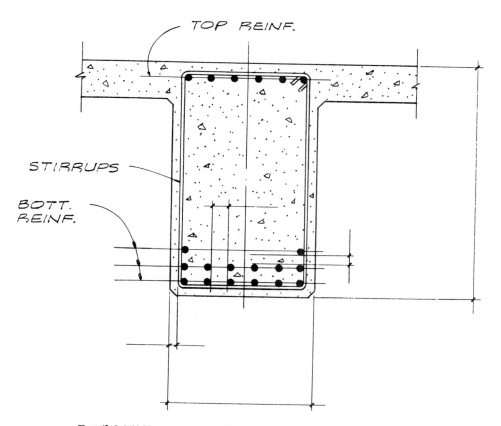

Detail 2-37(d). A concrete beam section; one layer of reinforcement at the bottom, two layers of reinforcement at the top.

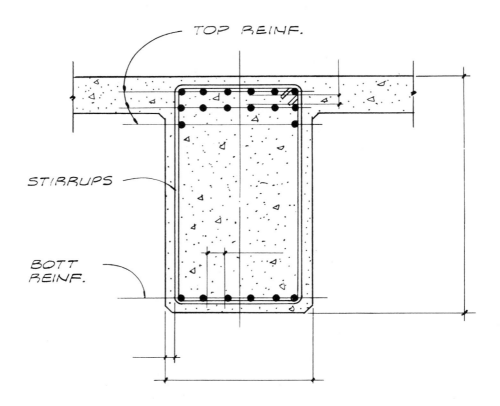

Detail 2-37(e). A concrete beam section; one layer of reinforcement at the bottom, three layers of reinforcement at the top.

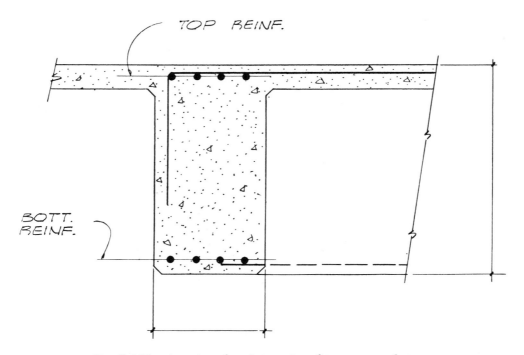

Detail 2-38. A section of an intersection of two concrete beams. The top end reinforcing bars of the intersecting beam are bent down into the supporting beam as shown. The bottom bars of the intersecting beam extend a minimum of 6″ into the supporting beam.

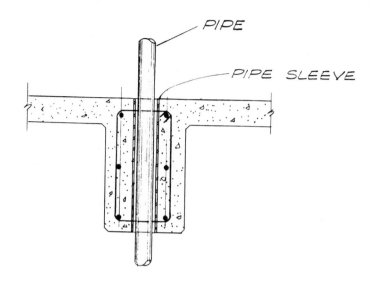

Detail 2-39(a). A section of a pipe passing vertically through a concrete beam. The pipe is sleeved. Extra reinforcing bars are added to the beam to compensate for the concrete cross-sectional area removed by the pipe. The amount of added reinforcing bars and stirrups is determined by calculating the bending and shear in the reduced beam section.

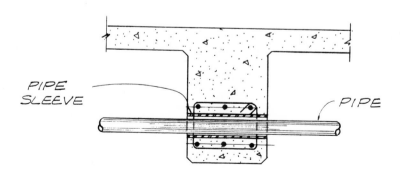

Detail 2-39(b). A section of a pipe passing horizontally through a concrete beam. The pipe is sleeved. Extra reinforcing bars are added to the beam to compensate for the concrete cross-sectional area removed by the pipe. The amount of added reinforcing bars and stirrups is determined by calculating the bending and shear in the reduced beam section.

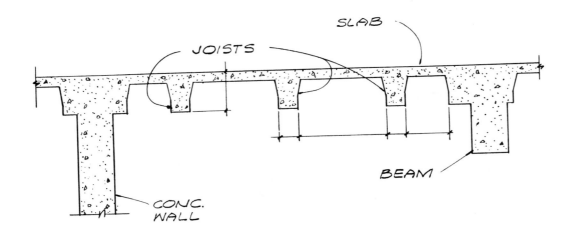

Detail 2-40. A section of a concrete slab and joists formed by inverted metal pans and wood soffits. The depth of the joists is varied by adjusting the height of the wood soffit form. The slab thickness depends on the load and the span between the joists. The ends of the concrete joists can be flared 2″ on each side for a length of 36″ to increase the width in order to reduce the shear stress. The width of the joist depends on the nominal width of the wood soffit form used. The pan form widths vary in increments of 10″, 15″, 20″, and 30″. The slab and joist reinforcement are not shown.

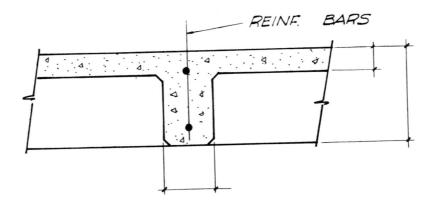

Detail 2-41. A section of a concrete pan joist bridge. The number of rows of bridging is determined by the local building code. The depth and width of the bridge section are equal to the depth and width of the joists.

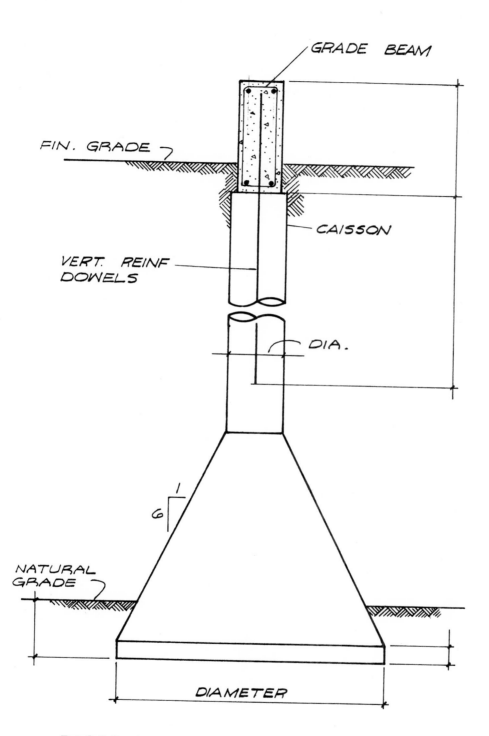

Detail 2-42. An elevation of a concrete caisson supporting a concrete grade beam. The grade beam is connected to the caisson shaft with vertical reinforcing dowels. The caisson shaft diameter depends on the length required to reach acceptable bearing soil below grade. The bell diameter at the base of the caisson is determined by the load on the caisson and the allowable bearing capacity of the soil. The depth of the bell base into the bearing soil is determined by calculation and the local building code. See Details 2-43(a) and (b).

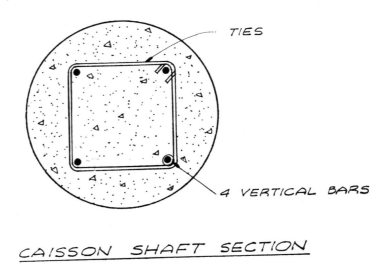

TIES

4 VERTICAL BARS

CAISSON SHAFT SECTION

Detail 2-43(a). A plan section of a caisson shaft. The shaft is reinforced with a minimum of four vertical bars tied together in the same way as required for a rectangular concrete column. See Detail 2-49(a).

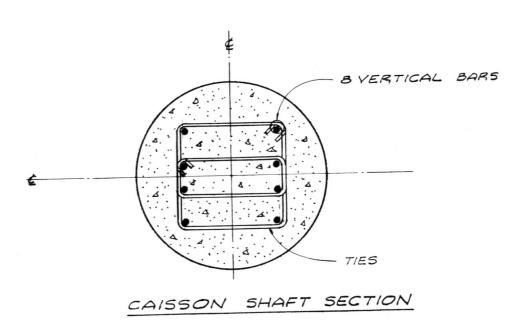

8 VERTICAL BARS

TIES

CAISSON SHAFT SECTION

Detail 2-43(b). A plan section of a caisson shaft. The shaft is reinforced with eight vertical bars tied together in the same way as required for a rectangular concrete column. See Detail 2-49(a). The arrangement of the vertical reinforcement permits the caisson shaft to resist axial and bending loads.

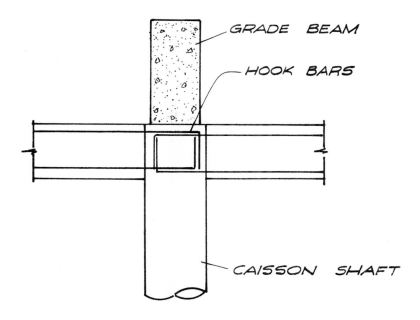

GRADE BEAM

HOOK BARS

CAISSON SHAFT

Detail 2-44(a). An elevation of concrete tie beams connected to the top of a caisson shaft. The tie beams restrain the caisson shaft laterally in each direction. The tie beam reinforcing bars are lapped and bent at the top of the caisson shaft as shown. See Detail 2-44(b).

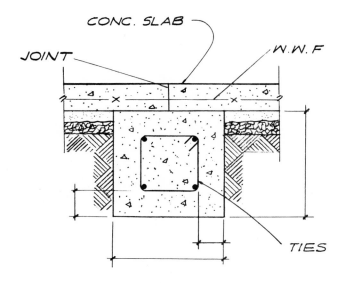

CONC. SLAB

JOINT

W.W.F

TIES

Detail 2-44(b). A section of a concrete tie beam. See Detail 2-44(a). The minimum reinforcement in the tie beam is four #4 bars and #2 ties spaced the same as for a rectangular concrete column. See Detail 2-49(a).

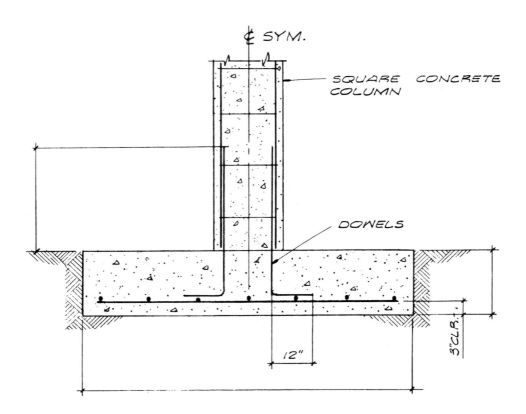

Detail 2-45. A concrete spread footing supporting a rectangular concrete column. The column is connected to the spread footing by reinforcing dowels. The reinforcing dowels lap the column vertical reinforcement 40 bar diameters or not less than 24″. The size and spacing of the footing reinforcement are determined by calculation. The depth and the area of the spread footing depend on the soil conditions.

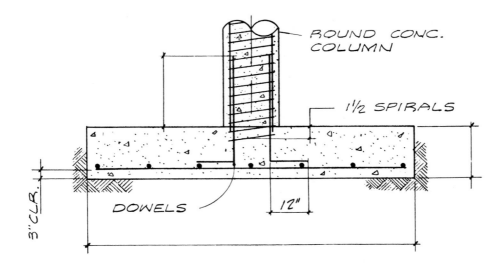

Detail 2-46. A concrete spread footing supporting a round concrete column. The column is connected to the spread footing by reinforcing dowels. The reinforcing dowels lap the column vertical reinforcement 40 bar diameters or not less than 24″. The column spirals extend 1½ turns into the top of the spread footing. The size and spacing of the footing reinforcement are determined by calculation. The depth and the area of the spread footing depend on the soil conditions.

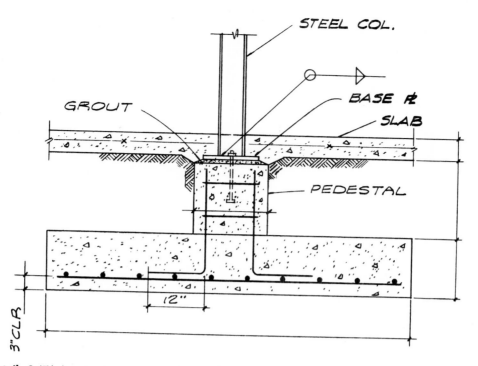

Detail 2-47(a). A concrete spread footing supporting a wide-flange steel column. The column base plate is set on a layer of grout. The column load is transferred to the spread footing by a rectangular concrete pedestal. The height of the pedestal is determined by the depth of the footing into the soil. The pedestal is reinforced with a minimum of four vertical bars tied together in the same way as required for a rectangular concrete column. See Detail 2-49(a). The size and spacing of the footing reinforcement are determined by calculation. The depth and the area of the spread footing depend on the soil conditions.

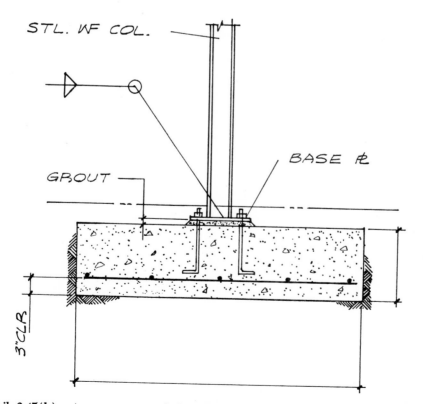

Detail 2-47(b). A concrete spread footing supporting a wide flange steel column. The column base plate is set on a layer of grout. The size and spacing of the footing reinforcement are determined by calculation. The depth and the area of the spread footing depend on the soil conditions.

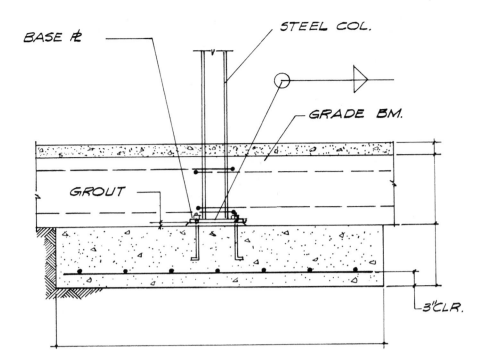

Detail 2-47(c). A concrete spread footing supporting a wide flange steel column through a concrete grade beam. The column base plate is set on a layer of grout. The concrete grade beam is poured around the base of the steel column. The grade beam reinforcing bars are bent 90° around the column as shown. The grade beam permits the column to resist axial loads and bending in the direction of the grade beam. The size and spacing of the footing and grade beam reinforcement are determined by calculation. The depth and the area of the spread footing depend on the soil conditions.

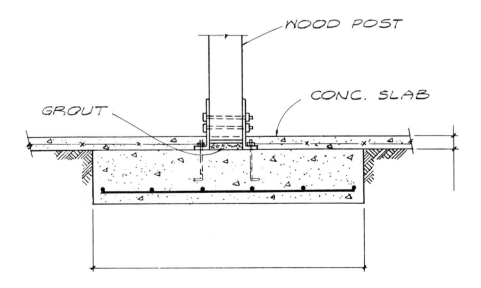

Detail 2-47(d). A concrete spread footing supporting a wood post. See Detail 1-86(a). The size and spacing of the footing reinforcment are determined by calculation. The size and the depth of the spread footing depend on the soil conditions.

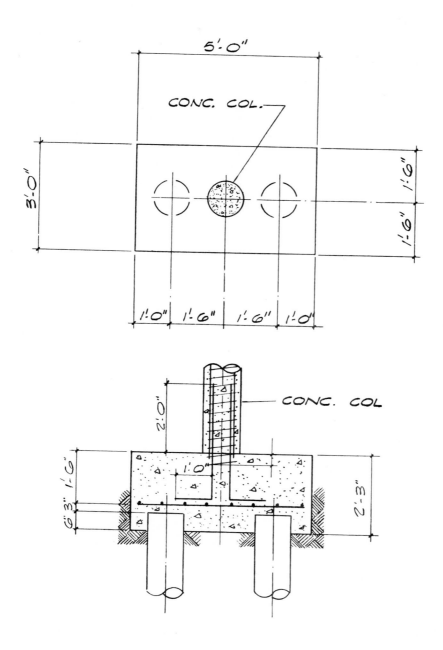

Detail 2-48(a). Two piles.

Detail 2-48. Concrete pile cap plans and sections. The pile cap may be used for concrete, wood, or steel piles. The pile spacing shown on each plan is for a 12″ dia. concrete pile. The spacing between piles depends on the size of the pile. Larger diameter piles require an increased pile spacing. A total friction pile cluster capacity depends on the pile size, the number and spacing of the piles, and the soil conditions. The pile cap may support a steel or a concrete column. The concrete column shown is connected to the pile cap by reinforcing dowels. The reinforcing dowels lap the column vertical reinforcement 40 bar diameters or not less than 24″. The column spirals extend 1½ turns into the top of the pile cap. The size and spacing of the pile cap reinforcement are determined by calculation.

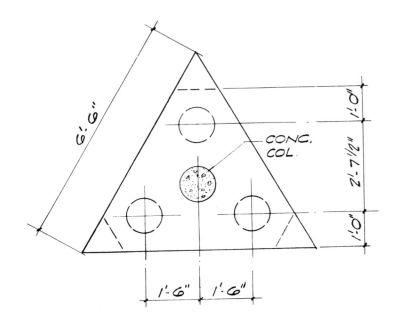

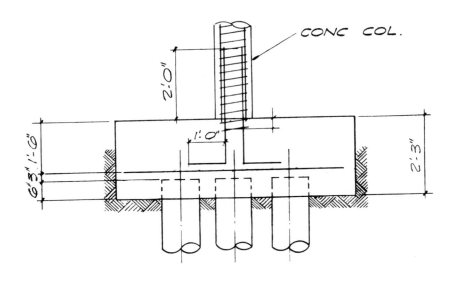

Detail 2-48(b). Three piles.

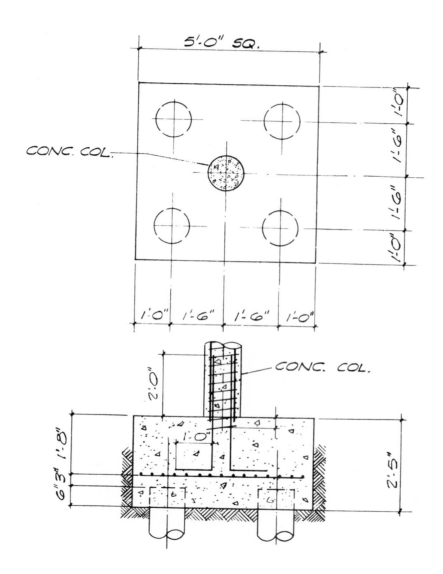

Detail 2-48(c). Four piles.

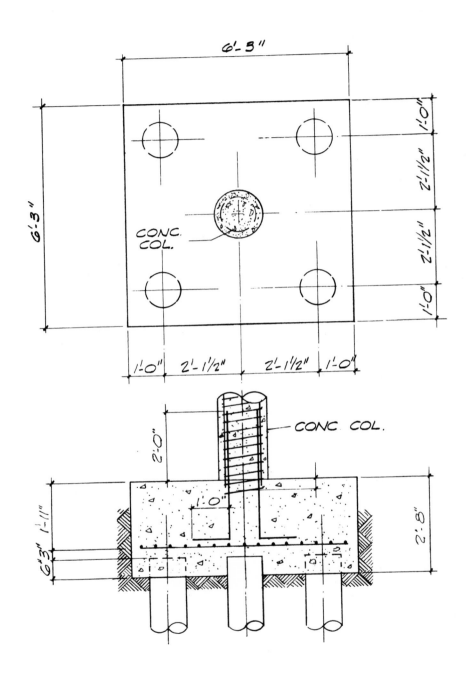

Detail 2-48(d). Five piles.

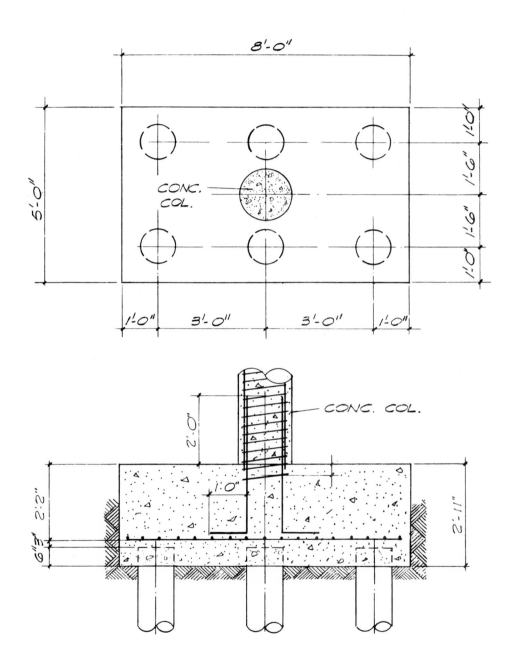

Detail 2-48(e). Six piles.

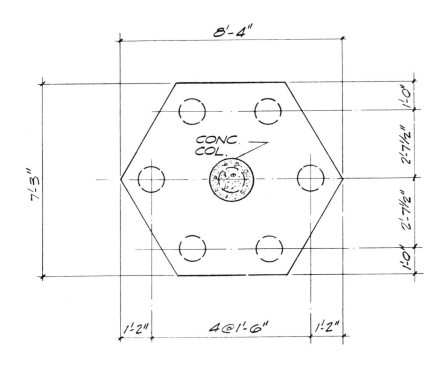

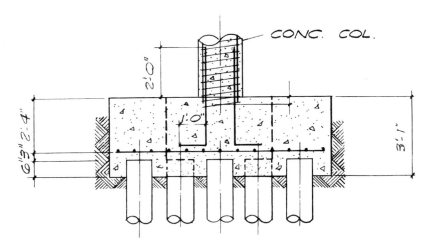

Detail 2-48(f).   Seven piles.

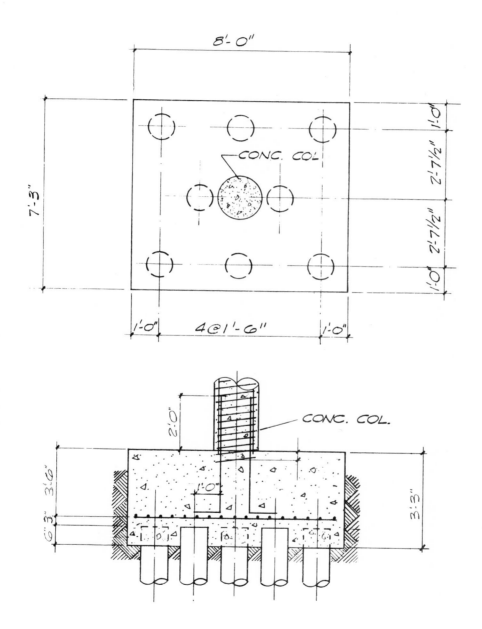

8'-0"

7'-3"

1'-0"

2'-7½"

2'-7½"

1'-0"

1'-0"   4@1'-6"   1'-0"

CONC. COL.

CONC. COL.

2'-0"

3'-6"

6'-3"

1'-0"

3'-3"

Detail 2-48(g).   Eight piles.

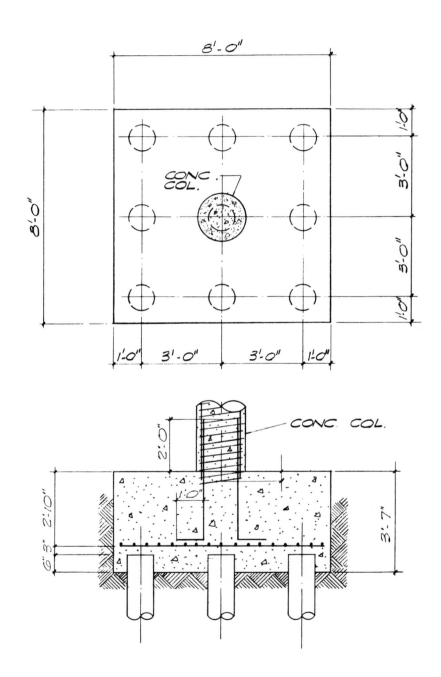

Detail 2-48(h). Nine piles.

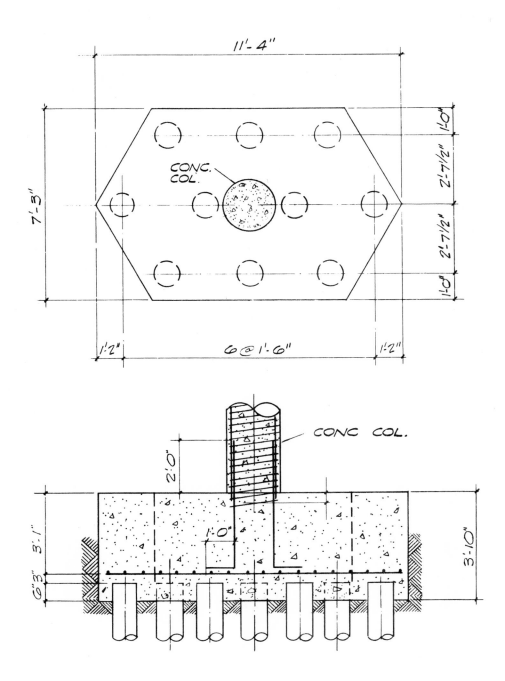

11'-4"

7'-3"

CONC.
COL.

1'-0"
2'-7½"
2'-7½"
1'-0"

1'-2"   6 @ 1'-6"   1'-2"

CONC COL.

2'-0"

3'-1"   6"3"3"   3'-10"

1'-0"

Detail 2-48(i). Ten piles.

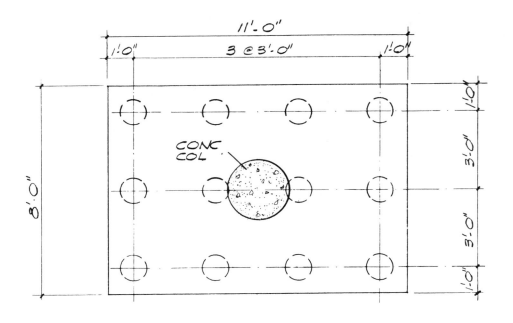

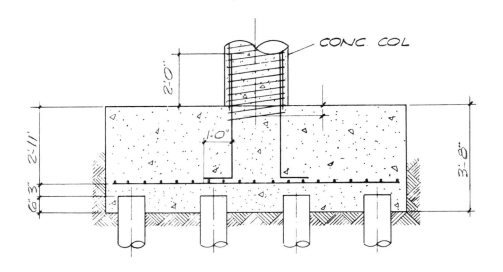

Detail 2-48(j). Twelve piles.

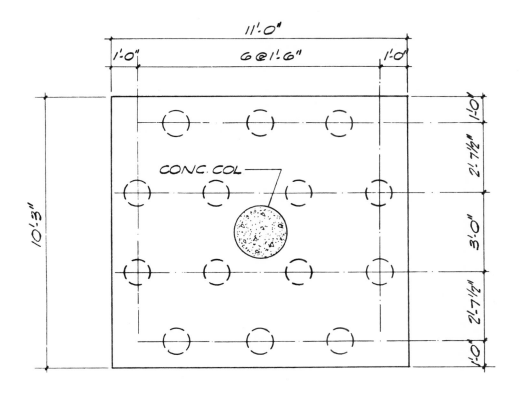

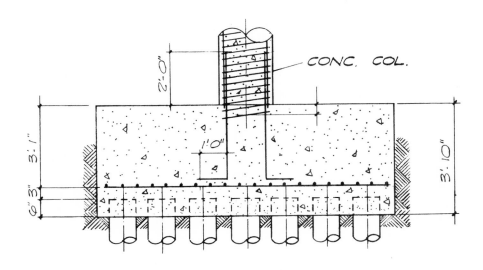

Detail 2-48(k). Fourteen piles.

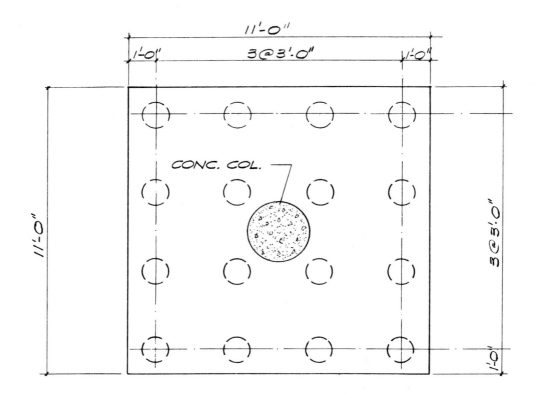

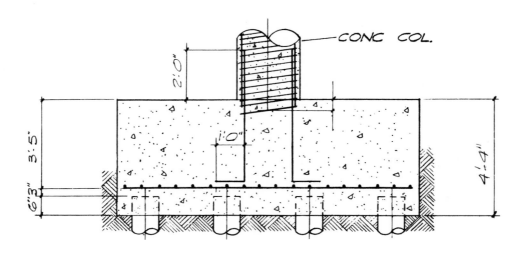

Detail 2-48(1). Sixteen piles.

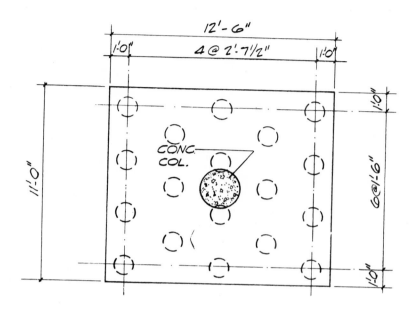

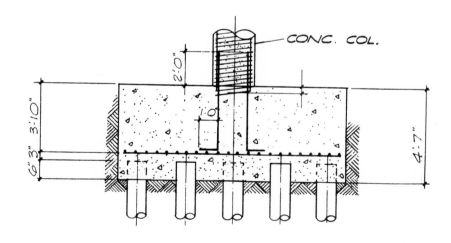

Detail 2-48(m). Eighteen piles.

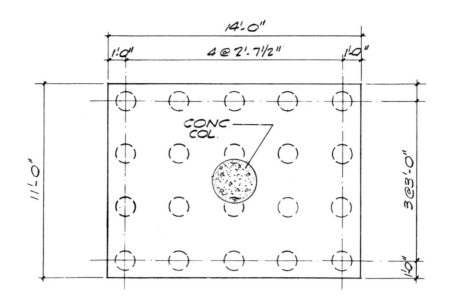

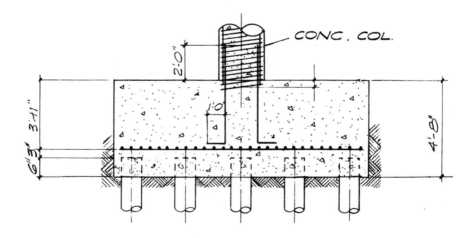

Detail 2-48(n).   Twenty piles.

4 VERT BARS

6 VERT BARS

8 VERT BARS

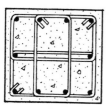

10 VERT BARS

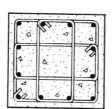

12 VERT BARS

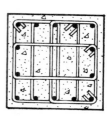

14 VERT BARS

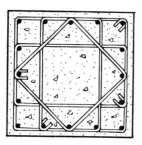

16 VERT BARS

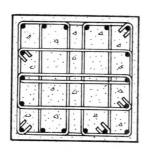

18 VERT BARS

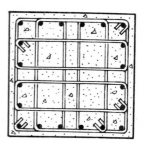

20 VERT BARS

Detail 2-49(a). Plan sections of square or rectangular concrete columns. The number of vertical reinforcing bars are shown for each particular column. The vertical reinforcement in square or rectangular concrete columns is not less than 1% or not more than 4% of the column cross section, or not less than four #4 reinforcing bars. Every vertical reinforcing bar is secured firmly in place and is laterally supported by a 90° bend of a reinforcing tie bar. The minimum tie bar is ¼″ dia. rod. The maximum tie-bar spacing is 48 tie-bar diameters, 16 vertical-bar diameters, or not more than the least dimension of the column. The minimum distance between the vertical reinforcing bars is 2½ times the diameter of the vertical bar, or not less than 1½″ clear. Pairs of reinforcing bars of a lapped splice may be in contact with each other. The minimum clear concrete cover of the reinforcement is 1½″.

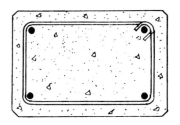

4 VERTICAL BARS

Detail 2-49(a).

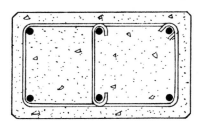

6 VERTICAL BARS

Detail 2-49(a).

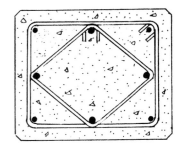

8 VERTICAL BARS

Detail 2-49(a).

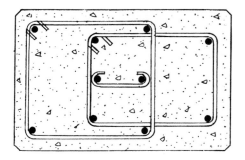

10 VERTICAL BARS

Detail 2-49(a).

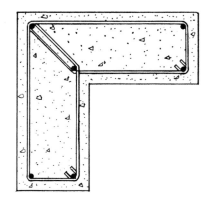

CONC. COL. SECTION

Detail 2-49(b). A plan section of a wall corner used as a concrete column. The reinforcement is placed as shown, and as required in Detail 2-49a. The capacity of the column depends on the cross-sectional area, the amount of vertical reinforcement, and the column slenderness ratio.

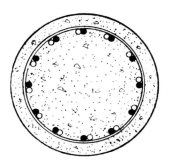 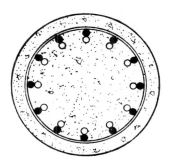

Detail 2-50(a). A plan section of a round concrete column. The minimum column diameter is 12″. The vertical reinforcement in a round concrete column is not less than 1% or not more than 8% of the column cross section, or not less than five #4 reinforcing bars. The vertical reinforcing bars are held in place by the column spiral steel. The spiral reinforcement consists of evenly spaced continuous rod. The minimum spiral size is ¼″ dia. for rolled bars or No. 4 U. S. Steel wire gauge for cold-drawn steel. The spiral spacing or pitch is not more than ⅙ of the column core diameter. The clear spacing between spirals is not more than 3″ or less than 1⅜″ and not less than 1½ times the maximum size of the coarse aggregate. The spirals extend 1½ turns past the top and bottom of the column. The spirals may be spliced by butt welding or by lapping 1½ turns. The spiral reinforcement is held in place by vertical metal spacers. The number of vertical spacers required depends on the spiral core diameter. The minimum distance between the vertical reinforcing bars is 2½ times the diameter of the vertical bar, or not less than 1½″ clear. Pairs of reinforcing bars of a lapped splice may be in contact with each other. The minimum clear concrete cover of the reinforcement is 1½″. The bars shown as open circles represent the reinforcing bars from the column below.

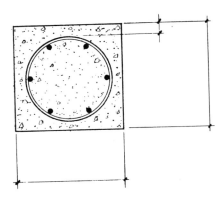

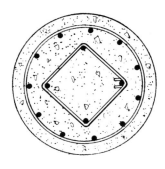

Detail 2-50(b). A square concrete column section with the round concrete column reinforcement arrangement. See Detail 2-50(a) for reinforcement requirements.

Detail 2-50(c). A plan section of a round concrete column with vertical reinforcing bars and spirals in the outer ring, and vertical bars and ties in the core of the column. See Details 2-50(a) and 2-49(a).

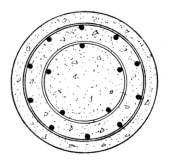

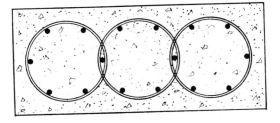

Detail 2-50(d). A plan section of a round concrete column with two cores of vertical reinforcement and spirals. See Detail 2-50(a).

Detail 2-50(e). A plan section of a rectangular concrete column. The reinforcing bars are arranged in three sets of round column reinforcement.

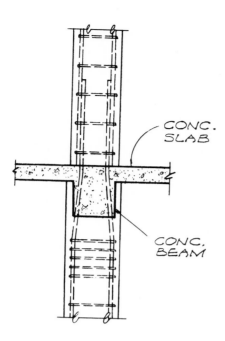

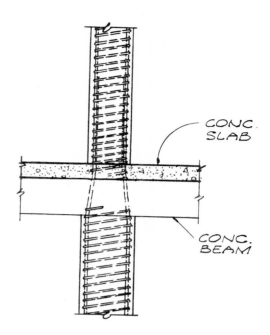

Detail 2-51. An elevation of a lap splice of a square or rectangular concrete column. The vertical bars may be bent at a slope of 1″ horizontally to 6″ vertically starting at the top of the slab. The lapped reinforcing bars may be in contact with each other. The length of the lap is 40 bar diameters or nor less than 24″.

Detail 2-52. An elevation of a lap splice of a round concrete column. The vertical bars may be bent at a slope of 1″ horizontally to 6″ vertically starting at the top of the slab. The lapped reinforcing bars may be in contact with each other. The length of the lap is 40 bar diameters or not less than 24″. The spirals are lapped 1½ turns.

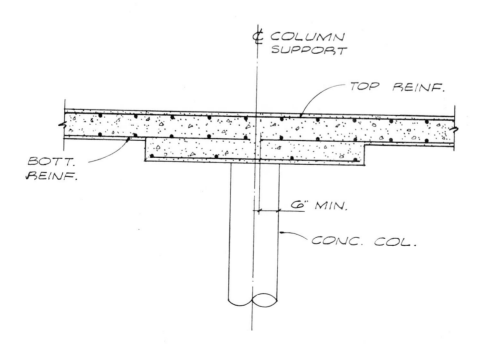

Detail 2-53. A section of a flat slab drop panel at a round concrete column. The slab top reinforcement is continuous across the panel in each direction. The slab bottom reinforcement extends 6″ past the edge of the panel.

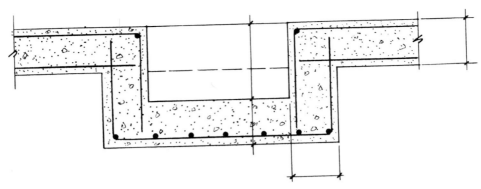

Detail 2-54. A section of a drop in a concrete slab. The size and spacing of the reinforcement are determined by calculation.

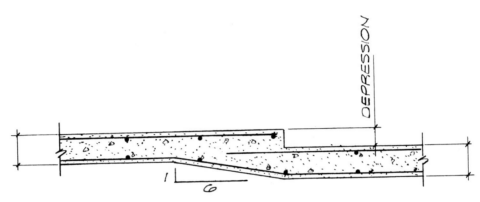

Detail 2-55. A section of a depression in a concrete slab. The reinforcing bars slope one vertical to six horizontal.

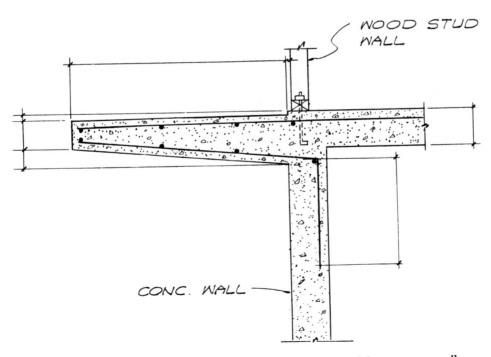

Detail 2-56(a). A section of a cantilevered concrete slab, a concrete wall, and a wood stud wall. The wood stud wall is set back to allow the exterior wall covering material to meet the top of the concrete slab. The exterior cantilevered slab is depressed below the interior floor slab to allow for waterproofing or flashing at the face of the stud wall. The thickness of the cantilevered slab and the size and spacing of reinforcement are determined by calculation.

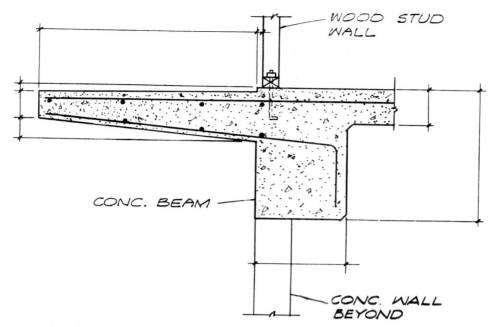

WOOD STUD WALL

CONC. BEAM

CONC. WALL BEYOND

Detail 2-56(b). A section of a cantilevered concrete slab, a concrete beam, and a wood stud wall. The wood stud wall is set back to allow the exterior wall covering material to meet the top of the concrete slab. The exterior cantilevered slab is depressed below the interior floor slab to allow for waterproofing or flashing at the face of the wood stud wall. The thickness of the cantilevered slab and the size and spacing of reinforcement are determined by calculation.

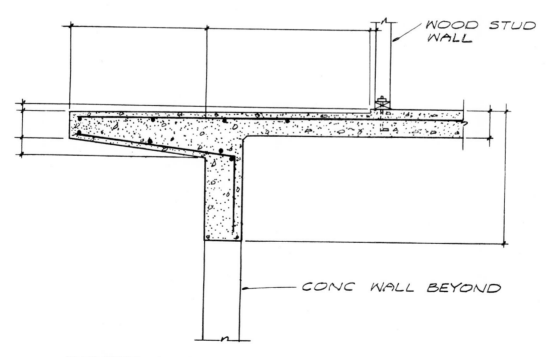

WOOD STUD WALL

CONC WALL BEYOND

Detail 2-56(c). A section of a cantilevered concrete slab, a concrete wall and a wood stud wall. The wood stud wall is supported by the interior concrete slab. The wood stud wall is set back to allow the exterior wall covering material to meet the top of the concrete slab. The exterior cantilevered slab is depressed below the interior floor slab to allow for waterproofing or flashing at the face of the wood stud wall. The thickness of the cantilevered slab and the size and spacing of reinforcement are determined by calculation.

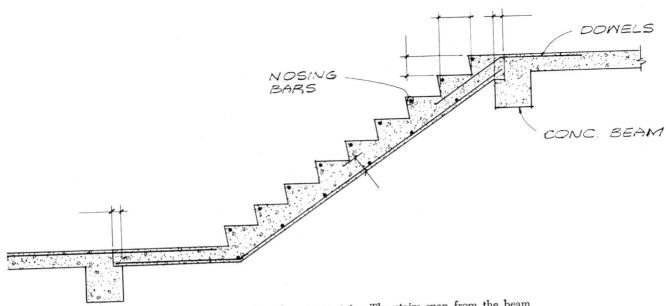

Detail 2-57. A section of concrete stairs. The stairs span from the beam at the top tread to the beam at the lower landing. The thickness of the slab and the size and spacing of the reinforcmeent are determined by calculation.

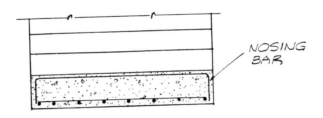

Detail 2-58. A section of concrete steps. The riser nosing bar is bent 90° at each end. See Detail 2-57.

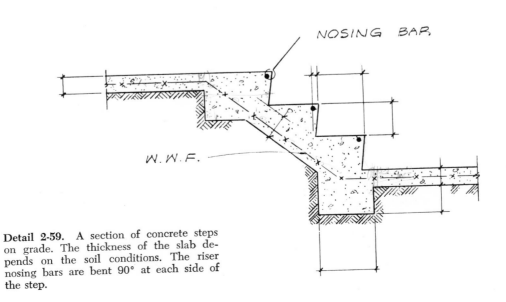

Detail 2-59. A section of concrete steps on grade. The thickness of the slab depends on the soil conditions. The riser nosing bars are bent 90° at each side of the step.

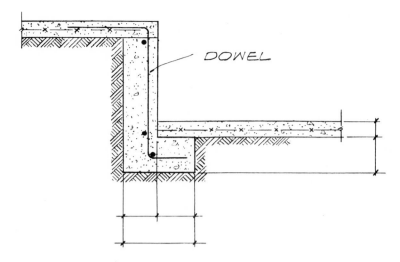

Detail 2-60.   A section of a step of a concrete slab on grade. The thickness of the vertical wall of the step depends on the difference in elevations of the slabs on grade. The top slab is connected to the wall by reinforcing dowels.

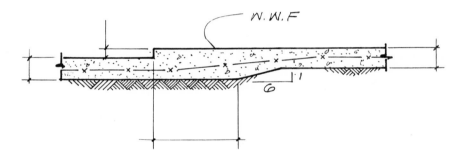

Detail 2-61.   A section of a depressed concrete slab on grade. The slab is thickened at the edge of the depression for a length of 12″.

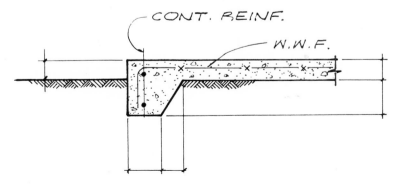

Detail 2-62.   A section of the edge of a concrete slab on grade. The welded wire fabric is bent at the edge of the slab as shown. The reinforcing bars are nominal bars to prevent the slab from cracking.

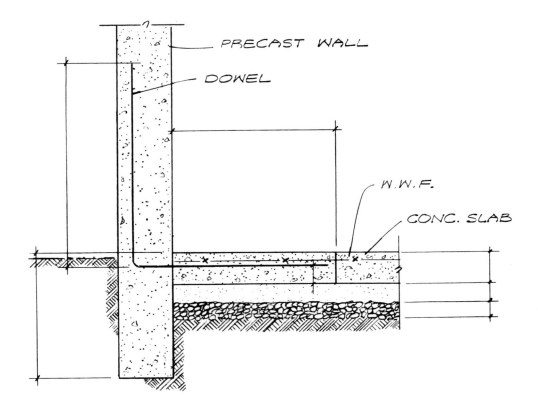

Detail 2-63(a). A section of the bottom of a precast concrete wall connected to a concrete slab on grade. The wall is connected to the slab by reinforcing dowels extending into the concrete slab and lapping with the slab welded wire fabric. The length of the dowel lap is determined by calculation. The perimeter of the slab is poured after the precast wall is erected in place.

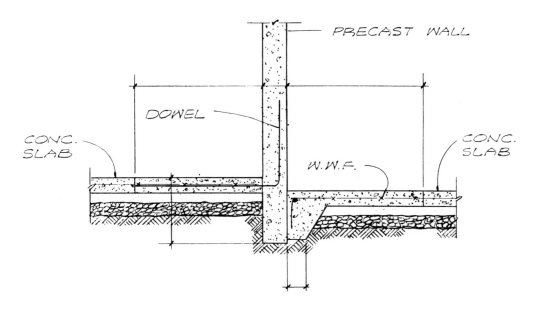

Detail 2-63(b). A section of a precast concrete wall connected to a concrete slab on grade similar to Detail 2-63(a).

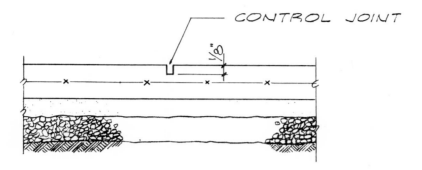

Detail 2-64(a). A section of a control joint in a concrete slab on grade. The depth and width of the joint is ⅛″. The purpose of this joint is to control the cracking of concrete slabs on grade.

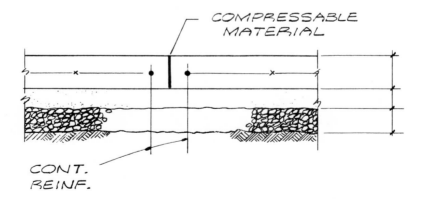

Detail 2-64(b). A section of a construction joint for a concrete slab on grade. The location of construction joints depends on the soil conditions and the use of the concrete slab.

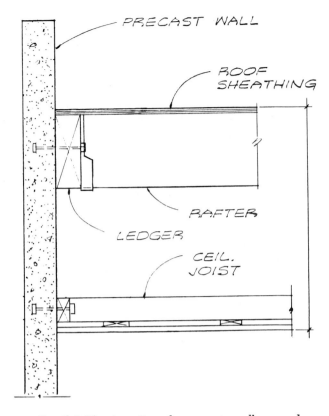

PRECAST WALL

ROOF SHEATHING

RAFTER

LEDGER

CEIL. JOIST

Detail 2-65. A section of a concrete wall, a wood roof and a wood ceiling. The roof rafters are connected to a 4″ wide wood ledger by joist hangers. The ledger is bolted to the concrete wall. The size and spacing of ledger bolts are determined by calculation. The ceiling joists are connected to a 2″ wide ledger bolted to the wall.

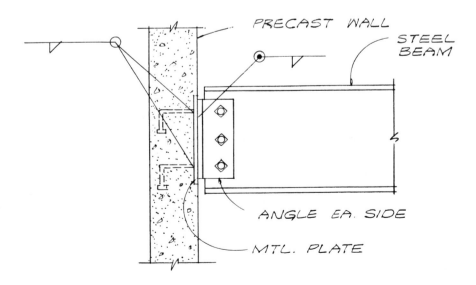

PRECAST WALL

STEEL BEAM

ANGLE EA. SIDE

MTL. PLATE

Detail 2-66. A section of a concrete wall and a steel beam. The clip angles are connected to the beam on each side of the web with bolts. The clip angles are connected to the wall by welding to a flat plate in the concrete wall.

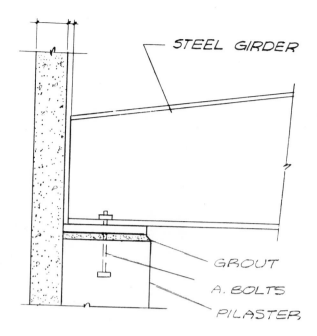

STEEL GIRDER

GROUT

A. BOLTS

PILASTER

Detail 2-67(a). An elevation of a tapered steel girder supported by a concrete pilaster. A space is provided between the end of the girder and the inside face of the concrete wall to allow for expansion and contraction of the girder. The girder is connected to the pilaster by a base plate set on a layer of grout. The anchor bolts pass through the bottom flange of the girder and the base plate. The bolt holes in the bottom flange of the girder are elongated to allow expansion and contraction movement. See Detail 2-67(b).

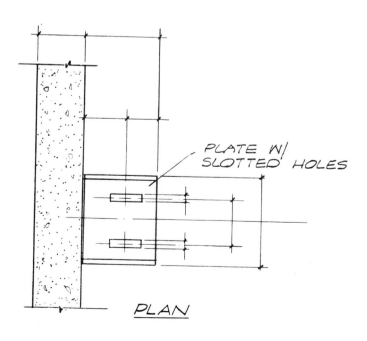

PLATE W/ SLOTTED HOLES

PLAN

Detail 2-67(b). A plan of the base plate used in Detail 2-67(a). The base plate holes are elongated as shown to permit the steel girder to move in expansion and contraction.

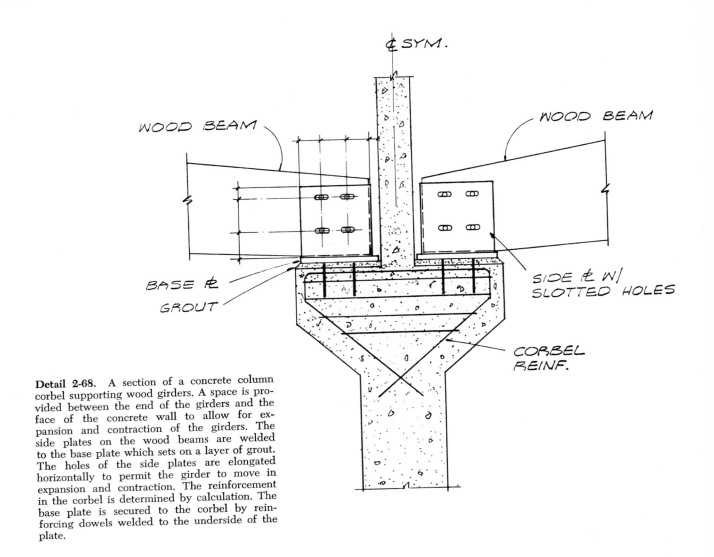

WOOD BEAM

℄ SYM.

WOOD BEAM

BASE ℄

GROUT

SIDE ℄ W/
SLOTTED HOLES

CORBEL
REINF.

Detail 2-68. A section of a concrete column corbel supporting wood girders. A space is provided between the end of the girders and the face of the concrete wall to allow for expansion and contraction of the girders. The side plates on the wood beams are welded to the base plate which sets on a layer of grout. The holes of the side plates are elongated horizontally to permit the girder to move in expansion and contraction. The reinforcement in the corbel is determined by calculation. The base plate is secured to the corbel by reinforcing dowels welded to the underside of the plate.

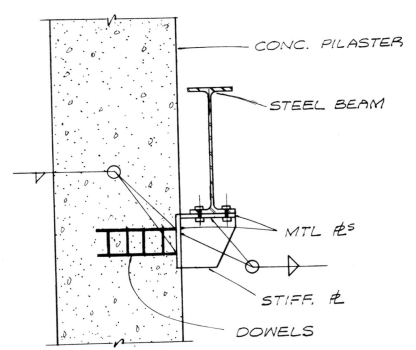

CONC. PILASTER

STEEL BEAM

MTL ℄ˢ

STIFF. ℄

DOWELS

Detail 2-69. A section of a concrete pilaster and a steel beam. The steel beam is supported by a metal bracket. The vertical stiffener of the bracket is welded to a flat plate in the concrete pilaster. The weld plate is connected to the pilaster with reinforcing dowels as shown. The pilaster reinforcement is not shown.

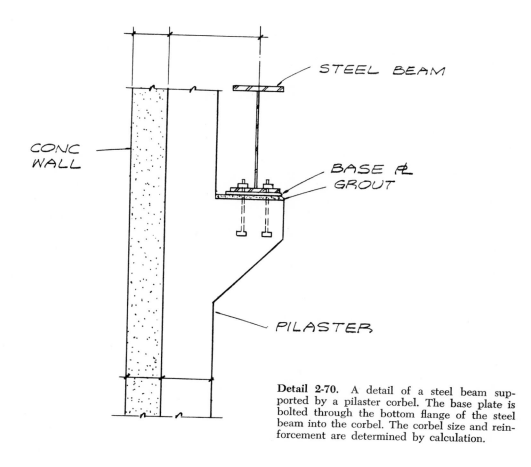

STEEL BEAM

CONC WALL

BASE ℞ GROUT

PILASTER

Detail 2-70. A detail of a steel beam supported by a pilaster corbel. The base plate is bolted through the bottom flange of the steel beam into the corbel. The corbel size and reinforcement are determined by calculation.

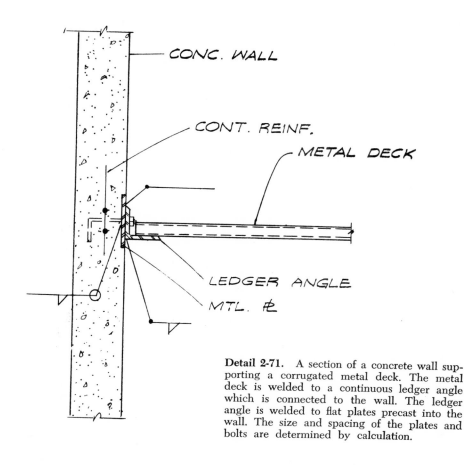

CONC. WALL

CONT. REINF.

METAL DECK

LEDGER ANGLE

MTL. ℞

Detail 2-71. A section of a concrete wall supporting a corrugated metal deck. The metal deck is welded to a continuous ledger angle which is connected to the wall. The ledger angle is welded to flat plates precast into the wall. The size and spacing of the plates and bolts are determined by calculation.

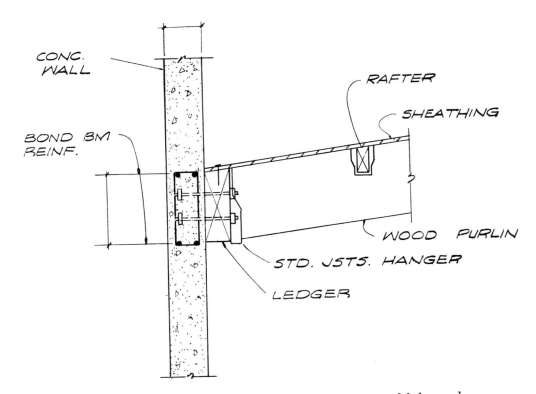

Detail 2-72. A section of a concrete wall supporting a wood ledger and purlin members of a panelized roof system. See Detail 1-9(a). The purlins are connected to the ledger by standard joist hangers. The ledger is connected to the wall by bolts. The size and spacing of the ledger bolts are determined by calculation. The reinforcing bars in the wall act as a bond beam to resist the diaphragm shear stress. See Detail 1-36.

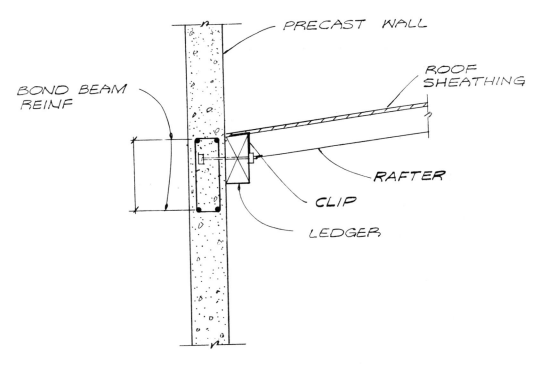

Detail 2-73. A section of a wall supporting the stiffener members of a panelized roof system. See Detail 1–9(a). The 4″ wide ledger is bolted to the precast wall. The size and spacing of the ledger bolts is determined by calculation. The reinforcing bars in the wall act as a bond beam to resist the diaphragm shear stress.

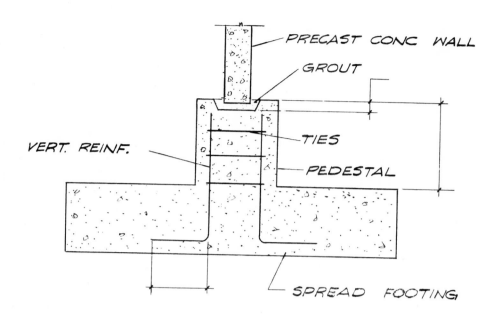

Detail 2-74(a). A section of a concrete spread footing and a precast concrete wall. The groove at the top of the pedestal is formed by a shaped 4″ wide wood member. The depth and width of the groove allow the precast wall to be placed and shimmed with metal plates to a level position. The groove is filled with grout after the precast wall is in place.

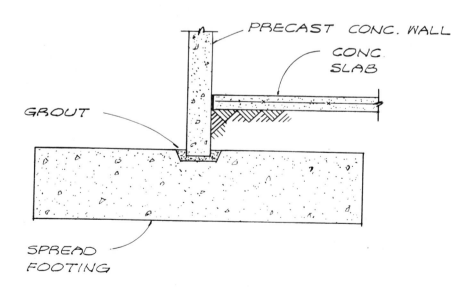

Detail 2-74(b). A section of a concrete spread footing and a precast concrete wall. The groove at the top of the footing is formed by a 4″ wide wood member. The depth and width of the groove allow the precast wall to be placed and shimmed with metal plates to a level position. The groove is filled with grout after the precast wall is in place.

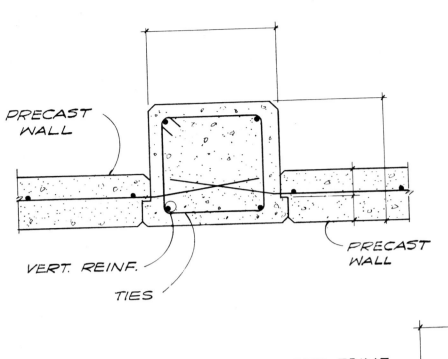

PRECAST WALL

VERT. REINF.

TIES

PRECAST WALL

Detail 2-75(a). A plan section of precast concrete walls connected to a poured concrete column. The walls are connected to the column by extending the wall horizontal reinforcing steel into the poured column 20 bar diameters.

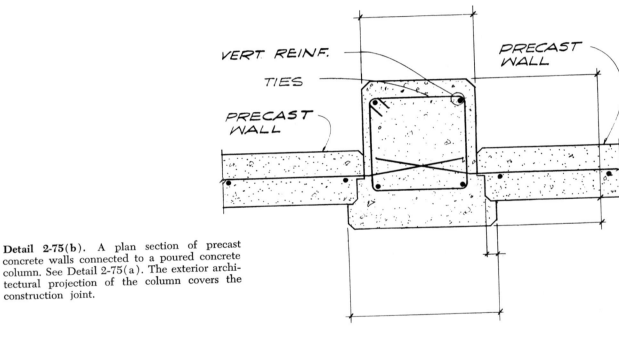

VERT. REINF.

PRECAST WALL

TIES

PRECAST WALL

PRECAST WALL

Detail 2-75(b). A plan section of precast concrete walls connected to a poured concrete column. See Detail 2-75(a). The exterior architectural projection of the column covers the construction joint.

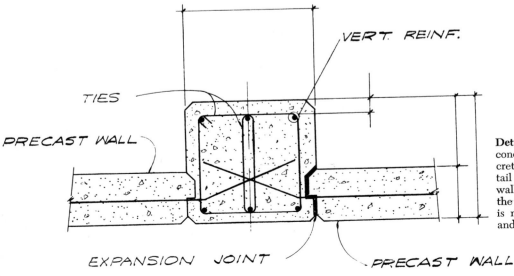

VERT. REINF.

TIES

PRECAST WALL

EXPANSION JOINT

PRECAST WALL

Detail 2-75(c). A plan section of precast concrete walls connected to a poured concrete column. This detail is similar to Detail 2-75(a). A joint between the precast wall and the column is made to permit the wall to expand and contract. The joint is made of a compressable solid material and coated with a waterproofing material.

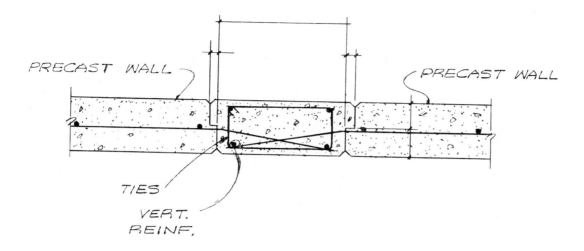

PRECAST WALL

PRECAST WALL

TIES

VERT.
REINF.

Detail 2-76(a). A plan section of precast concrete walls joined by a poured concrete splice connection. The horizontal bars of the precast wall are lapped 20 bar diameters in the poured splice. The poured splice is reinforced with four vertical bars as shown.

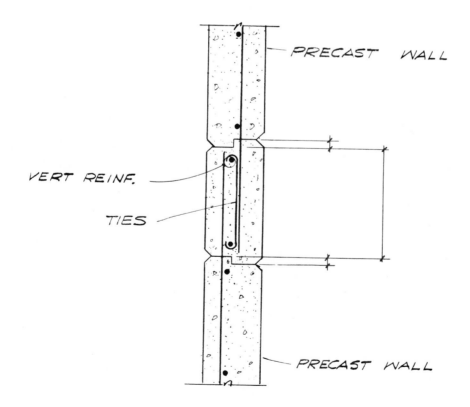

PRECAST WALL

VERT REINF.

TIES

PRECAST WALL

Detail-76(b). A plan section of precast concrete walls joined by a poured concrete splice connection. The horizontal bars of the precast wall are lapped 20 bar diameters in the poured splice. The poured splice is reinforced with two vertical bars as shown.

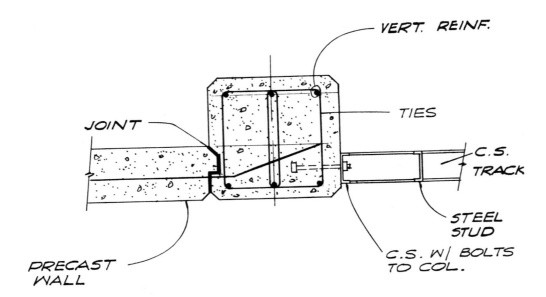

Detail 2-77. A plan section of a precast concrete wall and steel stud wall connected to a poured concrete column. The precast wall is connected to the poured concrete column as shown in Detail 2-75(c). The steel stud wall is connected to the poured column by bolting a channel track stud to the face of the column.

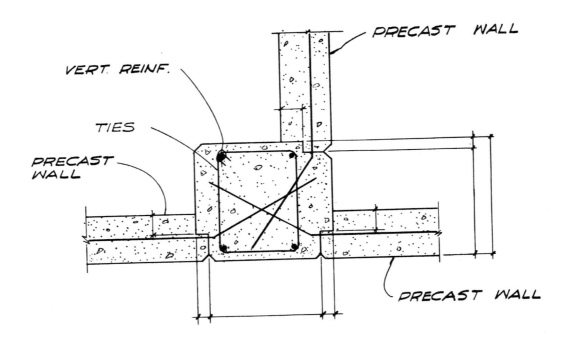

Detail 2-78. A plan section of precast concrete walls at a corner poured concrete column. The horizontal reinforcing bars of the walls are bent and lapped in the poured concrete column as shown.

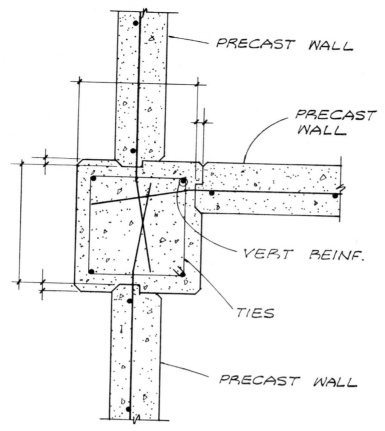

PRECAST WALL

PRECAST WALL

VERT. REINF.

TIES

PRECAST WALL

Detail 2-79. A plan section of precast concrete walls and a poured corner splice joint. The horizontal reinforcing bars of the precast walls are extended 20 bar diameters into the poured corner splice.

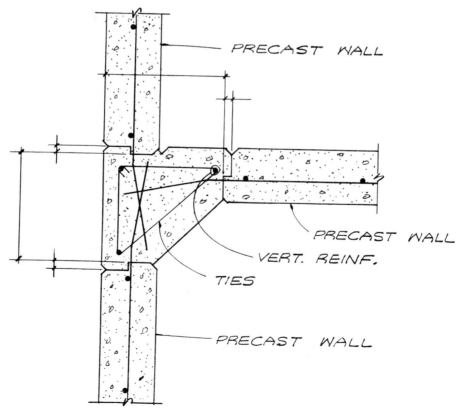

PRECAST WALL

PRECAST WALL

VERT. REINF.

TIES

PRECAST WALL

Detail 2-80. A plan section of three precast concrete walls intersecting at a poured concrete column. The horizontal reinforcing bars of the wall extend 20 bar diameters into the poured column.

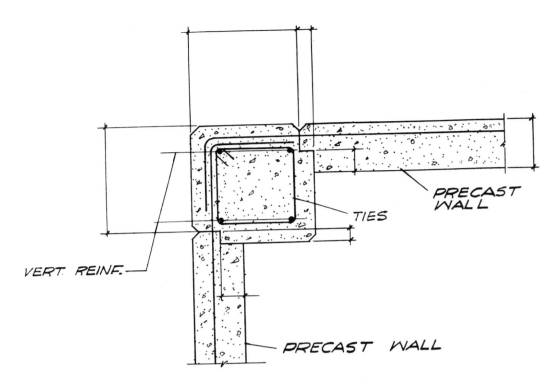

Detail 2-81. A plan section of three precast concrete walls intersecting at a poured concrete column. See Detail 2-80.

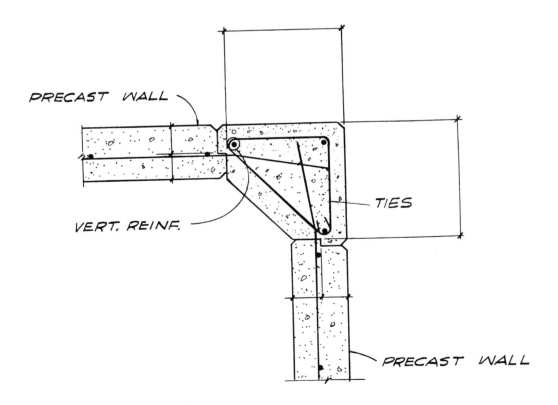

Detail 2-82. A plan section of three precast concrete walls intersecting at a poured concrete splice. See Detail 2-80.

3

MASONRY

The details in this chapter are divided into three different general categories. The first part of the chapter consists of drawings of hollow-unit masonry or concrete block construction. These details are arranged in the following sequence: wall intersections, columns and pilasters, wall opening lintels and jambs, wall sections with wood floors and roofs, and wall sections and concrete slabs. The second part of this chapter consists of drawings of brick details arranged in the following sequence: columns and pilasters, beam and lintel sections, typical masonry wall sections and reinforcing steel placement, wall sections and wood floors and roofs, wall sections and concrete slabs, and wall sections and steel-beam connections. The third section of this chapter is a series of drawings of concrete block retaining walls which are designed to support various grades and slopes.

Hollow masonry units are generally known as concrete blocks. The material used for the manufacture of this type of masonry unit consists of sand, cement, and natural crushed rock. Lightweight hollow masonry units use aggregates composed of coal cinders, slag, shale, or volcanic ash, depending on the materials available from natural sources where the units are manufactured. The sizes and shapes of the many standard manufactured hollow masonry units are shown in the drawings at the beginning of the detail drawings

of this chapter. These sizes and shapes are in accordance with the requirements of the Concrete Masonry Association of California.

Table 3–1 gives the A.S.T.M. designation numbers for the various types of concrete blocks.

Concrete hollow unit masonry is used to construct vertical structural members such as walls, beams, pilasters, columns, and foundation walls. The blocks are stacked vertically and joined to the adjacent block's horizontal and vertical surfaces by a mortar joint. Since the actual dimensions of the units are ⅜″ less than the nominal dimensions, the mortar joints are made so that the finished construction will equal an even inch. Except for ¾ length units, the nominal dimensions of the lengths of concrete hollow masonry units are in multiples of 8″. It is recommended that the design of concrete block construction be performed to utilize the vertical and horizontal nominal modular dimensions of the units. The width of concrete hollow unit masonry members

Table 3–1.
A.S.T.M. Specifications for Concrete Block Masonry

Masonry unit	Grade of concrete	A.S.T.M. Spec. No.
Hollow load bearing	A	C 90
Solid load bearing	A	C 145
Hollow non-bearing		C 129
Concrete building brick	A	C 53

is determined by the actual size of the block; however, it is designated by its nominal dimension. It is common practice to designate hollow masonry units in terms of the nominal dimensions in the sequence of width, height, and length.

Hollow unit masonry walls are constructed by lapping the units in the successive vertical courses by ½ the unit length to provide a vertical unobstructed core within the wall. This arrangement of the blocks, known as common bond, is the method most often used in the construction of masonry walls. A stack bond arrangement is constructed when the blocks of each successive vertical course are placed directly over each other and all the vertical cells are aligned. Stack bond construction requires that the wall be tied together with horizontal reinforcement or that open end blocks be used to obtain a bond between the blocks in the mortar head joints. The vertical core formed by the aligned cells of the masonry units provides a space for the reinforcing steel. Vertical cores that contain reinforcement should be not less than $2'' \times 3''$ in the horizontal dimensions and must be filled with cement grout.

Horizontal and vertical mortar joints of hollow masonry unit construction are ⅜″ thick. The horizontal surfaces of masonry units or bed joints have a full mortar cover on the exterior face shells of the unit and on the horizontal surfaces of cross webs of the blocks that are used to form vertical cores to contain reinforcement. Any mortar that may overflow into the vertical core should be removed to allow the cement grout to bond to the interior surface of the core and to permit proper clearance for the reinforcing bars. The vertical mortar joints, or the head joints, as they are called, should be filled with mortar for a distance in from the exterior face of the block equal to, but not less than, the thickness of the face shell of the block. The mortar joints between concrete blocks should be made straight and with a uniform thickness. Excess mortar that is squeezed from a joint as the result of positioning a block should be removed with a trowel. Concrete block is usually constructed with either a flush joint or a concave joint. Concave joints are made by tooling the surface of the joint so that the mortar will be compressed into the joint rather than its being removed from the surface; however, mortar joints should only be tooled

when the mortar is partially set and still plastic. Mortar joints should be made flush with the shell surface of the block when it is to be covered with a coat of plaster.

Horizontal and vertical cells of concrete blocks that contain reinforcing bars, ledger bolts, and other inserts must be filled solid with cement grout. Grout pours should not be made in lifts higher than 4′, and the grout should be well consolidated in place. Cleanout holes should be provided at the bottom of all cores that are to be filled, and 1 hr. should elapse between successive 4′ high pours. Grout pours should be stopped 1½″ below the top of the cell of a course so that a key for the succeeding pour can be formed. The grouting of masonry beams should be performed in one operation, and the tops of cells that are to remain unfilled with grout, which are directly below the cells of masonry beams, should be covered with metal lath to prevent grout leakage. Masonry beams and lintels should be supported in place with shores. It is recommended that these shores remain in place for a period of not less than seven days or at least until the member is capable of supporting its own weight and any construction load that may occur.

Many of the concrete hollow unit masonry details that are presented in this chapter are also presented as details constructed of reinforced grouted solid brick masonry. This type of construction consists of two or more wythes of bricks which are bonded together by mortar joints and by a solid vertical core of cement grout between the wythes. The grout, the mortar, and the bricks are bonded to each other to the degree that they will react as a unit and as a monolithic material. The structural capacity of reinforced grouted brick depends on the design, the quality of the mortar and the cement grout, the durability of the brick, the size and the compressive strength of the brick, and the water absorption factor. Bricks are manufactured by molding mixtures of clay and shale into oblong shapes which are then burned in a kiln to harden them. Although the materials used in the manufacture of bricks may vary, depending on the local source of supply, they must conform to the requirements of A.S.T.M. Spec. No. C 62–50. Also, bricks are produced with a variety of surface textures and colors, depending on the manufacturer. Table 3–2 lists the standard nominal modular sizes of bricks.

Table 3–2. Standard Nominal Modular Sizes of Brick

Thickness, in.	Face dimensions in the wall	
	Height, in.	Length, in.
4	2	12
4	2⅔	8
4	2⅔	12
4	4	8
4	4	12
4	5⅓	8
4	5⅓	12

Mortar joints of reinforced solid masonry should be straight and have a uniform thickness, the bricks should be laid in full head and bed joints, the joints should be not less than ½″ thick, and any excess mortar should be removed from the surface of the bricks after they are in place. Bricks should be dampened at the time they are laid to prevent the initial suction of the surface from removing too much water from the mortar or grout. The suction of the brick is a prime factor in creating the bond between the mortar and the brick; a mortar mixture that contains a larger amount of water will have a higher bond strength. When a brick member or wall is constructed of more than two wythes, the interior brick should be floated into place with not less than ¾″ of cement grout surrounding it. Brick walls are constructed with the same common bond or stack bond arrangement as that described for hollow unit masonry. The method of tooling mortar joints and the time required for soffit shoring of hollow unit masonry previously described also apply to reinforced grouted brick masonry.

Detail 3–35(a) and (b) show the minimum clearance required for reinforcing steel in grouted brick masonry walls. The grout space should not be less than the sum of the diameters of the ver-

tical and horizontal reinforcing bars plus ¼″ clear on each side of the bars. It is recommended that the grout space be not less than 2″ thick for rein-steel in grouted masonry is used in the same way as it is in reinforced concrete, that is, to resist tension or compression in a member that reacts to external forces by bending, compressing, or forced grouted masonry and not less than ¾″ thick in unreinforced grouted masonry. Reinforcing a combination of both. Therefore, the basic methods and principles of the structural design of grouted masonry are the same as those for reinforced concrete, except that the allowable working stresses are adjusted for the masonry materials used. Table 2–1 lists the various grades of reinforcing steel, and Table 2–2 lists the number designations of reinforcing bars and their respective physical properties. The reinforcing bars are embedded within the grout space between the brick tiers and are spaced and covered with grout or masonry as specified in Table 3–3. Grout pour requirements vary in different building codes; however, it is generally recommended that low-lift grout pours not exceed 12″ in height for vertical core widths less than 2″. It is also recommended that high-lift grout pours may be made when the vertical core is 2″ or more in width and the grout lift height should not exceed 48 times the core width for mortar grout, or 64 times the core width for pea gravel grout, or a maximum height of 12′0″. High-lift grout pours also require that the exterior tiers of the wall be tied together with rectangular ties of No. 9 gauge wire, 4″ wide by 2″ long and spaced 24″ o.c. horizontally and 16″ o.c. vertically, for walls using common bond of bricks. When a stacked bond of the bricks is used, the wire ties between the exterior tiers should be spaced 24″ o.c. horizontally and 12″ o.c. vertically. The grout pours

Table 3–3. Minimum Reinforcing Steel Spacing and Cover in Grouted Masonry

Location of reinforcment in masonry	Distance
Maximum spacing between reinforcing bars in walls	48″
Minimum spacing between parallel bars	1 bar diameter or not less than 1″
Minimum cover of reinforcing bars at the bottom of foundations	3″
Minimum cover of reinforcing bars in vertical members exposed to weather or soil	2″
Minimum cover of reinforcing bars in columns and at the bottoms or sides of girders or beams	1½″
Minimum cover of reinforcing bars in interior walls	¾″

Note: Reinforcing bars that are perpendicular to each other are permitted point contact at their intersection.

for reinforced masonry should be terminated 1½″ below the top of the bricks to form a key for the succeeding pour. The Uniform Building Code of the International Conference of Building Officials recommends that high-lift grout pours do not exceed 4′0″. Also, grout should be consolidated by vibrating or puddling to achieve a bond with the reinforcing bars and the masonry.

Grout and mortar are a mixture of water, portland cement, sand aggregate, and lime putty or hydrated lime. The proportions of the mixture are specified by the volume ratio of the ingredients. Mortar and grout are mixed in the ratio of 1 part portland cement, ¼ to ½ part lime putty or hydrated lime, and 2½ to 3 parts damp, loose sand. When the grout is to be poured in a space that is 3″ or more in width, the mix may be 1 part portland cement, 2 to 3 parts damp, loose sand, and 2 parts pea gravel or ⅜″ aggregate. Grout should have a fluid consistency when it is pumped into place; however, it should not be so fluid that the constituent aggregates of the mixture will segregate. Mortar should be used within 1½ hr. after it is mixed, but it may be retempered with water during that time to maintain a workable plasticity. Each building code specifies requirements for mortar and grout mixtures; however, the general requirements should conform to A.S.T.M. Spec. No. C 270. Since mortar and grout are composed of water and cement, the temperature conditions at the time it is placed can be critical. The temperature of masonry should be maintained at 50°F for 24 hr. for mixes composed of high early strength cement and 72 hr. for mixes composed of regular types of cement.

Acceptable construction of hollow unit masonry and grouted brick masonry depends a great deal on the quality of the workmanship in the field. Problems will often occur concerning the placement of reinforcing steel, the locations and the details for embedded conduits or pipes, the placing and aligning of construction joints, and the waterproofing of wall surfaces. The engineer should try to anticipate these conditions so that the construction will proceed without delays or extra costs. The size and location of reinforcing bars should be accurately dimensioned on the drawings; vertical reinforcement should be secured in place at the top and bottom and at intervals not exceeding 192 bar diameters apart; horizontal reinforcing bars should be placed in

bond beam or channel blocks in hollow unit masonry construction and within grout widths or as shown in Details 3–30 to 3–32(b); and reinforcing bars should be lapped 30 bar diameters or not less than 24″. Possible problems caused by locating pipes or conduits that pass through a masonry wall or are embedded within a wall can be avoided by coordinating the structural drawings with the requirements of the mechanical and electrical drawings. The location and the method of providing for the pipe or conduit in the wall should be shown on the structural drawings; all pipes that pass through masonry walls should be sleeved with a standard wrought iron pipe to prevent them from bonding with the masonry. Pipes and conduits in cores that are not filled with cement grout are not considered as embedded in the wall. However, when a pipe or conduit is embedded in masonry construction, care should be taken to ensure that it is not located at points of high shear or flexure stress and that it does not reduce the structural value of the wall.

Masonry walls will expand or contract, depending on the climate conditions and the composition of the material. The coefficient of thermal expansion of hollow masonry and brick masonry will vary in relation to the materials used in their manufacture; however, the engineer should consider the necessity of vertical construction joints in walls to allow for thermal growth, particularly in climates where the extreme temperature values will vary over a wide range. There are many recommended types and spacings of vertical wall joints. In general, a vertical wall joint should be of sufficient width to permit the free horizontal movement of the wall and also be capable of maintaining the structural capacity of the wall. This can be accomplished by aligning a full-height vertical joint through the wall cross section. The joint space is filled with a compressible bituminous or waterproof material, and the horizontal reinforcing bars are lapped across the joint but are not bonded to the grout on one side. The absence of expansion joints in masonry walls can be a source of severe cracking and therefore reduce the structural value of the wall.

Masonry is a comparatively porous material; if it is not waterproofed and it is exposed to normal weather conditions, it will allow a certain amount of moisture to permeate it, especially if the walls are approximately 8″ thick. The moisture that penetrates a wall from the exterior to the interior of the building will leave a white chalklike stain on the interior surface of the masonry. This phenomenon is caused by efflorescence, which occurs when the moisture that passes through the wall evaporates from the interior surface and leaves a white, dry, water-soluble salt residue that is derived from the masonry material. Efflorescence can be prevented by waterproofing the exterior surface of the wall and by sealing any cracks in the mortar joints by retooling them. Other sources of water intrusion in masonry walls can be traced to insert openings or cracks, to exposed grout surfaces at door and window openings, and to the tops of parapet walls. There are many commercial products available for the purpose of waterproofing masonry walls. The recommended methods and frequency of application of these materials are usually specified in their guarantee of performance. All masonry walls that are constructed below grade should be waterproofed with two layers of either asphalt or coal tar pitch material. Materials specifically manufactured for this purpose are also available and should be applied to the exterior surface of the wall in accordance with the manufacturer's recommendations. A definite method should also be provided to remove large amounts of water that may collect adjacent to walls below grade. This can be done either by installing perforated ceramic drain tiles adjacent to the bottom of the wall or by backfilling the area adjacent to the bottom of the wall with a continuous pocket of crushed rock or coarse aggregate. The tiles or crushed rock backfill should be sloped to permit the water to flow away from the wall. Exposed grout surfaces of masonry walls at windows, doors, and parapets should be covered with a galvanized sheet metal flashing. Jamb, sill, and header frames at doors and windows should be pressure caulked to the masonry surface. The layers of the roofing material should extend above the roof onto the surface of the parapet wall and should be either flashed into the wall or extended over the top of the wall and be covered by the parapet sheet metal flashing. Improper moisture protection of masonry walls can be a source of much damage within a building. Small leaks around windows and doors or through parapet copings may cause damage to large areas of finished plaster walls and ceilings and expensive floor covering materials; therefore it is quite important that positive steps be taken in the construction of a building to eliminate the possibility of water leakage.

Reinforced grouted masonry is designed by the same basic methods and principles used to design reinforced concrete. It is also assumed that grouted masonry will react to externally applied loads in the same manner that reinforced concrete will react, that is, that the masonry is not capable of resisting tensile stress, that the tension in a masonry member is resisted only by the reinforcing steel, and that the cement grout and the reinforcing steel are bonded together and will react as an analogous monolithic material. The primary difference between reinforced concrete and reinforced grouted masonry is the working stress values assigned to the grouted masonry by the various building codes or design criteria. These values are determined by compressive tests on the masonry and are specified as f'_m. The values of f'_m depend on the type of masonry used and on the quality of field workmanship during construction. The values of the allowable unit stresses of masonry acting in compression, shear, and bond are listed in the building codes for masonry construction performed with continuous inspection and without continuous inspection. Since the quality of field workmanship is an important factor for the strength of reinforced grouted masonry, the allowable unit working stresses with continuous inspection are double the allowable stresses that do not require continuous inspection. Valid continuous inspection requires that a registered deputy building inspector be on the job during the execution of all masonry construction and that he inspect and verify that the work is being performed in accordance with the building code requirements and that it complies with the engineer's structural design. The building code is not a design manual; it is a specification of the minimum safe design and construction requirements. Engineers, contractors, and field inspectors should bear this fact in mind when they use masonry as a construction material. This statement is not to be construed as meaning that masonry is not a good construction material; rather, it stresses that the quality of workmanship in the use of masonry as a structural material is a determining factor in the structural strength.

No construction is better than the least technically qualified person on the job, regardless of whether he is designing, drafting, supervising, or mixing mortar.

Masonry offers many advantages as a construction material since it is incombustible and has a high thermal insulation value. Depending on the structural requirements, the cost of masonry wall construction can be favorably compared with that of reinforced concrete construction since masonry walls can be constructed without the labor and material costs of concrete forms.

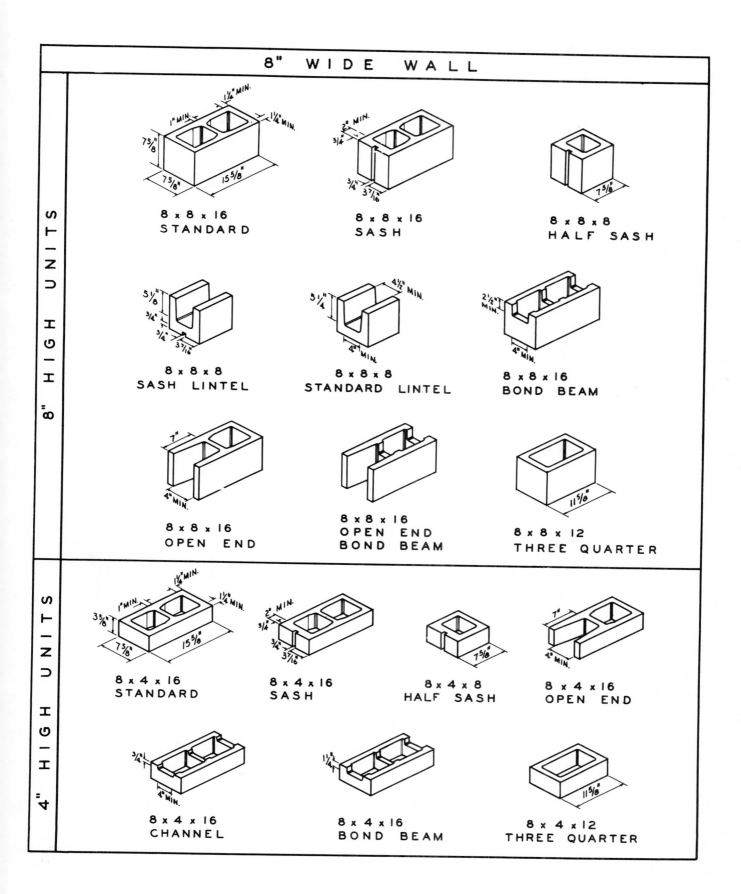

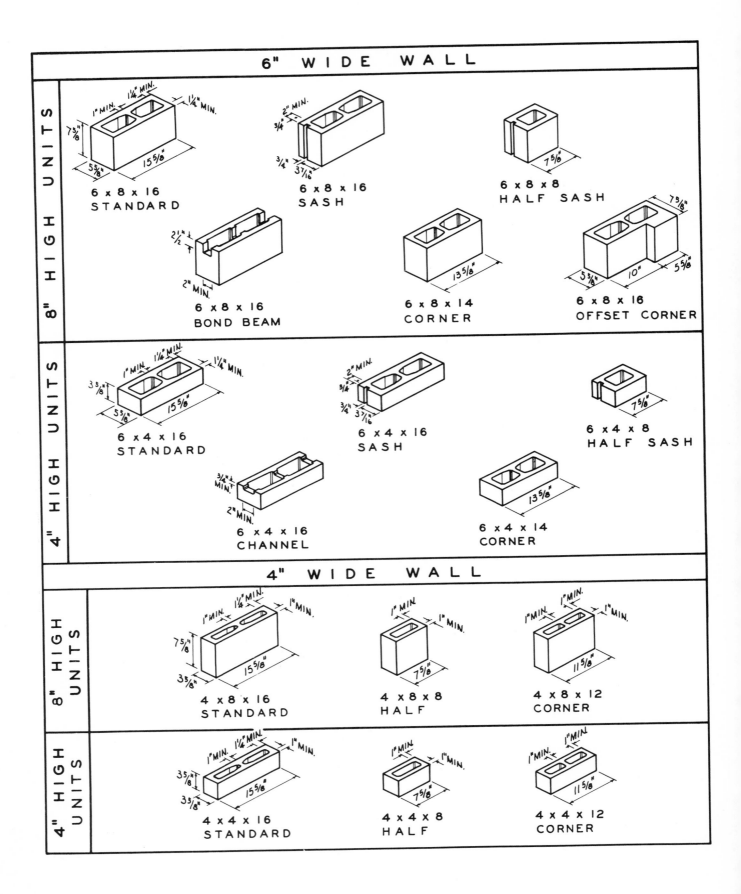

6" WIDE WALL

8" HIGH UNITS

6 x 8 x 16
STANDARD

6 x 8 x 16
SASH

6 x 8 x 8
HALF SASH

6 x 8 x 16
BOND BEAM

6 x 8 x 14
CORNER

6 x 8 x 16
OFFSET CORNER

4" HIGH UNITS

6 x 4 x 16
STANDARD

6 x 4 x 16
SASH

6 x 4 x 8
HALF SASH

6 x 4 x 16
CHANNEL

6 x 4 x 14
CORNER

4" WIDE WALL

8" HIGH UNITS

4 x 8 x 16
STANDARD

4 x 8 x 8
HALF

4 x 8 x 12
CORNER

4" HIGH UNITS

4 x 4 x 16
STANDARD

4 x 4 x 8
HALF

4 x 4 x 12
CORNER

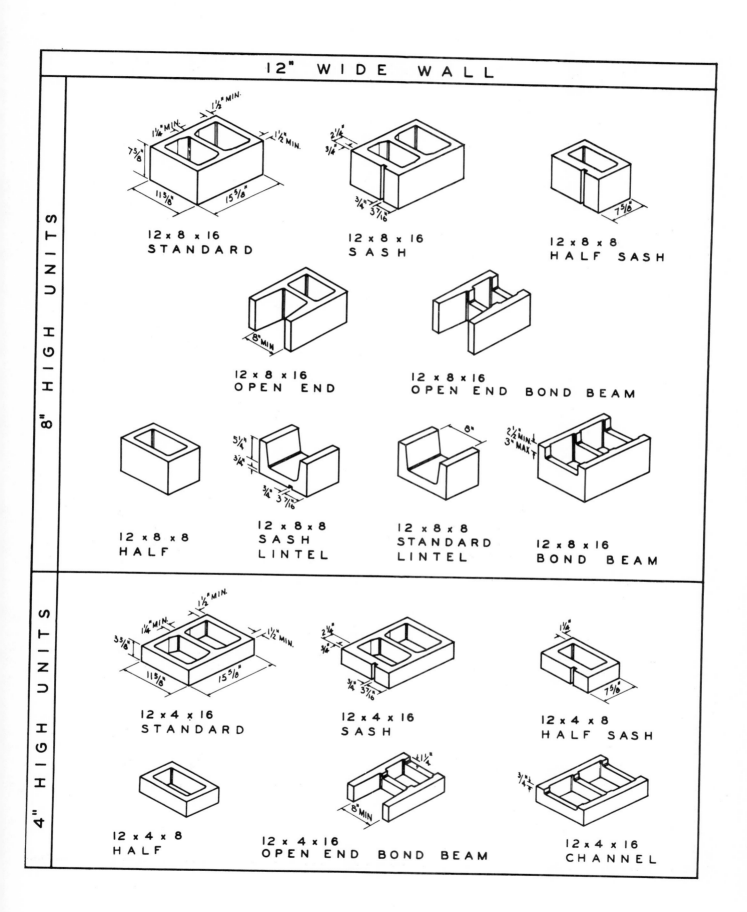

12" WIDE WALL

8" HIGH UNITS

12 x 8 x 16
STANDARD

12 x 8 x 16
SASH

12 x 8 x 8
HALF SASH

12 x 8 x 16
OPEN END

12 x 8 x 16
OPEN END BOND BEAM

12 x 8 x 8
HALF

12 x 8 x 8
SASH
LINTEL

12 x 8 x 8
STANDARD
LINTEL

12 x 8 x 16
BOND BEAM

4" HIGH UNITS

12 x 4 x 16
STANDARD

12 x 4 x 16
SASH

12 x 4 x 8
HALF SASH

12 x 4 x 8
HALF

12 x 4 x 16
OPEN END BOND BEAM

12 x 4 x 16
CHANNEL

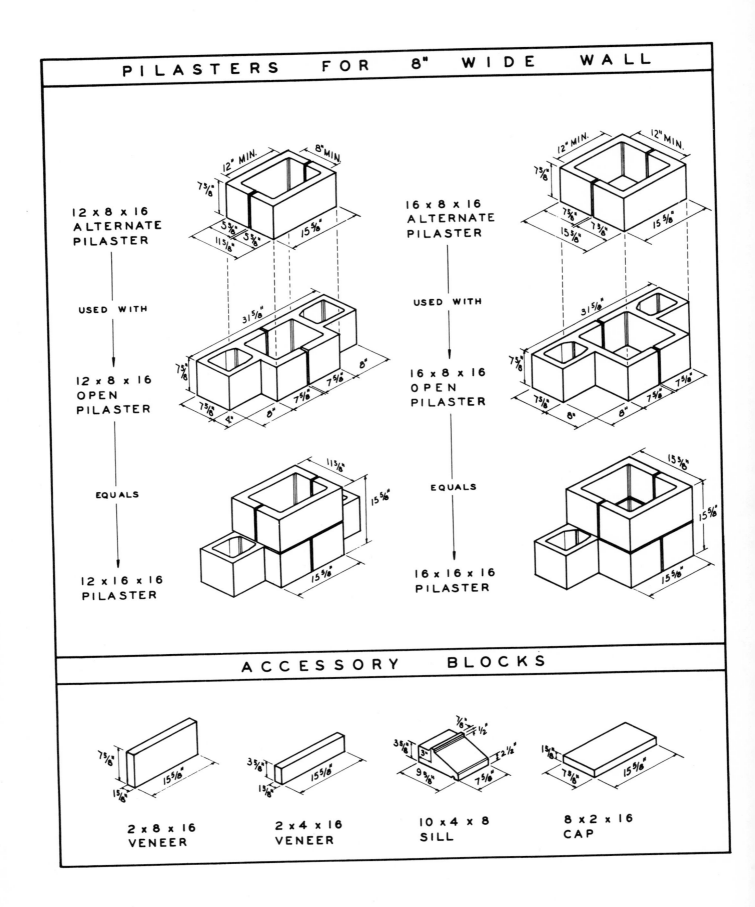

PILASTERS FOR 8" WIDE WALL

12 x 8 x 16
ALTERNATE
PILASTER

USED WITH

12 x 8 x 16
OPEN
PILASTER

EQUALS

12 x 16 x 16
PILASTER

16 x 8 x 16
ALTERNATE
PILASTER

USED WITH

16 x 8 x 16
OPEN
PILASTER

EQUALS

16 x 16 x 16
PILASTER

ACCESSORY BLOCKS

2 x 8 x 16
VENEER

2 x 4 x 16
VENEER

10 x 4 x 8
SILL

8 x 2 x 16
CAP

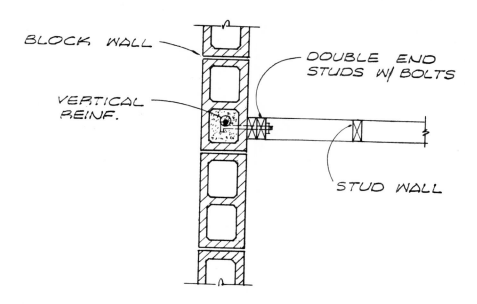

Detail 3-1. A plan section of a concrete block masonry wall intersected by a wood stud wall. The wood stud wall is nailed to a wood nailer that is bolted to the masonry wall as shown. One vertical reinforcing bar is placed in the wall at the line of the wall intersection.

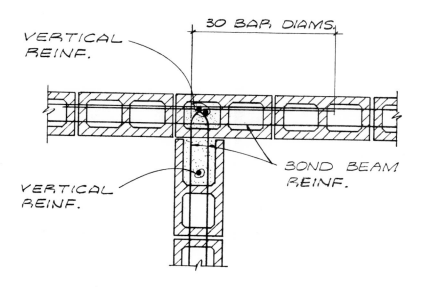

Detail 3-2. A plan section of the intersection of concrete block masonry wall bond beams. The vertical reinforcing bars are added to the wall at the line of the wall intersection. The bond beam reinforcing steel is lapped 30 bar diameters or a minimum of 24". Fill all masonry cells that contain reinforcement.

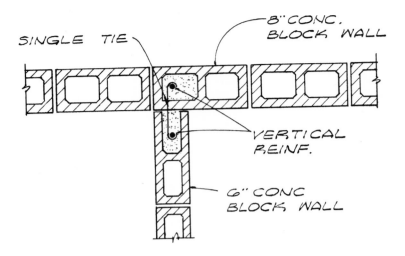

Detail 3-3. A plan section of the intersection of concrete block masonry walls. The walls are connected by dowels hooked to vertical reinforcing bars in each wall. Fill all masonry cells that contain reinforcement.

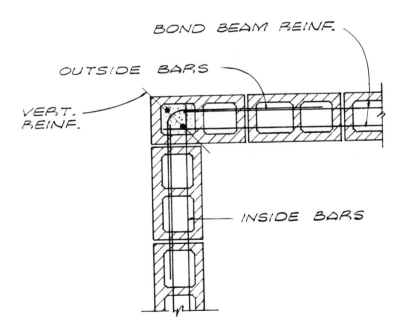

Detail 3-4. A plan section of the corner of a concrete block masonry wall. Two vertical reinforcing bars are added in the corner cell of the wall. The bond beam reinforcing bars at the outside face of the wall are lapped as shown. The reinforcing steel lap is 30 bar diameters or a minimum of 24″. Fill all masonry cells that contain reinforcement.

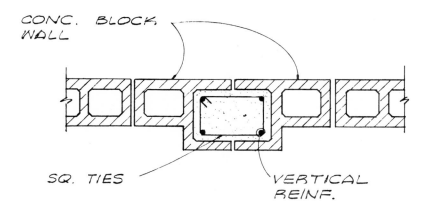

CONC. BLOCK WALL

SQ. TIES

VERTICAL REINF.

Detail 3-5(a). A plan section of a concrete block masonry wall rectangular pilaster. The pilaster is reinforced with a minimum of four vertical bars tied together in the same manner as is required for a rectangular concrete column. See Detail 2-49(a). Fill all masonry cells that contain reinforcement.

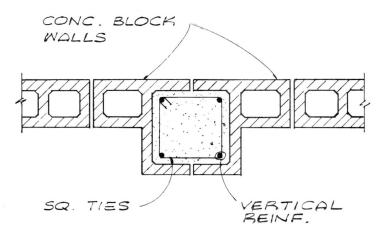

CONC. BLOCK WALLS

SQ. TIES

VERTICAL REINF.

Detail 3-5(b). A plan section of a concrete block masonry wall square pilaster. The pilaster is reinforced with a minimum of four vertical bars tied together in the same way as is required for a rectangular concrete column. See Detail 2-49(a). Fill all masonry cells that contain reinforcement.

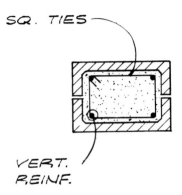

SQ. TIES

VERT.
REINF.

Detail 3-6(a). A plan section of a concrete block masonry rectangular column. The column is reinforced with a minimum of four vertical bars tied together in the same way as is required for a rectangular concrete column. See Detail 2-49(a). Fill all masonry cells that contain reinforcement.

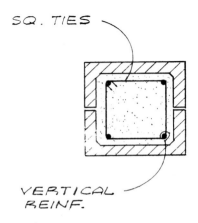

SQ. TIES

VERTICAL
REINF.

Detail 3-6(b). A plan section of a concrete block masonry square column. The column is reinforced with a minimum of four vertical bars tied together in the same way as is required for a rectangular concrete column. See Detail 2-49(a). Fill all masonry cells that contain reinforcement.

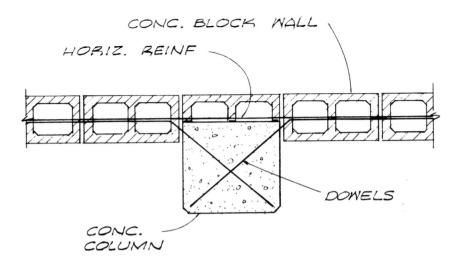

CONC. BLOCK WALL

HORIZ. REINF

DOWELS

CONC.
COLUMN

Detail 3-7. A plan section of a poured concrete column and a concrete block masonry wall. The wall is connected to the column by extending the horizontal reinforcing bars of the wall into the column as shown. The vertical reinforcing bars and ties of the poured column are not shown. See Detail 2-49(a).

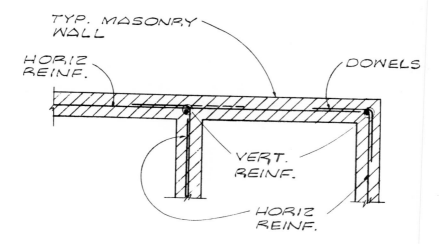

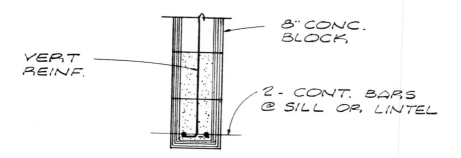

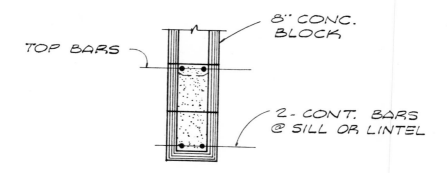

Detail 3-8. A plan section of a corner and of an intersection of masonry walls. The walls are connected by lapping the horizontal reinforcing bars as shown. The bars are lapped 30 bar diameters or a minimum of 24″.

Detail 3-9(a). A section of a concrete block masonry wall lintel. The size and number of reinforcing bars in the lintel depend on the span and the load and are determined by calculation. The horizontal reinforcing bars extend 24″ past the edge of the opening. The depth of the lintel is determined by the number of masonry cells filled with grout. All cells that contain reinforcing bars are filled with grout.

Detail 3-9(b). A section of a concrete block masonry wall lintel with reinforcing bars at the top and bottom. The size and number of reinforcing bars in the lintel depend on the span and the load and are determined by calculation. The horizontal reinforcing bars extend 24″ past the edge of the opening. All cells that contain reinforcing bars are filled with grout. See Detail 3-10(a).

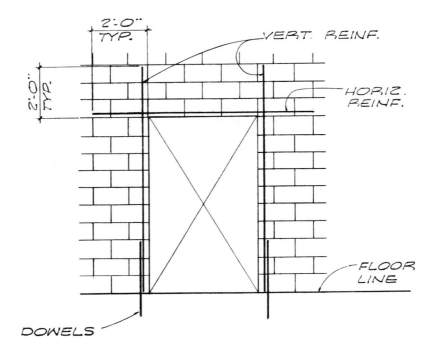

Detail 3-10(a). An elevation of an opening in a concrete block masonry wall. Vertical and horizontal reinforcing bars are added at the edge of the opening and extend 24″ past the edge of the opening. See Details 3-9(a) and (b) for lintel sections; see Detail 3-10(d) for a masonry jamb section.

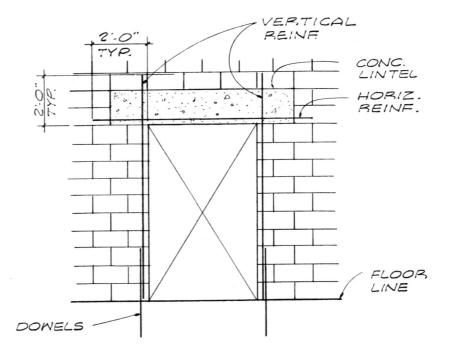

Detail 3-10(b). An elevation of an opening in a concrete block masonry wall. Vertical and horizontal reinforcing bars are added at the edges of the opening and extend 24″ past the edge of the opening. The lintel is a poured concrete beam. See Detail 3-10(d) for a section of the lintel and for a masonry jamb section.

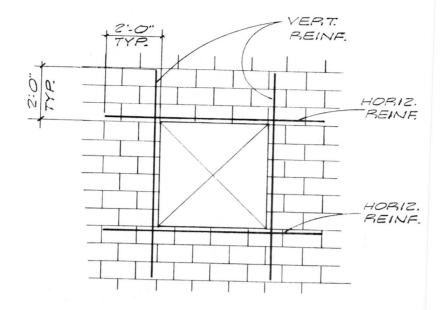

Detail 3-10(c). An elevation of an opening in a concrete block masonry wall. Vertical and horizontal reinforcing bars are added at the edge of the opening and extend 24″ past the edge of the opening. See Details 3-9(a) and (b) for masonry lintel sections; see Detail 3-10(d) for a masonry jamb section.

Detail 3-10(d). A section of a concrete lintel in a concrete block masonry wall, and a section of a jamb for an opening in a concrete block masonry wall.

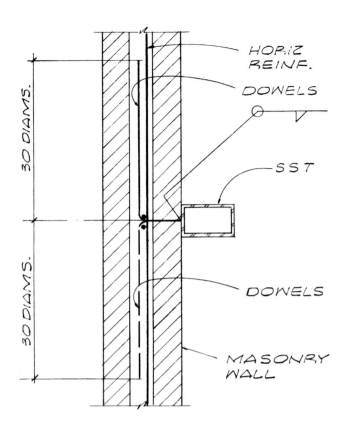

HORIZ REINF.

DOWELS

30 DIAMS.

SST

30 DIAMS.

DOWELS

MASONRY WALL

Detail 3-11. A plan section of a masonry wall and a structural steel tube column. The steel column is connected to the masonry wall by welding horizontal reinforcing dowels at the back face of the column and bending them into the masonry wall. A vertical reinforcing bar is added at the bend of the horizontal dowels. The size and spacing of the dowels into the masonry wall depend on the column forces to be resisted. The reinforcing dowels lap 30 bar diameters into the wall or not less than 24″.

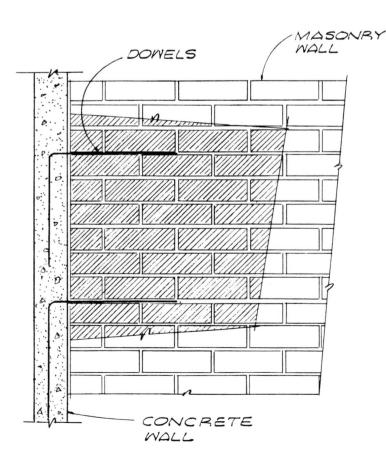

DOWELS

MASONRY WALL

CONCRETE WALL

Detail 3-12. A section of a concrete wall and an elevation of an intersecting masonry wall. The masonry wall is connected to the concrete wall by reinforcing dowels as shown. The dowel lap length is 30 bar diameters into the masonry and 40 bar diameters into the concrete or not less than 24″. The size and spacing of the reinforcing dowels depend on the lateral forces to be resisted by the walls.

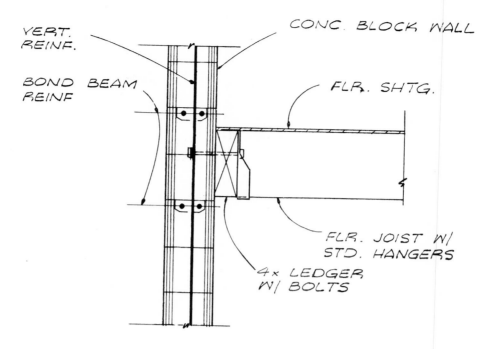

Detail 3-13. A section of a concrete block masonry wall supporting wood floor joists. The joists are connected to a 4″ wide wood ledger by standard joist hangers. The ledger is connected to the masonry wall by bolts. The size and spacing of the ledger bolts are determined by calculation. The horizontal reinforcing bars act as a bond beam in the masonry wall.

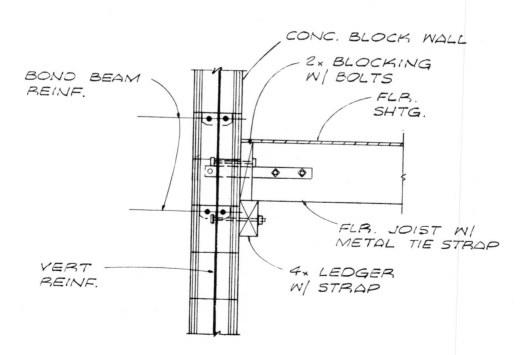

Detail 3-14. A section of a concrete block masonry wall supporting wood floor joists. The joists bear on a 4″ wide wood ledger which is bolted to the masonry wall. The size and spacing of the ledger bolts are determined by calculation. The joist continuous blocking is bolted to the masonry wall. A metal tie strap spaced at 4′0″ o.c. connects the floor to the masonry. The horizontal reinforcing bars act as a bond beam in the masonry wall.

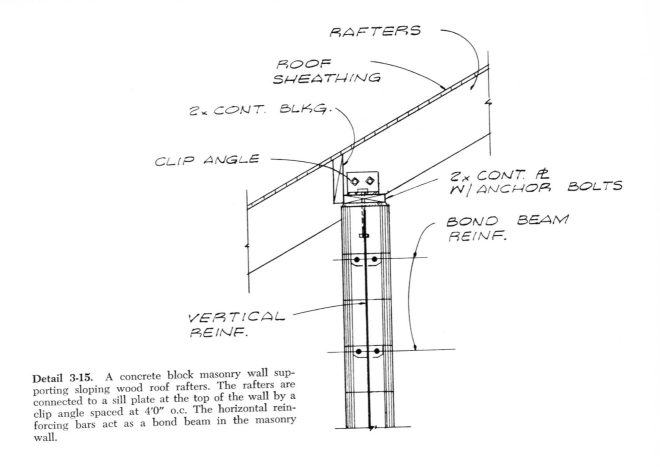

RAFTERS

ROOF SHEATHING

2x CONT. BLKG.

CLIP ANGLE

2x CONT. ℄ W/ ANCHOR BOLTS

BOND BEAM REINF.

VERTICAL REINF.

Detail 3-15. A concrete block masonry wall supporting sloping wood roof rafters. The rafters are connected to a sill plate at the top of the wall by a clip angle spaced at 4'0" o.c. The horizontal reinforcing bars act as a bond beam in the masonry wall.

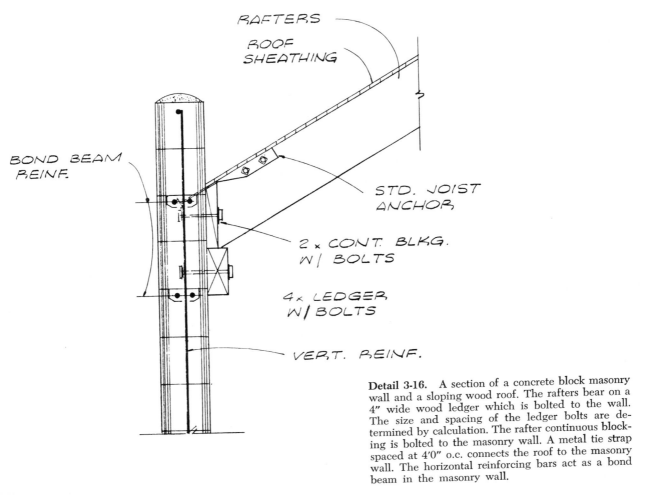

RAFTERS

ROOF SHEATHING

BOND BEAM REINF.

STD. JOIST ANCHOR

2x CONT. BLKG. W/ BOLTS

4x LEDGER W/ BOLTS

VERT. REINF.

Detail 3-16. A section of a concrete block masonry wall and a sloping wood roof. The rafters bear on a 4" wide wood ledger which is bolted to the wall. The size and spacing of the ledger bolts are determined by calculation. The rafter continuous blocking is bolted to the masonry wall. A metal tie strap spaced at 4'0" o.c. connects the roof to the masonry wall. The horizontal reinforcing bars act as a bond beam in the masonry wall.

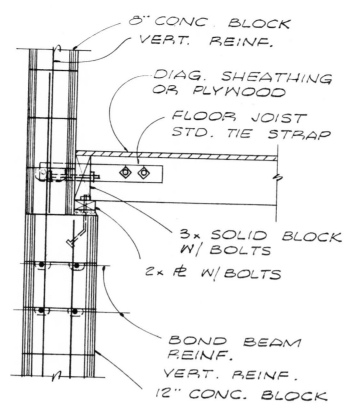

8" CONC. BLOCK

VERT. REINF.

DIAG. SHEATHING OR PLYWOOD

FLOOR JOIST

STD. TIE STRAP

3 x SOLID BLOCK W/ BOLTS

2 x ℄ W/ BOLTS

BOND BEAM REINF.

VERT. REINF.

12" CONC. BLOCK

Detail 3-17(a). A section of a 12″ concrete block masonry wall and an 8″ concrete block masonry wall supporting wood floor joists. The joists bear on a 4″ wide wood plate which is bolted to the top of the 12″ wall as shown. The joist continuous blocking is bolted to the 8″ wall. A metal tie strap spaced at 4′0″ o.c. connects the floor to the wall.

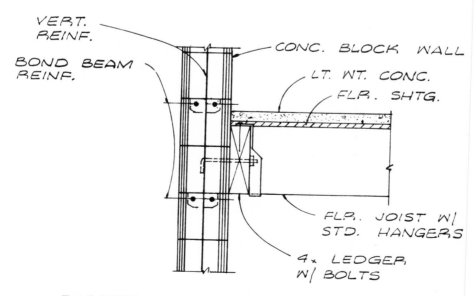

VERT. REINF.

BOND BEAM REINF.

CONC. BLOCK WALL

LT. WT. CONC.

FLR. SHTG.

FLR. JOIST W/ STD. HANGERS

4 x LEDGER W/ BOLTS

Detail 3-17(b). A section of a concrete block masonry wall, wood floor joists, and light-weight concrete over a wood floor. The floor joists are connected to a 4″ wide wood ledger by standard joist hangers. The ledger is bolted to the masonry wall. The size and spacing of the ledger bolts are determined by calculation. The floor sheathing is nailed to the ledger to transfer the floor diaphragm stress into the wall. The horizontal reinforcing bars act as a bond beam in the masonry wall.

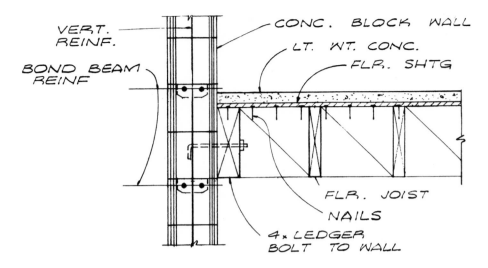

VERT. REINF.

BOND BEAM REINF

CONC. BLOCK WALL

LT. WT. CONC.

FLR. SHTG

FLR. JOIST

NAILS

4 x LEDGER BOLT TO WALL

Detail 3-18(a). A section of a concrete block masonry wall, floor joists, and light-weight concrete over a wood floor. The floor joists span parallel to the wall. The floor sheathing is nailed to a 4″ wide wood ledger to transfer the floor diaphragm stress into the masonry wall. The diaphragm stress may require that the perimeter floor joists be blocked and nailed as shown. The ledger is bolted to the masonry wall. The size and spacing of the ledger bolts are determined by calculation. The horizontal reinforcing bars act as a bond beam in the masonry wall.

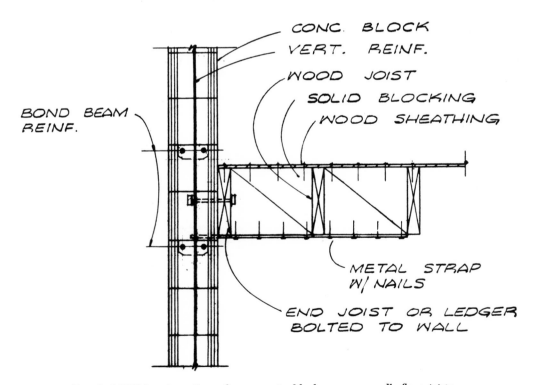

CONC. BLOCK

VERT. REINF.

WOOD JOIST

SOLID BLOCKING

WOOD SHEATHING

BOND BEAM REINF.

METAL STRAP W/ NAILS

END JOIST OR LEDGER BOLTED TO WALL

Detail 3-18(b). A section of a concrete block masonry wall, floor joists, and floor sheathing. The floor joists span parallel to the wall. The floor sheathing is nailed to a 4″ wide wood ledger to transfer the floor diaphragm stress into the masonry wall. The diaphragm stress may require that the perimeter floor joists be blocked and nailed as shown. The ledger is bolted to the masonry wall. The size and spacing of the ledger bolts are determined by calculation. A metal tie strap spaced at 4′0″ o.c. connects the floor to the masonry wall. The horizontal reinforcing bars act as a bond beam in the wall.

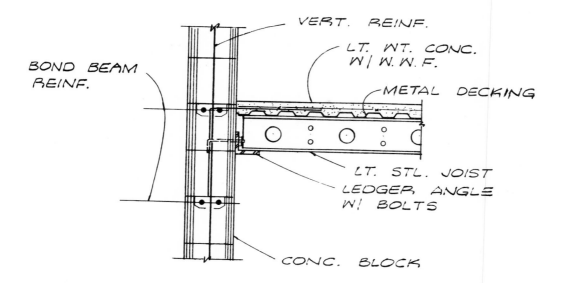

Detail 3-19. A section of a concrete block masonry wall, light steel joists, a continuous ledger angle, and metal decking with light-weight concrete. The steel joists bear on and are welded to the ledger angle which is bolted to the masonry wall. The size and spacing of the angle bolts are determined by calculation. The light-weight concrete slab is connected to the wall with reinforcing dowels. The horizontal reinforcing bars act as a bond beam in the masonry wall.

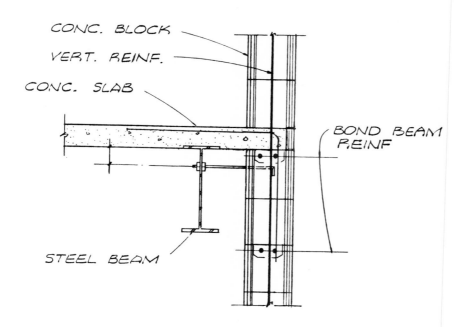

Detail 3-20. A section of a concrete block masonry wall and a concrete slab. The slab is supported by a steel beam. The slab diaphragm stress is transferred to the masonry wall by reinforcing dowels. Equally spaced rods between the web of the steel beam and the masonry wall restrain the beam laterally. The horizontal reinforcing bars act as a bond beam in the masonry wall.

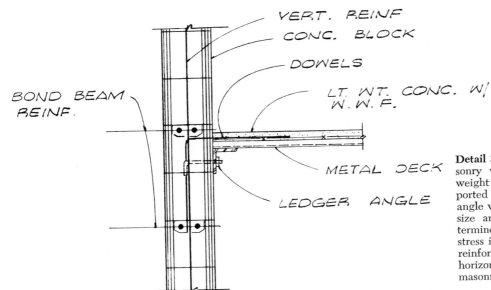

VERT. REINF
CONC. BLOCK
DOWELS
LT. WT. CONC. W/
W. W. F.
BOND BEAM REINF.
METAL DECK
LEDGER ANGLE

Detail 3-21. A section of a concrete block masonry wall and a metal decking with lightweight concrete. The metal decking is supported by and welded to a continuous ledger angle which is bolted to the masonry wall. The size and spacing of the angle bolts are determined by calculation. The floor diaphragm stress is transferred to the masonry wall by the reinforcing dowels and the ledger angle. The horizontal bars act as a bond beam in the masonry wall.

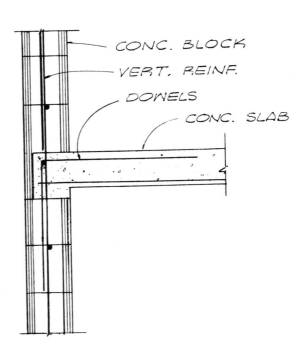

CONC. BLOCK
VERT. REINF.
DOWELS
CONC. SLAB

Detail 3-22. A section of a concrete block masonry wall and a poured concrete slab. The slab is cast into the wall for vertical support. The slab diaphragm stress is transferred to the masonry wall by the reinforcing dowels.

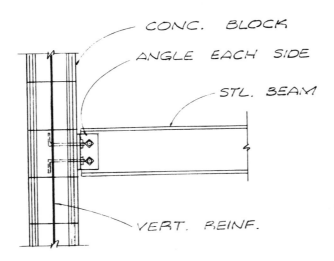

CONC. BLOCK
ANGLE EACH SIDE
STL. BEAM
VERT. REINF.

Detail 3-23. A section of a concrete block masonry wall supporting a steel beam. The steel beam reaction is transferred to the wall through clip angles bolted to each side of the beam web and into the masonry wall. The size of the angles and the size of the bolts are determined by calculation.

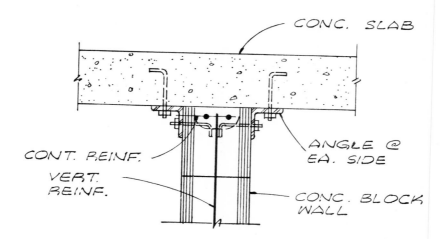

Detail 3-24(a). A section of the top of a concrete block masonry wall connected to a poured concrete slab. The wall is connected to the slab by continuous angles on each side of the wall. The angles are bolted to the slab and to the wall as shown. The size and spacing of the angle bolts are determined by calculation.

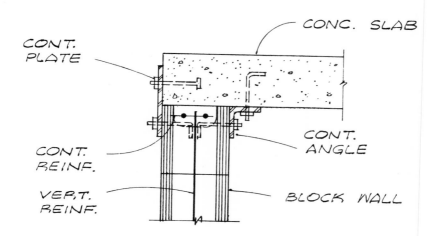

Detail 3-24(b). A section of the top of a concrete block masonry wall connected to the edge of a poured concrete slab. The wall is connected to the slab by a continuous angle and a continuous flat plate. The angle and plate are bolted to the slab and to the wall as shown. The size and spacing of the bolts are determined by calculation.

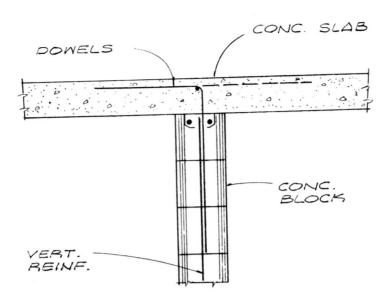

Detail 3-25(a). A section of a concrete slab supported by a concrete block masonry wall. The slab is connected to the wall by reinforcing dowels bent in alternate directions as shown. Continuous horizontal reinforcing bars are added at the top of the wall and at the top of the slab. The dowels lap 30 bar diameters in the masonry and 40 bar diameters in the concrete or not less than 24".

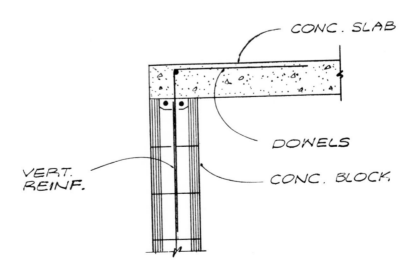

Detail 3-25(b). A section of a concrete slab supported by a concrete block masonry wall. The slab is connected to the wall by reinforcing dowels as shown. Continuous horizontal reinforcing bars are added at the top of the wall and at the top of the slab. The dowels lap 30 bar diameters in the masonry and 40 bar diameters in the concrete or not less than 24".

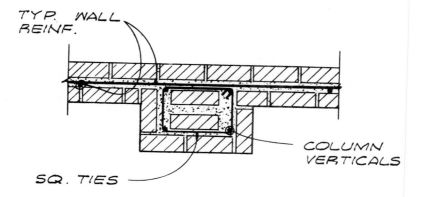

TYP. WALL REINF.

COLUMN VERTICALS

SQ. TIES

Detail 3-26(a). A plan section of a brick wall rectangular pilaster. The pilaster is reinforced with a minimum of four vertical bars tied together in the same way as is required for a rectangular concrete column. See Detail 2-49(a). The interior bricks shown in the pilaster plan may be omitted and the total section filled with grout or concrete.

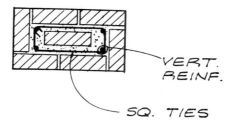

VERT. REINF.

SQ. TIES

Detail 3-26(b). A section of a rectangular brick column. The column is reinforced with a minimum of four vertical bars tied together in the same way as is required for a rectangular concrete column. See Detail 2-49(a). The interior brick shown in the column plan may be omitted and the total section filled with grout or concrete.

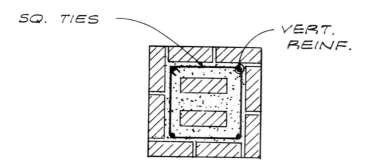

SQ. TIES

VERT. REINF.

Detail 3-26(c). A section of a square brick column. The column is reinforced with a minimum of four vertical bars tied together in the same way as is required for a rectangular concrete column. See Detail 2-49(a). The interior bricks shown in the column plan may be omitted and the total section filled with grout or concrete.

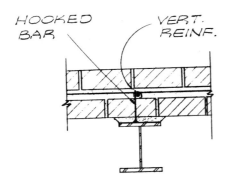

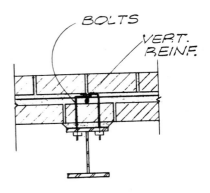

Detail 3-27(a). A plan section of a brick wall and a wide flange steel column. The column is connected to the wall by reinforcing bars bent as hooks, welded to the flange of the column, and hooked around a vertical reinforcing bar in the wall. The wall restrains the column laterally. The space between the face of the wall and the face of the column flange is filled with grout.

Detail 3-27(b). A plan section of a brick wall and a wide flange steel column. The column is bolted to the wall as shown. The wall restrains the column laterally. A vertical reinforcing bar is added in the wall at the line of the column connection. The space between the face of the wall and the face of the column flange is filled with grout.

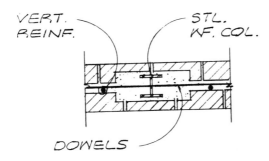

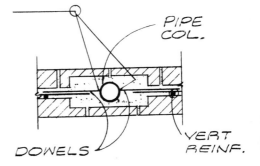

Detail 3-27(c). A plan section of a wide flange steel column inside a brick wall. Horizontal reinforcing dowels are welded to each side of the column web or pass through a hole in the web and extend 24" into the wall grout space. The horizontal dowels are spaced at 4'0" o.c.

Detail 3-27(d). A plan section of a steel pipe column inside a brick wall. Horizontal reinforcing dowels are welded to the column on each side and extend 24" into the wall grout space. The horizontal dowels are spaced at 4'0" o.c.

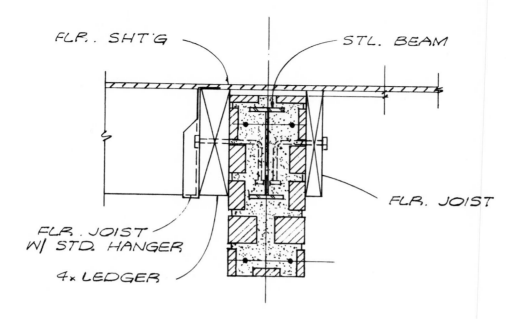

FLR. SHT'G

STL. BEAM

FLR. JOIST

FLR. JOIST
W/ STD. HANGER

4x LEDGER

Detail 3-28(a). A section of a composite brick and steel beam. The floors are connected to the beam as shown in Detail 3-36 and similar to Detail 3-39. A space is provided between the top of the brick beam and the bottom of the sheathing to allow for wood shrinkage.

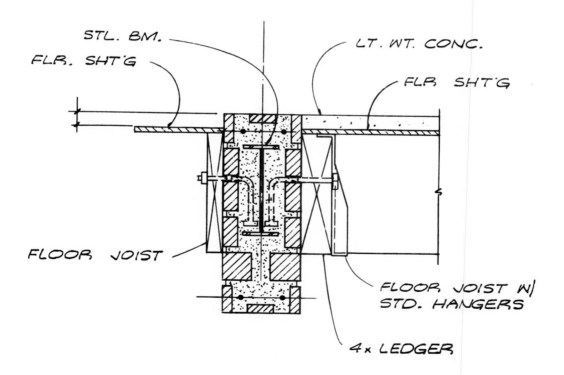

STL. BM.

FLR. SHT'G

LT. WT. CONC.

FLR. SHT'G

FLOOR JOIST

FLOOR JOIST W/ STD. HANGERS

4x LEDGER

Detail 3-28(b). A section of a composite brick and steel beam. The floor joists are connected to the beam as shown in Detail 3-36 and similar to Detail 3-39. The exterior wood floor is depressed below the top of the brick beam and the interior finished floor.

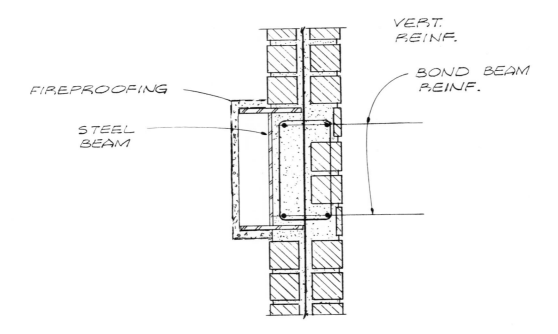

Detail 3-29. A section of a brick wall and a steel beam. The exterior surface of the steel beam is covered with a fireproof material. The inside face of the beam web acts as a form for the bond beam in the brick wall. The flange of the steel beam should not interrupt the vertical reinforcing of the brick wall; however point contact is permitted.

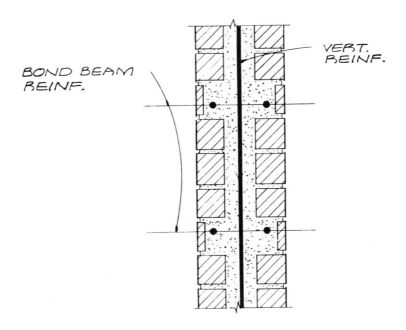

Detail 3-30. A section of a brick wall bond beam. The vertical distance between the horizontal reinforcement depends on the required area of the bond beam. The size of the horizontal reinforcement is determined by the load to be transferred through the masonry wall. The split bricks provide grout coverage of the reinforcing steel.

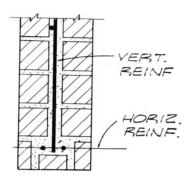

Detail 3-31(a). A section of a brick wall lintel or sill. The vertical reinforcement is stopped at the edge of the wall opening. The surface of the wall edge is covered by a split brick. The horizontal reinforcing bars extend 24″ past the edge of the opening.

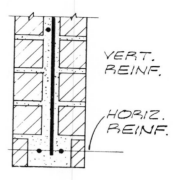

Detail 3-31(b). A section of a brick wall lintel or sill. The vertical reinforcement is stopped at the edge of the wall opening. The surface of the wall edge is covered by the grout fill. The horizontal reinforcing bars extend 24″ past the edge of the opening.

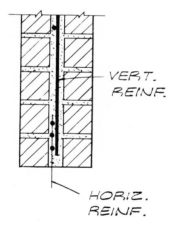

Detail 3-32(a). A section of a brick wall lintel or sill. The vertical reinforcement is stopped at the edge of the wall opening. The horizontal reinforcement is placed as shown. The horizontal reinforcing bars extend 24″ past the edge of the opening.

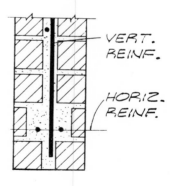

Detail 3-32(b). A section of a brick wall lintel or sill. The vertical reinforcement is stopped at the edge of the wall opening. The split bricks provide minimum grout coverage over the reinforcing steel. The horizontal reinforcing bars extend 24″ past the edge of the opening.

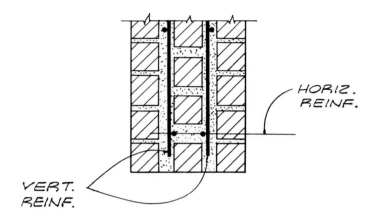

Detail 3-33(a). A section of a brick wall lintel or sill. The wall is constructed of three tiers of brick. The vertical reinforcement is stopped at the edge of the wall opening. The horizontal reinforcing bars extend 24″ past the edge of the opening.

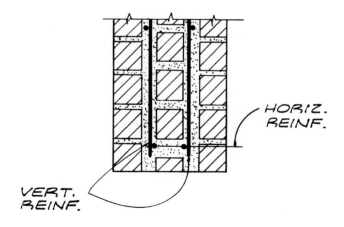

Detail 3-33(b). A section of a brick wall lintel or sill. The wall is constructed of three tiers of brick. The vertical reinforcement is stopped at the edge of the wall opening. A split brick is used at the surface of the edge of the wall to provide minimum grout coverage of the reinforcing steel. The horizontal reinforcing bars extend 24″ past the edge of the opening.

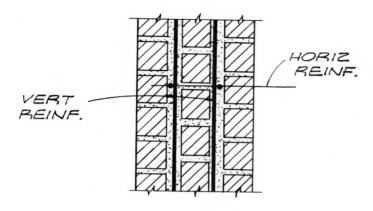

Detail 3-34(a). A typical section of a brick masonry wall three tiers wide and with two rows of horizontal and vertical reinforcement. See Detail 3-35(b) for the reinforcing bar clearance and grout coverage in masonry walls; see also Detail 3-34(b).

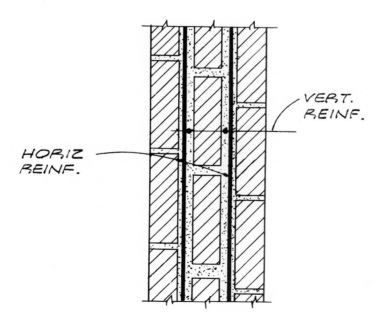

Detail 3-34(b). A plan section of a brick wall three tiers wide with two rows of horizontal and vertical reinforcement. See Detail 3-34(a).

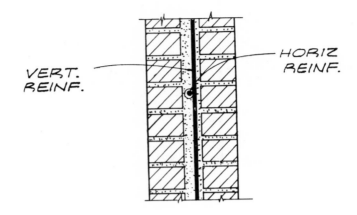

Detail 3-35(a). A typical section of a brick wall two tiers wide with one row of horizontal and vertical reinforcement. See Detail 3-35(b) for reinforcing bar clearance and grout coverage in masonry walls.

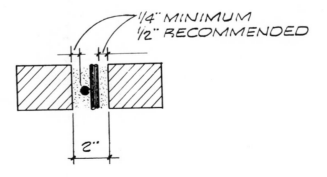

Detail 3-35(b). A section of brick masonry and reinforcing bars showing the required clearance between the brick surface and the reinforcing bars. The horizontal and vertical reinforcing bars are permitted point contact. It is recommended that the total grout space be not less than 2″.

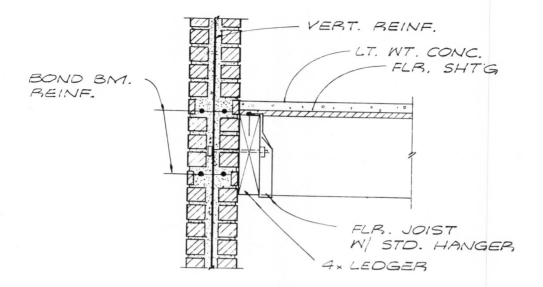

Detail 3-36. A section of a brick wall supporting floor joists and light weight concrete over the wood floor. The floor joists are connected to a 4″ wide wood ledger by standard joist hangers. The ledger is bolted to the wall. The size and spacing of the ledger bolts are determined by calculation. The floor sheathing is nailed to the ledger to transfer floor diaphragm stress into the wall. The horizontal reinforcing bars act as a bond beam in the masonry wall.

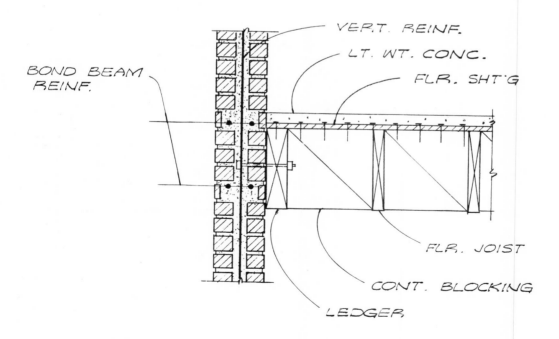

Detail 3-37. A section of a brick wall, floor joists, and light-weight concrete over the wood floor. The floor joists span parallel to the wall. The floor sheathing is nailed to a 4″ wide wood ledger to transfer the floor diaphragm stress into the wall. The diaphragm stress may require that the perimeter floor joists be blocked and nailed as shown. The ledger is bolted to the wall. The size and spacing of the ledger bolts are determined by calculation. The horizontal reinforcing bars act as a bond team in the wall.

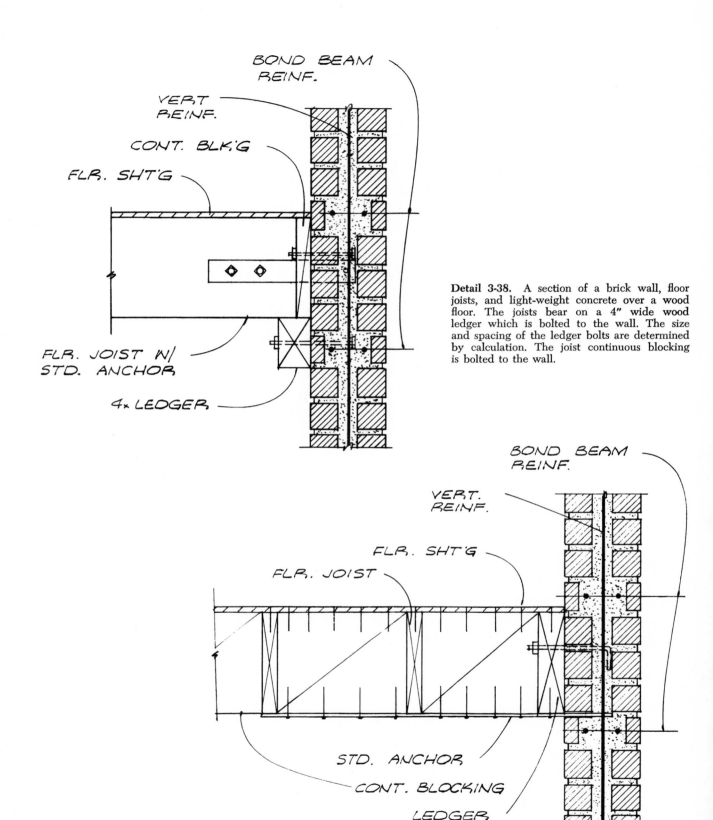

BOND BEAM REINF.

VERT REINF.

CONT. BLK'G

FLR. SHT'G

FLR. JOIST W/ STD. ANCHOR

4x LEDGER

Detail 3-38. A section of a brick wall, floor joists, and light-weight concrete over a **wood** floor. The joists bear on a 4″ wide **wood** ledger which is bolted to the wall. The size and spacing of the ledger bolts are determined by calculation. The joist continuous blocking is bolted to the wall.

BOND BEAM REINF.

VERT. REINF.

FLR. SHT'G

FLR. JOIST

STD. ANCHOR

CONT. BLOCKING

LEDGER

Detail 3-39. A section of a brick wall, floor joists, and floor sheathing. The floor joists span parallel to the wall. The floor sheathing is nailed to a 4″ wide ledger to transfer the diaphragm stress into the wall. The diaphragm stress may require that the perimeter floor joists be blocked and nailed as shown. The ledger is bolted to the masonry wall. The size and spacing of the ledger bolts are determined by calculation. The horizontal reinforcing bars act as a bond beam in the wall. A metal tie strap spaced at 4′0″ connects the floor to the wall.

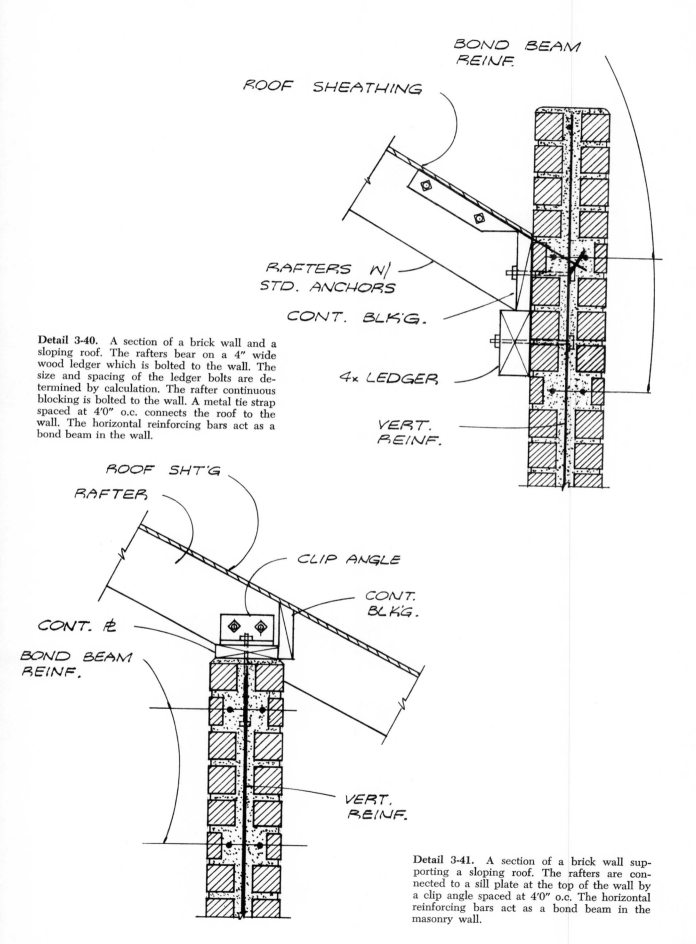

BOND BEAM REINF.

ROOF SHEATHING

RAFTERS W/ STD. ANCHORS

CONT. BLK'G.

4x LEDGER

VERT. REINF.

Detail 3-40. A section of a brick wall and a sloping roof. The rafters bear on a 4″ wide wood ledger which is bolted to the wall. The size and spacing of the ledger bolts are determined by calculation. The rafter continuous blocking is bolted to the wall. A metal tie strap spaced at 4′0″ o.c. connects the roof to the wall. The horizontal reinforcing bars act as a bond beam in the wall.

ROOF SHT'G

RAFTER

CLIP ANGLE

CONT. BLK'G.

CONT. ℔

BOND BEAM REINF.

VERT. REINF.

Detail 3-41. A section of a brick wall supporting a sloping roof. The rafters are connected to a sill plate at the top of the wall by a clip angle spaced at 4′0″ o.c. The horizontal reinforcing bars act as a bond beam in the masonry wall.

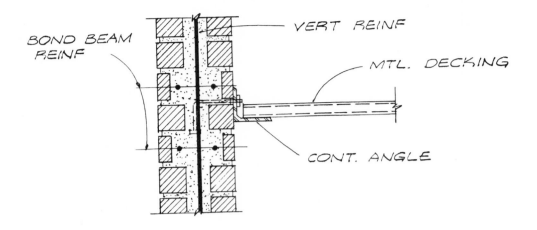

BOND BEAM REINF

VERT REINF

MTL. DECKING

CONT. ANGLE

Detail 3-42. A section of a brick wall and exposed metal decking. The decking is supported by and welded to a continuous ledger angle. The ledger angle is bolted to the wall. The size and spacing of the angle and bolts are determined by calculation. The horizontal reinforcing bars act as a bond beam in the wall.

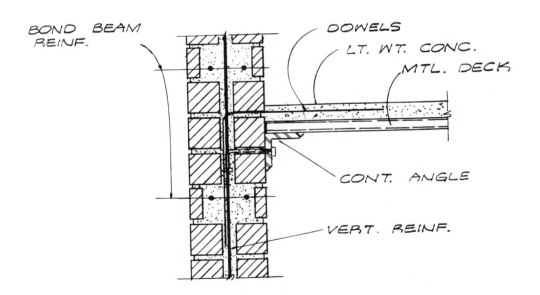

BOND BEAM REINF.

DOWELS

LT. WT. CONC.

MTL. DECK

CONT. ANGLE

VERT. REINF.

Detail 3-43. A section of a brick wall and metal decking with light-weight concrete. The decking is supported by a continuous ledger angle which is bolted to the wall. The size and spacing of the angle and bolts are determined by calculation. The slab diaphragm stress is transferred to the wall by the reinforcing dowels. The horizontal bars act as a bond beam in the wall.

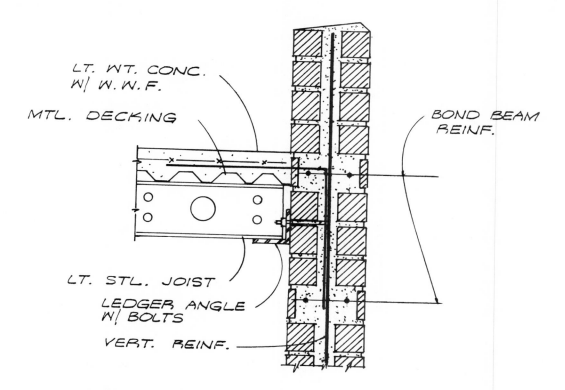

LT. WT. CONC.
W/ W.W.F.

MTL. DECKING

BOND BEAM
REINF.

LT. STL. JOIST

LEDGER ANGLE
W/ BOLTS

VERT. REINF.

Detail 3-44. A section of a brick wall, light steel joists, a continuous ledger angle, and metal decking with light-weight concrete. The steel joists bear on and are welded to the ledger angle which is bolted to the wall. The size and spacing of the angle and bolts are determined by calculation. The light-weight concrete slab is connected to the wall with reinforcing dowels. The horizontal reinforcing bars act as a bond beam in the wall.

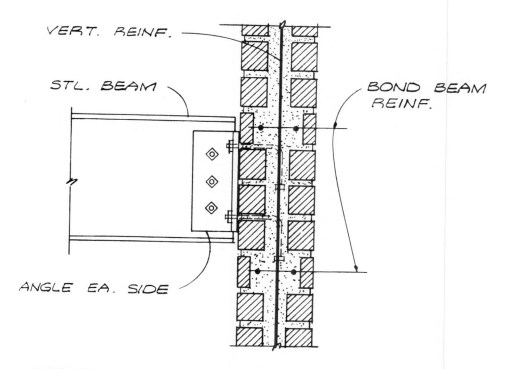

VERT. REINF.

STL. BEAM

BOND BEAM
REINF.

ANGLE EA. SIDE

Detail 3-45. A section of a brick wall supporting a steel beam. The steel beam reaction is transferred to the wall through clip angles bolted to each side of the beam web and into the wall. The size of the angles and the bolts are determined by calculation.

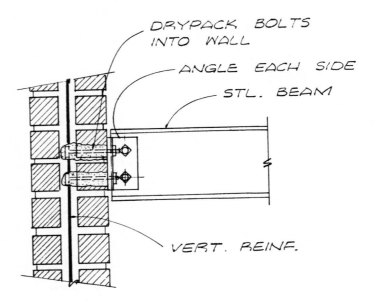

DRYPACK BOLTS
INTO WALL

ANGLE EACH SIDE

STL. BEAM

VERT. REINF.

Detail 3-46. A section of a brick wall supporting a steel beam. The steel beam reaction is transferred to the wall through clip angles bolted to each side of the beam web and into the wall. The size of the angles and the bolts are determined by calculation. This detail is used to connect steel beams to existing walls.

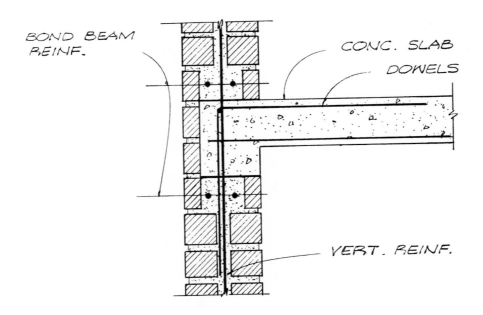

BOND BEAM
REINF.

CONC. SLAB

DOWELS

VERT. REINF.

Detail 3-47. A section of a brick wall and a poured concrete slab. The slab is cast into the wall for vertical support. The slab diaphragm stress is transferred to the wall by the reinforcing dowels.

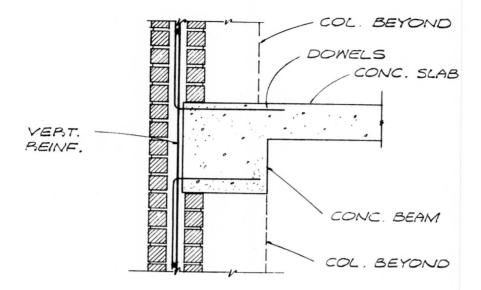

Detail 3-48. A section of a brick wall, a concrete slab, and a concrete spandrel beam. The spandrel beam is cast into the wall as shown. The wall is tied to the beam with reinforcing dowels. The beam and slab reinforcement is not shown.

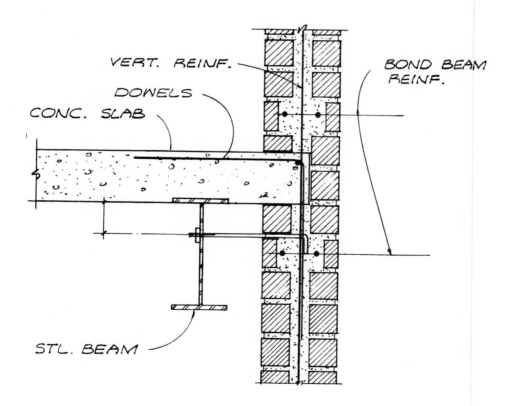

Detail 3-49. A section of a brick wall and a concrete slab. The slab is supported by a steel beam. The slab diaphragm stress is transferred to the wall by reinforcing dowels. Equally spaced rods between the web of the steel beam and the brick wall restrain the beam laterally. The horizontal reinforcing bars act as a bond beam in the wall.

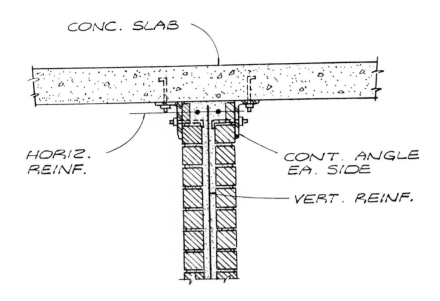

CONC. SLAB

HORIZ. REINF.

CONT. ANGLE EA. SIDE

VERT. REINF.

Detail 3-50(a). A section of the top of a brick wall connected to a poured concrete slab. The wall is connected to the slab by continuous angles on each side of the wall. The angles are bolted to the slab and to the wall as shown. The size and spacing of the bolts are determined by calculation.

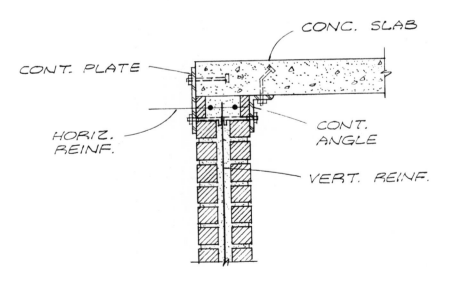

CONC. SLAB

CONT. PLATE

HORIZ. REINF.

CONT. ANGLE

VERT. REINF.

Detail 3-50(b). A section of the top of a brick wall connected to the edge of a poured concrete slab. The wall is connected to the slab by a continuous angle and a flat plate. The angle and plate are bolted to the slab and to the wall as shown. The size and spacing of the bolts are determined by calculation.

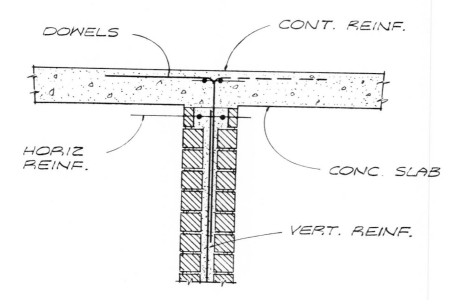

Detail 3-51(a). A section of a concrete slab supported by a brick wall. The slab is connected to the wall by reinforcing dowels bent in alternate directions as shown. Two horizontal reinforcing bars are added at the top of the wall and at the top of the slab. The dowels lap 30 bar diameters in the masonry and 40 bar diameters in the concrete or not less than 24″.

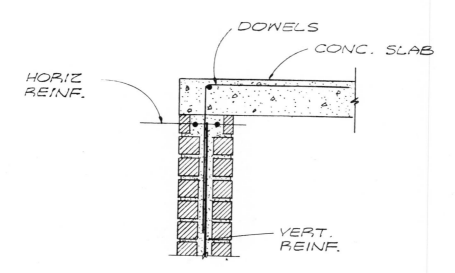

Detail 3-51(b). A section of a concrete slab supported by a brick wall. The slab is connected to the wall by reinforcing dowels as shown. Continuous horizontal reinforcing bars are added at the top of the wall and at the top of the slab. The dowels lap 30 bar diameters in the masonry and 40 bar diameters in the concrete or not less than 24″.

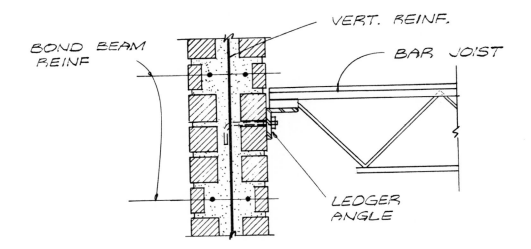

Detail 3-52. A section of a brick wall, metal decking, and steel bar joists. The bar joists are supported by and welded to a continuous ledger angle. The ledger angle is bolted to the brick wall. The size and spacing of the ledger bolts are determined by calculation. The concrete diaphragm stress is transferred to the wall by reinforcing dowels. The horizontal bars act as a bond beam in the wall.

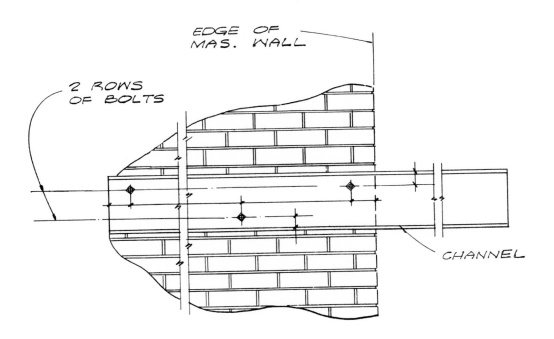

Detail 3-53. An elevation of a steel channel bolted to and cantilevered from the face of a masonry wall. The channel web is bolted to the wall as shown. The size and spacing of the bolts are determined by calculation.

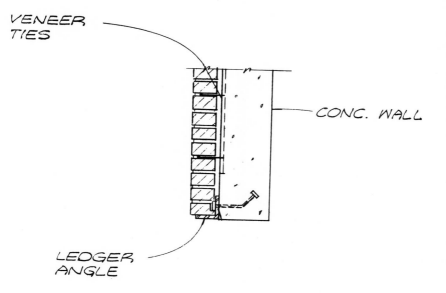

VENEER TIES

CONC. WALL

LEDGER ANGLE

Detail 3-54. A section of a concrete wall lintel supporting a brick veneer. The veneer is supported vertically by a continuous angle bolted to the concrete as shown. The size and spacing of the angle bolts are determined by calculation and by the local building code.

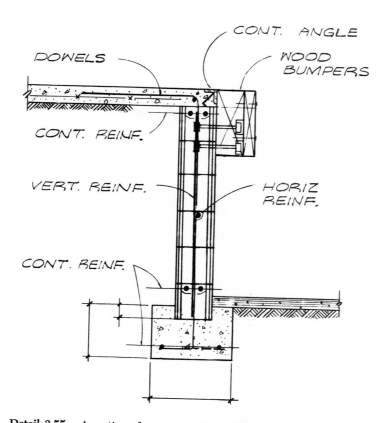

DOWELS

CONT. ANGLE

WOOD BUMPERS

CONT. REINF.

VERT. REINF.

HORIZ REINF.

CONT. REINF.

Detail 3-55. A section of a concrete block masonry loading dock wall. The wall is connected to the concrete slab on grade with reinforcing dowels. The vertical and horizontal reinforcing steel in the wall is determined by calculation. The depth and width of the wall footing depend on the soil conditions. The wood bumpers are bolted to the face of the masonry wall. The continuous angle at the top of the concrete slab prevents the concrete from spalling.

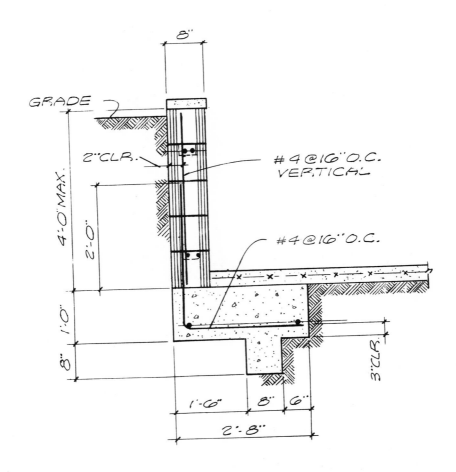

Detail 3-56(a). Stem height 4'0".

Detail 3-56. Sections of concrete block masonry retaining walls with soil at the exterior face of the stem. The walls retain a flat grade with no surcharge. The wall dimensions and the reinforcing steel size and spacing are determined by calculation. All concrete block masonry cells are filled with grout. Two #4 horizontal continuous reinforcing bars are placed at the top and the bottom of the wall stem. The minimum horizontal reinforcing in the stem wall and the footing is #4 at 24" o.c. The masonry head joint is omitted at 32" o.c. at the first course as a weep hole. The cement cap at the top of the wall is optional. The walls are designed for 30 lb per cu ft equivalent fluid pressure and a maximum soil bearing pressure of 1500 lb per sq ft. The resultant of the forces passes through the middle $\frac{1}{3}$ of the wall footing. The walls are designed to resist sliding and overturning. The overturning safety factor is 1.5. The concrete design stress is $f'c = 2000$ psi. The masonry design stress is $f'm = 600$ psi.

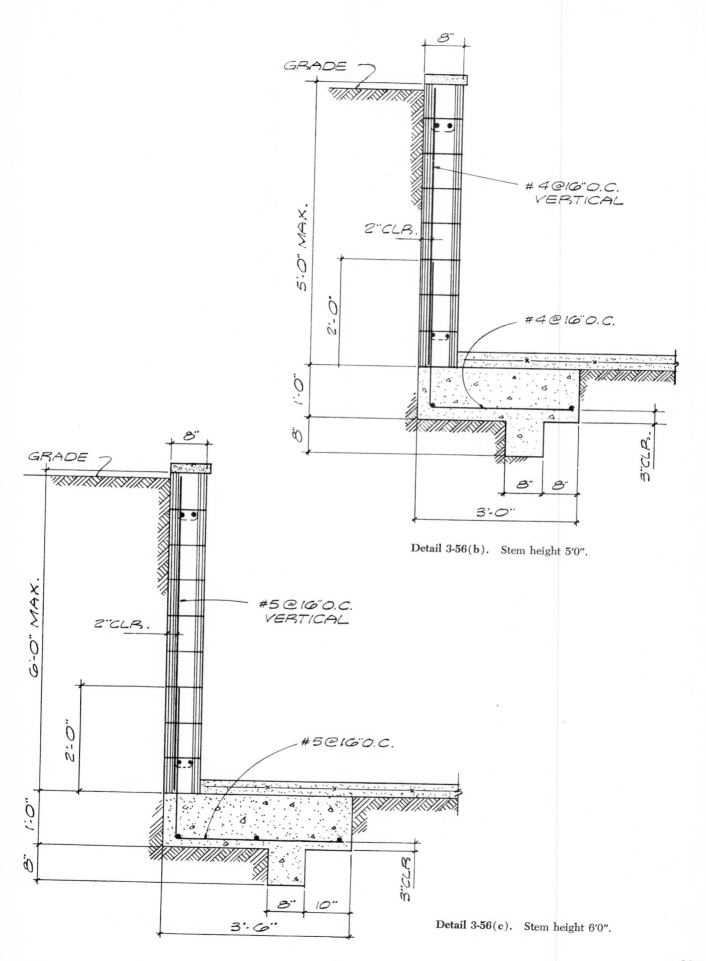

GRADE

#4@16"O.C.
VERTICAL

2"CLR.

#4@16"O.C.

5'-0" MAX.

2'-0"

1'-0"

8"

8"

8"

8"

3"CLR.

3'-0"

Detail 3-56(b). Stem height 5'0".

GRADE

#5@16"O.C.
VERTICAL

2"CLR.

#5@16"O.C.

6'-0" MAX.

2'-0"

1'-0"

8"

8"

10"

3"CLR.

3'-6"

Detail 3-56(c). Stem height 6'0".

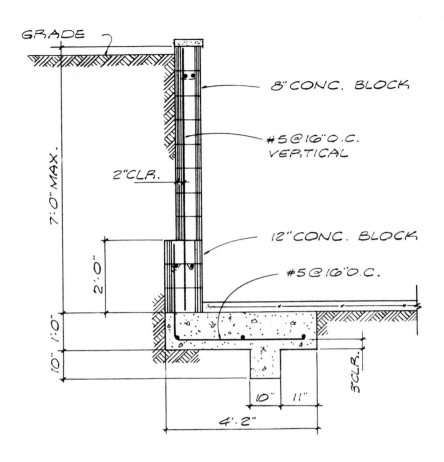

GRADE

8"CONC. BLOCK

#5@16"O.C.
VERTICAL

2"CLR.

12"CONC. BLOCK

#5@16"O.C.

7'-0" MAX.

2'-0"

1'-0"

10"   11"

4'-2"

3"CLR.

Detail 3-56(d).   Stem height 7'0".

GRADE

8" CONC. BLOCK

2"CLR.

#4@8"O.C.
VERTICAL

12"CONC. BLOCK

#4@8"O.C.

8'-0" MAX.

2'-0"

1'-0"   1'-0"

1'-0"   1'-2"

3"CLR.

5'-0"

Detail 3-56(e).   Stem height 8'0".

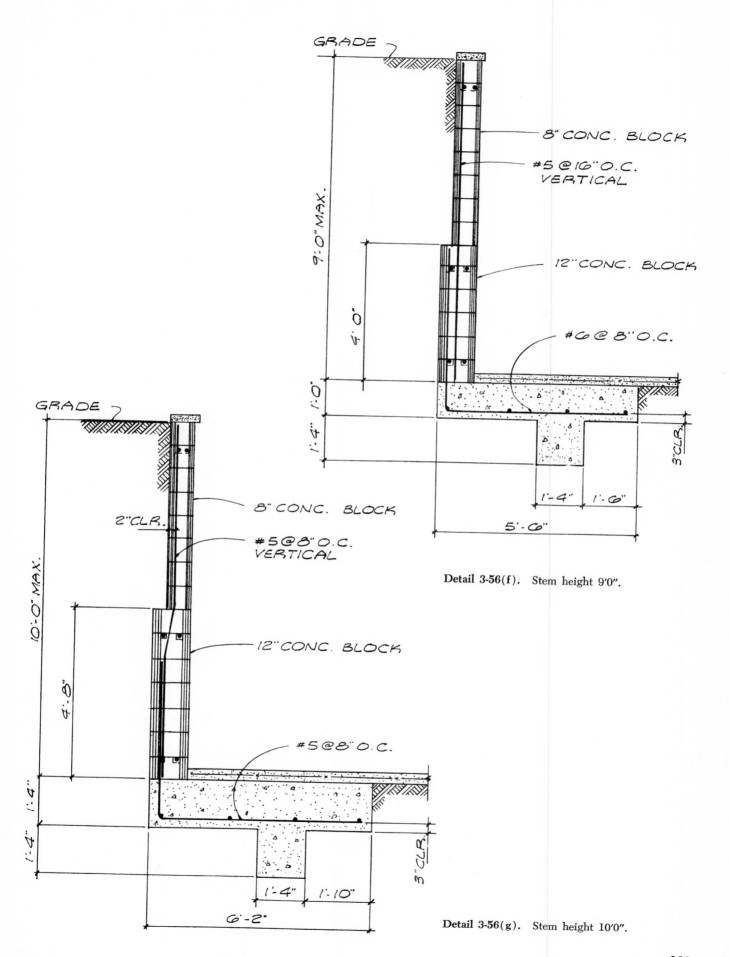

GRADE

8" CONC. BLOCK

#5 @ 16" O.C.
VERTICAL

12" CONC. BLOCK

#6 @ 8" O.C.

9'-0" MAX.

4'-0"

1'-0"

1'-4"

3" CLR.

1'-4"   1'-6"

5'-6"

Detail 3-56(f). Stem height 9'0".

GRADE

2" CLR.

8" CONC. BLOCK

#5 @ 8" O.C.
VERTICAL

12" CONC. BLOCK

#5 @ 8" O.C.

10'-0" MAX.

4'-8"

1'-4"

1'-4"

3" CLR.

1'-4"   1'-10"

6'-2"

Detail 3-56(g). Stem height 10'0".

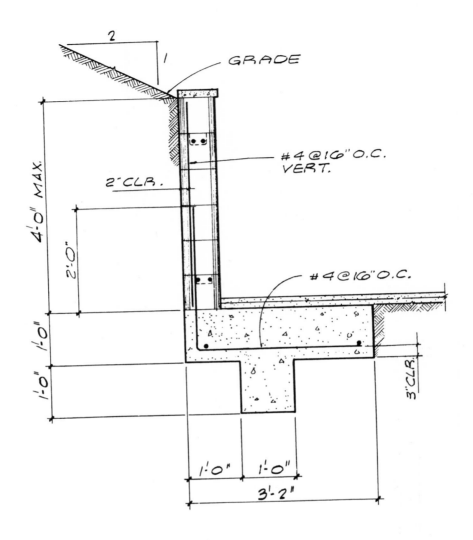

Detail 3-57(a). Stem height 4'0".

Detail 3-57. Sections of concrete block masonry retaining walls with soil at the exterior face of the stem. The wall retains a sloping grade of two horizontal to one vertical and no surcharge. The wall dimensions and reinforcing steel size and spacing are determined by calculation. All concrete block masonry cells are filled with grout. Two #4 horizontal continuous reinforcing bars are placed at the top and the bottom of the wall stem. The minimum horizontal reinforcing in the stem wall and the footing is #4 at 24" o.c. The masonry head joint is omitted at 32" o.c. at the first course as a weep hole. The cement cap at the top of the wall is optional. The walls are designed for 43 lb per cu ft equivalent fluid pressure and a maximum soil bearing pressure of 1500 lb per sq ft. The resultant of the forces passes through the middle $\frac{1}{3}$ of the wall footing. The walls are designed to resist sliding and overturning. The overturning safety factor is 1.5. The concrete design stress is $f'c = 2000$ psi. The masonry design stress is $f'm = 600$ psi.

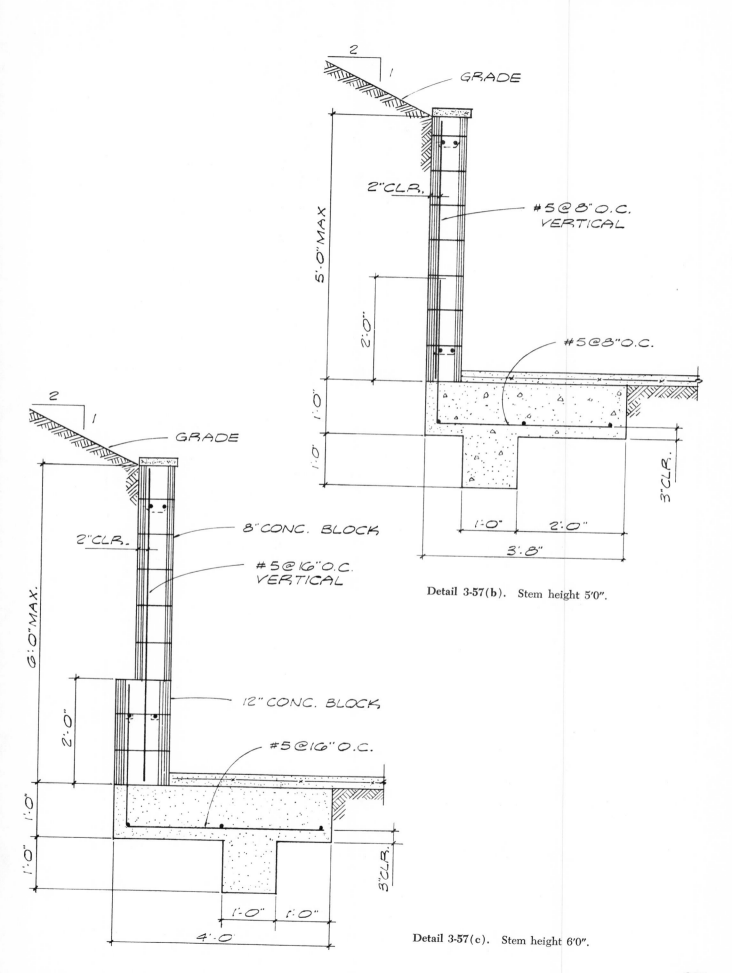

2

1

GRADE

5'-0" MAX.

2" CLR.

2'-0"

1'-0"

1'-0"

#5 @ 8" O.C. VERTICAL

#5 @ 8" O.C.

3" CLR.

1'-0"

2'-0"

3'-8"

Detail 3-57(b). Stem height 5'0".

2

1

GRADE

8" CONC. BLOCK

2" CLR.

#5 @ 16" O.C. VERTICAL

12" CONC. BLOCK

#5 @ 16" O.C.

6'-0" MAX.

2'-0"

1'-0"

1'-0"

3" CLR.

1'-0"

1'-0"

4'-0"

Detail 3-57(c). Stem height 6'0".

231

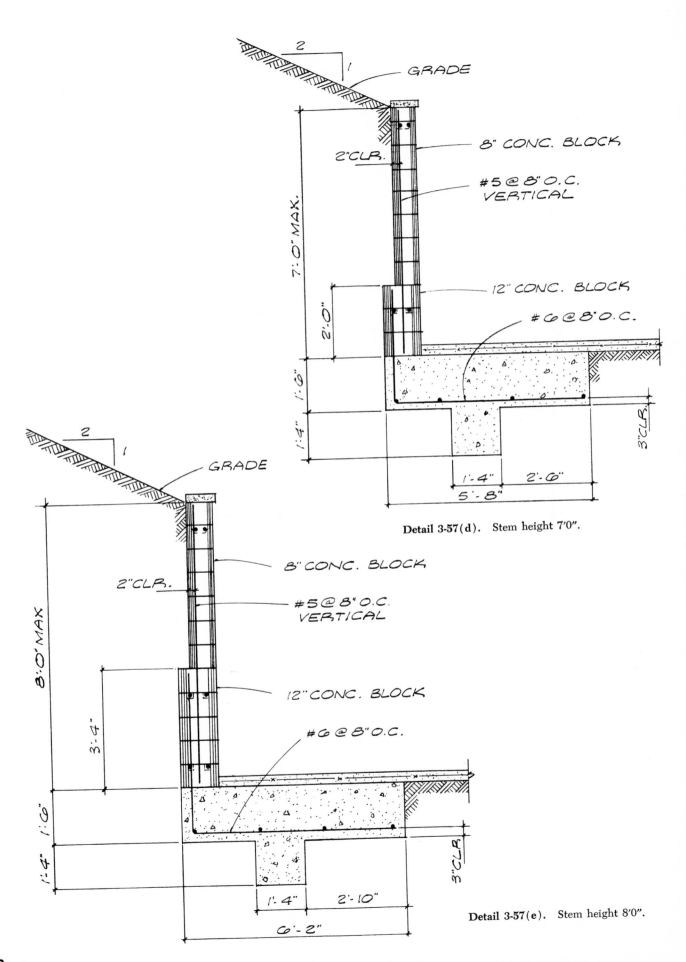

GRADE

8" CONC. BLOCK

2"CLR.

#5 @ 8" O.C.
VERTICAL

7'-0" MAX.

2'-0"

12" CONC. BLOCK

#6 @ 8" O.C.

1'-6"

1'-4"

3"CLR.

1'-4"   2'-6"

5'-8"

Detail 3-57(d). Stem height 7'0".

GRADE

8" CONC. BLOCK

2"CLR.

#5 @ 8" O.C.
VERTICAL

8'-0" MAX

3'-4"

12" CONC. BLOCK

#6 @ 8" O.C.

1'-6"

1'-4"

3"CLR.

1'-4"   2'-10"

6'-2"

Detail 3-57(e). Stem height 8'0".

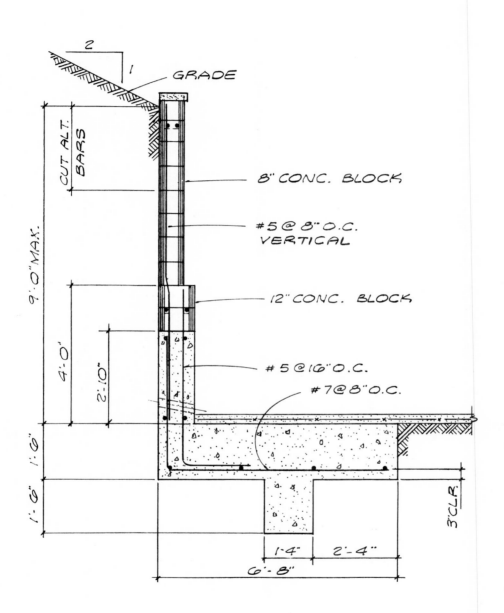

GRADE

2

1

CUT ALT. BARS

9'-0" MAX.

4'-0'

2'-0"

1'-0" 1'-0"

8" CONC. BLOCK

#5 @ 8" O.C.
VERTICAL

12" CONC. BLOCK

#5 @ 16" O.C.

#7 @ 8" O.C.

3" CLR.

1'-4"   2'-4"

6'-8"

Detail 3-57(f).   Stem height 9'0".

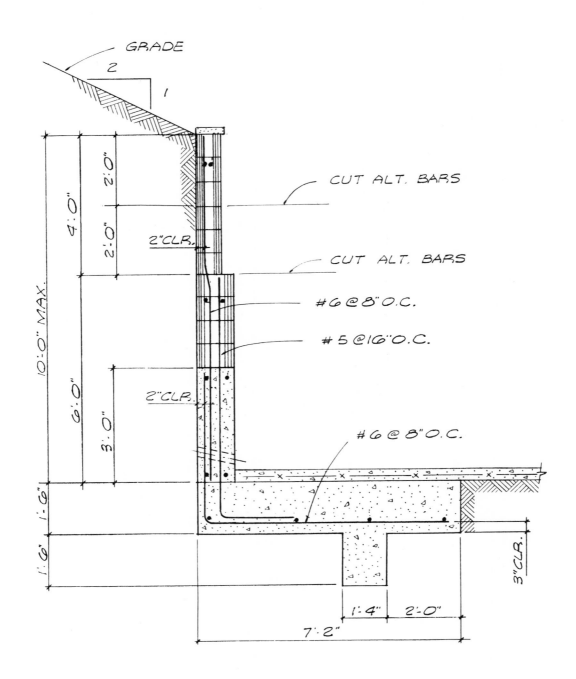

GRADE

2

1

CUT ALT. BARS

2"CLR.

CUT ALT. BARS

#6 @ 8" O.C.

#5 @ 16" O.C.

2"CLR.

#6 @ 8" O.C.

3"CLR.

4'-0"

2'-0"

2'-0"

10'-0" MAX.

6'-0"

3'-0"

1'-9"

1'-9"

1'-4"   2'-0"

7'-2"

Detail 3-57(g).   Stem height 10'0".

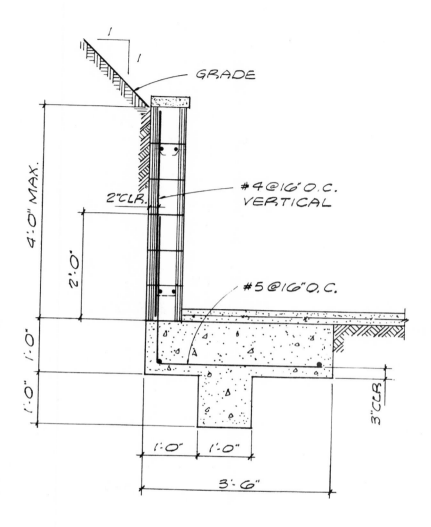

Detail 3-58(a). Stem height 4'0".

Detail 3-58. Sections of concrete block masonry retaining walls with soil at the exterior face of the stem. The wall retains a sloping grade with one horizontal to one vertical and no surcharge. The wall dimensions and reinforcing steel size and spacing are determined by calculation. All concrete block masonry cells are filled with grout. Two #4 horizontal continuous reinforcing bars are placed at the top and the bottom of the wall stem. The minimum horizontal reinforcing in the stem wall and the footing is #4 at 24" o.c. The masonry head joint is omitted at 32" o.c. at the first course as a weep hole. The cement cap at the top of the wall is optional. The walls are designed for 80 lb per cu ft equivalent fluid pressure and a maximum soil bearing pressure of 1500 lb per sq ft. The resultant of the forces passes through the middle ⅓ of the wall footing. The walls are designed to resist sliding and overturning. The overturning safety factor is 1.5. The concrete design stress is $f'c = 2000$ psi. The masonry design stress is $f'm = 600$ psi.

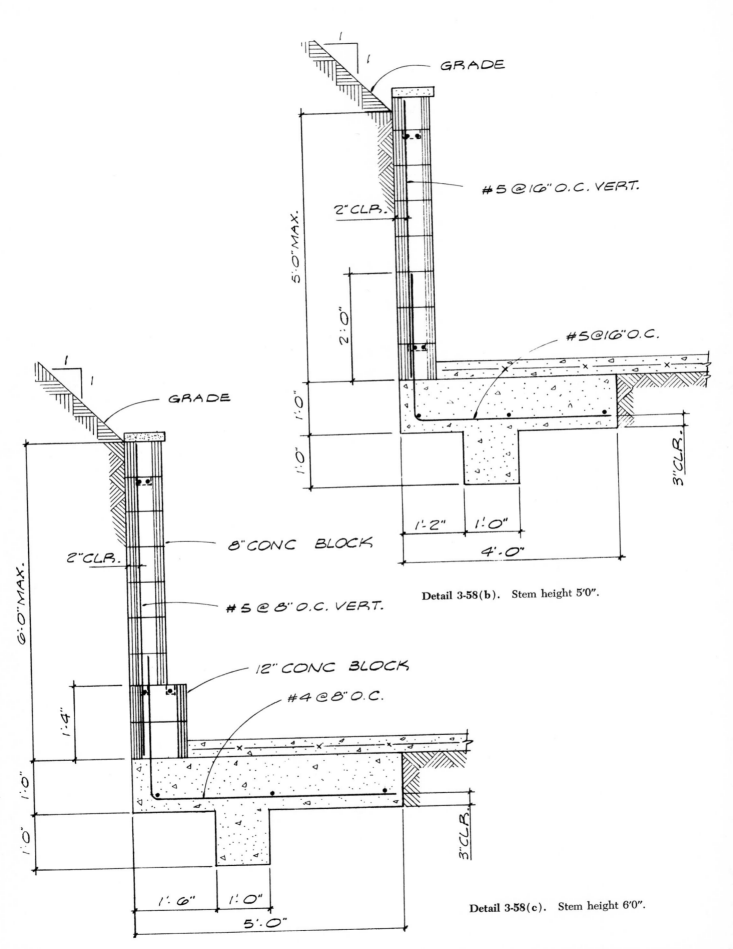

GRADE

#5 @ 16" O.C. VERT.

2" CLR.

5'-0" MAX.

2'-0"

#5 @ 16" O.C.

1'-0"

1'-0"

3" CLR.

1'-2"   1'-0"

4'-0"

Detail 3-58(b). Stem height 5'0".

GRADE

8" CONC BLOCK

2" CLR.

6'-0" MAX.

#5 @ 8" O.C. VERT.

12" CONC BLOCK

#4 @ 8" O.C.

1'-4"

1'-0"

1'-0"

3" CLR.

1'-6"   1'-0"

5'-0"

Detail 3-58(c). Stem height 6'0".

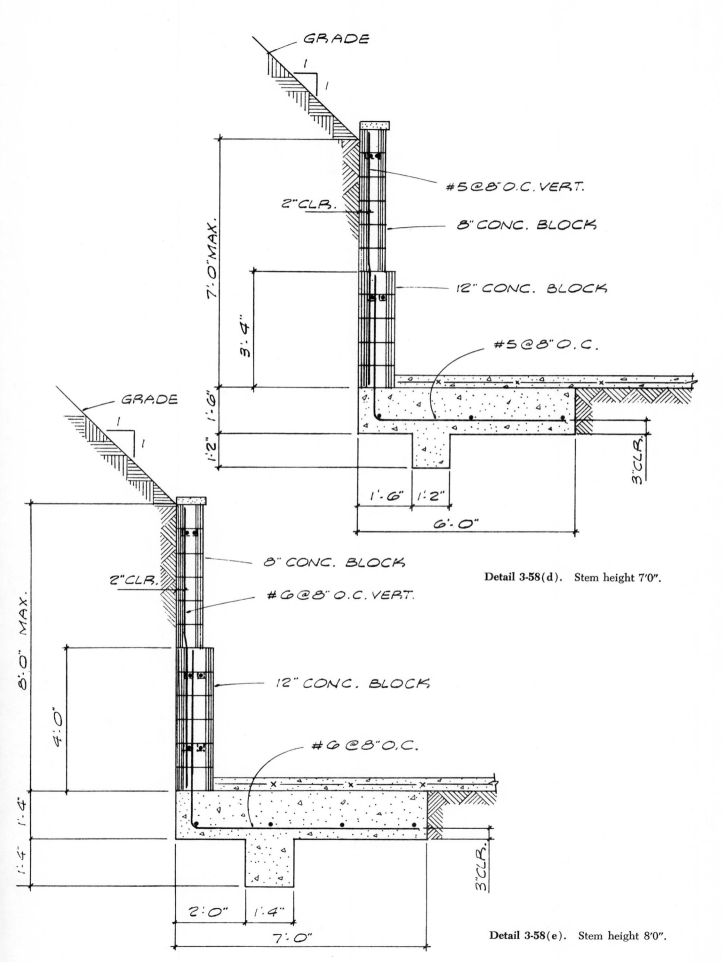

GRADE

#5@8"O.C.VERT.

2"CLR.

8" CONC. BLOCK

12" CONC. BLOCK

#5@8"O.C.

7'-0"MAX.

3'-4"

1'-6"

1'-2"

1'-6"

1'-2"

6'-0"

3"CLR.

Detail 3-58(d). Stem height 7'0".

GRADE

8" CONC. BLOCK

2"CLR.

#6@8"O.C.VERT.

12" CONC. BLOCK

#6@8"O.C.

8'-0" MAX.

4'-0"

1'-4"

1'-4"

2'-0"

1'-4"

7'-0"

3"CLR.

Detail 3-58(e). Stem height 8'0".

237

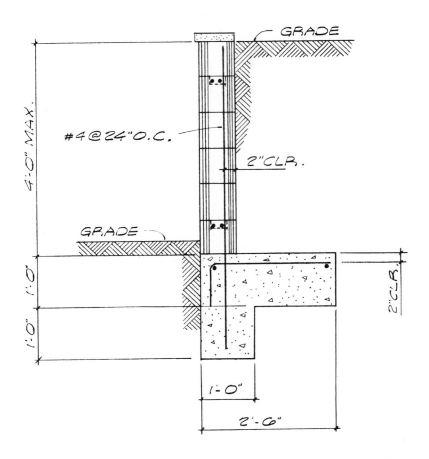

GRADE

#4 @ 24" O.C.

2" CLR.

4'-0" MAX.

GRADE

1'-0"

1'-0"

2" CLR.

1'-0"

2'-6"

Detail 3-59(a). Stem height 4'0".

Detail 3-59. Sections of concrete block masonry retaining walls with soil at the interior face of the stem. The walls retain a flat grade with no surcharge. The wall dimensions and reinforcing steel size and spacing are determined by calculation. All concrete block masonry cells are filled with grout. Two #4 horizontal continuous reinforcing bars are placed at the top and the bottom of the wall stem. The minimum horizontal reinforcing in the stem wall and the footing is #4 at 24" o.c. The masonry head joint is omitted at 32" o.c. at the first course as a weep hole. The cement cap at the top of the wall is optional. The walls are designed for 30 lb per cu ft equivalent fluid pressure and a maximum soil bearing pressure of 1500 lb per sq ft. The resultant of the forces passes through the middle ⅓ of the wall footing. The walls are designed to resist sliding and overturning. The overturning safety factor is 1.5. The concrete design stress is $f'c = 2000$ psi. The masonry design stress is $f'm = 600$ psi.

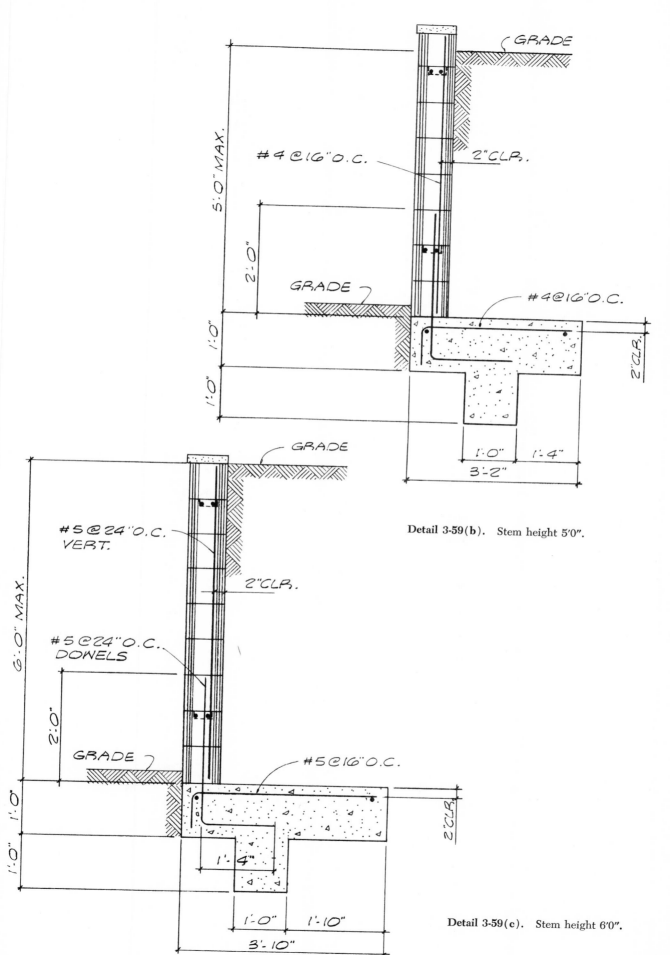

Detail 3-59(b). Stem height 5′0″.

Detail 3-59(c). Stem height 6′0″.

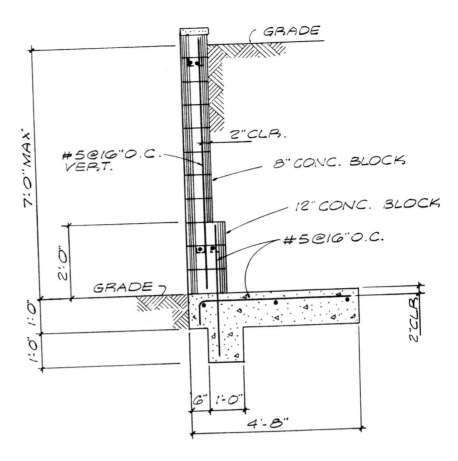

#5@16"O.C. VERT.

2"CLR.

8" CONC. BLOCK

12" CONC. BLOCK

#5@16"O.C.

GRADE

GRADE

2"CLR.

7'-0" MAX'

2'-0"

1'-0"

1'-0"

6"

1'-0"

4'-8"

Detail 3-59(d). Stem height 7'0".

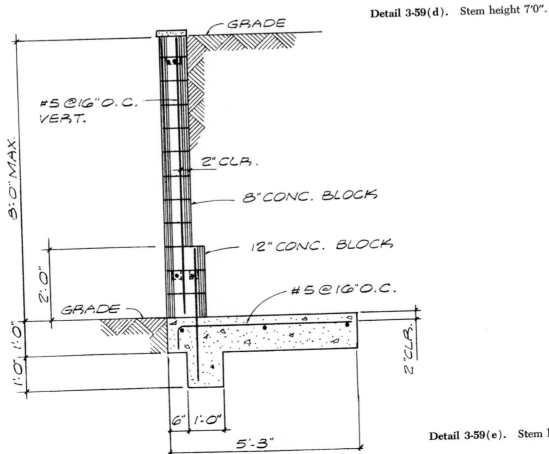

GRADE

#5@16"O.C. VERT.

2"CLR.

8"CONC. BLOCK

12"CONC. BLOCK

#5@16"O.C.

GRADE

2"CLR.

8'-0" MAX.

2'-0"

1'-0"

1'-0"

6"

1'-0"

5'-3"

Detail 3-59(e). Stem height 8'0".

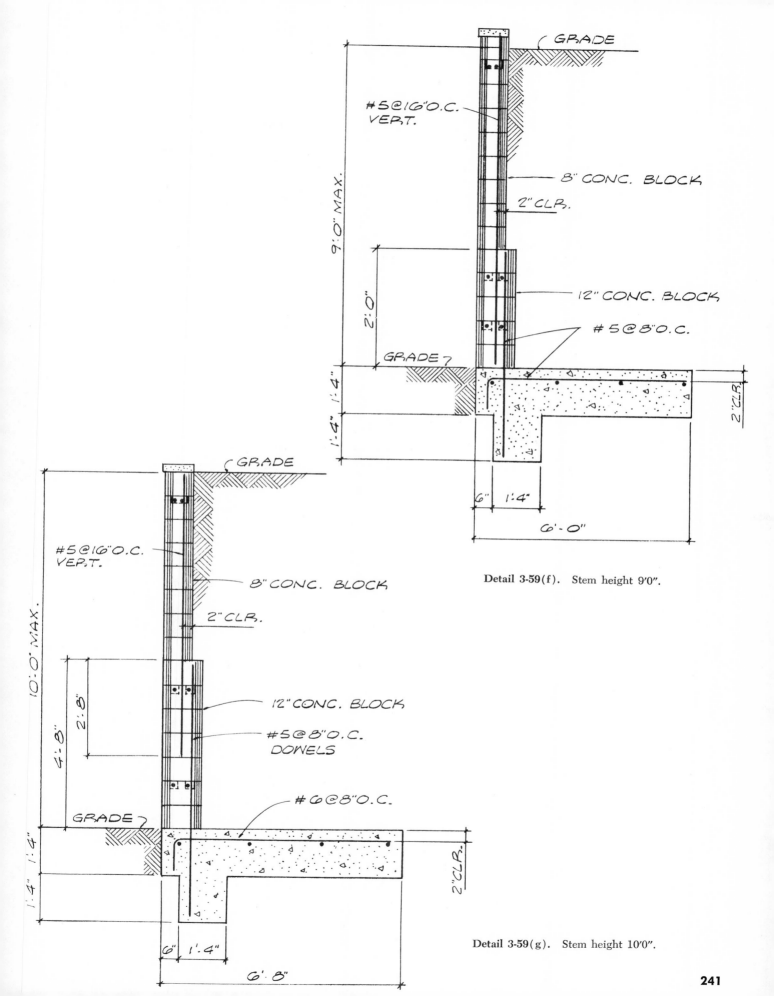

#5@16"O.C.
VERT.

8" CONC. BLOCK

2" CLR.

GRADE

9'-0" MAX.

2'-0"

1'-4" 1'-4"

12" CONC. BLOCK

#5@8"O.C.

2" CLR.

6" 1'-4"

6'-0"

Detail 3-59(f). Stem height 9'0".

GRADE

#5@16"O.C.
VERT.

8" CONC. BLOCK

2" CLR.

10'-0" MAX.

4'-8"

2'-8"

12" CONC. BLOCK

#5@8"O.C.
DOWELS

GRADE

#6@8"O.C.

2" CLR.

1'-4" 1'-4"

6" 1'-4"

6'-8"

Detail 3-59(g). Stem height 10'0".

241

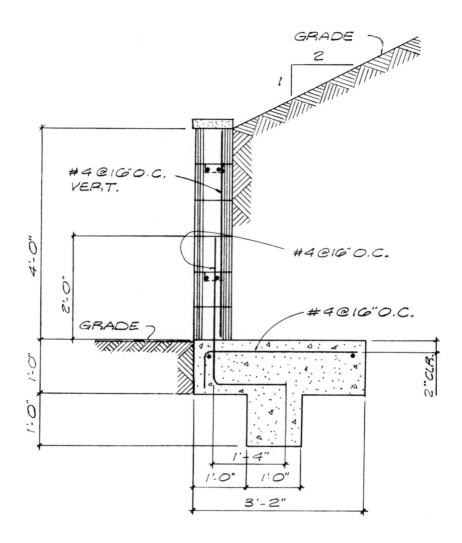

Detail 3-60(a). Stem height 4'0".

Detail 3-60. Sections of concrete block masonry retaining walls with soil at the interior face of the stem. The wall retains a sloping grade of two horizontal to one vertical and no surcharge. The wall dimensions and reinforcing steel size and spacing are determined by calculation. All concrete block masonry cells are filled with grout. Two #4 horizontal continuous reinforcing bars are placed at the top and the bottom of the wall stem. The minimum horizontal reinforcing in the stem wall and the footing is #4 at 24" o.c. The masonry head joint is omitted at 32" o.c. at the first course as a weep hole. The cement cap at the top of the wall is optional. The walls are designed for 43 lb per cu ft equivalent fluid pressure and a maximum soil bearing pressure of 1500 lb per sq. ft. The resultant of the forces passes through the middle ⅓ of the wall footing. The walls are designed to resist sliding and overturning. The overturning safety factor is 1.5. The concrete design stress is $f'c = 2000$ psi. The masonry design stress is $f'm = 600$ psi.

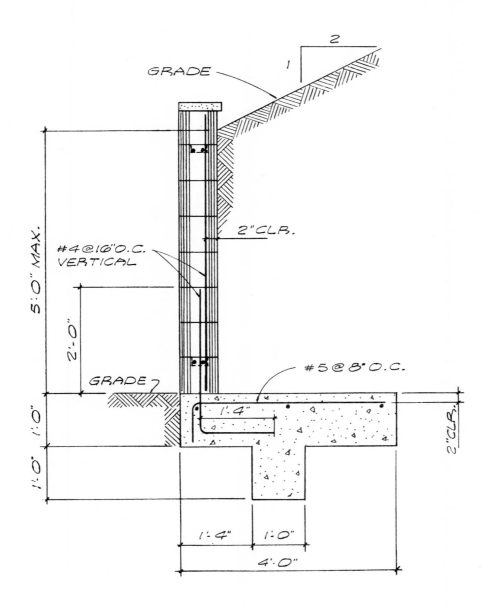

GRADE

2

1

5'-0" MAX.

#4 @ 16" O.C.
VERTICAL

2" CLR.

2'-0"

GRADE

#5 @ 8" O.C.

1'-4"

2" CLR.

1'-0"

1'-0"

1'-4"

1'-0"

4'-0"

Detail 3-60(b). Stem height 5'0".

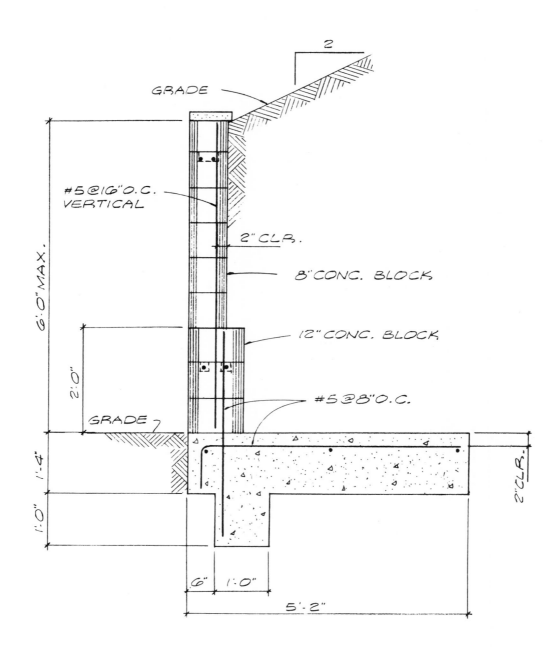

GRADE

2

#5@16"O.C.
VERTICAL

2" CLR.

8" CONC. BLOCK

12" CONC. BLOCK

#5@8"O.C.

6'-0" MAX.

2'-0"

GRADE

1'-4"

1'-0"

2" CLR.

6"

1'-0"

5'-2"

Detail 3-60(c). Stem height 6'0".

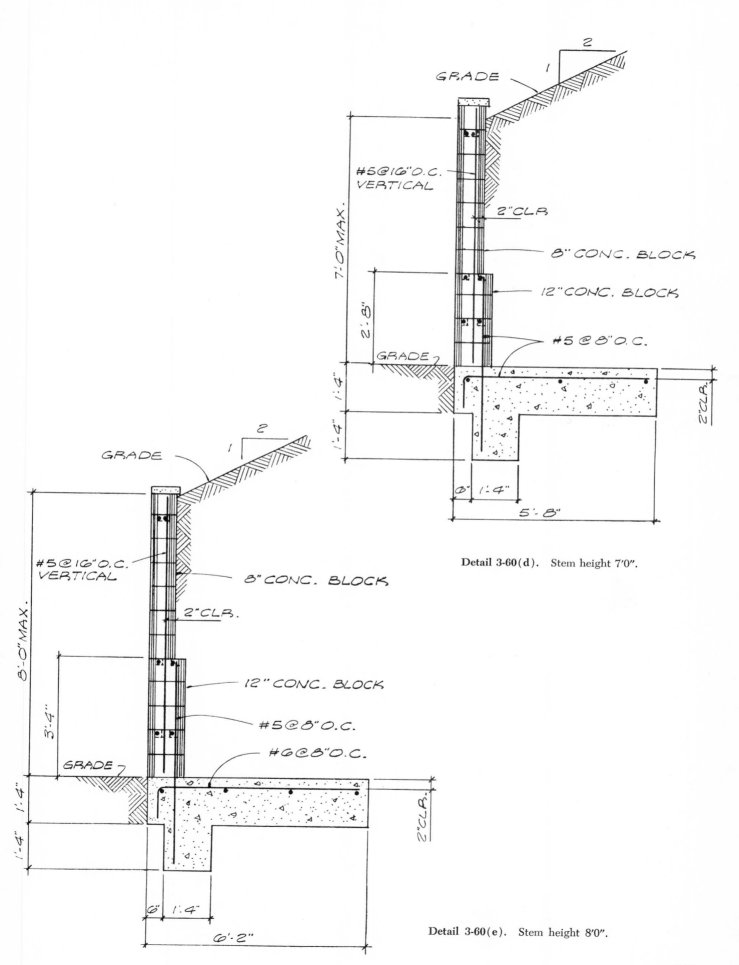

GRADE

2

1

#5@16"O.C.
VERTICAL

2"CLR.

8" CONC. BLOCK

12" CONC. BLOCK

#5@8"O.C.

7'-0"MAX.

2'-8"

GRADE

1'-4"

1'-4"

2"CLR.

6"

1:4"

5'-8"

Detail 3-60(d).   Stem height 7'0".

GRADE

2

1

#5@16"O.C.
VERTICAL

8" CONC. BLOCK

2"CLR.

12" CONC. BLOCK

#5@8"O.C.

#6@8"O.C.

8'-0"MAX.

3'-4"

GRADE

1'-4"

1'-4"

2"CLR.

6"

1:4"

6'-2"

Detail 3-60(e).   Stem height 8'0".

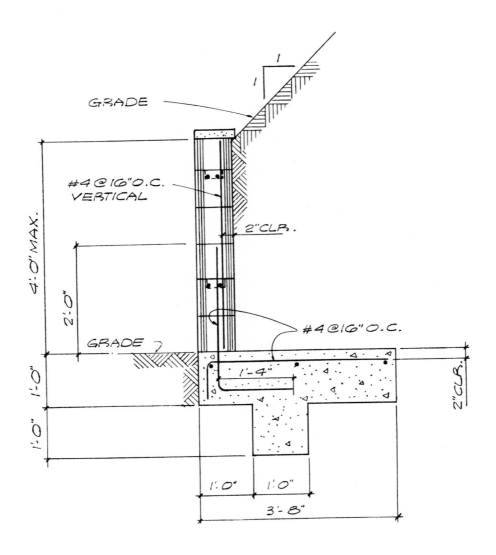

GRADE

#4 @ 16" O.C.
VERTICAL

2" CLR.

4'0" MAX.

2'0"

GRADE

#4 @ 16" O.C.

1'-4"

2" CLR.

1'0" 1'0"

1'0"

1'0" 1'0"

3'-8"

Detail 3-61(a). Stem height 4'0".

Detail 3-61. Sections of concrete block masonry retaining walls with soil at the interior face of the stem. The wall retains a sloping grade with one horizontal to one vertical and no surcharge. The wall dimensions and reinforcing steel size and spacing are determined by calculation. All concrete block masonry cells are filled with grout. Two #4 horizontal continuous reinforcing bars are placed at the top and the bottom of the wall stem. The minimum horizontal reinforcing in the stem wall and the footing is #4 at 24" o.c. The masonry head joint is omitted at 32" o.c. at the first course as a weep hole. The cement cap at the top of the wall is optional. The walls are designed for 80 lb per cu ft equivalent fluid pressure and a maximum soil bearing pressure of 1500 lb per sq. ft. The resultant of the forces passes through the middle $\frac{1}{3}$ of the wall footing. The walls are designed to resist sliding and overturning. The overturning safety factor is 1.5. The concrete design stress is $f'c = 2000$ psi. The masonry design stress is $f'm = 600$ psi.

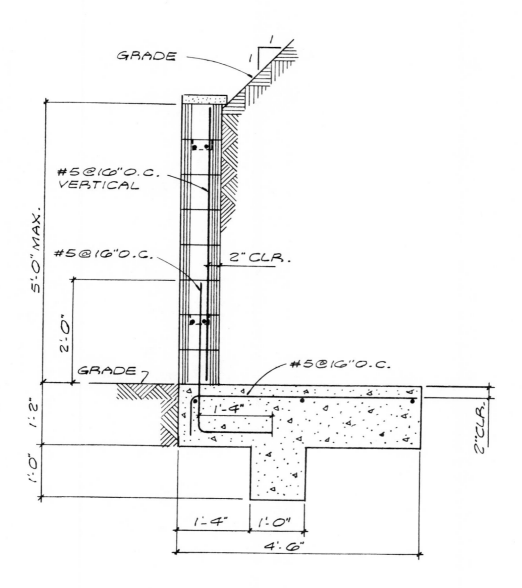

Detail 3-61(b). Stem height 5′0″.

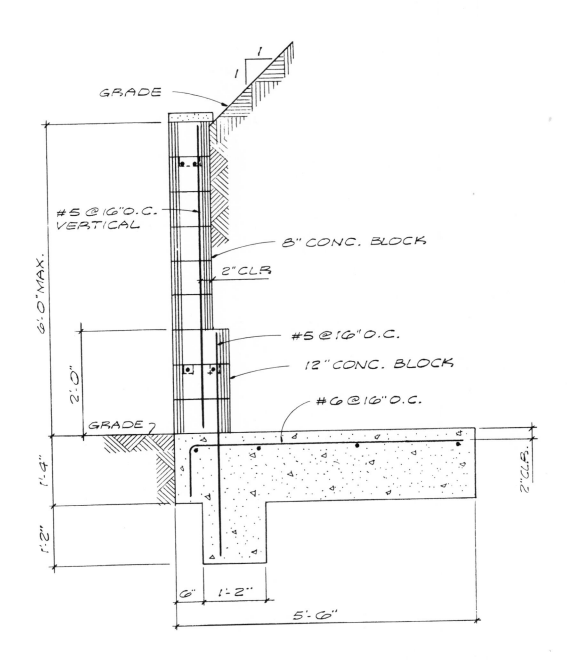

GRADE

#5 @ 16"O.C.
VERTICAL

8" CONC. BLOCK

2" CLR.

6'.O"MAX.

2'-O"

#5 @ 16"O.C.

12" CONC. BLOCK

#6 @ 16"O.C.

GRADE

2" CLR.

1'-4"

1'-2"

6"   1'-2"

5'-6"

Detail 3-61(c).   Stem height 6'0".

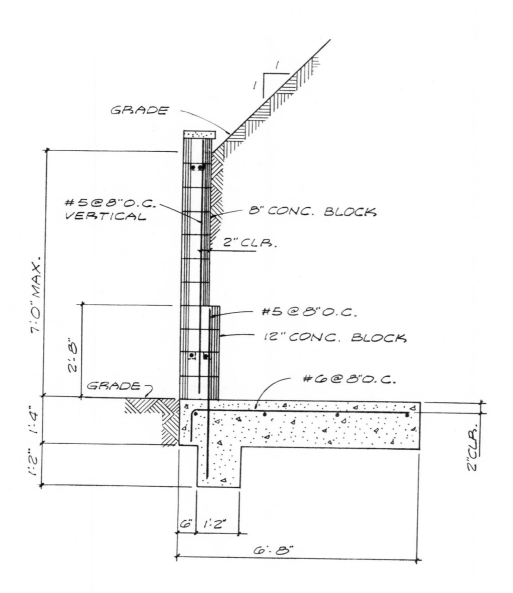

GRADE

#5@8"O.C.
VERTICAL

8" CONC. BLOCK

2" CLR.

7'0" MAX.

2'8"

#5@8"O.C.

12" CONC. BLOCK

#6@8"O.C.

GRADE

1'4"

1'2"

2"CLR.

6" 1'2"

6'8"

Detail 3-61(d).   Stem height 7'0".

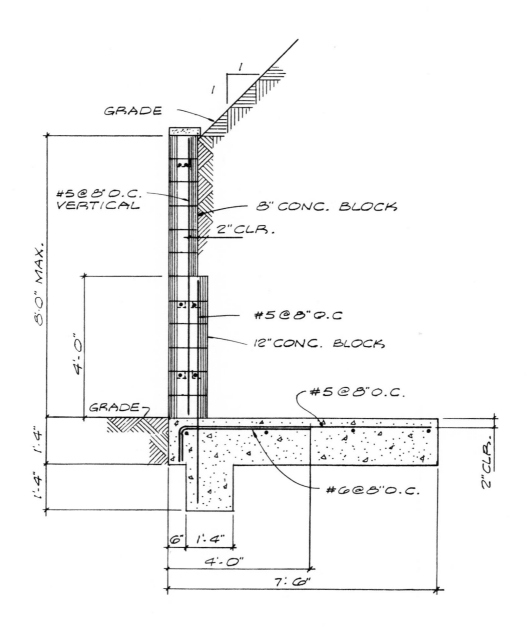

GRADE

#5@8"O.C.
VERTICAL

8" CONC. BLOCK

2" CLR.

#5@8"O.C

12" CONC. BLOCK

#5@8"O.C.

GRADE

#6@8"O.C.

2" CLR.

8'-0" MAX.

4'-0"

1'-4"

1'-4"

6" 1'-4"

4'-0"

7'-6"

Detail 3-61(e). Stem height 8'0".

4

STEEL

This chapter presents the drawings of the various alternate methods of connecting the component members of a building's structural steel frame. Each type of connection and its combinations of different size steel members is detailed and presented individually. The details, arranged in the sequence of their use in building construction, are classed in the following general categories: column base plates, column base connections, simple beam and column connections, rigid-frame beam and column connections, steel canopy details, column splices, composite steel beams and concrete slabs, steel member fire protection, light-steel stud and joist construction, steel stair details, and miscellaneous clevis connections.

The type and strength of structural steel used in the details shown in this chapter is not designated. Manufacturers and fabricators of structural steel rolled sections are required to conform to the American Institute of Steel construction specifications, which outline the standards for design, fabrication, and erection of steel structures. The type of steel used in construction is designated by an A.S.T.M. standards number. The "Manual of Steel Construction," compiled and published by the A.I.S.C., gives the A.S.T.M. designation number for each type of structural steel and the respective allowable working stresses (tension, compression, or shear)

for the method of use. Steel designated as A.S.T.M. Spec. No. A7 and A.S.T.M. Spec. No. A373 has a specific yield point stress of 33,000 psi and an allowable working stress in tension or compression from bending of 20,000 psi. A7 steel was the most widely used steel in the construction of buildings until recently. Steel designated as A.S.T.M. Spec. No. A36 is currently the most widely used steel since it has a higher specific yield point stress of 36,000 psi and a higher allowable working stress in tension or compression of 24,000 psi. The allowable working stresses from bending also depend on the shape of the structural section (a compact or noncompact section, determined by the width-to-thickness ratio of the compression flange) and the laterally unbraced length of the compression flange of a beam. The A.I.S.C. specified allowable working stresses for tension or compression from bending is equal to $0.66 f_y$ (f_y being the yield point stress of the steel as specified by the A.S.T.M.). High strength low-alloy steels are also used for structural steel members. This type of steel is designated as A.S.T.M. Spec. No. A242, A.S.T.M. Spec. No. A440, and A.S.T.M. Spec. No. A441 with minimum yield point stresses of 50,000 psi, 46,000 psi, and 42,000 psi, respectively. A242 steel is highly corrosive resistant; A440 steel is relatively corrosive resistant and is used in the construction of bolted or riveted structures; and

A441 steel is used for welded structures that may be subjected to high impact loads. The minimum yield point stress of high strength steel is also governed by the thickness of the material. That is, a thickness not greater than ¾″ has a yield point stress of 50,000 psi; thickness from ¾″ to 1½″ has a yield point stress of 46,000 psi; thickness from 1½″ to 4″ has a yield point stress of 42,000 psi. The above is a general statement concerning the types and strengths of the structural steels that are presently available for use in construction. Complete and specific data on this subject can be found in the "Manual of Steel Construction." Mill test reports may be supplied to the fabricator to verify the material quality control. These reports must be requested prior to the time the steel members are fabricated at the rolling mill.

Structural steel members are manufactured by extruding steel billets between a set of rolling dies in a series of forward and reverse passes until a uniform and standard size shape is produced. The nomenclature for steel shapes describes their cross section configuration, for example, wide flange beams, I beams, Tee sections, angles, and channels. The structural steel sections are fabricated to standard sizes and weights; however, each manufacturer's product

Table 4–1. Principal Steel Producers

B	Bethlehem Steel Co.
C	Colorado Fuel & Iron Corp.
I	Inland Steel Co.
J	Jones & Laughlin Steel Corp.
K	Kaiser Steel Corp.
N	Northwestern Steel & Wire Co.
P	Phoenix Steel Corp.
U	United States Steel Corp.
W	Weirton Steel Co., Div. Nat'l Steel Corp.

Section and weight per ft.	Producer code	Section and weight per ft.	Producer Code	Section and weight per ft.	Producer code
36WF—All	B-U	BP10 57-42	B-I-U	10B 19-15	B-I-N-U
33WF—All	B-U	BP8 36	B-I-U	10B 11.5	B-I-J-N-U
30WF—All	B-U	8 × 8M 34.3	K-U	8M 28-24	P
27WF—All	B-U	8 × 8M 32.6	K	8M 22.5	K
24WF 160-130	B-U	6WF 25.0	B-I-N-U-W	8M 20	P
24WF 120-68	B-I-U	6 × 6M 25.0	U	8M 18.5	K
21WF 142-82	B-U	6 × 6M 22.5	K-C	8M 17	P
21WF 73-55	B-I-U	6WF 20.0	B-I-N-U-W	8B 15-10	B-I-N-U
18WF 114-96	B-U	6 × 6M 20.0	C-K-U	6B 16-8.5	B-I-N-U
18WF 85-45	B-I-U	6WF 15.5	B-I-N-U	Ship and car channels	
16WF 96-88	B-U	5 × 5M 18.9	B-C-K-U	18 × 4 [—All	B-K-U-W
16WF 78-58	B-I-U	5WF 18.5-16.0	B-U	13 × 4 [—All	B-I-P-U
16WF 50-36	B-C-I-U-W	4WF 13.0	B	12 × 4 [50-35	B-I-P-U-W
14WF 426-61	B-U	4 × 4M 13.0	C-I-K-U	12 × 3½ [37-30.9	B-P-U
14WF 53-43	B-I-U-W	12JR 11.8	J	10 × 4 [41.1	B-U
14WF 38-30	B-C-I-U-W	10JR 9.0	J	10 × 4 [33.6-28.5	B-K-U
12WF 190-53	B-I-U	8JR 6.5	J	10 × 3½ [28.3-24.9	B-P-U
12WF 50-40	B-I-U-W	7JR 5.5	J	10 × 3½ [25.3-21.9	B-I-P-U
12WF 36-27	B-C-I-U-W	6JR 4.4	J	9 × 3½ [—All	B-P-U
10WF 112-49	B-I-U	12JR [10.6	J	8 × 3½ [& 8 × 3 [—All	B-P-U
10WF 45-33	B-I-U-W	10JR [8.4-6.5	J	7 × 3½ [& 7 × 3 [—All	B-I-P-U
10WF 29-21	B-C-I-N-U-W	16B 31-26	B-I-N-U	6 × 3½ [18.0	B-P-U
8WF 67-40	B-C-I-U	14B 26-22	B-I-N-U	6 × 3½ [15.3	B-I-P-U
8WF 35-31	B-C-I-U-W	14B 17.2		6 × 3 [& 6 × 2½ [—All	B-U
8WF 28-24	B-I-N-U	12B 22-16.5	B-I-U	4 × 2½ [13.8	U
8WF 20-17	B-C-I-N-U	12B 14	B-I-J-U	3 × 2⁵⁄₁₆ [7.6	B
BP14 117-73	B-U	10M 29.1-22.9	K	3 × 1⅞ [9.0	B-U
BP12 74-53	B-I-U	10M 21	P	3 × 1⅞ [7.1	B-I-U

SOURCE: Reproduced, with permission of the A.I.S.C., from the "Manual of Steel Construction."

Listings of American Standard beams and channels, as well as angles, are omitted from the above table since these shapes are generally procurable from all mills, including many not shown in the table heading.

Maximum lengths of shapes obtainable vary widely with producers, but a conservative range for all mills is from 60′ to 90′. Some mills will accept orders for lengths up to 120′, but only for certain shapes, and subject to special arrangement. Consult the producers for unusual length requirements.

Table 4–2. Methods of Designating Structural Steel Shapes

Group	Example	Group	Example
Wide flange shapes	24WF 76	Structural Tees (from B)	ST 6B 9.5
Light beams	14B 26	Structural Tees (from M)	ST 5M 10.5
Miscellaneous columns	8 × 8M 34.3	Structural Tees (from JR)	ST 6JR 5.9
Miscellaneous shapes	8M 17	Bearing piles	14BP 73
Junior beams	10JR 9.0	Car and ship channels	12 × 4 [45.0
Junior channels	12JR [10.6	Rolled Tees (flange × stem)	T 4 × 4½ × 11.2
American standard beams	24I 100	Zees (depth × flange)	Z 4 × 3 × 12.5
American standard channels	12 [20.7	Bulb angles	Bulb ∠ 6 × 3½ × 17.4
Equal leg angles	∠ 6 × 6 × ¾	Plates	PL 18 × ½
Unequal leg angles	∠ 6 × 4 × ⅝	Square bars	Bar 1 □
Structural Tees (from WF)	ST 18WF 115	Round bars	Bar 1¼ Φ
Structural Tees (from I)	ST 10I 32.7	Flat bars	Bar 2½ × ½

SOURCE: Reproduced, with permission of the A.I.S.C., from the "Manual of Steel Construction."

Designations shown above are intended primarily for use on design and detail drawings. When lists of material are prepared for ordering from the mills, the identification required by the respective mills should be observed.

may vary from another's by a small degree. The two major producers of structural steel in the United States are Bethlehem Steel Company and the United States Steel Company. Both companies manufacture the Regular Series Shapes, which are those shapes most frequently used, and the Special Series Shapes, which are not generally used and therefore are not continuously produced. There are certain structural steel sections that are manufactured exclusively by only a few steel producing companies, such as Jones & Laughlin Steel Corporation, Inland Steel Company, and Kaiser Steel Corporation. The primary considerations in specifying structural steel members for construction are strength, deflection, cost, and availability. The capacity of a steel member to resist stress and deflection is a function of its size and its shape and the yield point stress of the steel. Since steel is generally purchased by weight, it is economically important to use sections of the least weight that will be capable of sustaining the imposed loads and forces within the limits of the allowable working stresses and deflections. Table 4–1 gives the names of the companies that manufacture the various structural steel shapes. Table 4–2 gives the names and the methods of designating the different types of structural shapes.

Details 4–1 to 4–6(d) inclusive, show the various methods of connecting columns, base plates, and foundations. The function of a base plate is to transfer the column loads to the foundation. This can be achieved by designing the base plate with sufficient surface area and cross-sectional thickness. The contact surface between the top of the plate and the column should be flat to obtain a complete bearing area. Plates over 4″ thick should be milled to ensure a smooth surface; however, plates that are between 2″ and 4″ thick may be straightened by pressing. The bearing pressure on the bottom of the base plate is assumed to be equally distributed over the entire area of the plate. This pressure will cause the surface that is not directly beneath the column cross section to bend upward as a cantilever. The thickness of the plate is calculated to resist this bending. The column can be attached to the base plate by shop welding or by field welding; in either case the weld must be strong enough to resist the column lateral loads as well as bending and compression. The anchor bolts react against the base plate in bearing and in shear. The capacity of the anchor bolt to act as a resisting element depends on the size of the bolt, the thickness of the base plate, and the depth of embedment of the bolt in the concrete. The anchor bolts shown in Detail 4–6(a) to (d) are also used to transfer the column bending moments into the foundation by acting as resisting elements of a force couple. If the anchor bolts in this type of connection are to be completely effective as resisting elements, they must be capable of withstanding axial tension and compression loads. Further, anchor bolts must develop enough bond strength between the concrete of the foundation to prevent their slipping out or being pulled out. Base plates and anchor bolts are usually the first step in construction to coordinate the foundation with the steel superstructure; therefore, it is necessary that they be accurately placed. A small dimensional variation in elevation or horizontal location of the base plate will result in discrepancies in the superstructure connections. The columns can be plumbed to their final positions by setting the base plates on a relatively thin layer of nonshrinkable grout. The structural steel erector should verify the locations and elevations of the base plates in the field to ensure that the members will fit together as shown on the working drawings.

Details 4–9(a) to 4–12(d), 4–24(a) to (d), and 4–39(a) to 4–42 are drawings of simple beam to column connections. This type of connection is classified generally as a non-rigid, or simple, connection since it is assumed that it cannot restrain the end of the connected beam from rotating. The flexibility of simple connections depends on the stiffness of the connecting parts. A standard simple connection consists of two angles with each leg of each angle bolted through the beam web or with one leg of each angle bolted through the beam web and one leg bolted through the column flange or web. Non-flexible connections are classified as rigid frame connection. This type of connection is capable of resisting bending and shear, thus restraining the connected member from rotating independently. Rigid connection joints are defined by the fact that the angle between the connected parts or members will remain essentially the same after the members are deflected from flexure or shear. Details 4–13 to 4–20, inclusive, show rigid frame steel connections. It can be seen in these details that this type of connection is fabricated to resist both shear and bending. In rigid connections and simple connections, the vertical shear reaction of the beam is supported with angles or plates that are joined with bolts, rivets, or welds; however, in rigid type connections the bending in the joint can be resisted only by welds or by a bolt fastener that will not permit slippage between the connection parts. Details 4–26(a) and (b) and also Details 4–48(a) to (d) show simple beam to column connections with a seat angle. The seat angle is generally used as a temporary support for the beam during the erection of the steel frame. Details 4–48(c) and (d) use a structural Tee for a beam seat. This type of beam seat employs the web of the Tee as a stiffener plate. It is not necessary to make elaborate seat angle connections since they are rarely used as permanent connections, but rather to support the temporary construction dead and live loads. Engineers and draftsmen should pay particular attention to structural steel connections. Inadequate connections can be the source of serious structural failures or at least limit the amount of load a member may safely support.

The connections described in the previous paragraph can be fabricated by using bolts, rivets, or welds. The simple type connections are joined with unfinished, or machine, bolts of low-carbon steel, designated as A.S.T.M. Spec. No. A307–61T. Machine bolts can be easily identified by their square head and nut. In standard simple connections, the bolt shank reacts in bearing against the cross section of the web hole and transfers the load to the connecting angles by the shear resistance of the bolt shank cross section. The nuts are tightened in place with a spud wrench with sufficient force not to overstress the washer in bearing but to prevent the bolt from becoming loose from the connection. This type of connection can also be made by using hot-driven rivets or with bolts that are manufactured with ribbed or serrated shanks. The "Manual of Steel Construction" lists and diagrams the standard connections for the various size structural beams and the connection capacity for the different types of mechanical fasteners. It is important to use the minimum specified size angles in this type of connection. Thicker angles will reduce the flexibility of the joint and restrain the end of the beam as it bends.

High strength carbon-steel bolts are used in structural joints that require that the shear between the connecting parts be resisted by friction. This bolt is known as a friction type connector and is designated as A.S.T.M. Spec. No. A325–61T. Friction resistance in the connection is accomplished by mechanically tightening the nuts to develop a specified tension in the bolt shank that will clamp the contact surfaces of the connecting parts together. The friction resistance of the A325 fastener depends on the tension in the bolt and the condition of the contact surfaces, which must be free of paint or any coating that may permit slippage. Another type of bolt that is used in the same manner as the A325 bolt is designated as A.S.T.M. Spec. No. A490–63. This bolt is a high strength alloy-steel fastener used for connections of high strength steel members. Both types of bolts require that the nut be tightened to develop a specified tension in the shank.

A325 and A490 bolts can be identified by their hexagonal shaped heads and nuts and by their respective A.S.T.M. number and manufacturer's symbol. The thread length of friction type connector bolts or of high strength bolts should be excluded from the shear planes, except when they are used with thin adjacent connection parts. The A.I.S.C. specification for installing A325 bolts and A490 bolts require that they be tightened by using a calibrated torque wrench or by the "turn of nut method." The calibrated torque wrench may be power operated and set to cut off at a torque resistance that will correspond to the required tension in the bolt shank. The turn of nut method is performed manually with a wrench by successively tightening the bolts by rotating the nuts a certain amount after they are brought to a snug, tight condition. High strength bolt assemblies are required to have two hardened steel washers; however, A325 bolts do not require a hardened steel washer when they are installed by the turn of nut method. Where the connecting part's surfaces slope more than 1 to 20, the washers should be beveled to accommodate a snug fit of the bolts. The A.I.S.C. recommends that bolts or rivets be installed through holes that are 1/16″ larger in diameter than the bolt. Bolt or rivet holes may be reamed, punched, or drilled. The dimension between centers of bolts or rivets should be not less than 2⅔ times the nominal diameter of the bolt. The minimum recommended distance between bolt or rivet holes is 3″ o.c. The minimum distance between the edge of a structural steel part and the center of a bolt hole depends on the bolt diameter and on whether the edge is sheared or it is the edge of a rolled section or plate. Table 1.16.5 of the A.I.S.C. specifications gives the edge distance requirements for bolt diameters for sheared or rolled edges of plates and structural sections. The A.I.S.C. "Manual of Steel Construction" diagrams and tabulates the significant dimensions of all structural shapes. The clear dimension of the length of the web of a section is designated as "T." It is recommended that the length of a structural connection be not less than ½ the T dimension. Also, the gauge dimensions for spacing of bolt holes in flanges and webs of wide flange shapes and I beams and in the legs of angles are tabulated in the "Manual of Steel Construction."

Many of the details in this chapter require that the members or the parts of joints be connected by welding, particularly those members shown in Details 4–11 to 4–20, inclusive. Welding technology is a vast and complex subject and will not be completely covered in this text. The specific information that is ordinarily required in the structural design and drawing of steel buildings can be found in Sec. 1.17 of the A.I.S.C. specifications and in the "Welding Handbook" by the American Welding Society. Basically, structural welding is the process of uniting two metal surfaces by fusion from the heat of an electric arc. The electric-arc welding process consists of applying heat to the steel pieces to be joined by a low voltage, high amperage electric arc. The arc is maintained across the steel by an electrode which deposits a small amount of weld metal to the fused surfaces. Welding electrodes consist of a coated steel rod composed of a metal of the same chemical and mechanical properties as the steel to be joined. The strength of the weld also depends on the chemical composition of the rod coating.

When the shielded arc welding process is used, the arc deposits the weld metal on the surface, and the rod coating burns to create a gaseous shield within the immediate atmosphere around the weld and at the same time introduces a flux material into the molten metal. The effect of the gaseous shield is to prevent the hot weld material from combining with the oxygen and nitrogen in the air. Oxidation will make the weld porous and therefore weak, while nitrogen in the weld material will make it less ductile and therefore brittle. The flux in the rod coating is used as a purifying element to raise any impurities to the surface of the cooled weld. These impurities on the finished weld will take the form of a slag coating which should be chipped off before the welds are field painted. The shielded arc welding process is usually performed manually. Another welding process that is extensively used is the submerged arc welding process. Submerged arc welding refers to the fact that the arc is submerged in a layer of powdered flux material that is deposited in place as the work progresses. As in shielded arc welding, the flux raises the impurities to the surface of the weld as a slag. The slag that is formed by the submerged process is a loose scale and can be removed without chipping. In detailing welded connections, the designer should consider the direction and accessibility of the electrode relative to the work.

The strength and labor costs of welding can be affected by the position from which it is performed. There are four positions from which a weld can be made: flat, or down hand; horizontal; vertical; and overhead. The flat position is the most convenient position from which to weld and the least expensive. The overhead position of welding is slow, expensive, and inconvenient; this position will permit the molten weld metal to flow from the surfaces that are to be joined. The welds are designated on the drawings by standard symbols which approximate their cross section configuration. The weld drawings presented prior to the steel details in this chapter show the different types of welds and their symbols.

Details 4–32(a) to 4–38(b) inclusive, show various methods of splicing steel columns. In general, column splices are used in the construction of multistory buildings to coordinate the column sizes with the progressively increasing loads. The splices should be made several feet above the floor so that rigid connections of beams or girders to the column will not be affected and to allow enough clearance to erect the upper column. The splice connection must be capable of transferring the upper column moment, shear, and axial load to the lower column. The axial load is transferred to the lower column by bearing. The bearing surfaces of the members and connecting parts should be milled to ensure that they will have complete bearing on the cross sections. The shear on the upper column is usually transferred to the lower column through a bolted or riveted connection between the webs of the two members; however, the webs can be welded depending on the conditions of erection and the shear to be transferred. Column moments are transferred through splice plates attached to the upper and lower column flanges. These plates are bolted, riveted, or welded, depending on the moment load and the method of erection. The designer should endeavor to arrange all column splices in a multistory structure so that they occur at the same stories and to make the columns standard lengths. The length of steel columns is governed by fabrication, erection, and convenience of delivery to the job site.

Details 4–50(a) to (c) show sections of a concrete slab attached to the top flange of a steel beam. The method of attaching the two different materials allows them to react as a single structural element. This type of construction is known as composite beam construction. The A.I.S.C. specifications, Sec. 1.11.1, states: "Composite construction shall consist of steel beams or girders supporting a reinforced concrete slab, so interconnected that the beam and slab act together to resist bending." Part 2 of the "Manual of Steel Construction" gives many design examples of composite construction and tabulates the properties of sections of 4″, 4½″, and 5″ concrete slabs that are constructed integrally with the various steel beam standard sections. Section 1.11 of the A.I.S.C. specifications outlines the design and construction criteria for composite beams. This method of construction was first developed to be used for the deck slabs of highway bridges required to sustain heavy traffic loads. As the composite method of construction developed in bridge design, it was also found to be applicable to the design of steel buildings. The use of composite beams in building structures will result in lighter weight and smaller size steel beams, less floor deflection from live loads, and floors that are capable of supporting greater loads. Steel beams that are completely encased in concrete that is poured with the floor slabs will react as composite beams; however, mechanical shear connectors are not required between the top flange of the steel beam and the slab. The concrete cover over the entire beam serves as fire protection for the steel. The concrete slab at the top of the composite steel beam flange is analogous to a structural cover plate on the beam. The coverplate analogy requires that the composite section comply with two conditions: first, since concrete cannot resist tension, it will react with the total section only as part of the compression flange; second, the connection of the slab to the top flange of the steel beam must be capable of transmitting the horizontal shear that will result from the bending of the total section. The basic design of composite sections is performed by transforming the concrete slab area into an equivalent cross section of steel placed on the top flange of the steel beam. This is done by dividing the concrete area by the value n of concrete. The transformed section method of analysis of reinforced concrete defines n as the ratio of the modulus of elasticity of steel to the modulus of elasticity of concrete. The concrete slab is connected to the steel beam with shear connectors welded to the top flange of the beam. Detail 4–50(b) shows a section of a structural steel channel used as a shear connector; Detail 4–50(c) shows steel studs used as shear connectors. Spiral-bent bars can also be used as shear connectors. The size and spacing of the connectors is determined by calculation. Table 1.11.4 of the A.I.S.C. specifications gives shear values for the individual and different types of connectors.

Details 4–51(a) and (b) show methods of protecting structural steel members from being damaged from the extreme heat of a fire. Although structural steel is an incombustible material, an average temperature above 1000°F will appreciably reduce the yield point stress. The degree of fire protection required of structural members in a particular building depends on its area, height, type of construction, and location within a local fire zone and the use or occupancy of the building. Structural members are usually protected from fire damage by encasing them in concrete, as shown in Detail 4–51(a), or by applying a protective envelope of cement plaster, as shown in Detail 4–51(b). The use of either method of protection is determined by the number of hours required for the structural member to resist damage. The local building codes usually specify the type of protection required for structural members for the various types of construction. These requirements vary in each geographic region and in different cities; however, their basic criteria are developed by such agencies as the National Bureau of Standards and the Underwriters Laboratories, Inc.

Buildings that are required to be light, economical, and incombustible are usually constructed with light-gauge structural steel sections. Details 4–52(a) to 4–63, inclusive, show methods of framing with steel studs, light steel joists, bar joists, and metal decking. This type of construction is done with members fabricated from sheet or strip steel less than 3/16″ thick. The members are formed by bending or cold forming to the desired shape. The steel used in the manufacturing of light gauge members is designated as A.S.T.M. Spec. No. A245-T, Spec. No. A246-T, and Spec. No. A303-T, with minimum yield-point stresses of 25,000 psi, 30,000 psi, and 33,000 psi, respectively. The allowable working stress for tension or compression from bending can be determined by dividing the yield point stress by

a safety factor of 1.85. The "Light Gage Cold-formed Steel Design Manual," compiled and published by the American Iron and Steel Institute, gives the design and construction criteria for light steel members and tabulates the properties of the various shapes of structural sections. The major manufacturers of light gauge steel members also publish catalogues of their products which can be quite useful for structural designers and draftsmen.

The sequence of work for the design and construction of structural steel buildings consists of engineering design, shop drawings, shop fabrication, and finally field erection. The engineer is responsible for the structural design and the working drawings. He should check all working drawings to make certain that they comply with his design requirements. There are instances in which engineers relegate detail design decisions to draftsmen who may not be technically qualified for such work. This practice can lead to serious errors in the design and the drawings; even worse, it can result in structural failures. The engineer is responsible for all work performed under his supervision, including the clarity and completeness of working drawings as well as his own design calculations. The structural steel members are fabricated to conform to shop drawings which are prepared from information obtained from the engineer's working drawings. Working drawings that are not clear or complete will cause delays in preparing the shop drawings and increase the cost of fabrication of the members. The engineer should check the shop drawings of the members and connections prior to their shop fabrication to see that they agree with the working drawings. Any discrepancies or variations in member sizes or dimensions should be brought to the attention of the fabricator and corrected before the shop work begins.

Structural steel members are delivered to the job site with one coat of prime paint. Also, all steel members and connection parts will be marked in the shop with numbers and letters to correspond with a field erection diagram. Before the members are shop-painted, they are cleaned with a wire brush to remove rust, mill scale, and dirt. Areas of steel members that will be encased in concrete after the structure is completed should not be painted. This will permit the surrounding concrete to bond to the surface of the member. The shop coat of paint is only a temporary protection of the steel from weather exposure during erection. Some field painting may also be necessary for this purpose; in particular, field welds should be chipped free of surface slag and painted. The steel members should be shipped from the fabricator's shop in a sequence that will be convenient to expedite their erection.

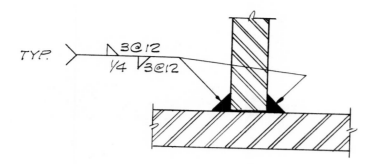

A typical weld. The contour symbol indicates a fillet weld. The offset of the near side and far side contour symbols indicates that the welds are staggered. 3 @ 12 indicates a 3″ long weld spaced at 12″ o.c. ¼ indicates the throat dimension of the fillet. The tail symbol which is indicated thus > is used to specify a process or note.

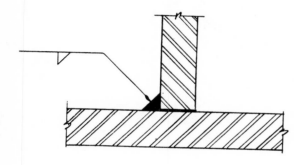

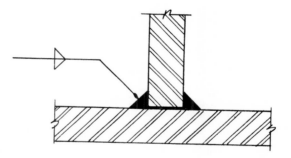

The contour symbol on the bottom of the leader line indicates that the weld is to be made on the near side of the member. If the contour symbol is on the top of the leader line, it would indicate that the weld is to be made on the far side of the member.

The contour symbol on the top and the bottom of the leader line indicates that the weld is to be made on the far side and the near side of the member to be joined.

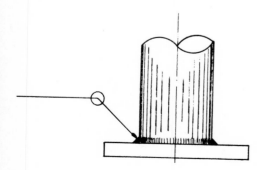

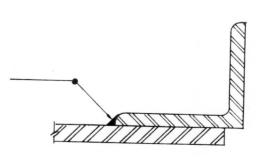

The open circle indicates that the weld is to be made all around the member to be joined.

The black dot indicates a field weld.

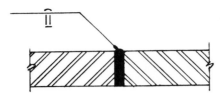

A square butt weld. The horizontal line at the bottom of the contour symbol indicates that the weld is to be made flush with the lower surface. The convex line at the top of the contour symbol indicates the shape of the weld surface at the top.

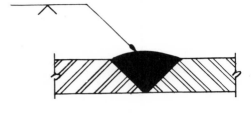

A "V" shaped weld.

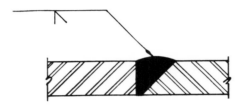

A bevel shaped weld.

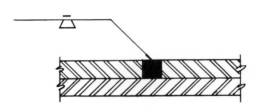

A plug weld or slot weld. The horizontal line at the top of the contour symbol indicates that the surface is to be flush.

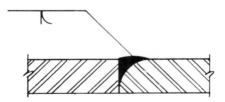

A flare bevel shaped weld.

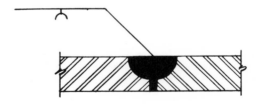

A "U" shaped weld.

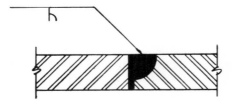

A "J" shaped weld.

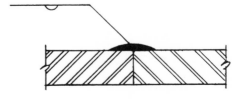

A back weld or surface bead weld.

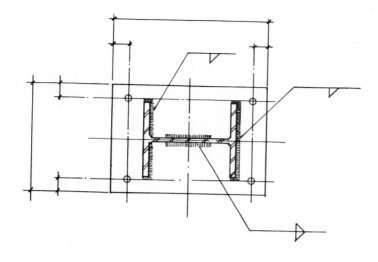

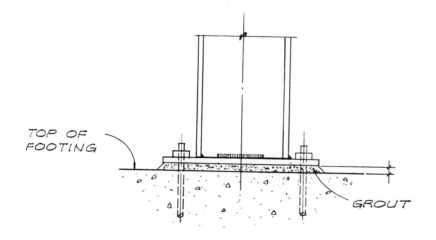

TOP OF
FOOTING

GROUT

Detail 4-1. A plan section and elevation of a steel column and base plate. The column is welded to the base plate as shown. The size and thickness of the base plate are determined by calculation. The base plate is set on a layer of grout and connected to the concrete foundation by four anchor bolts. The minimum edge distance of the anchor bolts through the base plate is 1½" or as required by the A.I.S.C. Spec. The base plate surface is finished as required by A.I.S.C. Spec. The end of the column is finished to obtain an even bearing surface on the base plate.

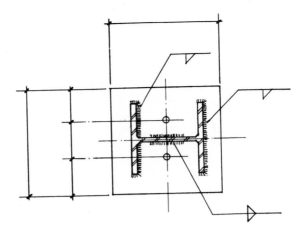

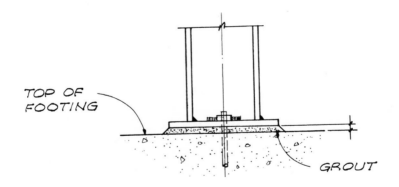

TOP OF
FOOTING

GROUT

Detail 4-2. A plan section and elevation of a steel column and base plate. The column is welded to the base plate as shown. The size and thickness of the base plate are determined by calculation. The base plate is set on a layer of grout and connected to the concrete foundation by two anchor bolts. The dimension between the anchor bolts on each side of the column web is the usual gauge dimension of the column. The base plate surface is finished as required by the A.I.S.C. Spec. The end of the column is finished to obtain an even bearing surface on the base plate.

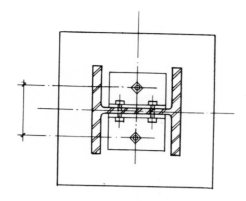

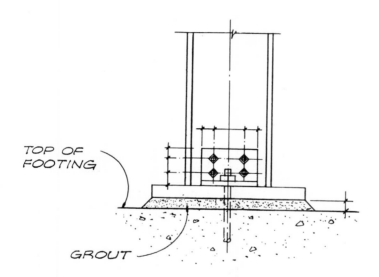

TOP OF
FOOTING

GROUT

Detail 4-3. A plan section and elevation of a steel column and base plate. The column is connected to the base plate by an angle on each side of the web. The vertical legs of the angles are bolted through the column web with four bolts. The horizontal legs of the angles are bolted through the base plate with two anchor bolts. The spacing of the bolts in the vertical legs of the angles is determined by the gauge of the angles or as required by the A.I.S.C. Spec. The size and thickness of the base plate are determined by calculation. The base plate is set on a layer of grout. The base plate surface is finished as required by the A.I.S.C. Spec. The end of the column is finished to obtain an even bearing surface on the base plate.

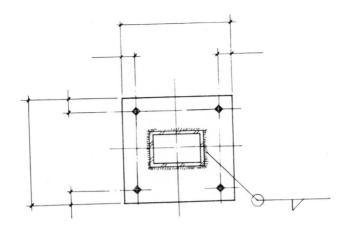

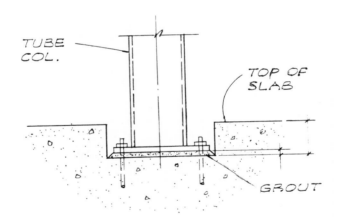

TUBE
COL.

TOP OF
SLAB

GROUT

Detail 4-4. A plan section and elevation of a structural steel tube column and base plate. The column is welded to the base plate as shown in plan. The size and thickness of the base plate are determined by calculation. The base plate is set on a layer of grout and connected to the concrete by four anchor bolts. The minimum edge distance of the anchor bolts through the base plate is 1½" or as required by the A.I.S.C. Spec. The base plate surface is finished as required by the A.I.S.C. Spec.

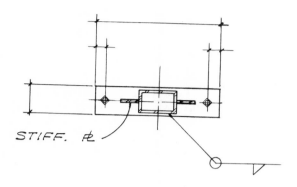

STIFF. ℄

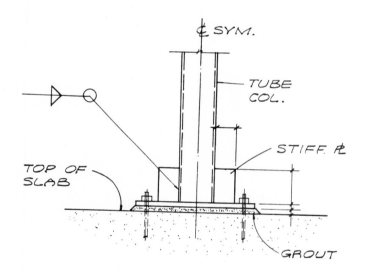

℄ SYM.

TUBE
COL.

STIFF. ℄

TOP OF
SLAB

GROUT

Detail 4-5. A plan section and elevation of a structural steel tube column and base plate. The column is welded to the base plate as shown. The width of the base plate allows the column to be placed within the limits of a stud wall. The size and thickness of the base plate are determined by calculation. The base plate is stiffened by vertical plates welded to the column and the plate. The base plate is set on a layer of grout and connected to a concrete foundation by two anchor bolts. The base plate surface is finished as required by the A.I.S.C. Spec. The end of the column is finished to obtain an even bearing surface on the base plate.

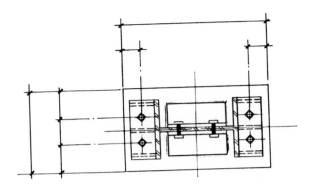

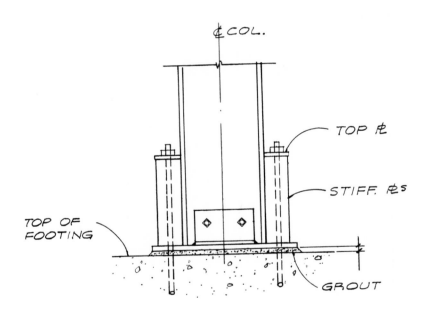

℄ COL.

TOP ℔

STIFF. ℔s

TOP OF
FOOTING

GROUT

Detail 4-6(a). A plan section and elevation of a steel column and base plate. The column web is connected to the base plate by two angles welded to the plate and to the column web. The column flanges are connected to a concrete foundation by anchor bolts extended above the top of concrete. The anchor bolts are connected to the flange plates and stiffener plates as shown. The size and thickness of the base plate are determined by calculation. The base plate is set on a layer of grout. The minimum edge distance of the anchor bolts through the base plate is 1½" or as required by the A.I.S.C. Spec. The base plate surface is finished as required by the A.I.S.C. Spec. The end of the column is finished to obtain an even bearing surface on the base plate.

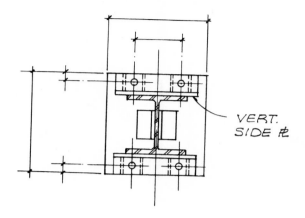

VERT.
SIDE ℄

℄ SYM.

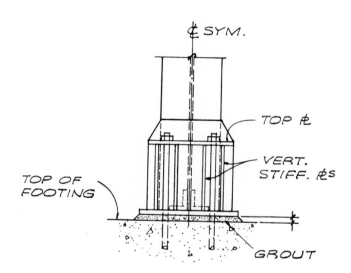

TOP ℄

VERT.
STIFF. ℄S

TOP OF
FOOTING

GROUT

Detail 4-6(b). A plan section and elevation of a steel column and base plate. The column web is connected to the base plate by two angles. The vertical legs of the angles are bolted through the web, the horizontal legs of the angles are welded to the base plate. The column flanges are connected to a concrete foundation by anchor bolts extended above the top of concrete. The anchor bolts are connected to the flange plates and stiffener angles as shown. The size and thickness of the base plate are determined by calculation. The base plate is set on a layer of grout. The minimum edge distance of the anchor bolts through the base plate is 1½″ or as required by the A.I.S.C. Spec. The base plate surface is finished as required by the A.I.S.C. Spec. The end of the column is finished to obtain an even bearing surface on the base plate.

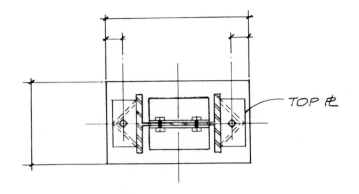

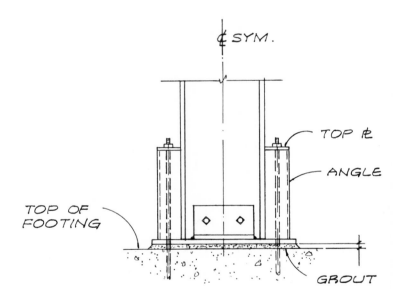

Detail 4-6(c). A plan section and elevation of a steel column and base plate. The column web is connected to the base plate by two angles. The vertical legs of the angles are bolted through the web; the horizontal legs of the angles are welded to the base plate. The column flanges are connected to a concrete foundation by anchor bolts extended above the top of concrete. The anchor bolts are connected to the flange stiffener plates as shown. The size and thickness of the base plate are determined by calculation. The base plate is set on a layer of grout. The minimum edge distance of the anchor bolts through the base plate is 1½″ or as required by the A.I.S.C. Spec. The base plate surface is finished as required by the A.I.S.C. Spec. The end of the column is finished to obtain an even bearing surface on the base plate.

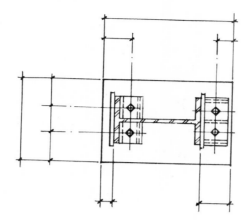

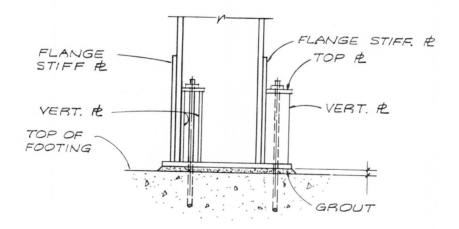

FLANGE STIFF. ℔

FLANGE STIFF. ℔
TOP ℔

VERT. ℔

TOP OF FOOTING

VERT. ℔

GROUT

Detail 4-6(d). A plan section and elevation of a steel column and base plate. The column is welded to the base plate as shown in Detail 4-1. The column flanges are connected to a concrete foundation by anchor bolts extended above the top of concrete. The anchor bolts are connected to the flange plates and stiffener plates as shown. The size and thickness of the base plate are determined by calculation. The base plate is set on a layer of grout. The minimum edge distance of the anchor bolts through the base plate is 1½" or as required by the A.I.S.C. Spec. The base plate surface is finished as required by the A.I.S.C. Spec. The end of the column is finished to obtain an even bearing surface on the base plate.

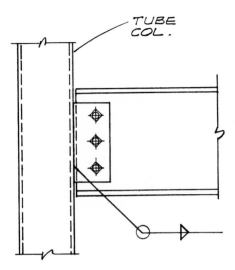

Detail 4-7(a). A connection of a steel beam to a continuous structural steel tube column. The beam is bolted to a plate on one side of the web and welded to the face of the column. The size and number of bolts, the size of the connection plate, and the size of weld are determined by calculation. The bolt spacing is 3″ o.c., and the edge distance is 1½″ or as required by the A.I.S.C. Spec.

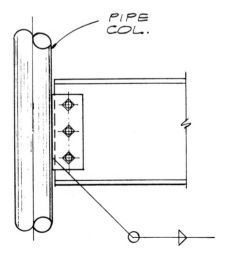

Detail 4-7(b). A connection of a steel beam to a continuous steel pipe column. The beam is bolted to a plate on one side of the web and welded to the face of the column. The size and number of bolts, the size of the connection plate, and the size of weld are determined by calculation. The bolt spacing is 3″ o.c., and the edge distance is 1½″ or as required by the A.I.S.C. Spec.

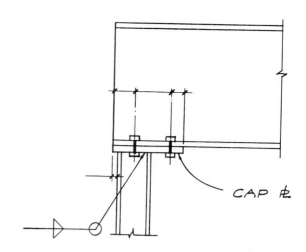

Detail 4-8(a). An end connection of a steel beam to a wide flange steel column. The bottom flange of the beam is bolted on each side of the web through the column cap plate. The cap plate is welded to the top of the column. The spacing of the bolts is determined by the A.I.S.C. Spec. The end of the beam extends ½″ beyond the flange of the column to provide a space for the weld.

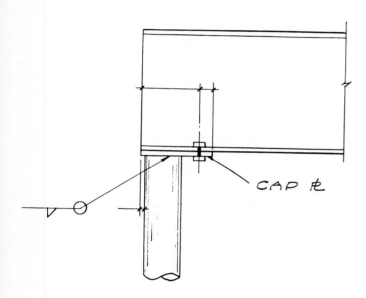

Detail 4-8(b). An end connection of a steel beam to a steel pipe column. The bottom flange of the beam is bolted on each side of the web through the column cap plate. The cap plate is welded to the top of the pipe column. The minimum edge distance of the bolts is 1½″ or as required by the A.I.S.C. Spec. The end of the beam extends ½″ beyond the column to provide a space for the weld.

Detail 4-8(c). An end connection of a steel beam to a structural steel tube column. The bottom flange of the beam is bolted on each side of the web through the column cap plate. The cap plate is welded to the top of the steel column. The minimum edge distance of the bolts is 1½″ or as required by the A.I.S.C. Spec. The end of the beam extends 1½″ beyond the face of the column to provide a space for the weld.

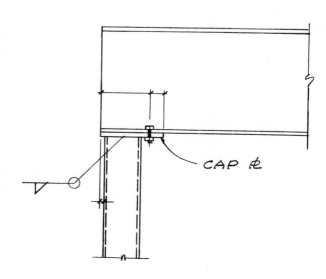

Detail 4-9. Sections and elevations of steel beams connected to the flanges of steel columns. The beams are connected to the columns by angles bolted through each side of the beam web and through the column flange. The size and number of bolts and the size of the angles are determined by calculation. The bolt spacing is 3″ o.c., and the edge distance is 1½″ or as required by the A.I.S.C. Spec.

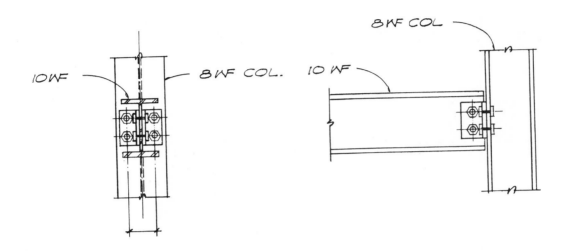

Detail 4-9(a). Steel beam connections to an 8″ wide flange column.

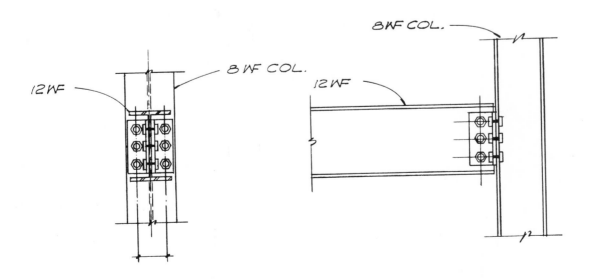

Detail 4-9(a). Steel beam connections to an 8″ wide flange column.

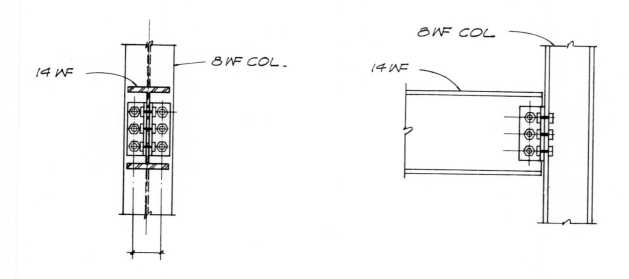

Detail 4-9(a). Steel beam connections to an 8″ wide flange column.

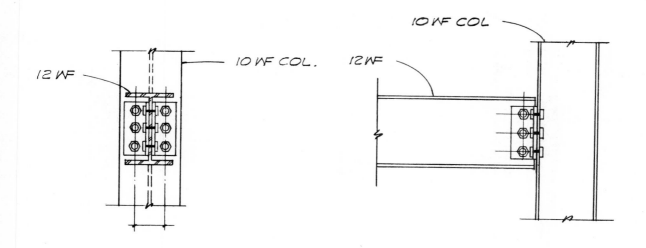

Detail 4-9(b). Steel beam connections to a 10″ wide flange column.

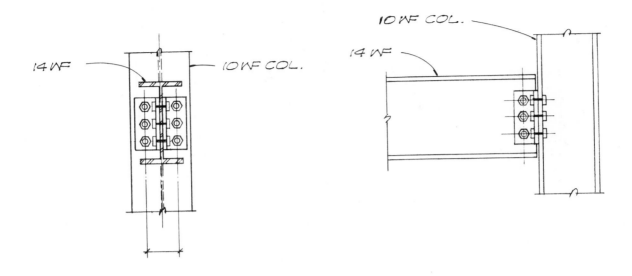

Detail 4-9(b). Steel beam connections to a 10″ wide flange column.

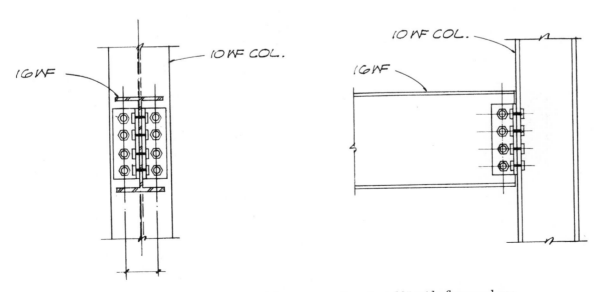

Detail 4-9(b). Steel beam connections to a 10″ wide flange column.

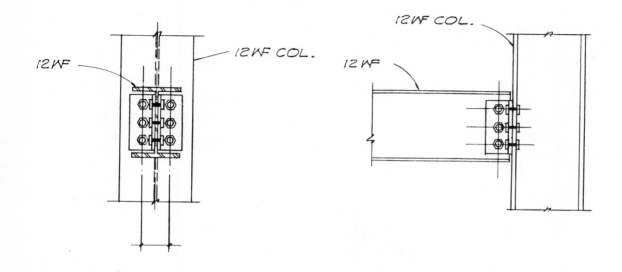

Detail 4-9(c). Steel beam connections to a 12″ wide flange column.

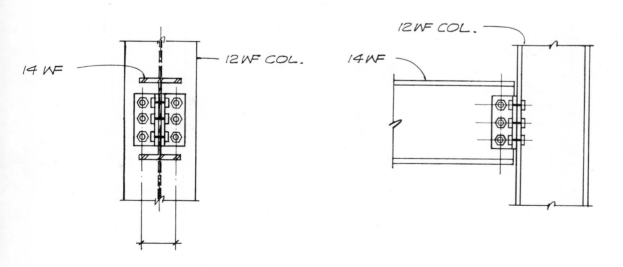

Detail 4-9(c). Steel beam connections to a 12″ wide flange column.

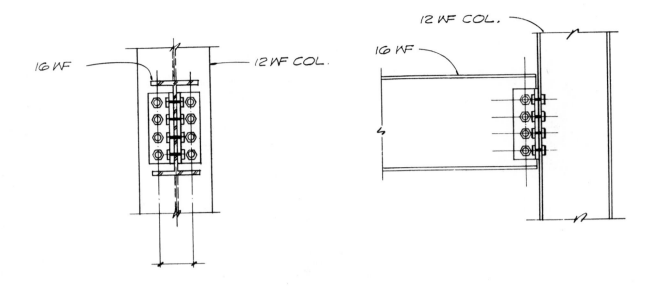

Detail 4-9(c). Steel beam connections to a 12″ wide flange column.

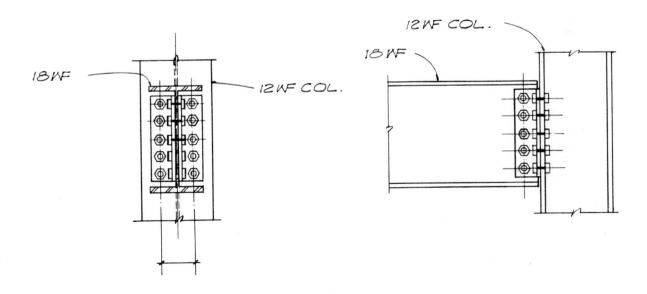

Detail 4-9(c). Steel beam connections to a 12″ wide flange column.

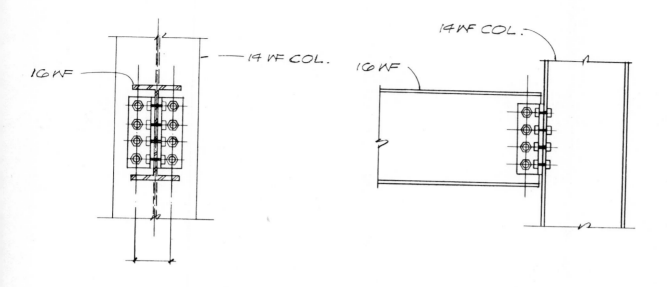

Detail 4-9(d). Steel beam connections to a 14″ wide flange column.

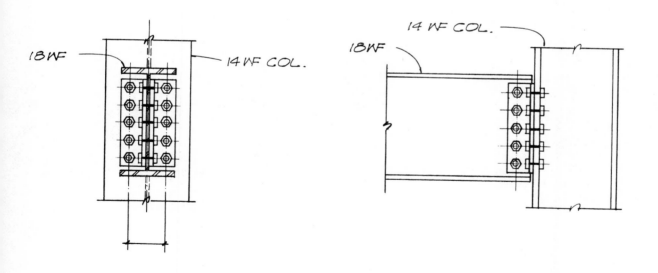

Detail 4-9(d). Steel beam connections to a 14″ wide flange column.

Detail 4-10. Sections and elevations of steel beams connected to the flanges of steel columns. The beams are connected to the columns by a structural T bolted through one side of the beam web and through the column flange. The size and number of the bolts and the size of the structural Tee are determined by calculation. The bolt spacing is 3″ o.c., and the edge distance is 1½″ or as required by the A.I.S.C. Spec.

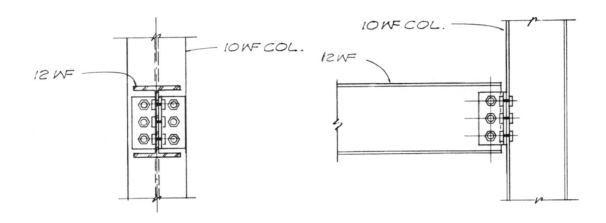

Detail 4-10(a). Steel beam connection to a 10″ wide flange column.

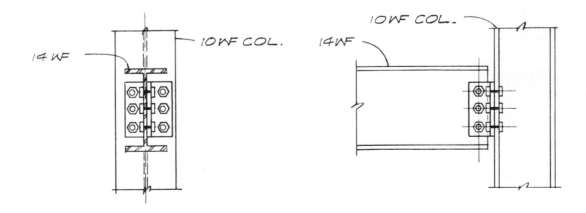

Detail 4-10(a). Steel beam connection to a 10″ wide flange column.

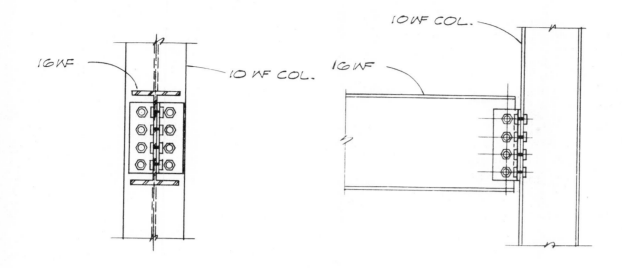

Detail 4-10(a). Steel beam connection to a 10″ wide flange column.

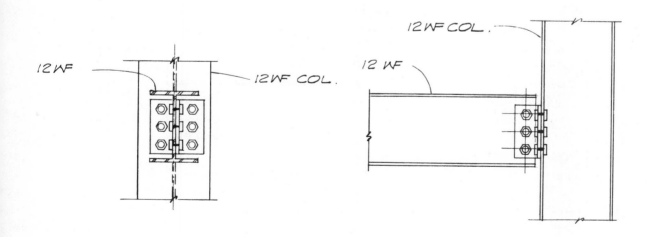

Detail 4-10(b). Steel beam connection to a 12″ wide flange column.

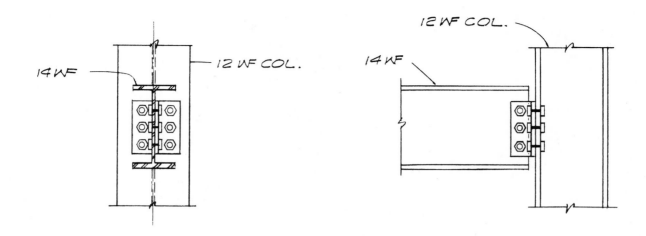

Detail 4-10(b).   Steel beam connection to a 12″ wide flange column.

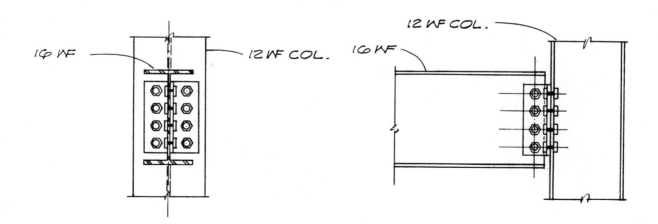

Detail 4-10(b).   Steel beam connection to a 12″ wide flange column.

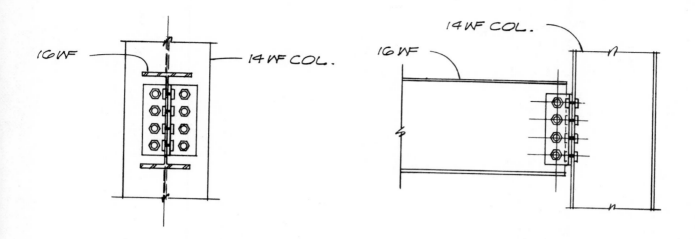

Detail 4-10(c). Steel beam connection to a 14″ wide flange column.

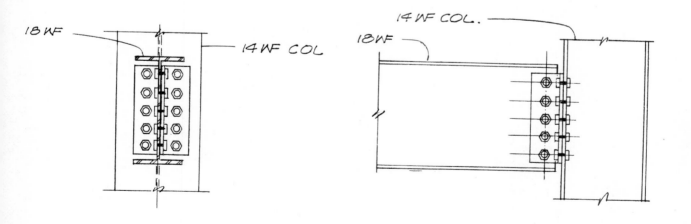

Detail 4-10(c). Steel beam connection to a 14″ wide flange column.

Detail 4-11. Sections and elevations of steel beams connected to the flanges of steel columns. The beams are connected to the column flange by angles welded to each side of the beam web and bolted through the column flange. The size and number of bolts, the size of the angles, and the size of the weld are determined by calculation. The bolt spacing is 3″ o.c., and the edge distance is 1½″ or as required by the A.I.S.C. Spec.

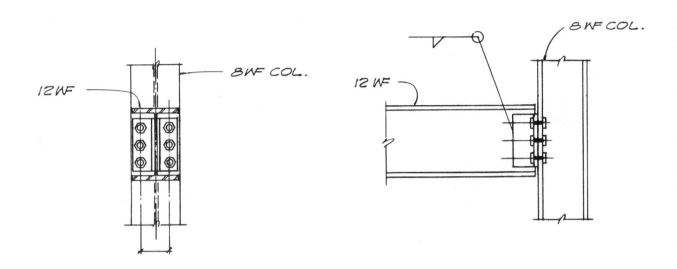

Detail 4-11(a). Steel beam connections to an 8″ wide flange column.

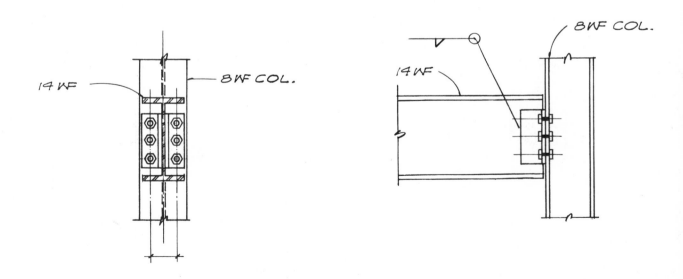

Detail 4-11(a). Steel beam connections to an 8″ wide flange column.

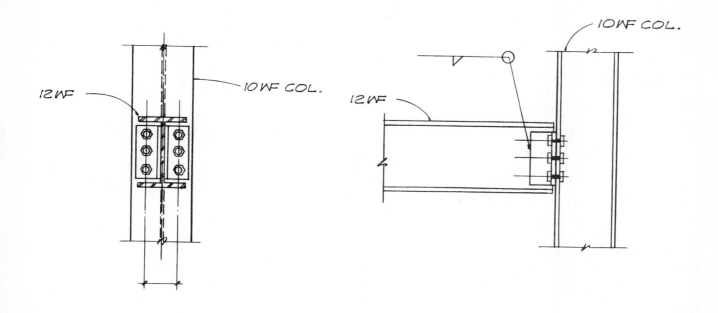

Detail 4-11(b). Steel beam connections to a 10″ wide flange column.

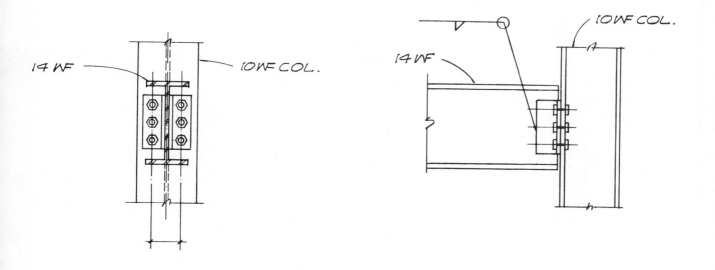

Detail 4-11(b). Steel beam connections to a 10″ wide flange column.

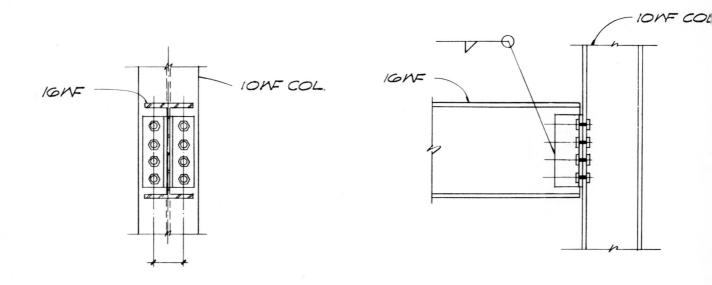

Detail 4-11(b). Steel beam connections to a 10″ wide flange column.

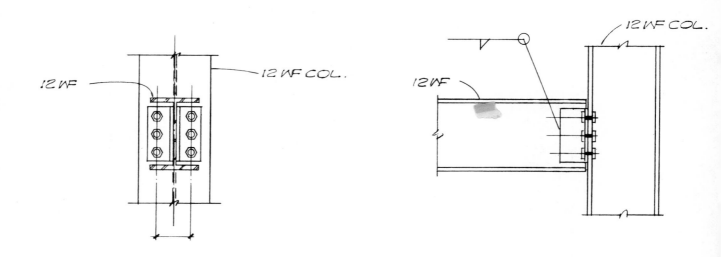

Detail 4-11(c). Steel beam connections to a 12″ wide flange column.

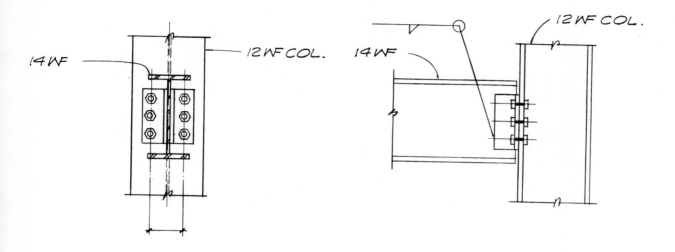

Detail 4-11(c). Steel beam connections to a 12″ wide flange column.

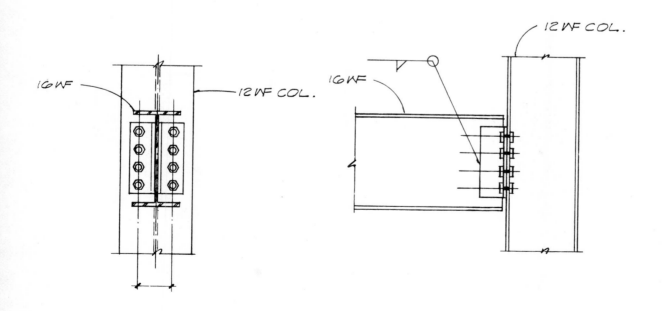

Detail 4-11(c). Steel beam connections to a 12″ wide flange column.

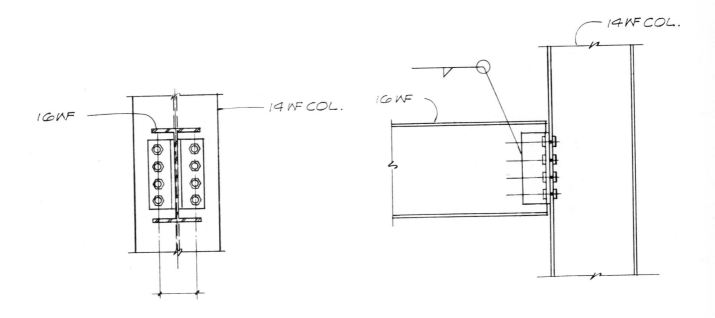

Detail 4-11(d).   Steel beam connections to a 14″ wide flange column.

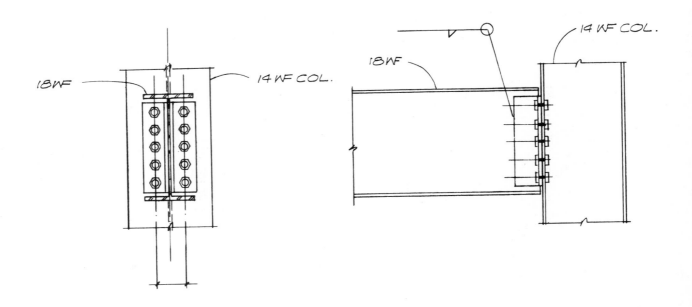

Detail 4-11(d).   Steel beam connections to a 14″ wide flange column.

Detail 4-12. Sections and elevations of steel beams connected to the flanges of steel columns. The beams are connected to the columns by a plate bolted through one side of the beam web and welded to the face of the column. The size and number of bolts, the size of the connection plate, and the size of the weld are determined by calculation. The bolt spacing is 3″ o.c., and the edge distance is 1½″ or as required by the A.I.S.C. Spec.

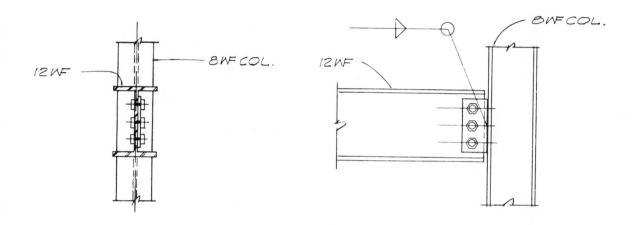

Detail 4-12(a). Steel beams connected to an 8″ wide flange column.

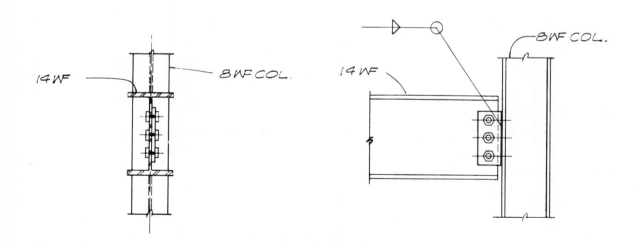

Detail 4-12(a). Steel beams connected to an 8″ wide flange column.

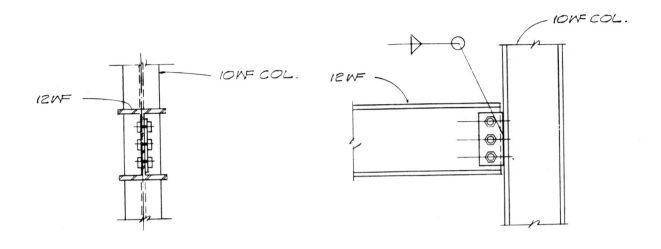

Detail 4-12(b). Steel beams connected to a 10″ wide flange column.

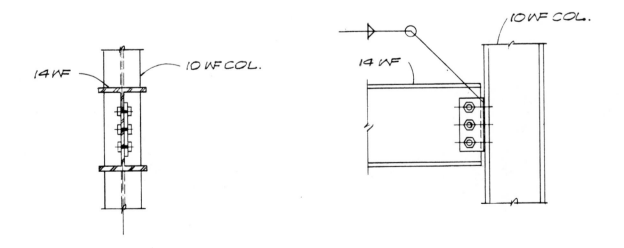

Detail 4-12(b). Steel beams connected to a 10″ wide flange column.

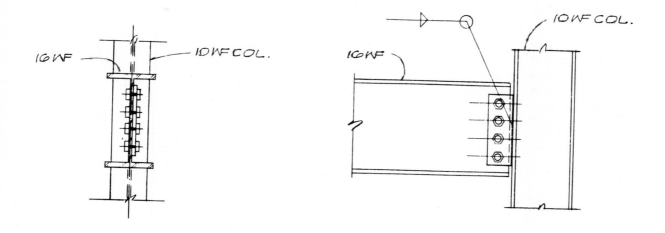

Detail 4-12(b). Steel beams connected to a 10″ wide flange column.

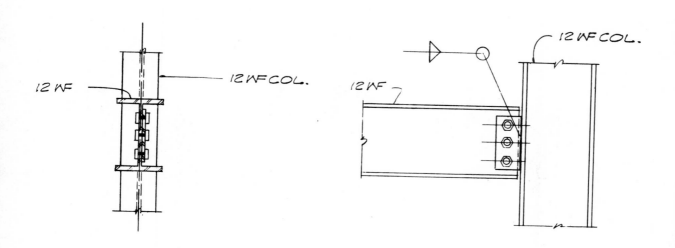

Detail 4-12(c). Steel beams connected to a 12″ wide flange column.

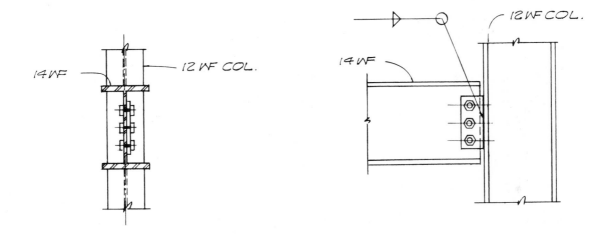

Detail 4-12(c). Steel beams connected to a 12″ wide flange column.

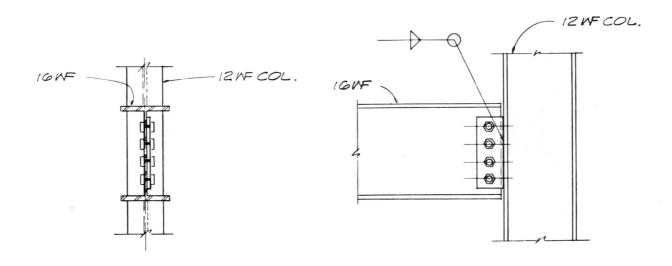

Detail 4-12(c). Steel beams connected to a 12″ wide flange column.

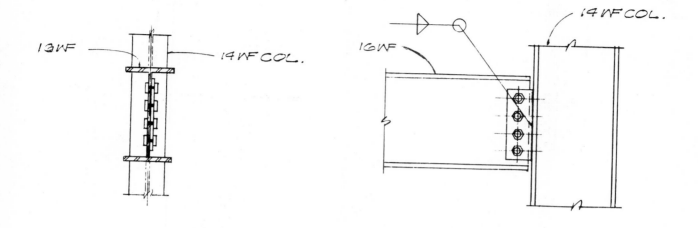

Detail 4-12(d). Steel beams connected to a 14" wide flange column.

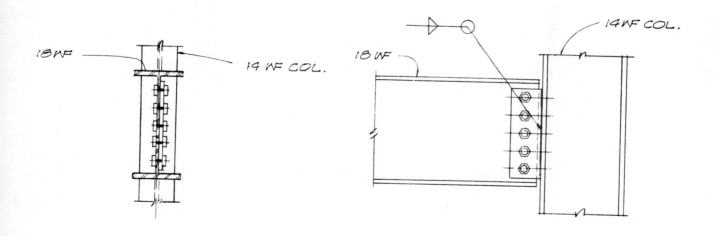

Detail 4-12(d). Steel beams connected to a 14" wide flange column.

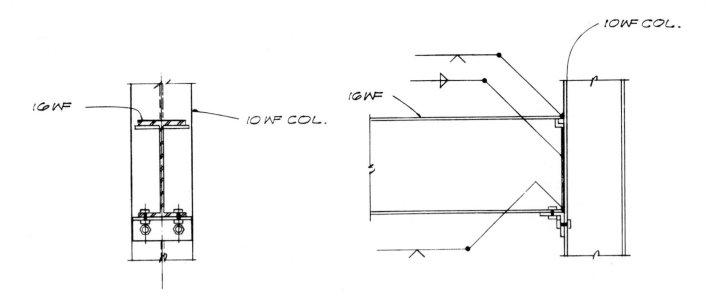

Detail 4-13. A steel beam connected to the flange face of a steel column. The connection can resist shear and bending. The beam shear is resisted by welding the web of the beam to the face of the column flange as shown. The beam bending is resisted by welding the edge of the top and bottom flanges of the beam to the face of the column. The top flange uses a backing strip to obtain a full penetration weld. The bottom flange is welded against the top of the seat angle. The seat angle is bolted to the face of the column and through the bottom flange of the beam. The vertical leg of the seat angle may be welded to the face of the column flange.

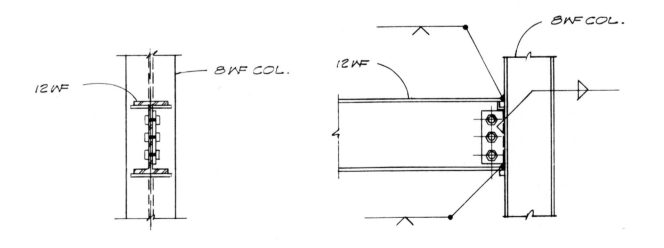

Detail 4-14(a). Steel beam connections to an 8" wide flange column.

Detail 4-14. Steel beams connected to the flange face of a steel column. The connection can resist shear and bending. The beam shear is resisted by a plate bolted through one side of the beam web and welded to the face of the column flange. The bolt spacing is 3" o.c., and the edge distance is 1½" or as required by the A.I.S.C. Spec. The size and number of bolts, the size of the connection plate, and the size of the weld are determined by calculation. The beam bending is resisted by welding the edge of the top and the bottom flanges of the beam to the face of the column flange. Backing strips are used as shown to obtain a full penetration weld.

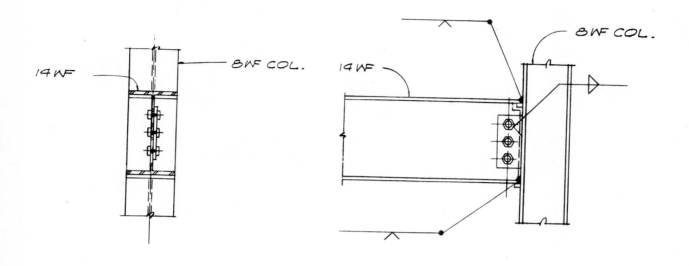

Detail 4-14(a). Steel beam connections to an 8″ wide flange column.

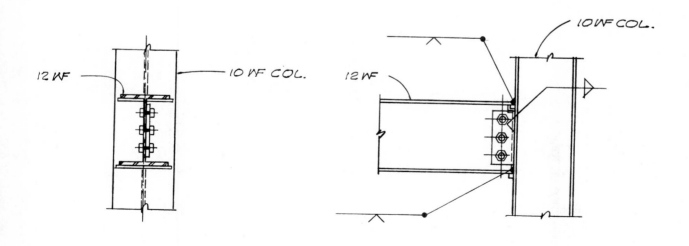

Detail 4-14(b). Steel beam connections to a 10″ wide flange column.

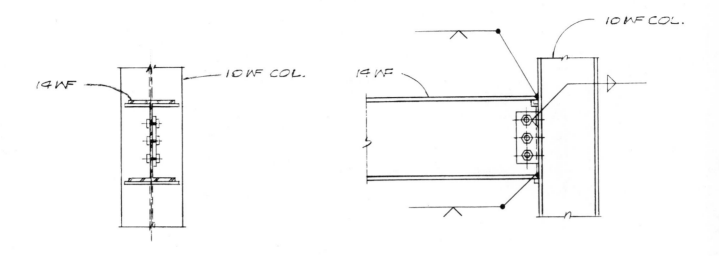

Detail 4-14(b). Steel beam connections to a 10″ wide flange column.

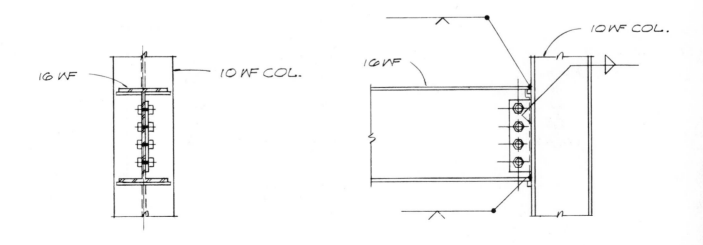

Detail 4-14(b). Steel beam connections to a 10″ wide flange column.

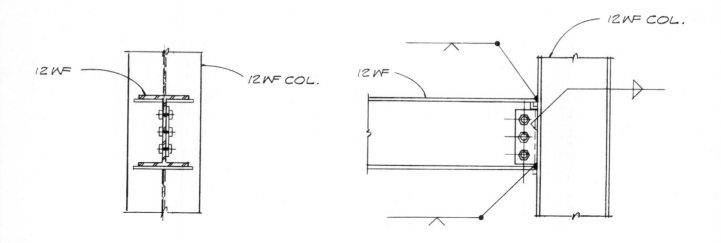

Detail 4-14(c). Steel beam connections to a 12″ wide flange column.

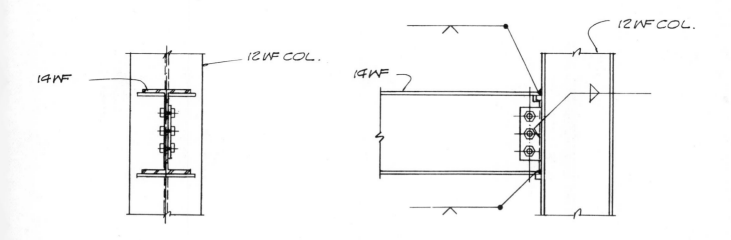

Detail 4-14(c). Steel beam connections to a 12″ wide flange column.

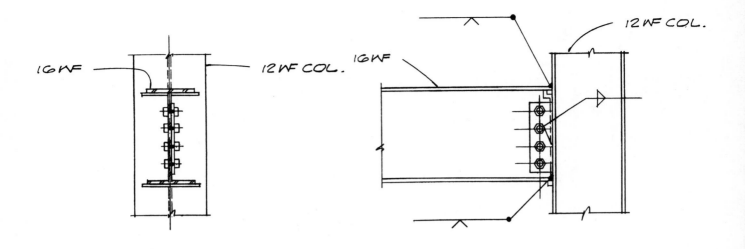

Detail 4-14(c). Steel beam connections to a 12″ wide flange column.

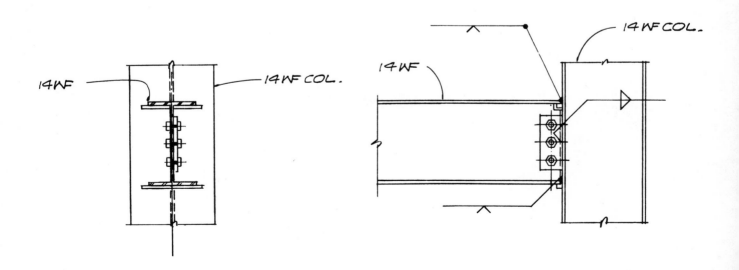

Detail 4-14(d). Steel beam connections to a 14″ wide flange column.

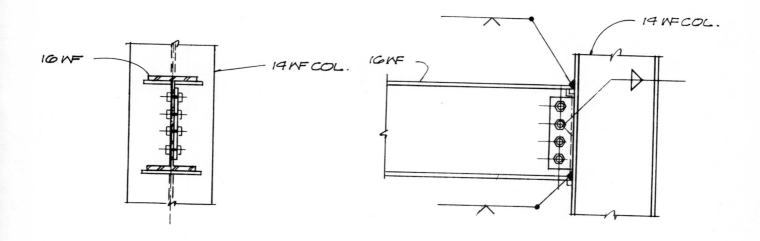

Detail 4-14(d).   Steel beam connections to a 14″ wide flange column.

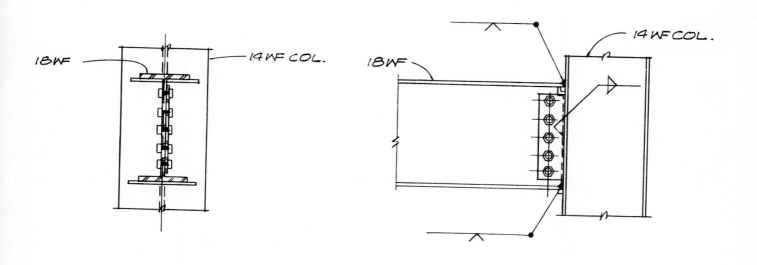

Detail 4-14(d).   Steel beam connections to a 14″ wide flange column.

Detail 4-15. Steel beams connected to the flange face of a steel column. The connection can resist shear and bending. The beam shear is resisted by a plate bolted through one side of the beam web and welded to the face of the column flange. The bolt spacing is 3″ o.c., and the edge distance is 1½″ or as required by the A.I.S.C. Spec. The size and number of bolts, the size of the connection plate and the size of the weld are determined by calculation. The beam bending is resisted by plates bolted to the top and bottom flanges of the beam and welded to the face of the column flange as shown. Backing strips are used to obtain a full penetration weld to the column flanges. The flange plates are bolted on each side of the beam web with a friction type connection. The size and number of the bolts and the size of the flange plates are determined by calculation.

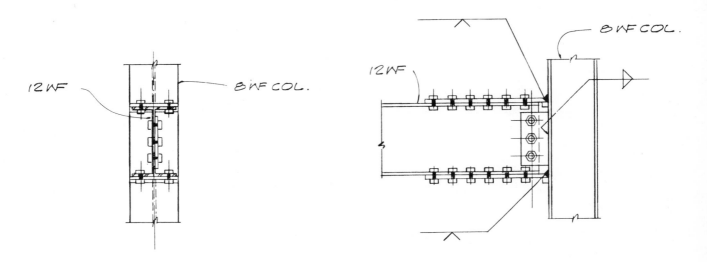

Detail 4-15(a). Steel beam connections to an 8″ wide flange column.

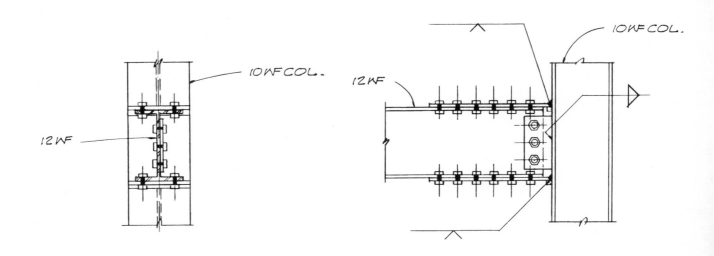

Detail 4-15(b). Steel beam connections to a 10″ wide flange column.

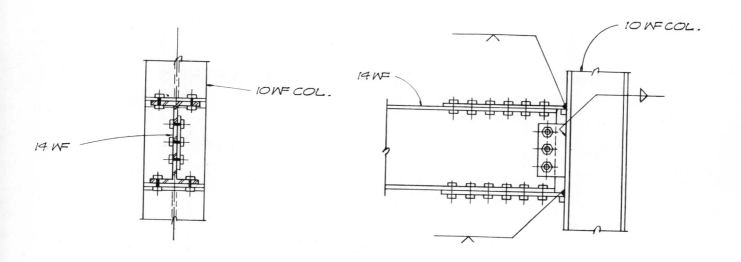

Detail 4-15(b). Steel beam connections to a 10″ wide flange column.

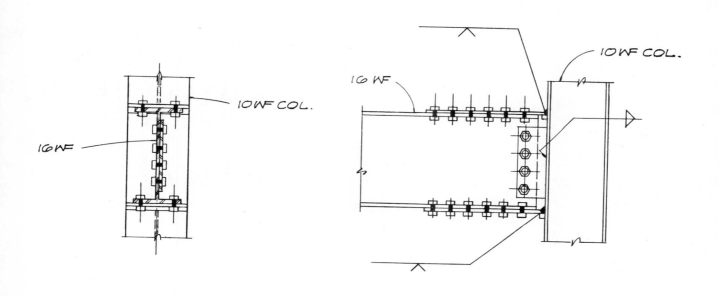

Detail 4-15(b). Steel beam connections to a 10″ wide flange column.

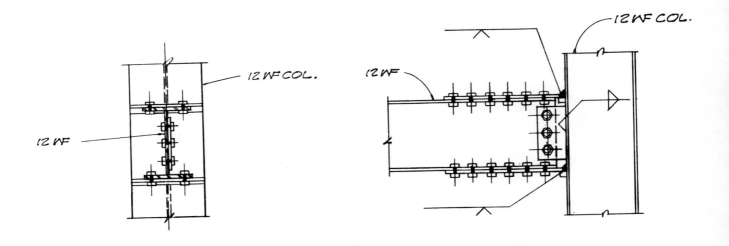

Detail 4-15(c). Steel beam connections to a 12″ wide flange column.

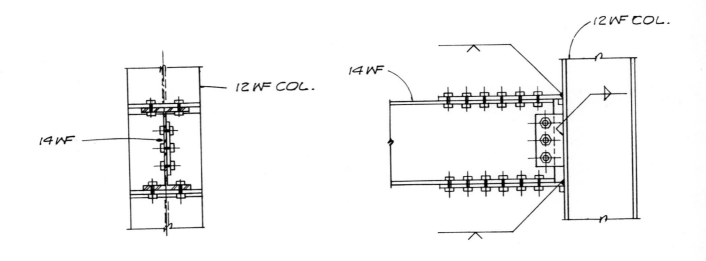

Detail 4-15(c). Steel beam connections to a 12″ wide flange column.

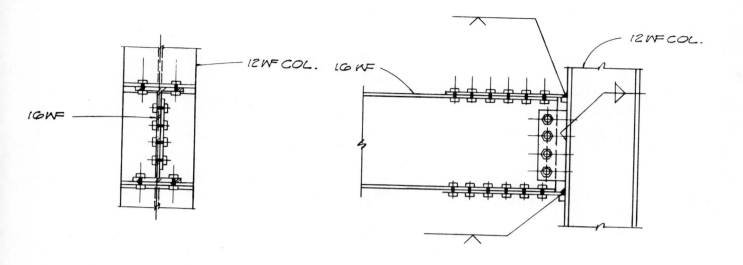

Detail 4-15(c). Steel beam connections to a 12″ wide flange column.

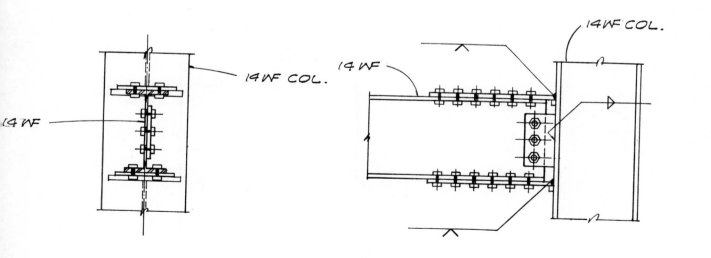

Detail 4-15(d). Steel beam connections to a 14″ wide flange column.

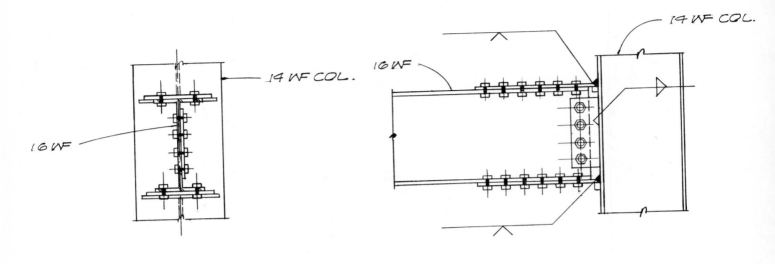

Detail 4-15(d). Steel beam connections to a 14″ wide flange column.

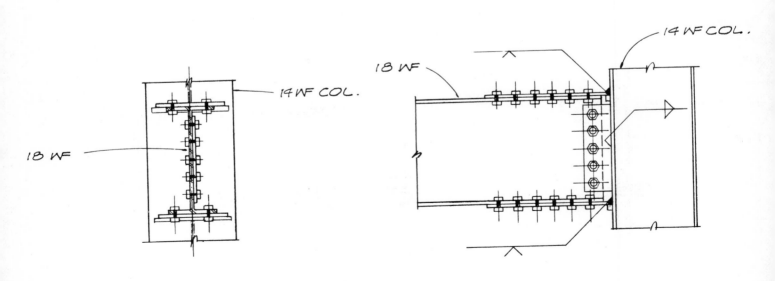

Detail 4-15(d). Steel beam connections to a 14″ wide flange column.

Detail 4-16. Steel beams connected to the web face of a steel column. The connection can resist shear and bending. The beam shear is resisted by a plate bolted through one side of the beam web and welded to the face of the column web. The bolt spacing is 3" o.c., and the edge distance is 1½" or as required by the A.I.S.C. Spec. The size and number of bolts, the size of the connection plate, and the size of weld are determined by calculation. The beam bending is resisted by welding the edge of the top and bottom flange plates to the inside face of the column flanges and to the face of the column web. The flange plates are bolted on each side of the beam web with a friction type connection. The size and number of bolts and the size of the flange plates are determined by calculation. Shim space is provided between the plates on the top and bottom flanges to allow for erection clearance.

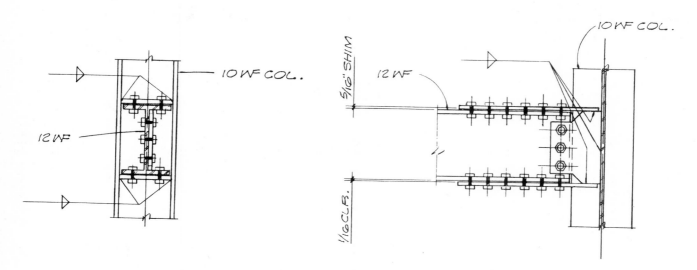

Detail 4-16(a). A steel beam connected to the web of a 10" wide flange column.

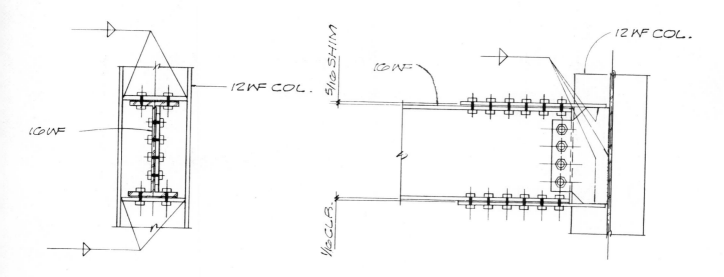

Detail 4-16(b). A steel beam connected to the web of a 12" wide flange column.

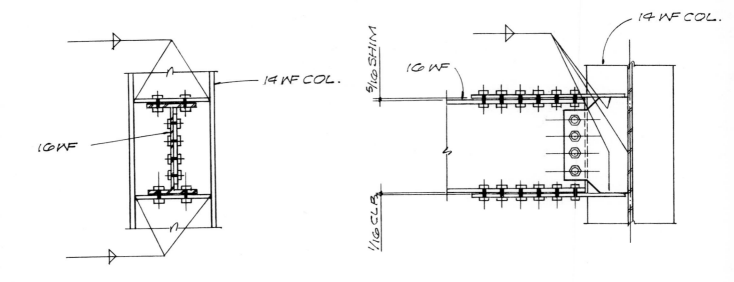

Detail 4-16(c). Steel beams connected to the web of a 14″ wide flange column.

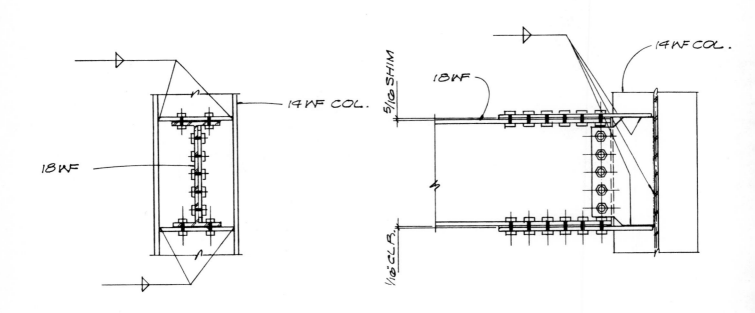

Detail 4-16(d). Steel beams connected to the web of a 14″ wide flange column.

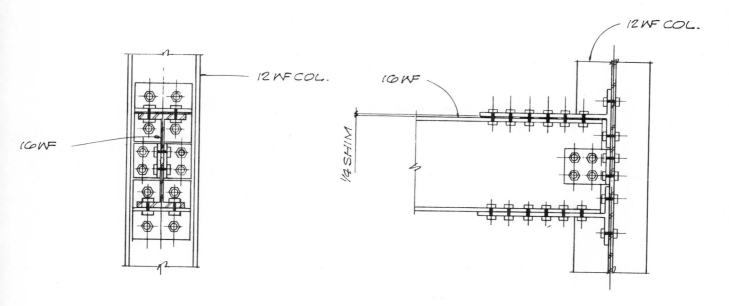

Detail 4-17(a). Steel beams connected to the web of a steel column. The connection can resist shear and bending. The beam shear is resisted by angles bolted through each side of the beam web and bolted through the column web. The size and number of bolts and the size of the angles are determined by calculation. The bolt spacing is 3″ o.c., and the edge distance is 1½″ or as required by the A.I.S.C. Spec. The beam bending is resisted by structural Tee sections. The web of the structural Tee section is bolted through the top and bottom flanges of the beam. The flanges of the structural Tee section are bolted through the column web. The webs of the structural Tees are bolted through the flanges on each side of the beam web with a friction type connection. The size and number of bolts and the size of the structural Tee section are determined by calculation. Shim space is provided at the top flange of the beam and the web of the structural Tee to allow for erection clearance.

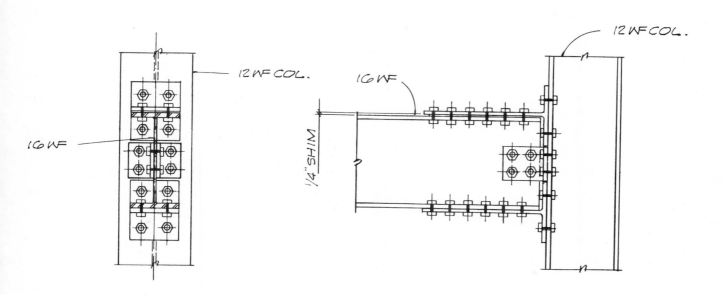

Detail 4-17(b). Steel beam connection to the flange of a steel column. The connection is similar to Detail 4-17(a).

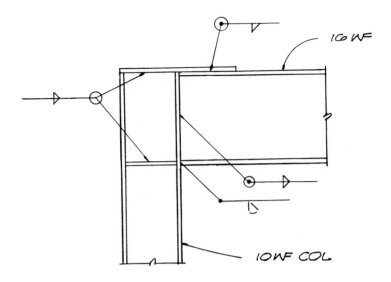

Detail 4-18(a). An end connection of a steel beam and a steel column. The connection can resist shear and bending. The bending is resisted by the stiffener and the side plates and by the welds. The size of the plates and the welds are determined by calculation.

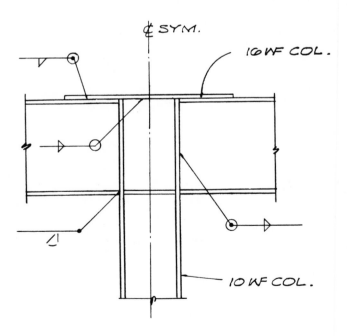

Detail 4-18(b). A connection of a steel beam to a steel column. The connection can resist shear and bending. The bending is resisted by the stiffener plates and the welds. The sizes of the plates and of the welds are determined by calculation.

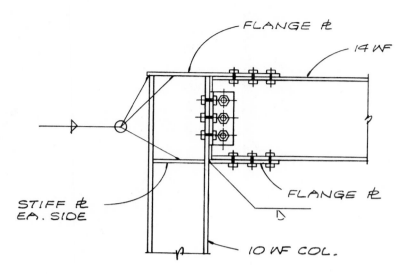

Detail 4-19(a). An end connection of a 14″ wide flange steel beam connected to a 10″ wide flange column. The connection can resist shear and bending. The bending is resisted by plates welded to the column and bolted through the beam flanges on each side of the beam web with a friction type connection. The size and number of the bolts, the size of the flange plates, and the size of the welds are determined by calculation.

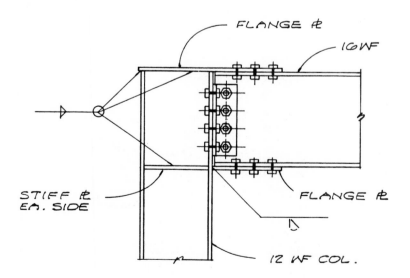

Detail 4-19(b). An end connection of a 16″ wide flange steel beam connected to a 12″ wide flange column. The connection can resist shear and bending. The bending is resisted by plates welded to the column and bolted through the beam flanges on each side of the beam web with a friction type connection. The size and number of the bolts, the size of the flange plates, and the size of the welds are determined by calculation.

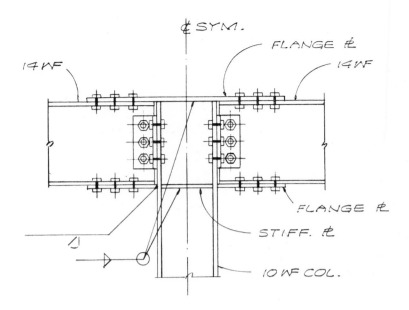

Detail 4-20(a). A connection of 14″ wide flange steel beams connected to a 10″ wide flange column. The connection can resist shear and bending. The bending is resisted by the top and bottom flange plates. The bottom flange plate is connected the same as shown in Detail 4-19(a). The top flange plate is welded to the column and bolted to the beam flange on each side of the beam web with a friction type connection. The size and number of the bolts, the size of the flange plates, and the size of the welds are determined by calculation.

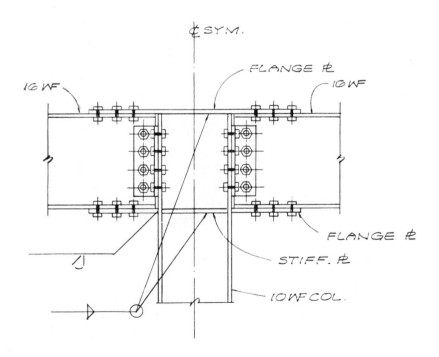

Detail 4-20(b). A connection of 16″ wide flange steel beams connected to a 12″ wide flange column. The connection can resist shear and bending. The bending is resisted by the top and bottom flange plates. The bottom flange plate is connected the same as shown in Detail 4-19(a). The top flange plate is welded to the column and bolted to the beam flange on each side of the beam web with a friction type connection. The size and number of the bolts, the size of the flange plates, and the size of the welds are determined by calculation.

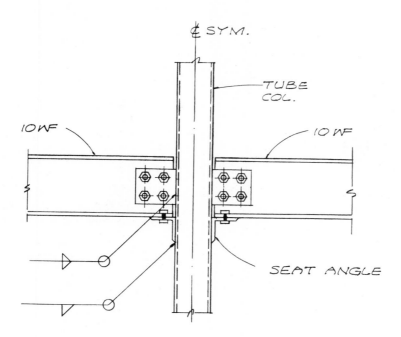

Detail 4-21(a). A connection of steel beams to a continuous structural steel tube column. The beams are connected to the column by plates bolted through one side of the beam web and welded to the face of the column. The size and number of the bolts, the size of the plates, and the size of the welds are determined by calculation. Seat angles are welded to the face of the column and bolted through the bottom flanges of the beams. The bolts are 3″ o.c., and the edge distance is 1½″ or as required by the A.I.S.C. Spec. The seat angles are for erection purposes and are optional.

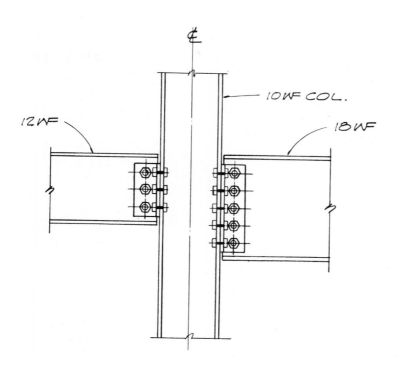

Detail 4-21(b). Steel beams connected to a continuous steel column. See Detail 4-9(b).

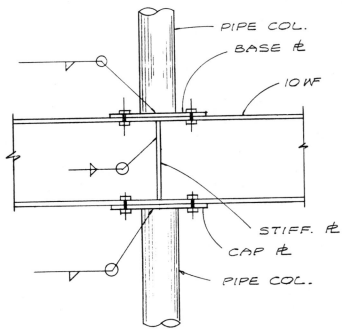

PIPE COL.

BASE ℞

10 WF

STIFF. ℞

CAP ℞

PIPE COL.

Detail 4-22(a). A connection of a steel pipe column supporting a continuous steel beam and another pipe column. The column plates are bolted through the beam flanges on each side of the web. The column plates are welded to the columns. The stiffener plates on each side of the beam web are determined by calculation.

TUBE COL.

BASE ℞

10 WF

STIFF ℞s

CAP ℞

TUBE COL.

Detail 4-22(b). A connection of a structural steel tube column supporting a continuous steel beam and another steel tube column. The column plates are bolted through the beam flanges on each side of the web. The column plates are welded to the columns. The stiffener plates on each side of the beam web are determined by calculation.

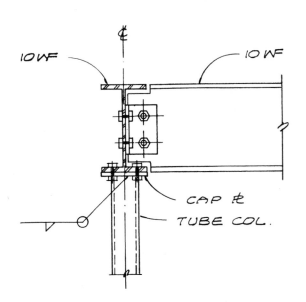

10 WF

10 WF

CAP ℞

TUBE COL.

Detail 4-23. A connection of intersecting steel beams supported by a structural steel tube column. The beams are connected as shown in Detail 4-39(b). The bottom flange of the beam shown in section is bolted on each side of the web through the column cap plate. The cap plate is welded to the top of the column.

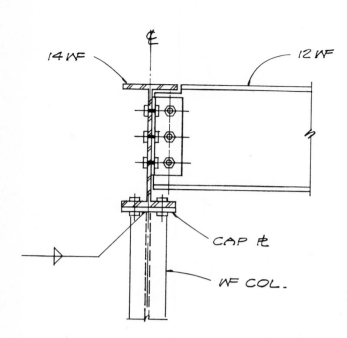

Detail 4-24(a). A connection of intersecting steel beams supported by a steel wide flange column. The beams are connected as shown in Detail 4-39(e). The bottom flange of the beam shown in section is bolted on each side of the web through the column cap plate. The cap plate is welded to the top of the column.

Detail 4-24(b). A connection of intersecting steel beams supported by a steel wide flange column. The beams are connected as shown in Detail 4-39(e). The bottom flange of the beam shown in section is bolted on each side of the web through the column cap plate. The cap plate is welded to the top of the column.

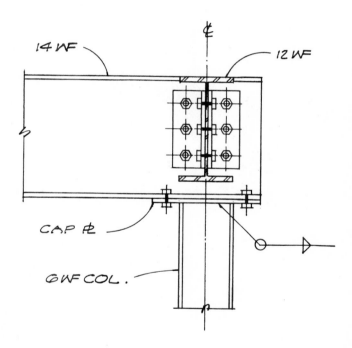

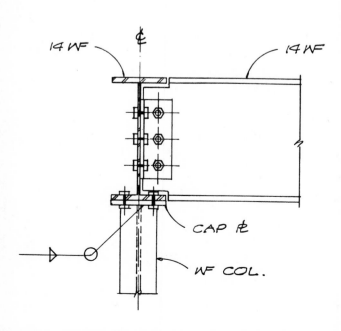

Detail 4-24(c). A connection of intersecting steel beams supported by a steel wide flange column. The beams are connected similar to Detail 4-39(f). The bottom flange of the beam shown in section is bolted on each side of the web through the column cap plate. The cap plate is welded to the top of the column.

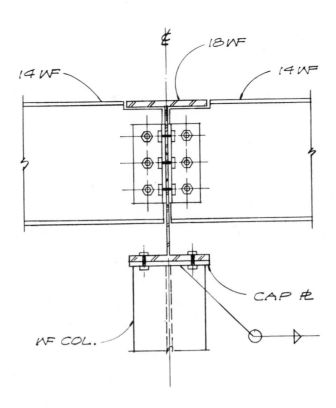

Detail 4-25(a). A connection of a steel beam supported by a steel column. The steel beams are connected to the 18″ beam similar to Detail 4-39(g). The bottom flange of the beam shown in section is bolted on each side of the web through the column cap plate. The cap plate is welded to the top of the column.

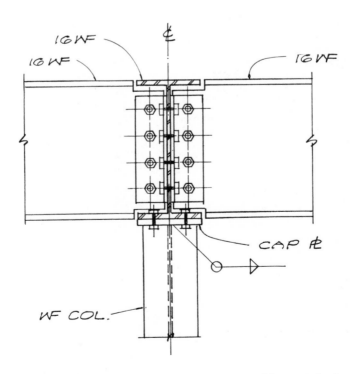

Detail 4-25(b). A connection of steel beams supported by a steel column. The steel beams are connected to the 16″ beam as shown in Detail 4-39(h). The bottom flange of the beam shown in section is bolted on each side of the web through the column cap plate. The cap plate is welded to the top of the column.

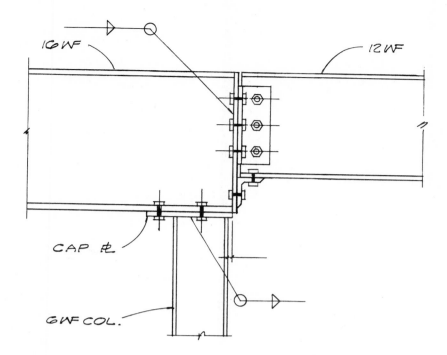

Detail 4-26(a). A connection of steel beams supported by a steel column. The 12″ steel beam is connected to the 16″ steel beam by angles bolted through each side of the beam web and through a plate welded to the end of the 16″ beam. The 16″ beam is connected to the steel column. The bottom flange of the 16″ beam is bolted on each side of the web through the column cap plate. The cap plate is welded to the top of the column. The 16″ beam extends ½″ beyond the flange of the column to provide a space for the weld. The seat angle supporting the 12″ beam is optional. The size and number of bolts and the size of the angles and plates are determined by calculation. The bolt spacing is 3″ o.c., and the edge distance is 1½″ or as required by the A.I.S.C. Spec.

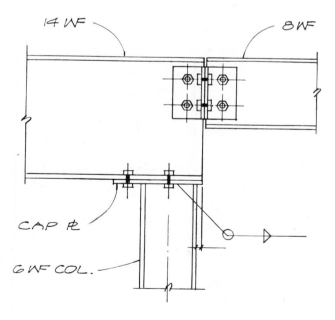

Detail 4-26(b). A connection of steel beams supported by a steel column similar to Detail 4-26(a). The beams are connected with angles bolted to the web of each beam.

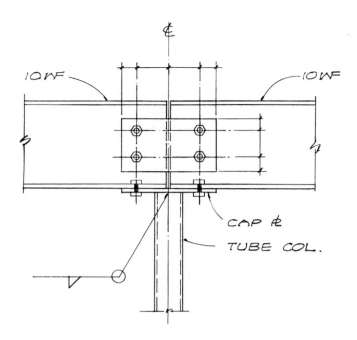

Detail 4-27(a). A connection of steel beams to a structural steel tube column. The steel beams are connected by plates bolted through each side of the beam web. The bottom flange of each beam is bolted on each side of the web through the column cap plate. The cap plate is welded to the top of the column.

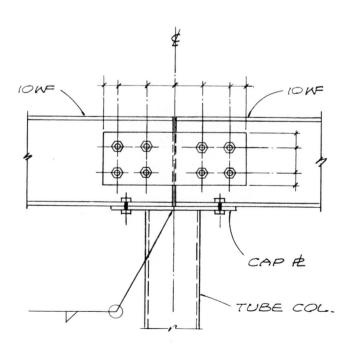

Detail 4-27(b). A connection of steel beams to a structural steel tube column. See Detail 4-27(a).

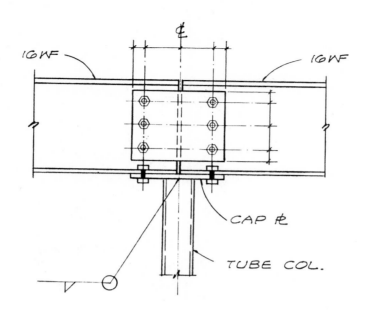

Detail 4-27(c). A connection of steel beams to a structural steel tube column. See Detail 4-27(a).

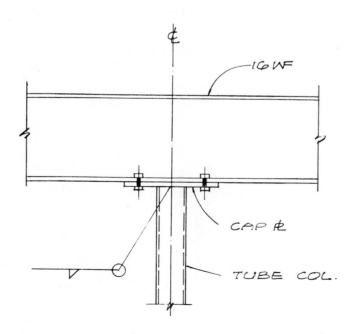

Detail 4-27(d). A connection of a continuous or cantilevered steel beam to a structural steel tube column. The bottom flange of the beam is bolted on each side of the web through the column cap plate. The cap plate is welded to the top of the column.

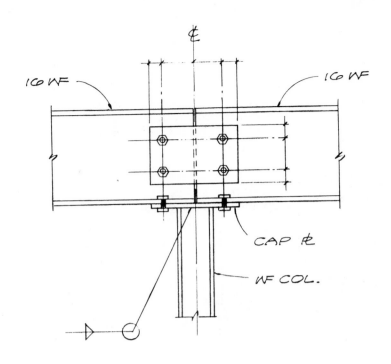

Detail 4-28(a). A connection of steel beams to a wide flange column. The steel beams are connected by plates bolted through each side of the beam web. The bottom flange of each beam is bolted on each side of the web through the column cap plate. The cap plate is welded to the top of the column.

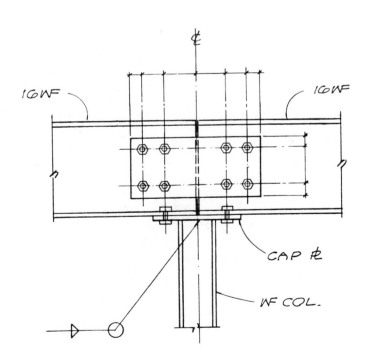

Detail 4-28(b). A connection of steel beams to a wide flange column. See Detail 4-28(a).

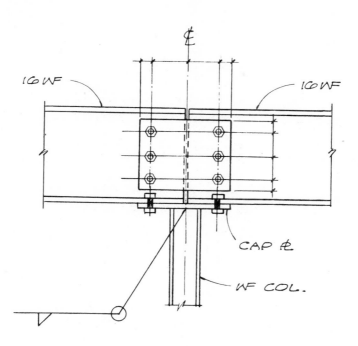

Detail 4-28(c). A connection of steel beams to a wide flange column. See Detail 4-28(a).

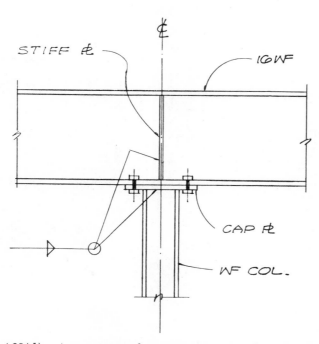

Detail 4-28(d). A connection of a continuous or cantilevered steel beam to a wide flange column. The bottom flange of the beam is bolted on each side of the web through the column cap plate. The cap plate is welded to the top of the column.

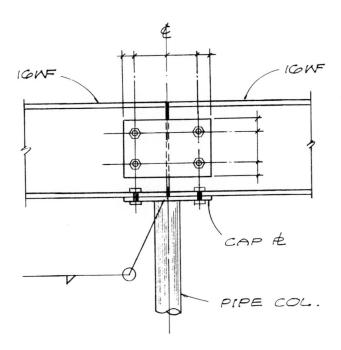

Detail 4-29(a). A connection of steel beams to a pipe column. The steel beams are connected by plates bolted through each side of the beam web. The bottom flange of each beam is bolted on each side of the web through the column cap plate. The cap plate is welded to the top of the column.

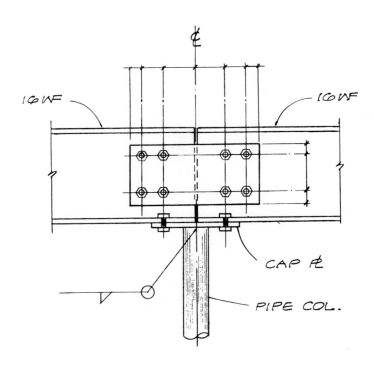

Detail 4-29(b). A connection of steel beams to a pipe column. See Detail 4-29(a).

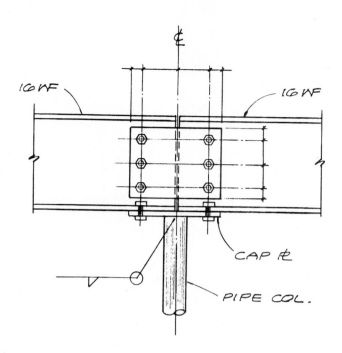

Detail 4-29(c). A connection of steel beams to a pipe column. See Detail 4-29(a).

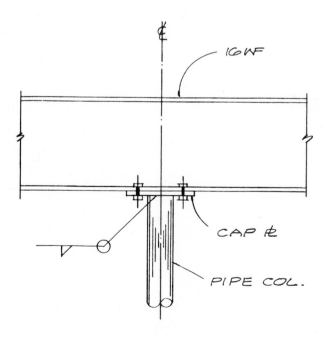

Detail 4-29(d). A connection of a continuous or cantilevered steel beam to a pipe column. The bottom flange of the beam is bolted on each side of the web through the column cap plate. The cap plate is welded to the top of the column.

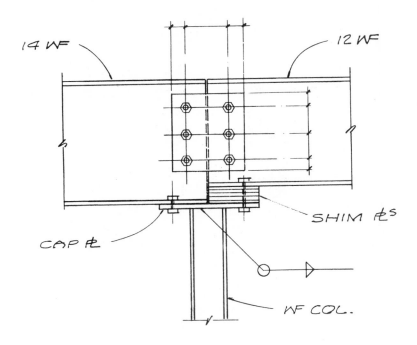

Detail 4-30. A connection of steel beams to a wide flange column. The steel beams are connected by plates bolted through each side of the beam webs. The bottom flange of each beam is bolted on each side of the web through the cap plate and the shim plates. The cap plate is welded to the top of the column. The shim plates are added to compensate for the unequal depth of the beams.

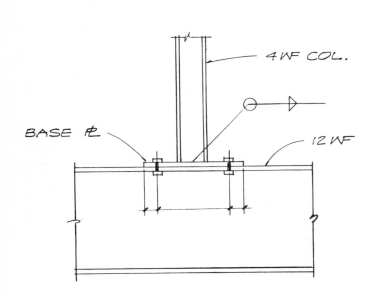

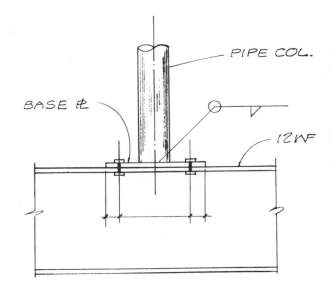

Detail 4-31(a). A detail of a steel beam supporting a steel column. A plate is welded to the bottom of the column and bolted through the top flange of the beam.

Detail 4-31(b). A detail of a steel beam supporting a steel pipe column. A plate is welded to the bottom of the column and bolted through the top flange of the beam.

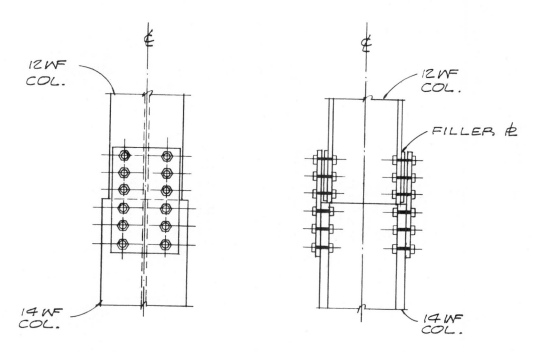

Detail 4-32(a). A column splice connection. The columns are spliced by flange plates bolted through the flanges of the upper and lower columns. Filler plates are added to the face of the upper column. A space of ⅛″ is provided between the splice plates and the filler plates to allow for erection clearance. The butting surfaces of the upper and lower columns are milled to permit full column bearing. The bolts used in the flange splice plates are friction type bolts. The size and number of bolts and the size of the flange plates are determined by calculation. The spacing of the bolts is determined by the A.I.S.C. Spec.

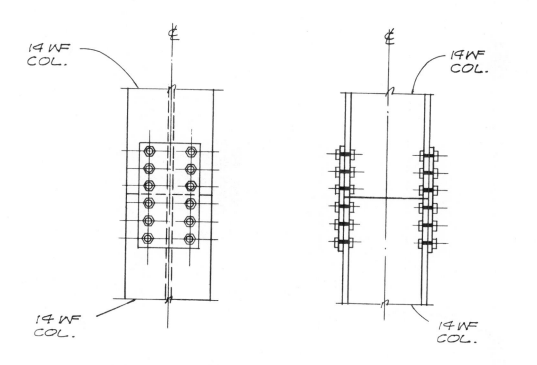

Detail 4-32(b). A column splice connection. The upper and lower columns are equal in size; filler plates are not required. See Detail 4-32(a).

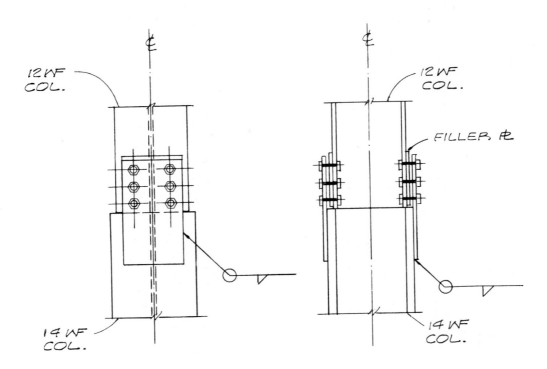

Detail 4-33(a). A column splice connection. The columns are spliced by welding the splice plates to the flange of the lower column and bolting through the flange of the upper column. Filler plates are added to the face of the upper column. A space of ⅛" is provided between the splice plates and the filler plates to allow for erection clearance. The butting surfaces of the upper and lower columns are milled to permit full column bearing. The bolts used in the flange splice plates are friction type bolts. The size and number of bolts, the size of the flange plates, and the size of the weld are determined by calculation. The spacing of the bolts is determined by the A.I.S.C. Spec.

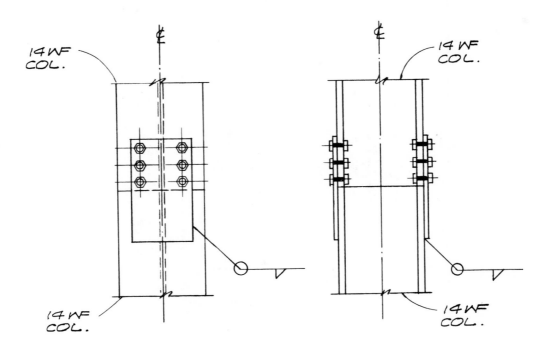

Detail 4-33(b). A column splice connection. The upper and lower columns are equal in size, filler plates are not required. See Detail 4-33(a).

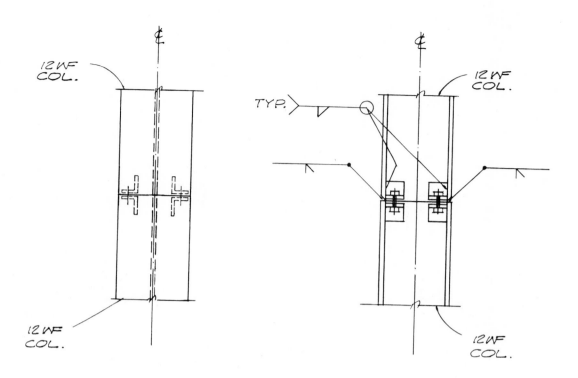

Detail 4-34. A column splice connection. The upper and lower columns are joined by bolts through angles welded to the inside faces of the column flanges. The column flanges are welded as shown. A space of ¼″ is provided between the horizontal legs of the connecting angles for erection clearance. The butting surfaces of the upper and lower columns are milled to permit full column bearing.

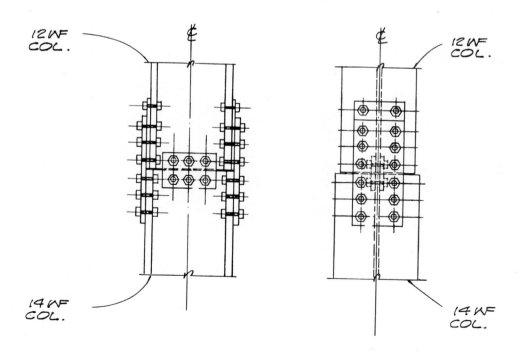

Detail 4-35. A column splice connection. The splice is the same as Detail 4-32(a). The column webs are connected by plates bolted through each side of the column web.

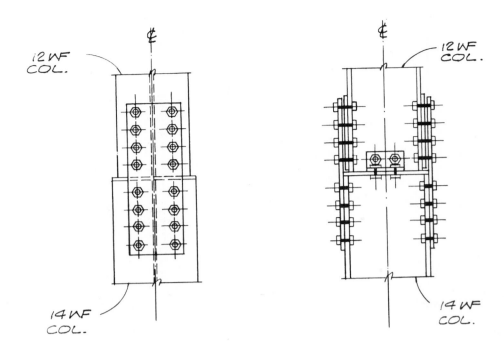

Detail 4-36. A column splice connection. The columns are connected with flange splice plates similar to Detail 4-32(a). A bearing plate is provided between the upper and lower columns. The web of the upper column is connected to the bearing plate with an angle on each side. The vertical legs of the angle are bolted through the column web. The horizontal legs of the angles are welded to the bearing plate.

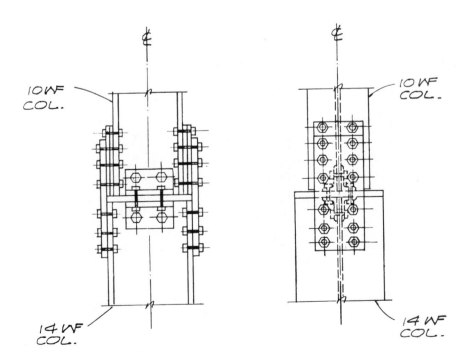

Detail 4-37. A column splice connection. The column flanges are connected as shown in Detail 4-32(a). A bearing plate is provided between the upper and lower column. The webs of the columns are connected to the bearing plate by angles bolted through the column webs and the bearing plate.

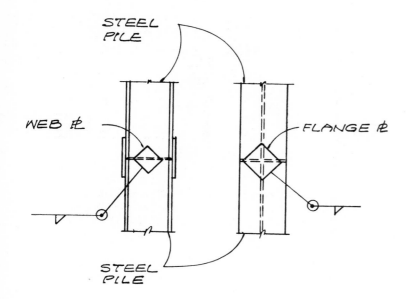

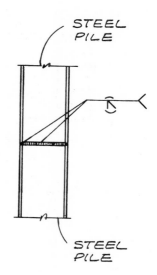

Detail 4-38(a). A steel pile splice connection. The pile is spliced by plates welded to each side of the flange face and to each side of the web. The size of the plates and the welds is determined by calculation.

Detail 4-38(b). A steel pile splice connection. The pile is spliced by a full penetration weld of the flanges and the web.

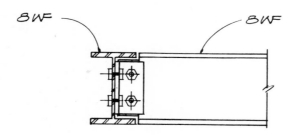

Detail 4-39(a). An 8″ wide flange beam connected to an 8″ wide flange beam.

Detail 4-39. Standard steel beam connections. The beams are connected by two angles with one vertical row of bolts through the web of each beam. The size and number of bolts and the size of the angles are determined by calculation. The bolt spacing shown is 3″ o.c., and the edge distance is 1½″ or as required by the A.I.S.C. Spec.

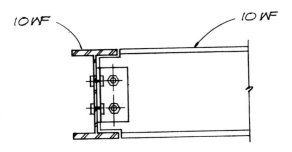

Detail 4-39(b). A 10″ wide flange beam connected to a 10″ wide flange beam.

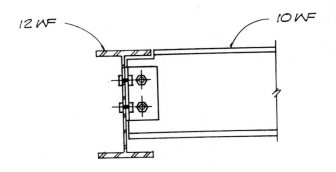

Detail 4-39(c). A 10″ wide flange beam connected to a 12″ wide flange beam.

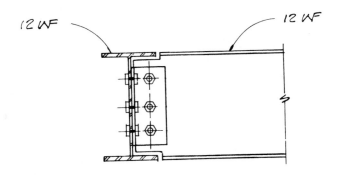

Detail 4-39(d). A 12″ wide flange beam connected to a 12″ wide flange beam.

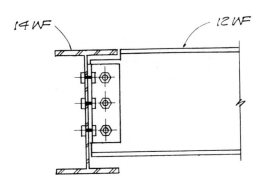

Detail 4-39(e). A 12″ wide flange beam connected to a 14″ wide flange beam.

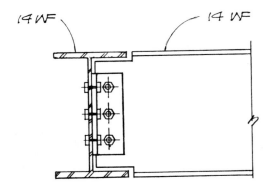

Detail 4-39(f). A 14″ wide flange beam connected to a 14″ wide flange beam.

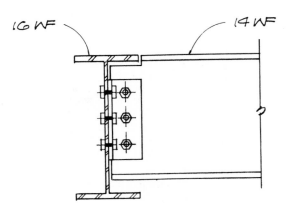

Detail 4-39(g). A 14″ wide flange beam connected to a 16″ wide flange beam.

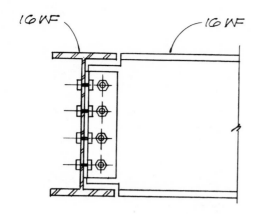

Detail 4-39(h). A 16″ wide flange beam connected to a 16″ wide flange beam.

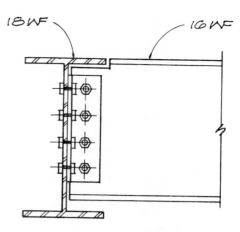

Detail 4-39(i). A 16″ wide flange beam connected to an 18″ wide flange beam.

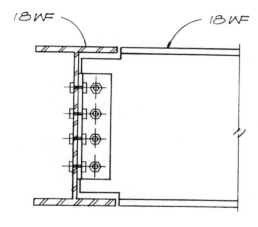

Detail 4-39(j). An 18″ wide flange beam connected to an 18″ wide flange beam.

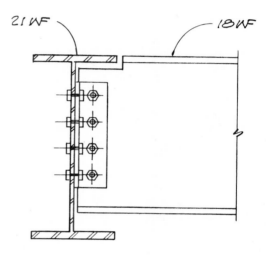

Detail 4-39(k). An 18″ wide flange beam connected to a 21″ wide flange beam.

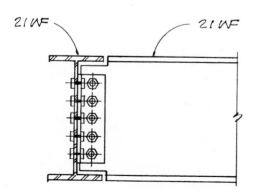

Detail 4-39(l). A 21″ wide flange beam connected to a 21″ wide flange beam.

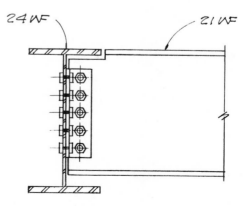

Detail 4-39(m). A 21″ wide flange beam connected to a 24″ wide flange beam.

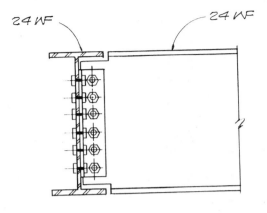

Detail 4-39(n). A 24″ wide flange beam connected to a 24″ wide flange beam.

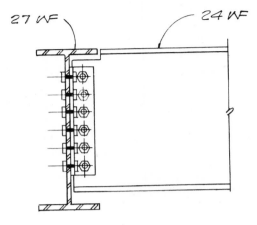

Detail 4-39(p). A 24″ wide flange beam connected to a 27″ wide flange beam.

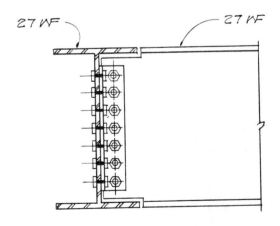

Detail 4-39(q). A 27″ wide flange beam connected to a 27″ wide flange beam.

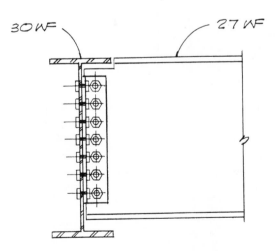

Detail 4-39(r). A 27″ wide flange beam connected to a 30″ wide flange beam.

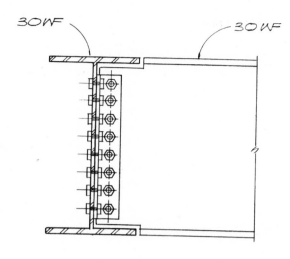

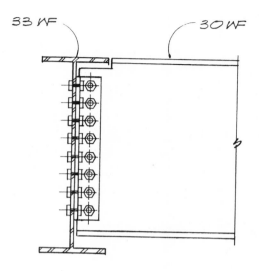

Detail 4-39(s). A 30″ wide flange beam connected to a 30″ wide flange beam.

Detail 4-39(t). A 30″ wide flange beam connected to a 33″ wide flange beam.

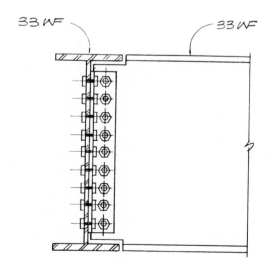

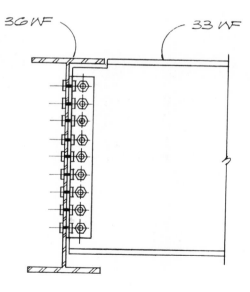

Detail 4-39(u). A 33″ wide flange beam connected to a 33″ wide flange beam.

Detail 4-39(v). A 33″ wide flange beam connected to a 36″ wide flange beam.

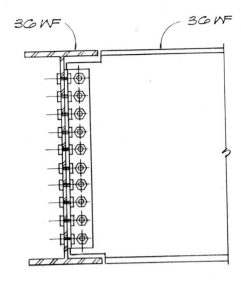

Detail 4-39(w). A 36″ wide flange beam connected to a 36″ wide flange beam.

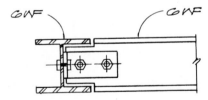

Detail 4-40(a). A 6″ wide flange beam connection.

Detail 4-40. Standard steel beam connections. The beams are connected by two angles with two vertical rows of bolts through the web of each beam. The size and number of the bolts and the angles are determined by calculation. The vertical bolt spacing is 3″ o.c. The spacing between the vertical rows of bolts is determined by the gauge of the angle and the edge distance is 1½″ or is as required by the A.I.S.C. Spec.

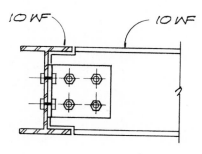

Detail 4-40(b). A 10″ wide flange beam connection.

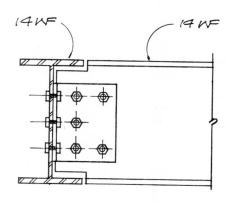

Detail 4-40(c). A 14″ wide flange beam connection.

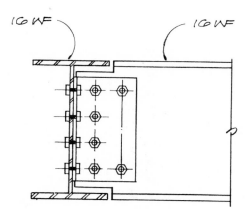

Detail 4-40(d). A 16″ wide flange beam connection.

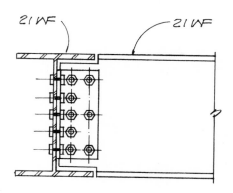

Detail 4-40(e). A 21″ wide flange beam connection.

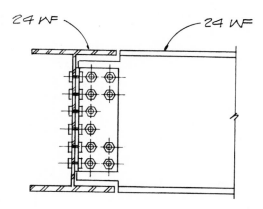

Detail 4-40(f). A 24″ wide flange beam connection.

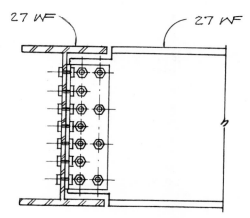

Detail 4-40(g). A 27″ wide flange beam connection.

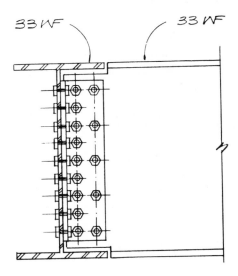

Detail 4-40(h). A 30″ wide flange beam connection.

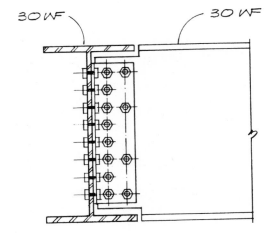

Detail 4-40(i). A 33″ wide flange beam connection.

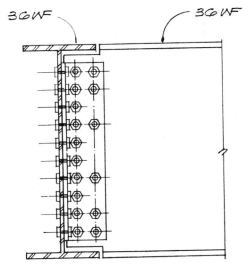

Detail 4-40(j). A 36″ wide flange beam connection.

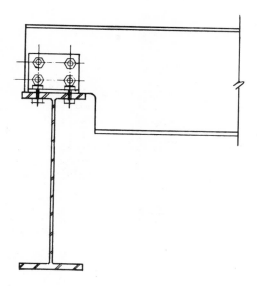

Detail 4-41. A section of a steel girder supporting a steel beam. The bottom of the steel beam is coped to adjust the top of steel height above the girder. The steel beam is connected to the girder by clip angles. The vertical legs of the angles are bolted through the web of the beam. The horizontal legs of the angles are bolted through the top flange of the girder. The spacing of the bolts is determined by the A.I.S.C. Spec.

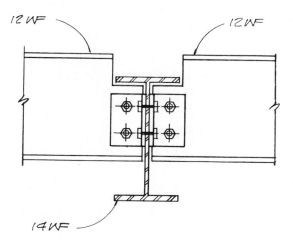

Detail 4-42. Connections of three steel beams. The steel beams shown in elevation are connected to the steel beam shown in section. The connection is made with angles bolted through the webs of each member. The size and number of bolts and the size of the angles are determined by calculation. The bolt spacing shown is 3″ o.c., and the edge distance is 1½″ or as required by the A.I.S.C. Spec.

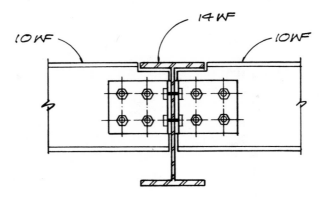

Detail 4-43. Connections of three steel beams. The steel beams shown in elevation are connected to the steel beam shown in section. The connection is made with angles bolted through the webs of each member. The size and number of bolts and the size of the angles are determined by calculation. The bolt spacing shown is 3″ o.c., and the edge distance is 1½″ or as required by the A.I.S.C. Spec.

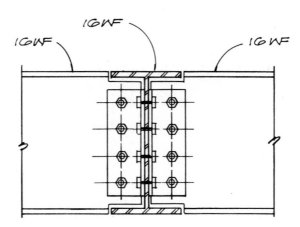

Detail 4-44. Connections of three steel beams. The steel beams shown in elevation are connected to the steel beam shown in section. The connection is made with angles bolted through the webs of each mmber. The size and number of bolts and the size of the angles are determined by calculation. The bolt spacing shown is 3″ o.c., and the edge distance is 1½″ or as required by the A.I.S.C. Spec.

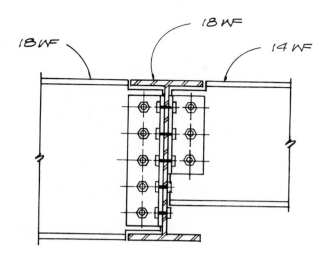

Detail 4-45. Connections of three steel beams. The steel beams shown in elevation are connected to the steel beam shown in section. The connection is made with angles bolted through the webs of each member. The size and number of bolts and the size of the angles are determined by calculation. The bolt spacing shown is 3″ o.c., and the edge distance is 1½″ or as required by the A.I.S.C. Spec.

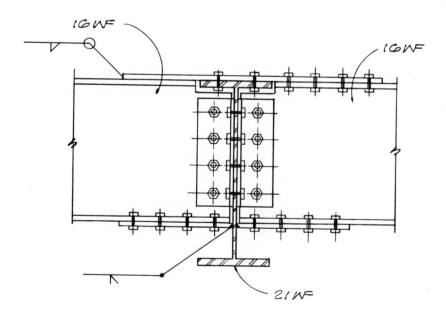

Detail 4-46. Connections of three steel beams. The connection can transfer shear and bending across the 21″ wide flange beam. The shear is transferred to the 21″ beam by angles bolted through each beam web. The size and number of bolts and the size of the angles are determined by calculation. The bending in the 16″ beams is transferred across the 21″ beam by a plate welded to the top flange of the beam on the left side and bolted through the top flange of the beam on the right side. The bending is transferred at the bottom of the 16″ beams by plates welded to the face of the web of the 21″ beam and bolted through the bottom flanges of each 16″ beam. The flange bolts are friction type bolts. The size and number of the bolts, the size of the flange plates, and the size of the welds are determined by calculation. The spacing of the flange bolts is determined by the A.I.S.C. Spec.

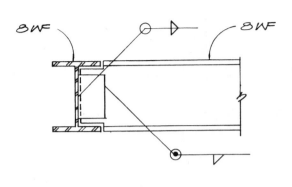

Detail 4-47(a). A steel beam connection. The intersecting beams are connected to each other with a plate welded to the web of each beam.

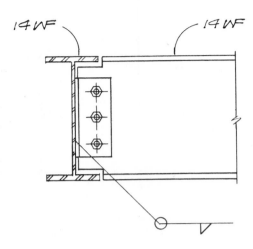

Detail 4-47(b). A steel beam connection. The intersecting beams are connected to each other with an angle welded to the web of one beam and bolted through the web of the other. The size and the number of bolts and the angles are determined by calculation.

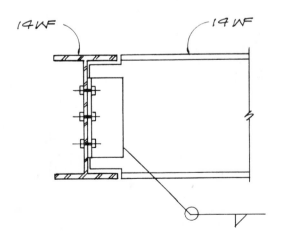

Detail 4-47(c). See Detail 4-47(b).

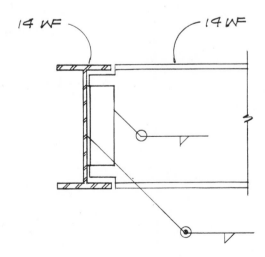

Detail 4-47(d). A steel beam connection. The intersecting beams are connected to each other with an angle welded to the web of each beam.

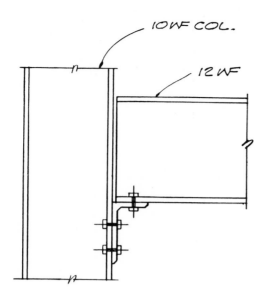
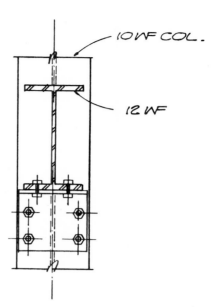

Detail 4-48(a). Two views of a steel beam supported by a seat angle. The vertical leg of the angle is bolted through a column flange. The horizontal leg of the seat angle is bolted through the bottom flange of the beam. The size of the angle and the bolts are determined by calculation.

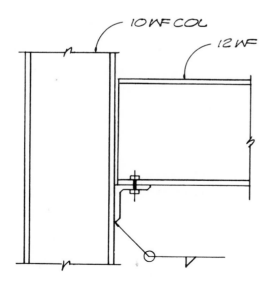
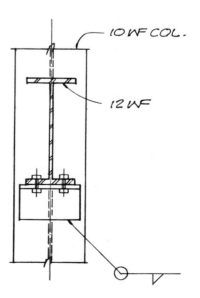

Detail 4-48(b). Two views of a steel beam supported by a seat angle. The vertical leg of the angle is welded to the face of the column flange. The horizontal leg of the seat angle is bolted through the bottom flange of the beam. The size of the weld and the size of the angle and the bolts are determined by calculation.

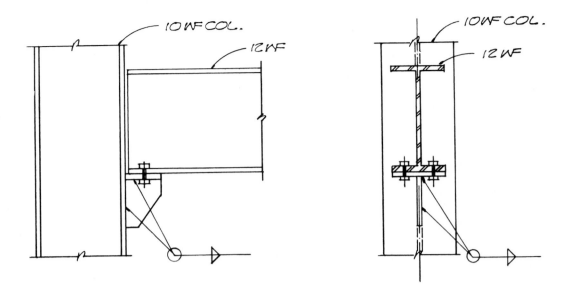

Detail 4-48(c). Two views of a steel beam supported by a shelf plate and a vertical stiffener plate. The shelf plate and the stiffener plate are welded to the face of the column. The shelf plate is bolted through the bottom flange of the beam. The sizes of the plates, welds, and bolts are determined by calculation.

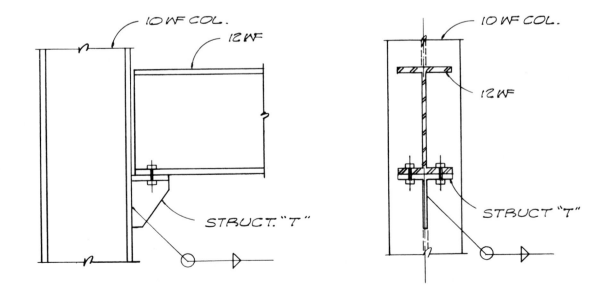

Detail 4-48(d). Two views of a steel beam supported by a structural Tee seat. The web of the structural Tee acts as a stiffener plate. The structural Tee is welded to the face of the column flange. The flange of the structural Tee section is bolted through the bottom flange of the beam. The sizes of the structural Tee section, welds, and bolts are determined by calculation.

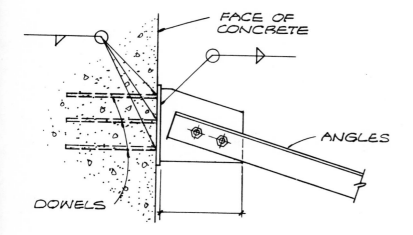

FACE OF CONCRETE

ANGLES

DOWELS

Detail 4-49(a). Steel canopy tie angles connected to a concrete pilaster. The angles act in tension to support a canopy beam and fascia as shown in Detail 4-49(b). The vertical legs of the angles are bolted through a gusset plate. The gusset plate is welded to a flat plate connected to the concrete pilaster with reinforcing dowels welded to the inside face of the plate. The dowels resist the tension of the angles by bond with the concrete.

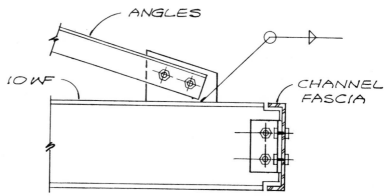

ANGLES

10 WF

CHANNEL FASCIA

Detail 4-49(b). A connection of canopy tie angles supporting canopy beams and a fascia. The vertical legs of the angles are bolted through a gusset plate which is welded to the top of the canopy beam. The fascia channel is connected to the canopy beam by bolts and angles as shown.

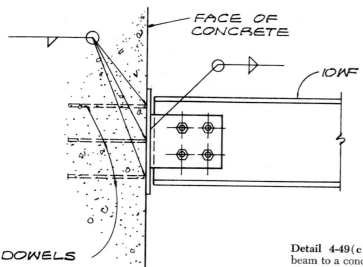

FACE OF CONCRETE

10 WF

DOWELS

Detail 4-49(c). A connection of a canopy steel beam to a concrete wall pilaster. See Detail 4-49(b). The web of the beam is bolted to a gusset plate. The gusset plate is welded to a flat plate connected to the concrete pilaster with reinforcing dowels welded to the inside face of the plate.

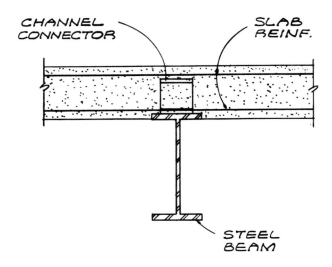

Detail 4-50(a). A section of a composite steel beam and concrete slab. The reinforcement in the slab is shown in the section. The top reinforcement is continuous over the steel beam. The bottom reinforcement laps over the steel beam as shown. See Detail 4-50(b).

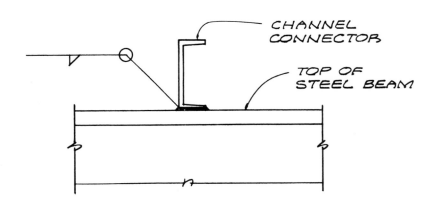

Detail 4-50(b). A detail of a structural steel channel welded to the top of a steel beam. The channel is used as a shear connector for the composite construction of a concrete slab and a steel beam. The size and spacing of the channel connectors are determined by calculation.

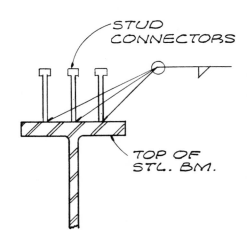

Detail 4-50(c). A section showing stud connectors welded to the top of a steel beam. The studs are used as shear connectors for composite construction of a concrete slab and a steel beam. The size and spacing of the studs are determined by calculation.

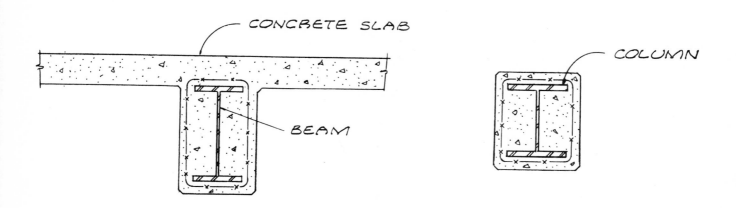

Detail 4-51(a). Sections of a steel beam and column covered with poured concrete for fireproofing. The amount of clear cover of concrete determines the fire rating of the steel member.

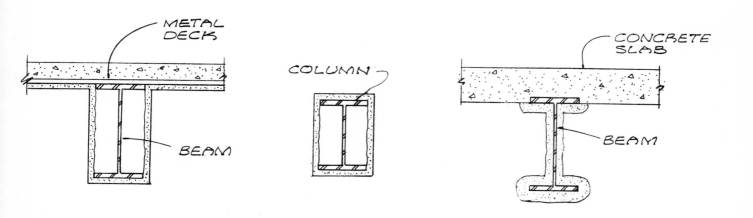

Detail 4-51(b). Sections of steel beams, metal decking and a steel column, fireproofed with a cement plaster material. The thickness of the plaster on the steel surface determines the fire rating of the steel member.

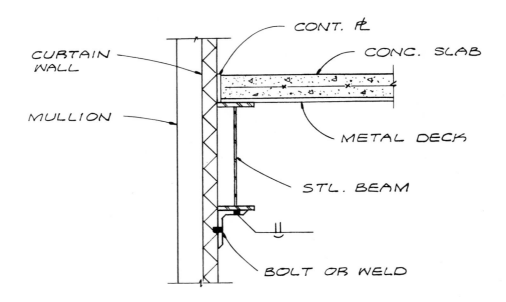

Detail 4-52(a). A section of a steel beam, metal decking and concrete, and an exterior curtain wall. The metal decking is filled with concrete and welded to the top flange of the steel beam. A continuous vertical metal strip at the edge of the top flange of the beam separates the concrete from the inside face of the curtain wall. The curtain wall is connected to the bottom flange of the steel beam by clip angles bolted or welded as required by the curtain wall manufacturer.

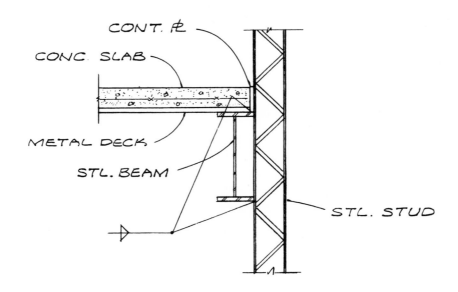

Detail 4-52(b). A section of a steel beam, metal decking filled with concrete, and an exterior steel stud wall. The metal decking is filled with concrete and welded to the top flange of the steel beam. A continuous vertical metal strip at the edge of the top flange of the steel beam separates the concrete from the steel stud wall. The steel studs are connected to the beam by welding the inside flange face of the stud to the edge of the steel beam flanges.

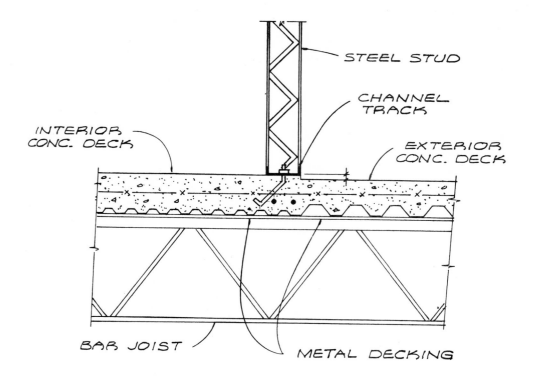

STEEL STUD

CHANNEL TRACK

INTERIOR CONC. DECK

EXTERIOR CONC. DECK

BAR JOIST

METAL DECKING

Detail 4-53. A section of a steel stud wall supported by metal decking with concrete on bar joists. The metal deck spans between and is welded to the top flange of the bar joists. The steel stud wall is connected to the concrete slab with anchor bolts. The exterior concrete roof slab is supported by a metal roof decking and is depressed below the interior floor slab to allow for waterproofing or flashing at the face of the wall.

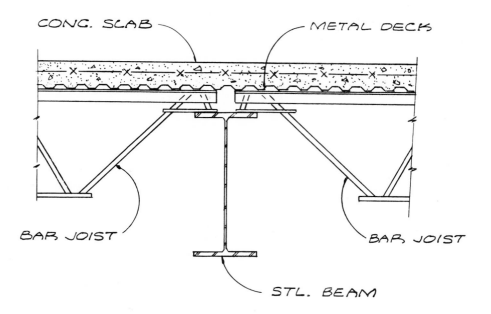

CONC. SLAB

METAL DECK

BAR JOIST

BAR JOIST

STL. BEAM

Detail 4-54. A section of a steel beam supporting bar joists, metal decking and a concrete floor. The metal decking spans between and is welded to the top flange of the bar joists. The size and spacing of the bar joists are determined by calculation. The bar joist is welded to the top flange of the steel.

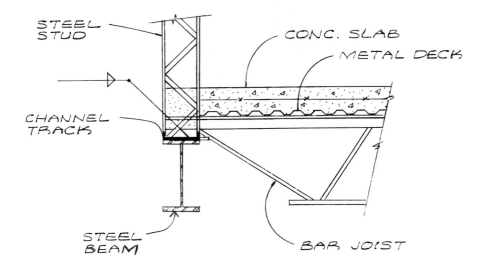

STEEL
STUD

CONC. SLAB

METAL DECK

CHANNEL
TRACK

STEEL
BEAM

BAR JOIST

Detail 4-55. A section of an exterior steel stud wall, metal decking with concrete, and a steel beam. The bar joists are connected to the top flange of the steel beam similar to Detail 4-54. The metal decking spans between and is welded to the top flange of the bar joists.

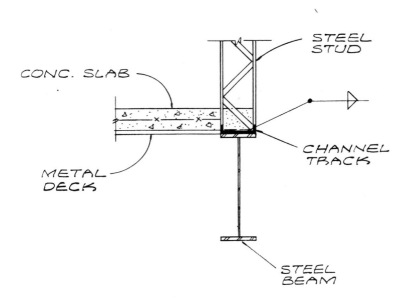

STEEL
STUD

CONC. SLAB

METAL
DECK

CHANNEL
TRACK

STEEL
BEAM

Detail 4-56. A section of an exterior steel stud wall, metal decking with concrete, and a steel beam. The metal decking is supported by and welded to the top flange of the steel beam.

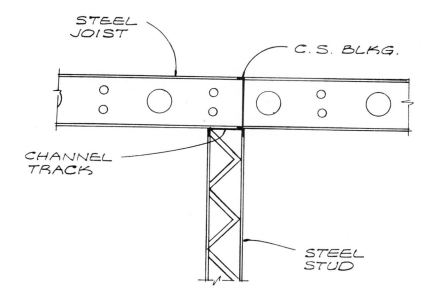

Detail 4-57. A section of a steel stud wall supporting light steel joists. The studs are tied together by the continuous channel stud track at the top of the wall. The joists are continuously blocked by a channel stud.

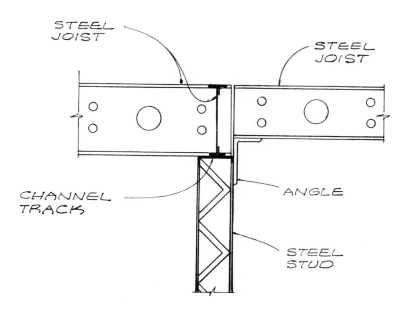

Detail 4-58. A section of a steel stud wall supporting light steel joists. The studs are tied together by the continuous channel stud track at the top of the wall. The joists are continuously blocked by a light steel joist. The smaller joist is supported by a continuous ledger angle welded to the stud wall.

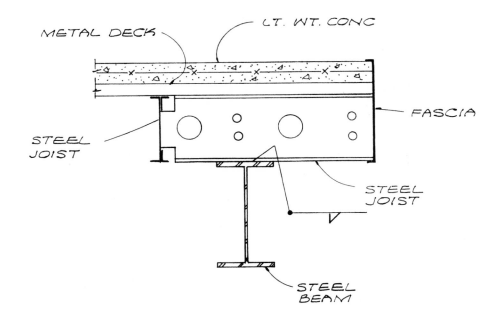

Detail 4-59. A section of a steel beam, metal decking with concrete, steel joist and a fascia. The light weight joists are welded to the top of the beam. The fascia is a light steel channel section.

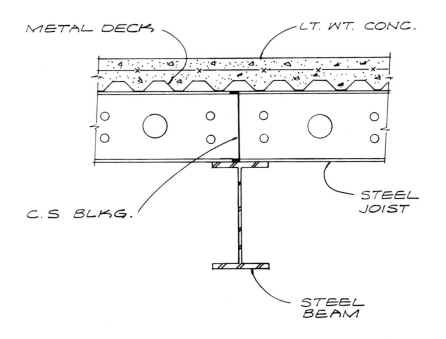

Detail 4-60. A section of a steel beam supporting light steel joists, and a metal decking with concrete. The joists are welded to the top flange of the steel beam and are blocked by a continuous channel stud.

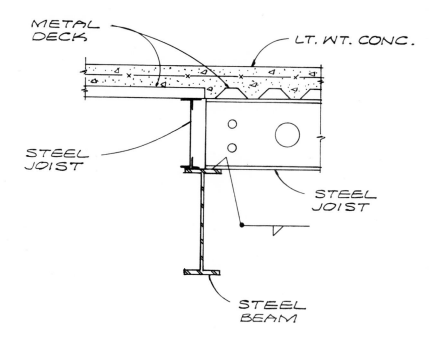

Detail 4-61. A section of a steel beam supporting metal decking and light steel joists. The steel joists are welded to the top flange of the beam.

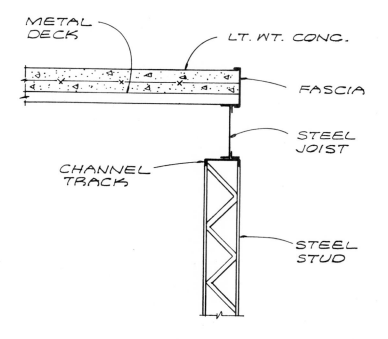

Detail 4-62. A section of the edge of a concrete slab on metal decking supported by a steel stud wall. The metal decking is supported by a continuous steel joist. A channel stud track is used as a fascia for the concrete slab.

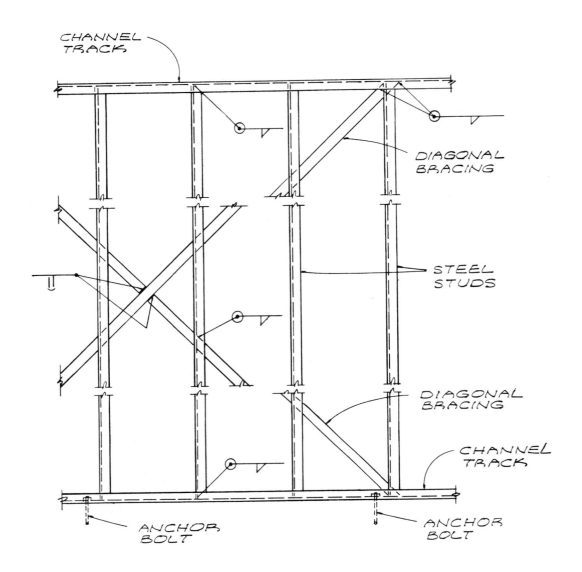

Detail 4-63. An elevation of a steel stud wall. The studs are spaced at 16″ o.c. and connected at the top and bottom by a horizontal channel stud track. The channel stud track at the bottom is bolted to the concrete as shown or welded to the top of a steel beam. The wall is diagonally braced by metal straps at 45°. The metal straps are welded to each face of the channel stud. The straps may be placed on either side of the wall.

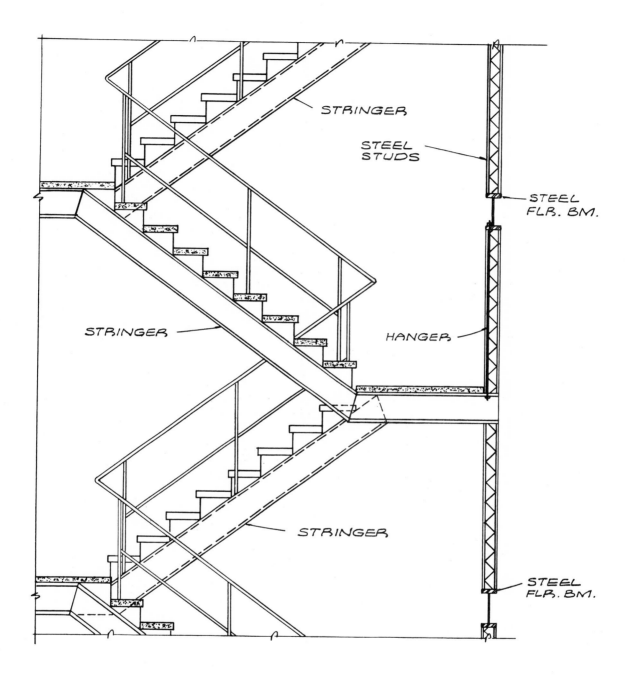

STRINGER

STEEL STUDS

STEEL FLR. BM.

STRINGER

HANGER

STRINGER

STEEL FLR. BM.

Detail 4-64. A section of a steel stair. The stair stringers are channels as shown in Detail 4-68. The stringer may be bent plates or rolled channel sections. The stringer bends at the landings are welded as shown in Details 4-68(b) and (c). The size of the stringers depends on the span and load and is determined by calculation. Stringers at the steel stud wall are supported from the floor beams by metal hanger rods as shown in Details 4-75(a) and (b). An alternate method of suspending the stair stringers from a steel beam can be seen in Detail 4-76. Detail 4-77 shows a method of suspending a steel stair stringer from a concrete beam, and Detail 4-66 shows a method of connecting the steel stringer to a concrete wall. Detail 4-65 shows an enlarged view of the steel stringers at the landing intersection. The treads and risers of the steel stairs can be constructed of welded metal plate or by rolled channel sections as shown in Detail 4-65. Detail 4-67 shows metal stairs supported to a channel stringer with no concrete cover.

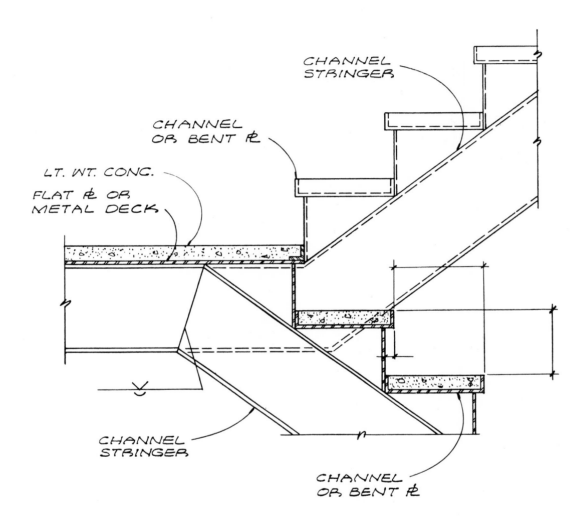

CHANNEL STRINGER

CHANNEL OR BENT ℞

LT. WT. CONC.

FLAT ℞ OR METAL DECK

CHANNEL STRINGER

CHANNEL OR BENT ℞

Detail 4-65. An enlarged view of steel stairs at the landing intersection.

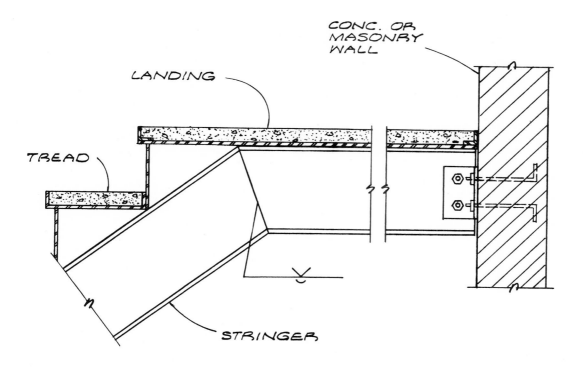

Detail 4-66. A section of a stair stringer connected to a masonry wall with clip angles.

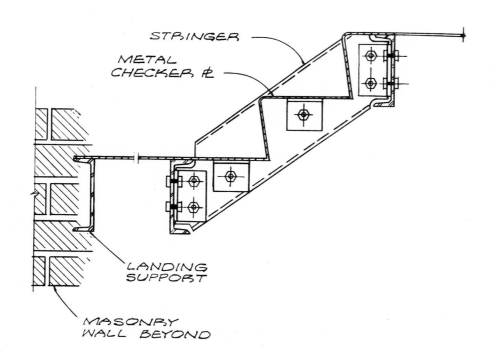

Detail 4-67. A section of metal stairs using metal checker plate for treads and risers. The landing deck is constructed of inverted channels or bent plate filled with concrete.

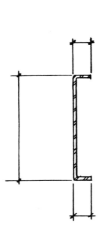

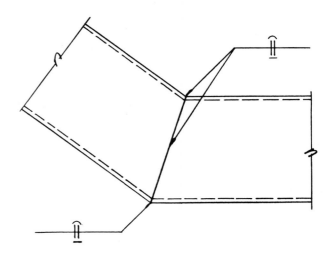

Detail 4-68(a). A section of a bent plate used for a steel stair stringer. The thickness and depth of plate depend on the span and load on the stringer, and are determined by calculation.

Detail 4-68(b). A detail of a steel stringer weld.

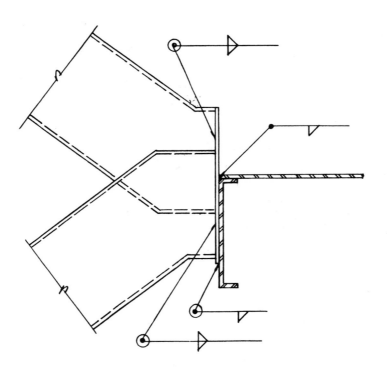

Detail 4-69. A detail showing steel stair stringers connected to a steel channel landing beam.

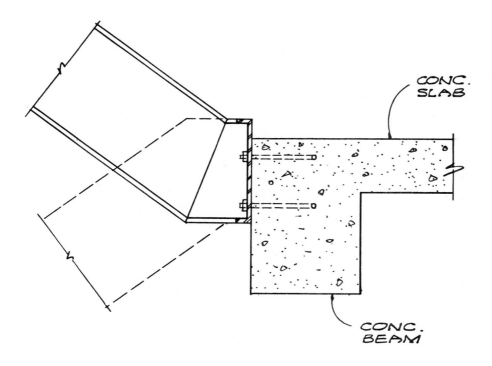

CONC.
SLAB

CONC.
BEAM

Detail 4-70. A detail showing steel stringers connected to a concrete beam at the landing.

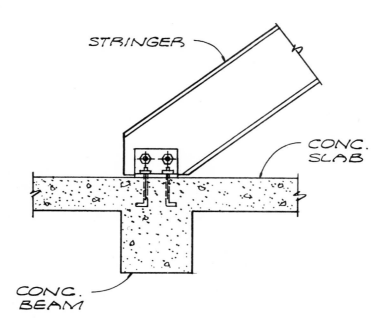

STRINGER

CONC.
SLAB

CONC.
BEAM

Detail 4-71. A detail showing a concrete beam supporting a steel stair stringer. The stringer is connected to the beam with a clip angle.

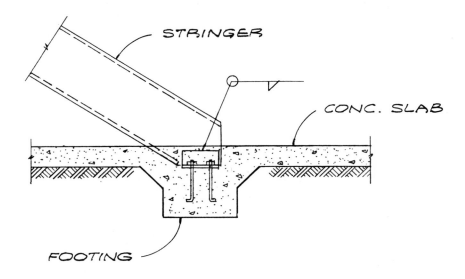

Detail 4-72. A detail of a steel stringer connected to a concrete slab on grade. The stringer is bolted to the concrete slab with clip angles. The vertical leg of the angle is welded to the face of the stringer. The horizontal leg of the angle is bolted to the concrete.

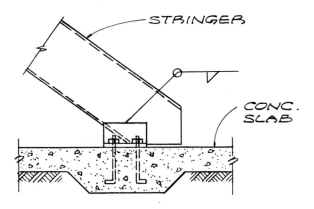

Detail 4-73. A detail of a steel stringer connected to a concrete slab on grade. The stringer is bolted to the concrete slab with clip angles. The vertical leg of the angle is welded to the web of the stringer. The horizontal leg of the angle is bolted to the concrete.

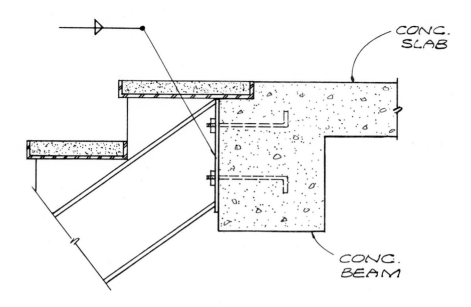

Detail 4-74. A detail showing a connection of a steel stringer to a concrete beam. The stringer is welded to a plate which is connected to the beam with anchor bolts. The size of the weld and the size of the bolts are determined by calculation.

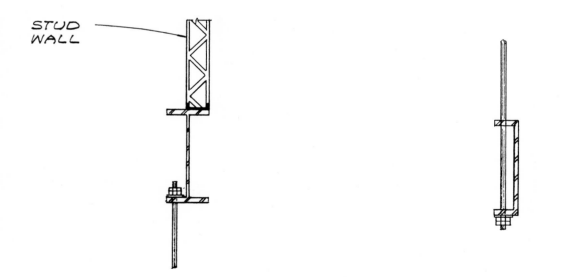

Detail 4-75(a). A section of a steel beam and a suspender rod supporting a steel channel stair stringer. See Detail 4-75(b). The rod is bolted through the flange of the steel beam and is secured in place by a washer and double nut. The size of the rod required is determined by calculation.

Detail 4-75(b). A section of a steel channel suspended from a steel beam by a rod. See Detail 4-75(a). The rod is bolted through the flanges and is secured in place by a washer and double nut. The size of the rod required is determined by calculation.

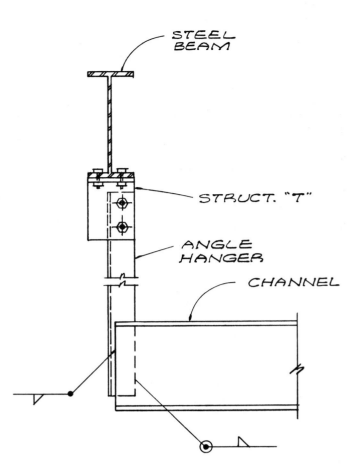

STEEL
BEAM

STRUCT. "T"

ANGLE
HANGER

CHANNEL

Detail 4-76. A detail showing an angle hanger connected to the bottom flange of a steel beam and suspending a steel channel. The suspender angle is connected to the steel beam with a structural Tee. The channel may be connected to the hanger either by welding or by bolting.

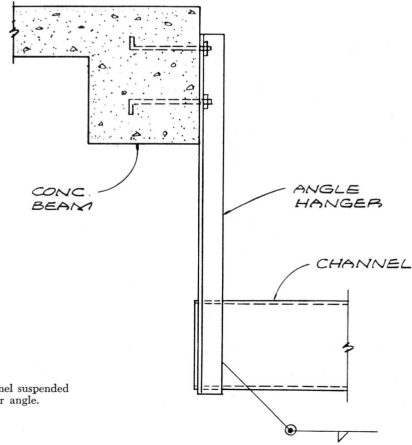

CONC.
BEAM

ANGLE
HANGER

CHANNEL

Detail 4-77. A detail of a steel channel suspended from a concrete beam by a suspender angle.

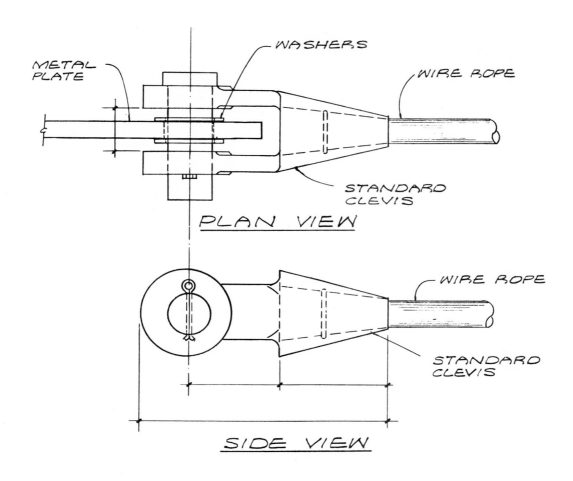

PLAN VIEW

SIDE VIEW

Detail 4-78. Two views of a steel clevis and clevis pin connected to a wire rope.

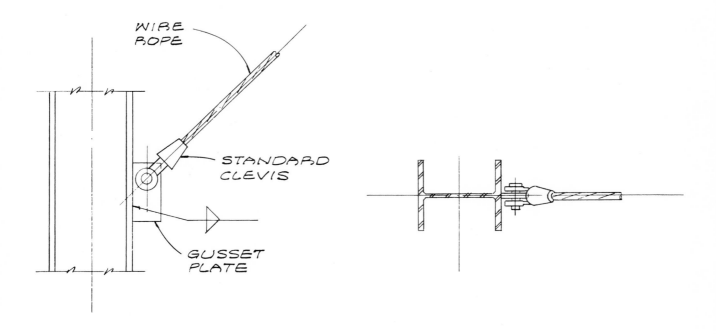

Detail 4-79. Two views of a connection of a standard clevis and wire rope to the flange of a steel column. The gusset plate is welded to the face of the flange, and the clevis pin is passed through a hole in the plate.

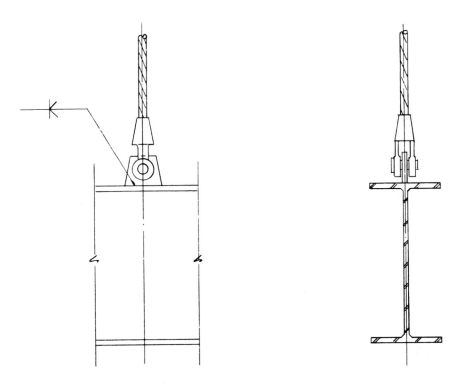

Detail 4-80. Two views of a clevis and wire rope connection used to suspend a steel beam. The clevis pin is passed through a gusset plate welded to the top flange of the beam.

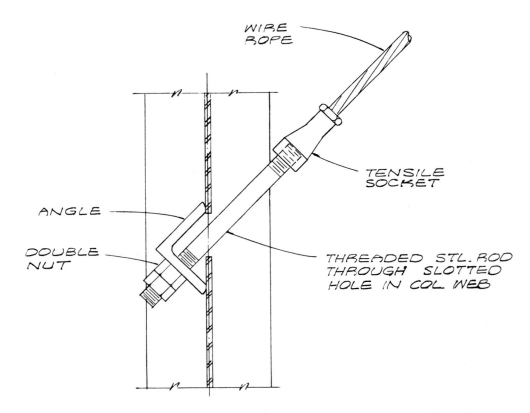

WIRE ROPE

TENSILE SOCKET

ANGLE

DOUBLE NUT

THREADED STL. ROD THROUGH SLOTTED HOLE IN COL WEB

Detail 4-81. A wire rope connected to a socket and used for diagonal bracing. The socket is connected to a threaded rod that passes through a hole in the column web.

INDEX